SMOKE
AND
MIRRORS

The 'Worker and Kolkhoz Girl' sculpture created by the famous sculptor Vera Mukhina (1989-1953), first went on display as part of the Soviet pavilion at the 1937 Paris International Exhibition. It was then moved to Moscow and became a universally recognised symbol of the Soviet regime for many years.

SMOKE
AND
MIRRORS

FROM THE SOVIET UNION
TO RUSSIA, THE PIPEDREAM
MEETS REALITY

LEONID SINELNIKOV

(Translation from the Russian by Paul Leathley)

UNICORN

This edition first published in the UK by Unicorn
an imprint of the Unicorn Publishing Group LLP, 2021
5 Newburgh Street
London W1F 7RG

www.unicornpublishing.org

10 9 8 7 6 5 4 3 2 1

ISBN 978-1-913491-35-2

Design by Vivian@Bookscribe

Printed by Latitude Press

ACKNOWLEDGEMENT:
The author would like to expresses his gratitude to Oleg Alexandrovich Smirnov,
CEO of the SNS Group of Companies for sponsoring publication of this book.

CONTENTS

INTRODUCTION:
For smokers and non-smokers

People's attitudes to tobacco cover a whole gamut of emotions, from "I can't live without a cigarette" to "I regard tobacco as one of the vilest enemies..."

If you ask me about tobacco, you will risk getting the answer, "Read my book!" – because in my case, tobacco has been my life's career. There is probably no point now in dwelling on whether or not I chose the right path. In any case, back when, as a freshly baked Moscow college graduate, I was sent to work at the tobacco factory, I had little choice in the matter. "I'll do a stint at the Yava factory", I told my parents, not imagining that this "stint" would go on for half a century.

I never thought that I would witness such changes in attitudes to smoking as we are seeing now the world over. Even in Russia, where people are fairly conservative in their habits, cigarette consumption is in decline. In the USSR, cigarettes were considered a vitally important product without which consumers simply could not live – a view borne out by the serious unrest that broke out whenever there were tobacco shortages. This is why the country's leadership paid great attention to ensuring that the country was properly supplied with tobacco products, putting tobacco on a par with bread and vodka. In the rest of the world too, of course, smoking was a major influence in society and something that governments kept a watch over, but the problems there were of a different nature from those in Russia.

Now, smokers are giving up or cutting down on cigarettes of their own accord. They are switching to electronic cigarettes or other products that mimic traditional smoking but without the burning of tobacco. I will touch upon this topic in the concluding part of the book. However, my main subject is much broader than the traditional production of cigarettes. In this book, dear reader, tobacco is also a pretext to describe the people I have known and the events that I have been involved in and witnessed, to talk about the difficult times our country has faced and about the fates of people who made their contribution to Russia's development.

Was the tobacco industry in the USSR just an anomalous weak point in a viable system, or were we all, by constantly plugging the holes in a shortage-based economy, propping up an illusion of the sustainability of the command system? To use an English expression, was it all just "smoke and mirrors"? That is for you to judge. The purpose of my account is to help the next generation draw the right conclusions from the lessons of history.

I began pondering over the fundamental problems of the system when it became clear that our country had hit a dead end. The sequence of deaths of one elderly General Secretary after another provided us with a fecund source of bleak jokes, but precious little in terms of hopes for the future. And when a new leader, Gorbachev, appeared atop the political Olympus, no one expected his appointment to turn the life of this vast country upside down. That era, which became popularly known throughout the world as "perestroika", may without any exaggeration be called the brightest period in the history of the USSR. Events that brought long-established stereotypes crashing down and had life-changing consequences for the whole country occurred in rapid succession. The man who instigated and inspired these momentous changes was the General Secretary himself, Mikhail Gorbachev, who very astutely identified the primary targets of long-overdue reforms.

Almost immediately after he came to power, concepts that were fundamentally new to Soviet power were suddenly proclaimed as policy. Perestroika and glasnost were designed to overcome the worst vices of the Brezhnev era: stagnation and the concealment of the real state of affairs in the country from the people. There was particular awe over the way Mikhail Sergeyevich interacted with members of the public. People sat in astonishment at television reports covering Gorbachev's visits to various places around the country. It was in the course of Mikhail Sergeyevich's frank and open engagement with the public that the catchphrase "we cannot live like this" was born.

I think that those of my compatriots who these days like to criticise Gorbachev, accusing him of all the mortal sins, would do well to remember how we lived before he bravely took on the challenge and responsibility of breaking a monstrously vicious circle.

CHAPTER I.

A CONDENSED HISTORY OF MY COUNTRY: FROM STALIN TO BREZHNEV

I shall begin with what I remember well, with an account of my earliest impressions of the country in which I was born and raised. I was thirteen when Stalin died. Did I understand then, as a studious secondary school pupil, that the death of the tyrant would offer a way out of the brutal totalitarianism under which we had been living? Of course not. It had never entered my head that the poverty in which we lived resulted from the way we were governed. Indeed, it was only later that I realised how badly we had been living. But at the time? Poverty was the norm, and thoughts about material well-being did not even arise. We had been taught that we had to work in the interests of the state, to help rebuild the country after the devastation of the war. As for material comforts – that was all bourgeois prejudice.

My family lived in a two-storey building next to Rizhsky (then Rzhevsky) railway station. The rooms led off a communal corridor. There were eight families living along our corridor. Heating came from coal-fired stoves. No one had a kitchen. The women of each household would cook on a kerosene stove on a little table positioned next to the door of her apartment. The toilet and washbasin were located at the end of the corridor next to the cold stairwell. There was no question of a shower. Each morning, when everyone was in a rush to get to work, a queue would form to the so-called communal facilities.

It amazes me to this day to think how my parents managed to get through those unthinkable times. They would go to work early in the morning and come home at around eight in the evening. While mama began to cook, my father would put on a bodywarmer, fetch firewood and coal from the shed and set about heating the stove. The air was damp, and the warmth did not linger long. By the time I got home from school, it was cold in our room. My most fervent wish was that it could be warm and cosy.

The working week lasted six days. On the only day off – Sunday – my father and I would go to the market to buy food, and then the whole family would go to the bathhouse. Getting into the bathhouse meant standing in a queue for several hours. And so life would go on, week after week. This was how the majority of Muscovites lived. It was no better for those who lived in packed communal flats (*kommunalki*)[1]. Strangely enough, the presence of a shared kitchen in dwellings of that kind was actually a cause of conflict, with daily fights and quarrels among women competing for use of the gas cooker or sink. The so-called "Stalin high-rises"[2] were reserved for important officials. But even then, there was a price to pay, since people in that category were at an especially high risk of falling victim to repressive measures. These living arrangements were in keeping with the Stalinist ideology of extending the principles of collectivism even to citizens' personal lives, so that people spent as little time as possible on their own or in the family circle and had minimal opportunity for heart-to-heart conversation.

Wages were only just enough to make ends meet. Next to our building was the Rizhsky *gastronom*, or food store. Inside, the counters groaned under the weight of myriad delicacies. Most people, however, unable to avail themselves of this splendour, stood in long queues for cheap products. I myself, I recall, would try to help my parents by standing in queues for hours to buy cheap curd. So that people didn't lose their place in the queue, numbers were written on palms with a purple copying pencil. Living conditions were so crude that some of our neighbours would carry canisters to the station to have them filled with free boiled water. And yet, state propaganda was forever singing Stalin's praises on account of the latest reductions in food prices. People trusted Stalin. They deified him for the care he took of them. For of course, he sat in the Kremlin day and night thinking of nothing else but the welfare of the Soviet nation and its citizens. Discipline in the country was maintained through fear: fear of losing work, of being repressed for incautious utterances, of facing conviction for petty theft.

My mother worked at the USSR Ministry of Agriculture. According to her accounts of that time, people hesitated to leave their desks when the working day ended. They were afraid that their boss or a Party secretary would say, "If you're leaving on the dot, there's clearly not enough for you to do, so we can let you go". People were afraid of losing their jobs. Moving from one job to another was not something that the authorities encouraged. People who did so were

---

1   A dwelling similar to the one already described, but with a separate kitchen room.
2   A small number of relatively high-quality apartment buildings built in the 1930s–1950s.

judged erratic and unreliable and immediately fell under the scrutiny of the authorities. If a person lost his job, he could be convicted for parasitism.

When people joined an enterprise or organisation, they were mentally prepared to work there for their entire lives. This meant that, from the moment they took their first independent steps until the moment they retired, people were effectively tied to one place of work. This made it a lot easier to keep tabs on people. At home, their behaviour was monitored by the local police officer, who would question neighbours in detail about the conduct of anyone who had fallen under suspicion. At work, this role was fulfilled by the personnel department, which acted as a sort of filter for recruitment and played an important role in any later promotions. Personnel officers were disliked and feared, because it was known that they liaised with the security services and had to keep them constantly informed of the situation at an enterprise or organisation. The personnel department worked closely with the so-called "special departments", which effectively consisted of NKVD[1] officials. At secret and classified enterprises these would be large divisions. At food enterprises it would be a single person – the head of the "special unit". As a rule, the people appointed to such posts were former security service officers, very closed people whose thoughts were difficult to read.

People accepted these conditions without a murmur. The important thing was that the war had ended – and life was bound to get better! Regular price reductions instilled hope in the popular masses and strengthened their faith in Stalin.[2] Soviet propaganda was rather effective. From morning to evening, national radio would pump out songs glorifying the great leader. I remember that, as a primary school pupil, I sincerely considered Stalin to be a great leader and teacher, imagining him as a superhuman figure endowed with unearthly qualities. Stalin rarely appeared in public, and his every word was worth its weight in gold. The only time you could actually see him, from a distance at least, was during workers' parades on public holidays. The columns of marchers consisted of representatives of various institutions, organised by district. Participation in the parade was an essential way of asserting your loyalty to the government. Mama often took me along with her, and we marched in the Agriculture

---

1 NKVD – the People's Commissariat for Internal Affairs, which acted as the country's political police force.

2 "Stalin's price reductions" – after the war, in the late 1940s and early 1950s, a series of price reductions were implemented with much fanfare.

Ministry's column. The parade lasted eight to ten hours. It was exhausting, but people proceeded with great enthusiasm, singing patriotic songs and dancing. From the ministry's location, where the column assembled, to Red Square was not far at all, but the route was contrived to make it a long march. People had to experience hardships even on a public holiday. When the weary marchers reached Red Square, all minds were preoccupied with the same question: "Was Comrade Stalin on the Mausoleum?" In truth, it was difficult to see anything or make out what was going on, as the columns filed across Red Square, encircled by security officers, almost at a run. Nonetheless, everyone felt inspired and happy if they thought that Stalin was standing on the tribune! All of which goes to show that even parades were organised in such a way as to demean and belittle people.

The manic adulation of the leader reached its zenith, of course, on the days over which his funeral took place. It was early in the morning when the death of Stalin was announced to the Soviet people to the accompaniment of funereal music. The outpouring of grief among simple people was entirely genuine. According to the established custom, our leader lay in state in the Hall of Columns in the House of Unions.[1] Driven by some insuperable force, and for all that I was, generally speaking, an obedient son and a diligent pupil, I abandoned my school lessons and resolved to pay my respects to Stalin come what may. It was a very frosty day. The city centre and Gorky Street from Pushkin Square onwards had been closed off by soldiers. The queue to the Hall of Columns began from the Pushkin monument and stretched in the direction of Pushkin Street, at the end of which was the House of Unions building. It was not a huge distance. The people in the queue were mostly calm, advancing patiently and very slowly. But after five o'clock in the afternoon, when the working day ended, the situation abruptly changed. Demented crowds broke through the soldiers' barriers, pouring onto Pushkin Street through the arches of apartment buildings and toppling people who had been standing in the queue. Some even descended from rooftops. Within a few minutes, the peaceful queue had been transformed into a frenzied, stampeding mass of bodies. It was very frightening. A grown-up tried to help me avoid getting pinned to the walls – or, even worse, to the display windows – of buildings that stood along Pushkin Street. I vaguely remember somehow managing to leap free of that deadly stream.

---

1 A hall in what used to be the building of the Moscow Assembly of the Nobility, built by M.F. Kazakov c. 1775, now the Hall of Columns, a venue for major official functions.

I walked home along the boulevards via Trubnaya, Samotechnaya and Kolkhoznaya Squares, heading for Rzhevsky Station. What I witnessed was terrible. A gigantic, solid stream of crazed people was heading in the opposite direction towards the House of Unions. Still etched on my mind are the heaps of galoshes I encountered on the way as evidence of the chaotic, possibly tragic, events. It was past one o'clock at night by the time I arrived home. My parents had guessed where I was, knew what was happening in the city, and had prepared themselves for all eventualities. They did not scold me or ask me questions. They got me warm, fed me and put me to bed. It was said that a lot of people had been killed or injured that night in Moscow. As always in such cases, rumours went around that there had been deliberate sabotage in the arrangements for the lying-in-state, which was why things had got out of hand. The official channels of information, as always, maintained a complete silence about it all.

A little less than three years later, in February 1956, the Twentieth Party Congress took place. The man now in power, Nikita Khrushchev, gave a speech denouncing Stalin's cult of personality. The country was apprised of mass repressions and other transgressions of the rule of law. Despite this, the authority of the country's ruling Communist Party remained wholly intact. Khrushchev's speech paved the way for new processes in Soviet society. The victims of Stalin's repressions began to be rehabilitated, and profound changes occurred in the mentality of Soviet people.

Those changes were driven by the intelligentsia. "Thick" magazines[1] began publishing all sorts of materials that gave a truthful view of everything that had happened in the country. People learned the truth about how Stalin had come to power, about the repressions of 1937, the lack of preparation for the war, the genuine heroism of the Soviet people and the innocent victims of Stalin's actions after the war. Literary works appeared that painted an accurate picture of life as it really was and what was happening to the country and its people. After the suffocating censorship that had gone before, these publications were like a breath of fresh air. People's whole way of thinking was literally turned upside down. They started to believe in the possibility of change. The young, in particular, were profoundly affected by these processes. A new generation was growing, less inhibited by the constraints of Party doctrine. This immensely important time in the country's history later became known as the "Khrushchev

---

1 Meaning literary and socio-political magazines such as *Novy mir*, *Zvezda* and *Znamya*.

thaw",[1] while the representatives of the new generation of intelligentsia were dubbed the "Sixtiers".

Cracks had begun to show in the iron curtain built under Stalin. After all, it was only possible to hold the people of a vast country in submission by keeping them fully insulated from real life. Compared with his predecessor, Khrushchev was an outward-facing politician. He made numerous state visits to various countries. These trips received wide coverage in the press. Because of this, the country began to feel itself a part of the wider world, and this changed people's psychology.

Nothing brings people together more than culture. After a long period of isolation, the Soviet Union began to play host to cultural figures from abroad, who displayed a keen interest in visiting our country. One recalls, for example, the wonderful American pianist Van Cliburn winning the first International Tchaikovsky Competition in 1958. He captivated the Moscow public with his performances and became a hugely popular figure in the country. In 1957 the World Festival of Youth and Students took place in Moscow. This was a landmark event for the USSR. Young people from all over the world flocked to the capital city. And although the Soviet youth remained ideologically blinkered, the possibility of having this kind of open contact with their foreign peers had been unthinkable up to that point.

Party policies began to change. People no longer wanted to be cogs in a machine, and a certain amount of democratisation began to take place in the Party. Calls to heed the people and focus on their needs began to ring out ever more often in Party documents. For the first time in its history, the USSR embarked on a large-scale programme of housing construction. Residential construction under Stalin had centred around luxury high-rises for the elite, designed as visual symbols of the might of the Communist regime. Meanwhile, ordinary people lived in dreadful conditions – in cellars, barracks and overcrowded communal flats. The Khrushchev era saw a mass relocation of people into new apartments. The quality of the accommodation was poor: five-storey panel buildings without lifts; small, low-ceilinged apartments with a simplistic layout and combined bathroom and lavatory... But they were separate apartments! Although Khrushchev was later slated for organising the construction of such low-quality structures, and the buildings themselves were disparagingly referred to as *khrushchovki*, the progress in people's lives was plain

---

[1] The "thaw" epithet for the ten years from 1954 to 1964 was coined by the writer Ilya Ehrenburg.

to see. Given the standard of residential construction as it was then, there was no other way of resolving a truly catastrophic situation. The inhabitants of our building, which fell short of elementary housing standards, likewise gradually began to move out to new apartments.

Another important factor that altered people's mindset was the reform of the pension system. In Stalin's time, pensions had been extremely meagre, to the point of beggarly. Under Khrushchev, pensions were raised significantly, to as high as 120 roubles, which was good money in those times. People stopped fearing retirement, instead seeing it as a new phase in their lives. It was even joked that an unmarried pensioner on a pension of that size could "be of interest" to a younger woman. A great deal changed for the better in people's everyday lives. Dry-cleaners and amenity centres opened. Shops began to sell higher-quality food at affordable prices. The bakery in our building began selling lots of new kinds of baked goods. I was amazed to see fresh bread and rolls being delivered in baskets to people's apartments. Attention to people's needs was manifested in all sorts of ways and was especially noticeable after the complete absence of civil rights and disdainful neglect of people's problems that had prevailed in the Stalin era. Cafés began to open, as did beer bars and dumpling (*pelmeni*) cafeterias. Those who liked a stronger tipple could go to a *ryumochnaya* (liquor bar). The leaders began to pay attention to the ordinary issues of everyday life, rather than concentrating solely on larger, strategic problems. For example, Khrushchev began to devote much attention to agriculture. The crop that particularly interested him was corn, which is good cattle fodder and could therefore help improve food supplies to the public. Of course, Nikita Sergeyevich took this idea a little too far, as he did with many things, by giving orders for corn to be grown in places where the conditions did not allow it. People joked about Khrushchev's obsession, calling him *kukuruznik* (the corn man). But this was an indication of the fundamental changes in government policy. The groundwork was laid for the development of the food industry.

As he persevered with these serious reforms, Khrushchev found himself unable to win support among top Party figures. The devolution of economic decision-making from Party-managed ministries to regional economic councils (*sovnarkhozy*) weakened the Communist Party's role in administering the country. This was bound to provoke concern among top Party officials. In addition, Khrushchev himself was a contradictory figure, having emerged as a strongman during the Stalin cult of personality period. While he pursued a policy of decentralising the administration of the economy, he was in no hurry to reform the country's political system or to share the unlimited power that was concentrated in his hands. As a result, there were ominous signs of a cult of personality being formed around Khrushchev himself. This was seized upon by Party apparatchiks led by Leonid Brezhnev. Khrushchev was accused of "voluntarism", of making important state decisions without having due regard for the laws of the system. At a specially convened plenary session of the CPSU[1] Central Committee, Khrushchev was removed as leader. The goal of Brezhnev and the people who brought him to power was to restore the centrally administered economy and the dominant role of the CPSU Central Committee in governing the country and bring about the gradual rehabilitation of Stalinism. The *sovnarkhozy* were dissolved, their powers handed back to revived state committees, ministries and Gosplan[2] as the central economic planning authority. But Khrushchev's reforms had already changed the face of the country and the trajectory of its development.

My personal entrance into adult life effectively coincided with this period: in 1962, two years before Brezhnev came to power, I graduated with a degree from the Moscow Technological Institute of the Food Industry (MTIPP) as a "food production mechanical engineer". For my graduate placement[3] I was offered two options: design engineer at the leading design institute, VNIIEKIPRODMASH, or machine shop supervisor at the well-known Yava tobacco factory. After giving it some thought, I chose the factory.

---

1   CPSU – the Communist Party of the Soviet Union.

2   Gosplan – the State Planning Commission.

3   Graduate placement – the compulsory job placement requirement that existed in the Soviet period for graduates of educational establishments.

Chapter 2.

The Yava Factory – A Group B Industrial Enterprise

My choice was guided not only by the placement requirement. At that time, I firmly believed that industry experience was an important first step towards becoming a good specialist in one's field. I was also attracted by the idea of working at such a unique enterprise.

The institute I had graduated from was not a particularly prestigious establishment. Nonetheless, we received a decent education. Lectures were given by major authorities who, for one reason or another, had found themselves exiled from the big-name colleges to the food institute. People tended to think of the food industry as something primitive. A neighbour of ours, a retired colonel, reacted with astonishment on learning that I was studying at the food institute: "What on earth can they teach you there? How to open a bottle of champagne?" Views of this sort were in large measure shaped by the way in which the food industry was regarded by the state itself, i.e. as a second-class industry.

In the Soviet economy, all enterprises were divided into two groups: A and B. Group A included industrial enterprises geared to making "means of production", i.e. materials and equipment. Group B was for the "production of articles of consumption", meaning food and consumer goods. Ever since the days of the "industrialisation of the entire country", state policy had been weighted towards developing the manufacture of means of production. Group B enterprises were financed with whatever was left. Since they were last in line to receive funds for development, it was hardly surprising that the quality of consumer goods remained poor.

When I arrived to sign up for work, I did not even notice a nondescript fence fronting 3 Yamskovo Polya Street. Harbouring quite different expectations at the time, I at first plunged into a smart-looking building, only to find myself at the checkpoint of a "closed"[1] defence enterprise called Nauka. The Yava factory was over the fence on the opposite side of the road.

---

1 "Closed" here means that it had a special, strict admission system.

I must say that my first impression was somewhat grim. The factory entrance was on the first floor of a dilapidated two-storey building that bore little resemblance to the lobby of a prominent enterprise. The personnel department and security office were also housed here. Once on the premises, the first thing I saw was the single-storey wooden warehouses used to store paper. The factory's first production building had been erected at the time of its opening at the end of the nineteenth century. The others had been built at different times during the Soviet period. They were disparate structures that did not meet the requirements that existed even at that time for contemporary enterprises. The equipment and technology were outdated too. I later found out that all tobacco factories were in this condition, as indeed was the Soviet food industry as a whole.

Yava was founded in 1856 by the Karaite merchant Samuil Gabay.[1] The name of the factory is easy enough to explain. Starting in 1912, the factory produced *papirosy*[2] using tobacco supplied from the Indonesian island of Java. In 1922, now under Soviet rule, it was decided to name the factory after the place from which its tobacco had originally been sourced.

Tobacco factories generally made *papirosy* using equipment dating from the early twentieth century. The main unit was the *papirosy* production (or "*papirosy* stuffing") shop, which worked three shifts. The working conditions there were hard, the rhythm exceedingly intense. The workers often developed hypertonia and hearing problems.

I was appointed shift supervisor in the machine shop, working on a shift basis: days one week, evenings the next. Sometimes I had to work nights, too. There was a system whereby engineering staff occasionally had to work as duty attendant in charge of the night shift. The factory attendant was stationed in the control room, which was in the production shop. I remember what a terrifying first impression it made on me. All the dividing walls shook from the vibration. The noise level was ninety-four to ninety-five decibels, compared to a regulatory limit of eighty-five. It was impossible even just to sit in that room. The dust concentration, which was subject to a limit of 4 mg/m^3, reached 8–9 mg just in the aisles. It is frightening to think what it must have been

---

1 The Karaites are an ethnic group professing a special, non-Talmudic, form of Judaism.

2 *Papirosa*, plural *papirosy* – a Russian-invented cigarette-like smoking article consisting of a tissue paper-wrapped "cartridge" of tobacco into which a cardboard mouthpiece was inserted.

in the work areas! Seventeen *papirosy* production lines were working virtually non-stop, day and night. The machines kept on running, while the workers sometimes cleaned up a little between shifts.

Work in the primary processing section was also hard. The processes used had not changed since pre-revolutionary times. There were bins known as *harmans*[1] in which the tobacco was blended and moistened. The tobacco arrived in compressed form (in bales). Its moisture content was 10–12 per cent. At this level, the tobacco was dry and brittle, making it difficult to process. It had to be manually divided into leaves, after which five or six grades would be put together for blending and moistened. The tobacco leaves were placed in layers in the *harmans*, then moistened with water from hoses, measured by eye. All this was done manually, without any mechanisation. Then the tobacco blend from the bins was transferred into crates and fed, again by hand, into the loading unit of the cutting mill. The workers' hands were constantly covered in wounds.

I was there to see the start of the factory's renovation. Assembly lines were installed to process the tobacco, and the moistening and blending began to be done mechanically. The baled tobacco was delivered to preparation tables. Each table was assigned a particular grade of tobacco for processing. Women workers broke the bales into leaves and fed them onto a common conveyor. The leaves then entered a rotating drum. In the drum, the different grades were mixed together and moistened with a vapour spray. The equipment was of the simplest kind, manufactured in the engineering workshops of the Yaroslavl Tobacco Factory. But even this was regarded as a major technical achievement for our country's tobacco industry. It was the first time that elements of modern technology had been incorporated into the primary processing stage. Moreover, at around the same time, vacuum pumps for the humidification of baled tobacco were purchased from Czechoslovakia. Yava was the first to have them installed. It proved to be a very effective process that enabled the entire mass of tobacco to be properly moistened. The tobacco acquired an elasticity, and the bale would fall apart itself without having to be broken up. This was a big step forward in terms of improving product quality and making working conditions more bearable. The advent of the new technology was a major event for the director, Mikhail Demyanovich Voitsekhovich. They even laid a marble floor in the primary section, which made our director movingly proud.

---

1 Probably derived from the Turkish word *harman*, signifying the process of threshing grain.

The cigarette-making shop operated a single shift using DK and DKO machines brought over from Germany as part of reparations in 1946. But the public was used to *papirosy*, and demand for cigarettes was limited. There were only a few factories that made them, including Yava and Ducat in Moscow. The cigarettes were unfiltered.

The machine shop made spare parts for the production machinery. Although the shop was classed as an auxiliary unit, it was actually a very important part of the factory. The equipment in the main workshops was outdated: parts quickly wore out and broke. From early in the morning the technical managers of the production shops would form a queue to our workshop to order replacements for parts that had broken, causing machines to stand idle. These orders had to be dealt with straight away so as to get everything back up and running as quickly as possible. The workshop answered to the chief mechanic's office. The machine tools were old, too, but they were in working condition. There were around sixty-five to seventy people employed in the workshop. There was a separate unit for the quenching and forging of workpieces, which people referred to as the "hot shop". I must say that the technical staff were quite highly skilled at what they did.

At the institute I had trained in engineering disciplines. I had taken an optional course on "Programmed control of metal-cutting machines". I wanted to do something modern and advanced, to make changes for the better. I began to see where the problems lay. The orders from the production shops for the manufacture of spare parts were poorly organised, meaning that we were constantly having to "put out fires". The technical managers were practical workers with no specialised technical education. They had a good understanding of the equipment but their organisational skills were poor. In this respect they had not advanced beyond the level they had achieved when they first started working at the factory. I realised that it was essential to organise statistical records of the consumption of spare parts, and I set about doing just that.

The formation of the factory's workforce dated from the end of the nineteenth century when the Gabay partnership had moved its operations to 3 Yamskovo Polya Street next to Belorussky (then Brest) Station. At that time, large-scale industry was only just beginning to appear in Moscow. The population lived compactly in historically known districts and was divided into Arbatians, Tverians, Zamoskvorechians, and so on. When an enterprise started up, it was sometimes the one and only source of work, and people treated it as a second home. At the Gabay factory, too, the workforce was mostly made up of residents of the area around it. It was also at that time that the traditions of family bonds within the labour collective began to take shape, along with feelings of factory patriotism and pride in one's enterprise.

When I came to the Yava, those traditions were still in place. The kernel of the workforce comprised people who had begun their working life before or just after the war. Tobacco production was a stable job that came with good wages and a variety of benefits. A service record of eighteen to twenty years was at the low end. People had worked for thirty, forty, even fifty years. It was a somewhat monolithic group. Everyone was in some way connected with everyone else; they were like family to each other. They would have relatives and neighbours working alongside them. They would bring their children to work there. If a vacancy came up, there was already a queue of people waiting to take it. People considered it a great blessing to be able to work at a factory like that. As at other Soviet enterprises, the managerial staff were mostly trained and promoted from among existing employees. They would come to the factory at a young age, usually as adolescents, learn the skills of their trade, then the most capable of them would gradually climb the ranks. This meant that the managers came from among the workforce's "own", from yesterday's factory hands. They were mainly practical workers or specialists with an intermediate technical education. While still working they would do courses at the food industry evening college, which had a branch in the training centre located directly on the factory's premises. This maintained the family, patriarchal traditions of relationships within the workforce. It was all for one. This was something that those at the top would take into account. When a new director had to be appointed at the enterprise, they did what they could to nominate someone from the factory's staff.

Our director, Mikhail Demyanovich Voitsekhovich, came to the factory after leaving factory-and-works college at the end of the 1920s. He became chief mechanic, shop foreman, chief engineer and, finally, director. As people used to say, he had "gone through all the stages of production". It was written on his CV that he had an "unfinished higher education". With all his practical experience, it did not seem essential for him to have a higher education as well. Mikhail Demyanovich was a demanding person, a man of "strong character" as they used to say at the factory. He did not hold back from giving a tongue-lashing, and people were afraid to disobey him. He had worked with these people virtually all his life, and this was bound to manifest itself in the relationship he had with his subordinates. The director was determined to keep order, anxious to ensure that the factory remained the leading enterprise in the industry. He demanded a lot from his workers, but he also supported them. I should add that his own brother was a simple worker in the primary processing section, and his wife was an engineer in the economic planning department. The same went for other managerial staff, and particularly the shop foremen, who were in charge of large groups of employees. Relationships between management and workers were informal. I remember times when, after hearing complaints from some of the women workers, the director personally intervened to talk sense into their errant husbands and reconcile the spouses. And it all worked very well. Sackings were extremely rare. Everyone on the workforce knew each other's weaknesses and did what they could to keep them in check.

There were numerous occasions on which I saw people show a great sense of responsibility towards their work and act as true patriots of the factory. I remember a time when a fire broke out at the factory at night. Many workers lived nearby and came along themselves, collecting water after the fire had been extinguished. The older workwomen wept, wailing "What will become of the factory now?" And this was despite the fact that they lived and worked in dreadful conditions. Many women had serious family problems: their husbands drank, and money was usually tight.

Work was paid on a piece-rate basis, and people tried to earn as much as they could. The main conflicts arose when workers were down on earnings because the machinery had stopped working or for other reasons. The administration was at pains to fulfil the plan, otherwise bonuses might not be paid, or the director might even lose his position. This would mean the "family" losing its "papa". I will describe later how Voitsekhovich faced dismissal. People fought for him. One of our more determined workwomen managed to deliver a collective letter to the Kremlin. The loss of "our director" was a threat to the whole family.

This was in the Khrushchev reform period, when the so-called *sovnarkhozy* (regional economic councils) were set up. Khrushchev had set a goal of decentralising the economy and promoting more energetic development of the regions. Each region had its own administrative authority – the *sovnarkhoz* – which had the power to resolve many local issues without consulting Moscow.

There were even little ditties, or *chastushki*, about this: *"Now we find that all our woes are settled by the* sovnarkhoz". The regions gained greater access to resources, and the centre's power to redistribute them was severely limited. I will give an example. The metal-cutting equipment was hopelessly outdated. When I became head of the machine shop, I put in a request to the management for new machine tools to be allocated. There were a lot of machine tool-building enterprises in the Moscow region. Previously, however, machine tools had only been supplied to Group A enterprises based on distribution orders from the centre. The factory was visited by the head of the Moscow *sovnarkhoz*, Comrade Doyenin. We showed him the outdated machines in the machine shop, on which it was difficult to make parts to repair equipment. After the chairman's visit, the Moscow *sovnarkhoz* allocated five new metal-cutting machines for Yava. It was an astonishing victory. The workers could hardly believe their eyes when the new machines arrived at the factory. This was only possible thanks to Khrushchev's reforms. But these were small, local-level achievements. The reforms did not bring serious improvements to the efficiency of the Soviet economy. Where did Khrushchev go wrong? After decentralising administration, he should have let go of the economy. It was a mistake to try to combine decentralisation with a command economy based on the Party system.

After starting work in the machine shop, I soon realised that our machine operators were a unique breed. Yes, they all liked to drink, but they were consummate professionals, very proud and very intelligent. They had interesting opinions. They had pride in their work. They were incapable of doing work badly. Having come to the factory as mere boys, they had learned through hard experience what real work meant, what quality meant. Another thing that typified these people was their lack of faith in positive change. They were used to living in hardship and regarded it as just the way things were. This is why even the appearance of new machine tools was something akin to a miracle as far as they were concerned. Somehow or other we managed to procure a modern boring machine, a unique piece of equipment. And the workers looked after it.

I remember an episode that helped boost my standing among the workers. From my very first days at the workshop I had noticed that the workers were dressed in any old clothes. It transpired that the regulations did not provide for overalls to be allocated to machine shop employees – which was why they went about in rags. I was young and full of hope. Having grown up in a reasonably well-to-do family, I had naturally seen little of reality and was somewhat naïve. Accordingly, I thought that everything ought to be resolved in accordance with common sense. After learning that the decision depended on the deputy director for commercial matters, I went to see him. His name was Garnik Kegamovich Azizyan. He was quite an elderly man by then, very learned, with an interesting background. He had previously worked at the USSR Ministry of Food, where he had been deputy head of the Chief Supply Office (Glavsnab). He had even been close to Mikoyan[1] when the latter was the Food Minister of the USSR. Khrushchev had instigated a campaign to "purify" the Party ranks. It was declared that it was not becoming for a true Communist to enjoy material excesses in his personal life. There was a point at which any officials who possessed large dachas came in for censure. And Azizyan had a mammoth dacha in Bolshevo in the Moscow suburbs: almost a hectare of land. He was summoned to the Party organisation and asked to turn over his dacha to the state, but he refused. He was expelled from the Party, sacked from the ministry and "exiled" to the post of deputy director at Yava.

And so it was he whom I went to see. He welcomed me in, bade me sit on a leather sofa, and began to ask me questions. I told him that workers in the machine shop were not issued overalls despite the fact that they were constantly in contact with metal shavings, coolant, and so on. He responded very good-naturedly and promised to see what he could do. And he actually succeeded. At his own risk and peril (contrary to the regulations), he ordered overalls to be issued to the entire machine shop. This was my first victory. The workers could scarcely believe it when I said to them, "Here are your overalls". They saw that I really was working in their interests. As I said before, people had little faith that things could be changed for the better.

A good wage was considered to be in the region of 150–160[2] roubles. If it came out at 120–130 roubles, there would be conflicts between workers and department managers, with daggers drawn over those extra 20–30 roubles. That was how things were wherever the piece-rate system was used. People fought for every last kopeck. They had no expectations beyond this. Incorrect output

---

1   Anastas Ivanovich Mikoyan (1895–1978). Influential Soviet statesman and politician. Held a number of ministerial posts and was a member of the Politburo of the Central Committee of the Communist Party of the USSR – the country's highest administrative authority.

2   In 1963 the official exchange rate was 1 rouble to US$0.29 However, that was an artificially inflated rate which bore no relation to reality.

quotas, equipment downtimes for reasons beyond the workers' control, lack of spare parts, poor-quality paper, damp tobacco: these issues were raised at every meeting. The whole of life revolved around these problems.

Soon after I arrived at the factory, I was invited to attend a function in celebration of the forty-fifth anniversary of the October Revolution. It took place in the building of the Pushkin Theatre, where a show was put on that evening especially for our staff. All the invited employees came with their wives and husbands. It was very grand, and people looked very dignified. This was decent society in the old mould, in contrast to work gatherings in the 1970s–80s, when many people inevitably drank themselves into a stupor by the end of proceedings.

As a young engineer, I was introduced to the former director of the factory, Maria Andreyevna Ivanova, a pleasant, now elderly woman who had retired in 1961 (a year before I had joined the factory). She had been made director in the 1930s, entering the ranks of "Stalin's recruits" rather than repressed "enemies of the people". During the war years, when equipment and remaining staff had to be evacuated to the Kuybyshev (now Samara) Tobacco Factory, she became one of the so-called "golden pool", or crème de la crème, of managers of major enterprises of the food industry, and enjoyed great authority in the eyes of government and industry leaders.

The war period must have been a very hard time to work. Even now, I am at a loss to understand (thinking of my parents and neighbours) how people survived that terrible time. Yava had to evacuate the factory out of Moscow and at the same time keep the army supplied with smokes. Tobacco meant even more to the soldiers at the front than their hundred grams ration of vodka. Stalin himself was never without a pipe in his hands as he worked through the night. He would fill his pipe with tobacco taken from Herzegovina Flor *papirosy* made at Yava. The top generals, meanwhile, usually opted for Yava's Kazbek brand. It was a huge responsibility: everyone is aware of the consequences that could ensue in Stalin's time even for minor errors and omissions. I am sure that a fair number of difficult work situations must have arisen during that period, but all issues were resolved internally, ensuring that the managers did not fall victim to repressions. I imagine that it was the family atmosphere at Yava that helped the workers to survive and keep going in those difficult years. Old-timers gave detailed accounts of how Herzegovina Flor *papirosy* were made for the Great

Leader. The whole process took place under the total control of the NKVD, with members of the work crew rigorously vetted beforehand for reliability. On the appointed day, in the presence of representatives of the authorities, the manufacturing process would begin. Before anything else was done, the workers would thoroughly clean the machines with alcohol. The materials and tobacco would be inspected in advance in a laboratory outside the factory, presumably to check for any poisonous substances. The quality of the finished *papirosy* was checked by the factory's quality control department. They were then taken away by NKVD officials to a special depot. I feel certain that further inspections would have been carried out there: Stalin became increasingly paranoid towards the end of his life.

Maria Andreyevna was a remarkable woman who had managed to guide a large enterprise through those difficult years and become its matriarch. Naturally, she had her confidants – people who acted as her eyes and ears among the workers. This enabled her to feel relatively at ease. The head of the factory's economic planning department, who had worked at Yava during the war while still a girl, recounted to me how she had once taken some papers into the director's office, only to find Maria Andreyevna sitting on the sofa playing cards with her favourite grandson. All the same, she lived very modestly towards the end of her life.

At the end of the 1960s, memories of the Great Patriotic War were still fresh in people's minds. In 1965 the country marked the twentieth anniversary of the victory. A celebratory evening was organised at the factory. Government awards were issued to war veterans. I was amazed to discover that around 250 of the factory's employees had served in the Great Patriotic War. Everyone came wearing suits and displaying their orders and medals. Seated at tables, they enjoyed drinks and snacks in the time-honoured way. It felt very festive and very moving.

Mikhail Demyanovich Voitsekhovich held the position of chief engineer until he took over as director of the factory after Maria Andreyevna's retirement. I think that he adopted many of his predecessor's ways of doing things. Essentially, it was the same "family" but with a new "head of household". He too had a circle of confidants on whom he relied: the chief accountant, the head of the personnel department, the shop foremen. The engineering divisions became the "stepchildren", in that they were the first to be blamed for any failures or problems. This meant that the inner circle always had a supply of scapegoats – which was important, as one of the primary tasks of management was to shape public opinion within the workforce and manage people's moods.

Yava had what was considered a large Party organisation.[1] Being a Party member carried prestige, and admission was subject to strict rules. The factors considered were not only the candidate's productivity and discipline, but also his or her social activism and understanding of the Party's goals and objectives. Applications had to be accompanied by recommendations from two Party members with a certain number of years' service behind them. The final decision was made by a vote at a general meeting of the factory.

Party membership gave the most active workers the opportunity to express their views at Party meetings and thereby influence what went on at the enterprise. Party meetings could be boisterous affairs. A lot of criticism was aired. The managerial staff were obliged to reckon with the opinion of the Party organisation – "to pay attention and respond in a timely manner to criticism from Communists". The last thing they would have wanted was for disagreements within the workforce to reach the ears of the *raikom*, or district Party committee.[2] Criticism at Party meetings was regarded as a sign of healthy and constructive relationships within the workforce. The important thing was that it did not cross certain boundaries. For example, if the director was criticised, this was an indication of systemic disagreements between management and the Party organisation. Maintaining a good balance in matters of administration was a delicate matter. This made it especially important to nominate a suitable person as Party secretary. The candidate had to satisfy the *raikom* and be accepted by Party members – but most importantly, the management had to be sure that the power placed in his hands would not induce him to pull any unexpected tricks.

Managing a workforce of this kind was no easy matter. Tobacco factories were considered the most technologically advanced enterprises in the food industry. They had a more skilled workforce. People who had worked at the factory for thirty to forty years understandably felt that they had a stake in the enterprise. It was important to take this into account, listen to what the workers had to say and show them respect. Relations with the workforce were mostly handled through public organisations, namely the Party bureau and the trade union

---

1   Shop floor Communist Party organisations were set up at all major enterprises.
2   The district Party committee (*raikom*) was senior to the shop floor organisation.

committee. The director kept full control over these matters. There were many worthy people among the workers. There were obvious leaders who commanded respect within the labour collective. First and foremost among them were the machine adjusters in the *papirosy* production shop. These were highly regarded people of advanced years with a long record of service at the factory. Some of them had emerged as personalities even before the Revolution. They were people of the old school, known for their maturity and sense of responsibility. They set great store by their reputation and valued the respect accorded to them by the bosses. To a large extent, the way they conducted themselves set the tone of relationships within the workforce. Whenever I talked to them, even I found myself trying to pull my socks up on some instinctive level. The best-known representative of this group of workers was Vasily Markovich Morozov, who had worked at Yava for over fifty years. Vasily Markovich was well-known within the tobacco industry, and by order of the ministry he had been awarded the highest government honour – the Order of Lenin. He was a fine professional, a mentor who had trained many young workers, and an active member of the Party. As people used to say then, he was "ideologically well-trained". When talking about the factory's affairs he often used expressions such as "interests of the state", "Party discipline and responsibility", "ideological guidance", etc. These were not just words, but reflected his way of thinking and the strength of his convictions. At that time, the most devoted Party members still believed in the triumph of Communist ideas.

People were not in a hurry to leave the factory after their shift ended. The environment at the enterprise tended to draw people together socially. There were always various kinds of social gatherings, whether it be Party and trade union meetings or get-togethers with workmates. People hung around to seek advice on some personal matter or request help from the trade union committee. On the factory's grounds was a small garden with a few large trees, a survival from the olden days, where people could sit and chat in a relaxed atmosphere. There was a large library, and the workers did actually read the books in it. The pursuit of learning was viewed as something honourable, and the authorities actively encouraged it. No one could have imagined then that cardinal changes were afoot which would lead to the dismantling of the patriarchal family structure at the factory.

The year 1964 saw the start of another radical overhaul of the economic system. As I mentioned before, the *sovnarkhozy* (economic councils) were set up as regional bodies, but the economy remained centrally managed. Enterprises within one industry came under different *sovnarkhozy*. This hampered the development of industries, which is why the *sovnarkhoz* system ultimately proved unviable. The basic idea was good, but the necessary economic framework was never put in place. When Khrushchev was removed, one of the charges levelled against him was that, because of the *sovnarkhozy*, control over industries had been lost. The decision was made to go back to sectoral administration and revive the old ministries and chief directorates (*glavki*).[1] This created a need for administrative personnel. Yava's chief engineer was moved to the post of chief engineer at Rosglavtabak – the chief directorate for the tobacco industry within the Food Ministry of the RSFSR.[2] The chief engineer post at the factory thus became vacant. The "family" pondered over what to do. They did not want to take on someone from the outside, a stranger. But they had no candidates among themselves. They were all practical workers with only secondary education. They would not be approved by the ministry. For around six months, the factory carried on without a chief engineer. By that time, I was foreman of the machine shop. I had managed to do quite a lot in terms of organising the supply of parts and had raised the need for greater thoroughness in the preparation of shop orders. This required me to show character and argue with my colleagues. At that time, life had not yet taught me how to be flexible, and there were quite a few occasions on which I was rather too forceful in making my point.

Then, out of the blue, I was summoned to the director, who said, "Leonid, I have been thinking and thinking. You are a young man with plenty of energy. I want to offer you the post of chief engineer". This came as a complete surprise. I was twenty-six years old. I did not know all that much about the factory's core business. Of course, I had done my best to get to grips with some of the issues involved, but I still had a lot to learn. Anyway, I answered that I would have to think about it and seek advice, since it was a very serious decision. I was not yet sure that working at an industrial plant was the path I wanted to take. Literally a week before this happened, I had received an invitation to do a postgraduate traineeship in the institute's metalworking faculty. On the other hand, I understood that this

---

1   *Glavk* was the common name for a sectoral directorate under the direct jurisdiction of a ministry.
2   RSFSR – the Russian Soviet Federal Soviet Republic (also referred to as the Russian Federation and the Russian Republic).

tempting offer of the position of chief engineer at a well-known enterprise was a once-in-a-lifetime opportunity. I had been given a chance to prove myself. In the end, therefore, I decided to give it a go and gave my agreement. And I turned out to be right – it really was the opportunity of a lifetime.

The country was undergoing intensive restructuring of its administrative system. My appointment had to be approved by the ministry's collegium. When submitting my nomination, the minister said, "The Yava factory is going to be renovated, so it is good that we are appointing a young man". Not long afterwards, however, our director found himself in trouble. I was still a mere *Komsomolets*[1] at that time. It was unthinkable for someone who was not a Party member to be appointed to a position of such responsibility. Evidently, amid all the administrative changes going on in the country, the Party bodies had taken their eye off the ball. The director was summoned to the *raikom* and asked to explain how he could have appointed a *Komsomolets* to such a position. The secretary of the Party organisation invited me to come and see her and asked me to submit an application. I answered that I was not yet morally prepared, that people might think that I was joining the Party just to further my career. Having only just been appointed, I needed to prove my worth and demonstrate that I was up to the job. In the end, I remained a *Komsomolets* for another year or more. When I think back to that time, I must assume that my appointment was only made possible by the Khrushchev thaw, when the country suddenly breathed more freely after the Stalinist tyranny. How did it come about that such a young man, of Jewish ethnicity, was appointed chief engineer of such a large enterprise, the leader of its industry? It could only have happened as a consequence of the weakening of the influence of the Communist Party. I think that it was precisely that fear of losing Party control over the economy that led to Khrushchev being ousted as a result of an internal plot hatched by party leaders.

I have some interesting memories of my first director. Mikhail Demyanovich Voitsekhovich was certainly a striking character. A very good-looking man, he was extremely fond of women. He had a number of favourites among the most attractive women at the factory. His wife knew all about it, of course. She worked as an engineer in the factory's economic planning department, used her maiden name, Vedeneyeva, and pretended not to notice anything. They made a

---

1   *Komsomolets*, i.e. a member of the *Komsomol*, the Communist Union of Youth – the CPSU's youth organisation.

curious couple. At work they always used the polite plural to address each other. At that point in time, Voitsekhovich had become something of a heavyweight. He was at the peak of his influence. When Kosygin embarked on his reform programme,[1] Voitsekhovich was one of the few directors to be included in the working group to discuss the drafts of the relevant government resolutions. He had been abroad and had extensive contacts. This would later help him create the well-known packaging for Yava cigarettes, which was designed in Finland at his personal request. Once, the directors of the tobacco factories were summoned by Dymshits,[2] the first deputy chairman of the government and the head of the Supreme Economic Council[3] under Khrushchev. It was explained that the budget was underfunded, and one of the quickest and most reliable ways of raising revenue might be to exceed the targets for sales of tobacco products. Dymshits asked the directors to increase output. He promised each director a brand-new Volga. This was in 1964. The tobacco bosses kept their side of the bargain and increased output as requested. Our director received a swanky new Volga. Then something curious happened. We received a visit from the director of the Kursk Tobacco Factory (it was common for directors to come to Yava for various reasons). The car he drew up in was a Moskvich. He explained that when his Volga had arrived, he had immediately been summoned to the provincial Party committee to be told: "Who do you think you are? We don't have Volgas, and you expect to drive around in a Volga?!" They gave him a Moskvich and confiscated the Volga. This was the sort of thing that went on. He was lucky to get the Moskvich.[4]

Our director had a distinctive style of management. He lived close to the factory and usually came to work very early. Every morning he would do the rounds and rattle off a ton of observations, generally couched in somewhat coarse language. He would berate the engineers and shop foremen. The workers saw

---

1 Alexei Nikolayevich Kosygin (1904–1980) – chairman of the Council of Ministers of the USSR from 1964. Attempted to reform the Soviet economy by giving enterprises and their employees a greater stake in their performance.
2 Veniamin Emmanuilovich Dymshits (1910–1993) – a major figure in politics and industry in the period 1959–1986. A member of the CPSU Central Committee.
3 The Supreme Council of the National Economy of the Council of Ministers of the USSR – the highest state institution for the administration of industry and construction in the country.
4 Volga here refers to the GAZ-21 model, and Moskvich to the Moskvich-408. There were very few privately owned Volgas about, contrary to the impression created in the 1962 film, *Watch Out for the Car*.

this. They knew that the director was a good man, that he was on the side of the workers. His behaviour acted as an incentive. In fact, he was not the only one who employed this approach. Many directors acted in a similar way. It was a question of maintaining a balance in the relationship between managers and workers. Voitsekhovich might have been quick to give people a telling-off, but when it came to serious disputes, he would stand up for his own people and have their backs. I grew to understand this way of running things. I had to learn to take account of all these nuances. Sometimes I had to learn the hard way, too. The chief engineer was also the first deputy director. It was a highly responsible role.

The factory produced a total of fifteen billion units of tobacco products each year, 85 per cent of which were *papirosy*. The main brand of *papirosy* was Belomorkanal. There was keen demand for Yava's "Belomor" alongside *papirosy* produced by the Uritsky factory in Leningrad. *Papirosy* are a purely Russian product. In the nineteenth century they were even smoked by businessmen in Europe: I noticed this recently while reading Thomas Mann's novel, *Buddenbrooks*. They were probably of a decent quality. The equipment and methods for manufacturing them were developed in Russia.[1] First, a tube-making machine was invented (for the manufacture of *papirosy* tubes). The inventors were Russian engineers, the Kurkevich brothers. Another version was proposed by an engineer called Semyonov. The development of the machines earned the Kurkeviches the Grand Prix at the World Exhibition in Brussels in 1904. It was a unique design. The basis of the *papirosa* consisted of a cylindrical "shirt" made from *papirosa* paper (thin cigarette paper). A mouthpiece was inserted into the lower part of the shirt with the aid of a special device, while the upper part formed the "*papirosa* tube" into which the tobacco was stuffed. The cylindrical shirt (i.e. the tube) was made without any glue, the seam being formed by a special lock with the aid of an original component known as a *maletka*. This was know-how. This was what was being achieved in Russian engineering at the beginning of the twentieth century! I have been fortunate enough to see an original Semyonov-designed tube-making machine in operation. They were actually called "Semonyov machines". Yava had three such machines, which were used to make high-grade *papirosy*. It was a pleasure to see them in operation. There was no noise or vibration, and the quality of the *papirosy* was irreproachable.

---

1 The first known mention of *papirosy* in official documents dates from 1844.

A feature of Soviet times was the practice of "intensifying" the use of equipment to make it more productive. Tube-making machines were initially designed to produce forty to fifty tubes per minute. The tubes were arranged in special containers ("carriages") and sent to be stuffed with tobacco, a process that was done manually. Later, *papirosy*-stuffing machines were developed (designed by the engineer Katsnelson). Until the mid-1950s there were two *papirosy* production shops at the factory: the "tube-making shop" and the "packing shop". It was in the packing shop that the tubes were filled with tobacco and the finished *papirosy* were put into packs. After the war, the production of *papirosy* had to be substantially stepped up. The rural population smoked roll-ups made using *makhorka* tobacco. People in rural areas grew *makhorka* themselves and produced home-made *makhorka* tobacco by drying and cutting the leaves. There was also a *makhorka* industry. *Makhorka* was grown in the Tambov, Lipetsk and Kursk regions, and was industrially processed by factories in Yelets, Usman, Kursk and Morshansk (in the Tambov region) to make *makhorka* tobacco, which went on sale and was used for roll-ups. *Makhorka* is much stronger than normal tobacco and has a very coarse flavour. The paper used was ordinary newsprint, which is very harmful when burned. People in the army had smoked roll-ups during the war. But times were moving on. The rural population was decreasing, and city folk smoked *papirosy*. The rural youth followed their example and switched to factory-made products. There was a pressing need to increase production of *papirosy*, and it was to meet this need that assembly lines were created in the post-war period. One assembly line comprised ten units. Each unit consisted of interconnected tube-making and stuffing machines and produced finished *papirosy*. The *papirosy* from each unit were fed onto a common conveyor, and from there to the PUCh packing machine, which assembled the *papirosy* into packs of twenty-five. This, of course, was a revolution. It meant the complete reconfiguration of the entire production process and entirely different arrangements for organising labour and equipment maintenance. A single unit could produce up to 300 *papirosy* per minute, and the total line output was 1,200,000–1,300,000 *papirosy* over eight hours. Of course, operating the equipment at this intensity degraded the quality of the *papirosy*, caused parts to wear out more quickly and made working conditions harder to bear for the factory's workers (owing to the increased vibration and dust concentration). But there were not enough resources to implement real modernisation or develop new manufacturing processes. These practices may have been referred to as "modernisation" in all the documents, but really it was just plain and simple "intensification": in other words, they pushed the equipment to attain higher rates of productivity but without making any serious changes to its design. In effect, it was the way in which the *papirosy* lines were operated that caused the problems that subsequently had to be wrestled with. Every day was spent labouring to overcome difficulties resulting from the adoption of the assembly lines. But the main objective – increasing production at whatever cost – was achieved.

When the chief directorates took over from the *sovnarkhozy* (regional economic councils), things got more complicated. Under the *sovnarkhozy* we had felt relatively unsupervised. But after the ministries were reinstated, the factory came under the control of Rosglavtabak, the chief directorate for the tobacco industry under the Food Ministry of the RSFSR. The director of the Uritsky factory in Leningrad, Nikita Ivanovich Karakozov, was appointed head of the chief directorate. A very experienced manager, he assembled a competent team. The chief directorate began setting tougher targets for enterprises, imposing higher demands. The first meeting of the core members of Rosglavtaba*k* was held at Yava to review the factory's performance. Officials from the directorate arrived and found a host of deficiencies. It was interesting to observe the factory's "family" attempting to defend itself. The shop foremen made speeches and tried to make their voices heard, but their arguments were rather feeble. They blamed everything on external difficulties. This was the way dealings between enterprises and the ministry usually went.

The factory was a relatively smooth-running establishment. The workers knew their equipment inside out, and all spare parts were made in the machine shop. I remember how the overhauling of *papirosy*-stuffing and tube-making machines was carried out. The machine would be completely dismantled to its bare frame, and after a good scraping down, all the parts would be put back together again. A complete overhaul would take between three and five days. All the process materials (tube, mouthpiece and pack paper) were supplied by Soviet enterprises. Tobacco was supplied in the quantities required from Union republics (Moldavia, Azerbaijan, Uzbekistan and Georgia) or imported from other countries (India, Bulgaria, Greece and Turkey). It was hard to get a job in Moscow in those days, and so labour discipline was high, and people took a responsible attitude to their work. The flip side of this apparent stability was that hardly anything changed over a long period of time. Stagnation had set in at the enterprise. The factory's staff found themselves dealing with the same old problems year after year. People got used to this state of affairs.

Perhaps the most pressing issue was getting hold of corrugated packaging (containers) in which to place *papirosy* and cigarette packs before they were shipped for retail. New corrugated packaging was in short supply, and the plan required the enterprise to use "return" (used) containers for 40 per cent of its needs. These were supposed to be brought to the factory by Avtomattorg stores, which sold tobacco products. But they were slow about doing this and did not always bring as much as they were meant to (because of difficulties in collecting and transporting the containers), as a result of which the factory had to make its own arrangements to get the used packaging delivered. Because of the shortage of containers, the work crews often had to store products on the floor next to the production line until there were containers to put them in. This situation arose virtually every week and was a source of great stress for workers and management alike, because apart from the additional labour involved, all this extra moving around had a detrimental effect on the products themselves.

Meeting the target for shipments to the far north was a major problem. At that time, the government paid special attention to this matter, and everything had to be done in time to fit in with the short navigation period in which ships could deliver cargoes to those remote areas. Tough targets were set for volumes to be supplied. The packing methods used had to ensure that the goods were hermetically sealed for the sea journey. When I joined, boxes were still waxed (coated in paraffin wax) before being placed in special wooden crates, which were also made at the factory. All these laborious operations were done by hand. Making the wooden crates was especially problematic. The idea of mechanising this process was raised from time to time, but there was not enough space for even the simplest machinery. Fulfilling the plan for supplies to the far north was extremely difficult: it meant getting all hands on deck and borrowing extra workers from other departments. But not fulfilling it was not an option.

"Special orders" were another important responsibility. It was the Yava factory that traditionally supplied tobacco products to the special depots (501 and 208) responsible for provisioning the canteens of the CPSU Central Committee and other top Party and government agencies. It need hardly be said that there were special delivery conditions for these products, and quality requirements were more stringent than normal. Everything was closely monitored. The whole staff bent over backwards to ensure that no deficiencies would be found.

In the Russian Federation, tobacco products were distributed via local branches of Rosbakaleya, the distribution division of the Trade Ministry, which was responsible for sales of confectionery, sugar and salt as well as tobacco products. Yava's products were sold through Rosbakaleya's Moscow office. What was the process by which products reached sales outlets? Rosbakaleya rented a space at the factory as a shipping room for finished products. As soon as boxes of tobacco products made it to the shipping room, the factory regarded them as sold. The products were then taken either to Rosbakaleya's warehouses or directly to Avtomattorg sales outlets. The next day, money would enter the factory's account. Because tobacco products were in short supply, everything was bought up on virtually the same day as it reached the sales outlets. It seemed simple enough. But glitches arose at individual points in the supply chain. The shipping room was too small for anything much to be stored in it. Boxes were put straight into trucks, which meant that the rate at which goods were taken out was wholly dependent on the efficiency of transport operations. And this was where problems arose: generally speaking, the quantity of goods taken off the premises each day was less than the quantity being manufactured. As a result, a large number of boxes amassed in the workshops over the course of the week. They were piled up in the aisle spaces between the production lines. This made working conditions very difficult and disrupted the rhythm of production. People grew very stressed over this issue, and it was something that the management had to keep a constant watch over.

The enterprise was judged chiefly on whether it met production and economic targets: physical volume of production, gross output, sales and profits, supplies to far north areas, and special orders. There were also a lot of additional parameters, such as fulfilment of quality requirements, meeting of targets for savings on materials, avoidance of payroll overspending, and fulfilment of the plan for bringing in new equipment and new types of products. All this was communicated in the form of an itemised assignment. Fulfilling the government plan was an absolute must. The payment of the bonus for engineering and technical staff, popularly referred to as the *progressivka*, was dependent on it. Although this payment was called a bonus, it was actually a part of planned salary. In Soviet times the monthly pay of engineers and technicians was very low. An engineer received 100–120 roubles per month, the chief engineer 180 roubles, the director 200 roubles. This meant that engineers were highly incentivised to ensure that they got their *progressivka* (which amounted to 40 per cent of basic pay), since it was difficult to support a family on basic pay alone. Fulfilling the plan was critically important for the enterprise's engineering and management staff. Machine operators were generally paid on a piece-rate basis. Output quotas were set for every crew working on a production line. Members of the crew would only receive a bonus if the quotas were fulfilled. If they were overfulfilled, the bonus would be increased. If all lines (crews) fulfilled their output quotas, this meant that the production plan for the enterprise as a whole would be fulfilled. That was how the system worked: the machine operators strove to overfulfil the output quota, while engineers and technicians concerned themselves with the fulfilment of all the obligations of the enterprise as a whole. Production efficiency was measured by the indicator of "achieved average productivity of equipment", or "equipment output" as it was sometimes called. High equipment outputs ensured that the enterprise was on course to fulfil the production plan, which was why the bonus system at the factory was aimed at encouraging the achievement of higher equipment outputs, and why "socialist" competition between different crews, shifts and workshops in this regard was actively used as a form of incentive.

Quality assurance was an important factor. The Yava factory's reputation as a producer of high-quality products had been duly earned: the enterprise placed great emphasis on this matter. The Quality Control Department (QCD) had considerable authority, and there was a very effective quality evaluation system in place. The QCD was staffed by the most skilled employees, who had worked at all the production stages at Yava. The head of the department was the veteran worker Tamara Ilyinichna Mozdgrishvili, who had worked at the factory back when the Gabays were in charge. She was highly respected and commanded great authority. In her office stood "Gabay's chair", made by the famous Russian craftsman Shutov.[1] The back of the chair was in the form of a shaft bow from a horse's harness, while the elbow rests were in the form of hatchets. On the

---

1   Vasily Petrovich Shutov (1826–1887) – Petersburg joiner and woodcarver. In 1870 he received the bronze medal at the All-Russian Industrial Exhibition for his "Shaft bows, hatchets and mittens" armchair, which sealed his reputation as a master craftsman.

seat there were two mittens, and the back was inscribed with the words "Slow and steady wins the race". We interpreted this to mean that success is achieved by working hard and taking the time to get things right. This acted as a sort of motto for Yava. Work crews were only paid a bonus if they produced products of good or excellent quality. Samples of *papirosy* and cigarettes were taken several times per shift for inspection by the process laboratory and the QCD. Particular attention was paid to the quality of products made for "special" orders and for the far north. It was the strict quality control system, combined with the long-standing traditions of the Yava labour collective, that earned the factory's products such a high rating. Besides the popular mainstream brands of *papirosy*, such as Belomorkana*l* and Kazbek, Yava was famed for the premium brands Tri bogatyrya (Three bogatyrs), Sputnik and Herzegovina Flor. These were of a higher quality than the mass varieties. They were manufactured by the old methods on Semyonov's machines, wrapped in foil and packed in attractive cartons. The carton itself was then wrapped in a thin transparent paper. They were intended as gift products. The production volumes were small, as all the manufacturing operations were done by hand. Yava was the only factory in the country to make Zolotoye Runo (Golden Fleece) flavoured cigarettes. The distinctive taste was achieved by treating the uncut tobacco with a special sauce that included unusual ingredients: prunes, honey and walnuts. Zolotoye Runo were well-known throughout the country, and even non-smokers noticed their unusually pleasant aroma.

I think that the popularity of Yava's products was largely down to the highly professional and conscientious work ethic of its staff. One might say that the workers acted as custodians of the quality of the Yava brand. If anything fell short of the standards set, there would be all sorts of unpleasant scenes. People would admonish each other, insisting that things be done the right way. It was all achieved through intense, stressful work.

Such was the factory at which I found myself appointed chief engineer. The factory administration was housed in an old two-storey building erected by the factory's founder, the first-guild merchant Samuil Gabay. The ground floor had once accommodated the factory's office, while the first floor served as apartments for the owner's family. At the time of my arrival at the factory, the ground floor was occupied by the management, while upstairs were the Party bureau's room, the trade union chairman's office, a small meeting room and a very good library.

The chief engineer's office was just opposite the director's; between them was a shared reception area. Every Monday, a supervisors' meeting would take place in the director's office. The director would preside over the meeting, seated at the head of a vast carved table, with the chief engineer and the commercial managers sitting to his right and left on large, high-backed armchairs. The shop foremen, department heads and chief specialists sat on ordinary chairs. Usually, the chief supervisor would report on operating results and problems, and then there would be discussions about specific issues. I remember how psychologically difficult it was at first to bridge the short distance from my usual place as shop foreman to the chief engineer's chair at the director's right-hand side.

What sorts of things were usually discussed at the supervisors' meeting? The fulfilment of targets, the quality of output, the execution of special shipments, supplies of packaging, materials and parts. I regret to say that there was a propensity for each manager to try to explain any malfunctions in terms of failings on the part of related departments. This made it difficult to reach the right decisions. The managers of the workshops responsible for putting out finished products (the *papirosy* and cigarette production shops) usually attributed any lags in fulfilling the plan to the poor performance of the departments on which they relied, i.e. excessively damp or dry tobacco, the shortage or poor quality of spare parts, mistakes made by the supply department, and so on. These problems did exist. The tobacco treatment process was far from perfect. The quality of humidification was dependent on the attention and diligence of the staff. The people who worked in the primary processing section were quite highly skilled and did their best, but it was genuinely impossible to keep the quality at a constant level. The supply department worked at full strain. Suppliers were constantly hampered by difficulties in procuring raw materials and operated erratically. Corrugated containers were supplied to us by the Moscow Cardboard and Printing Plant (known among us as the *kartonazhka*). It frequently happened that the plant's box-making line stopped working for lack of cardboard, causing supplies to the factory to be interrupted. The workshops had to place products on the floor. The supply department rang around all the trade outlets and mobilised vehicles to go and collect any containers that had become available. Used containers were usually damaged and had to be repaired. It was impossible to get by on used boxes alone. Then, the *kartonazhka* would get a delivery of raw materials and organise work on a three-shift basis. Talks would begin with the manager of the plant as to who would be first in line for the new containers: the confectioners, the tobacconists or someone else (the plant even made boxes for the packaging of television sets). If necessary, they would get the ministry involved. It was very stressful. Meanwhile, production was thrown into disarray, the workers were on edge, and a lot of extra work was needed to sort things out. Complications of this kind occurred quite regularly. If it wasn't the corrugated packaging, it would be some other emergency, and these pressures demanded a lot of time and effort, or non-productive expenditure, as it was called. The factory had a catchphrase coined by the chief supervisor, the veteran worker Ivan Fedotovich Kuleshov, which he used when addressing his subordinates (who were mostly women): "Cheer up, Maria, things are bound to get worse!"

I had to look into all manner of problems, including production issues, performance targets and finances. As regards technical equipment, which was the main concern of the chief engineer, there were serious problems. When I moved to the chief engineer's office, the first person to come and see me was the head of the electrical department, a competent worker but an incurable pessimist. "Leonid Yakovlevich," he said. "How could you agree to take this post? Do you realise that we are sitting on a powder keg that could blow up at any moment?" He was referring to the parlous state of the factory's power substation. Sure enough, when I went to make a closer inspection, I was horrified. It was a dismal facility with outdated equipment (including, crucially, the transformers themselves). The factory's power needs were constantly rising, but nothing was being done about updating the substation. Power cuts were becoming more and more frequent, and the overload on the system made the temperature of the oil in the transformers go through the roof, especially in the summer, which was extremely dangerous. All the distribution boards had been crudely rigged up and fitted with outdated and worn-out equipment. The same went for the power cables. It was symptomatic of the closed-environment nature of the factory: they tried to do everything internally. Urgent measures had to be taken. For the first time, Yava brought in an electrical installation contractor, which set about putting the electrical fixtures in order, step by step. After that, the factory began using contractors on a regular basis in other areas too.

It was the electrical division that worried me the most. The staff were very low-skilled. They were simple electricians, who knew how to change a motor or a fuse, but what we needed were electronic engineers. It was around this time that pneumatic loading systems were introduced for the *papirosy* lines. Until then, the *papirosy* machines had been loaded by hand. Not only did this cause a lot of tobacco to be lost, but it also reduced the quality of the *papirosy*, as it was difficult to ensure that the tobacco was evenly loaded at such a high production speed. The pneumatic loading system (which basically consisted of receiver chambers in which the tobacco was placed, piping and tobacco "feeders") had been developed in the factory's design bureau. The chambers were mounted on the *papirosy*-making machines. At a signal received from the machine's photosensor, the loading of tobacco would begin. This was a fairly rudimentary control system with simple electronic components, but the factory had only one specialist who was capable of maintaining it. Something had to be done as soon as possible.

Enterprises had to fend for themselves where many problems were concerned, since the state made no effort to support the technical development of industries. It was a sign of the devaluation of engineering work that nothing was done to encourage the development of engineering creativity. The situation in mechanical engineering for the food industry was one of complete stagnation. The only factory in the USSR that made equipment for the tobacco industry was Lenmashzavod.[1] The quality of design and manufacturing was low. In the main, attempts were made to copy the designs of foreign manufacturers. For example, KTS cutting mills were copied from similar equipment made by the well-known West German firm Hauni.[2] But even the copying was not done well: the mill was constantly malfunctioning because of serious structural defects. At Yava we preferred to use outdated German TB machines until they were later replaced with imported models. The Leningrad plant also made cigarette packing machines, the design for which was copied from another German firm, Schmermund.[3] There were running jokes among the operators of these machines about their technical defects. But what could the factories do? Cigarettes had to be manufactured and packed. There was no option but to buy these semi-finished articles, as one might call them. Once they got to the factories, the mechanics tried to iron out the kinks in the process of using them.

---

1   Founded in 1882 as the N.Ya. Pal Machine and Ironworks.
2   Founded in 1946. Hauni Maschinenbau GmbH headquartered in Hamburg.
3   Maschinenfabrik Alfred Schmermund GmbH, headquartered in Gevelsberg.

Production equipment at tobacco factories had not been updated. It was worn out and obsolete. The country needed to increase its output of tobacco products, but plainly did not have the production facilities needed to achieve this. Moreover, in 1964, after protracted debates, *papirosy* production went over to a two-shift system. Working conditions were indeed very hard, and the intensity of the three-shift operation made recruiting workers, especially women machinists, very problematic. The transition to the two-shift regime was greeted with huge relief. However, it made the shortage of *papirosy* even worse. The situation was particularly serious in the Russian Federation. In order to balance trade, *papirosy* were imported into the Russian Republic from Ukraine. When the ministries were formed, the pressure on enterprises intensified. Gosplan set very high target plans for Russia's tobacco industry, based on 100 per cent capacity utilisation. I remember my first involvement in the discussion of the 1968 plan for the manufacture of tobacco products, which took place at a meeting of Rosglavtabak. The assigned target of 217 billion units of tobacco products really was beyond all possibility. The factory directors protested and presented arguments and calculations to show that fulfilling a "state assignment" of that magnitude was impossible. The new head of the chief directorate (the former Yava chief engineer, V.A. Grigoryev) was forced to acknowledge the directors' arguments. The next stage was the meeting with the minister, A.P. Klemenchuk. At first, the directors behaved quite confidently and openly expressed their opinions – an after-effect, evidently, of the more liberal relationship with the authorities that had developed during the *sovnarkhoz* period. The ministries, with their inclination towards administrative pressure, were still settling into their role. But Klemenchuk, an experienced apparatchik, was quick to take charge of the situation. After hearing the directors' arguments, he evidently decided to start by "breaking down" the head of the chief directorate. He asked him what his opinion was. I did not envy Vadim Alexandrovich at that moment. I suppose he must have been a little lacking in experience, because he proceeded somewhat hesitantly to express support for the directors' arguments. This was honest of him, but completely flew in the face of the bureaucratic style of management. The minister accused him of opportunism, declaring that he would not be able to work with him if that was the attitude he took, and as a result the state assignment was approved. In a command economy, where there are no real stimuli for increasing output, forceful decision-making was the only thing that worked.

The main objective of enterprise directors was to keep targets as low as possible so as to make the plan more realistically achievable for the workforce, i.e. to ensure that incentives and bonuses would be received and the director would keep his job. This reminds me of the joke about the Soviet and American directors who temporarily swapped places. When they later met to swap back again, both were horrified. The American had taken on large orders, which prompted the Soviet director to clutch his head, exclaiming "How am I going to fulfil them?" For his part, the Soviet director boasted that he had managed to cut production substantially. "You've ruined me!" exclaimed the American. This joke reflected the diametrically opposite approaches to the functioning of the Soviet and Western economies.

The deficiencies of Soviet planning were evidently well known to the country's top Party and economic officials. Even after Khrushchev had been ousted, the thaw period continued. The introduction of a new system of economic administration was a logical development. The USSR's new prime minister was Alexei Nikolayevich Kosygin, a highly experienced economic administrator who had previously been in charge of various sectors of the Soviet economy. In October 1965, the CPSU Central Committee and the USSR Council of Ministers issued a joint decree "On the Improvement of the Administration of Industry, the Enhancement of Planning and the Raising of Economic Incentives for Industrial Production". The main purpose of the reforms was to encourage enterprises to commit to higher targets and provide them with incentives to develop production. This was to be achieved by making enterprises more independent. The quantity of assigned targets was significantly reduced. Volume of output sold was established as the key indicator. To encourage enterprises to take on higher targets, they were allowed to set up production development funds and material incentive funds. The size of these funds was determined by the strength of production figures. Enterprises were free to decide for themselves how to use the funds to develop production and award material incentives to their staff. It was also permitted to pay employees annual bonuses as long as targets for a given year were met (the so-called "thirteenth salary"). This was a very important decision, because the lack of incentives was the main obstacle to enhancing employees' motivation.

It was all very well, but the notion of giving enterprises independence was at odds with the course set by the Party leadership to restore the command economy. The specific rates of allocations to the funds were set by the ministries, whose guiding principle was "don't give them an inch". If an enterprise started to pull ahead, it had to be stopped. For managers of an enterprise to be earning more than ministry officials was completely unacceptable.

It was just as this reshaping of the administrative system was going on that I began in my role as chief engineer. This was a watershed moment in the country's development, and with the right political will, things could have gone very differently. For Yava, too, it proved to be a pivotal time – one that had fateful repercussions for the factory and its workforce and to a large extent determined what lay ahead. When I was summoned to the director and offered the post of chief engineer, I could not have imagined that I would be caught up in such a whirl of events.

Chapter 3.

Yava Cigarettes – the Leap to Western Technology

Mikhail Demyanovich Voitsekhovich was one of those directors who realised that cardinal changes were afoot in the country's political course. Thanks to the Khrushchev thaw, he had been able to travel abroad, where he had seen for himself how far tobacco production in the USSR was lagging behind the rest of the world in technological terms. America and Europe had wholly gone over to manufacturing modern products, meaning filter cigarettes. By comparison, Soviet tobacco products looked outmoded and primitive. During Khrushchev's reforms the USSR had begun to develop trade and economic relations with other countries, and the Soviet elite had enthusiastically embraced foreign-made cigarettes, which were purchased for distribution among a privileged few. The rest of the population continued to smoke *papirosy* and unfiltered cigarettes. It was reasonable to suppose that there would soon be moves to modernise tobacco enterprises with a view to bringing their output up to date, especially as the state supported the development of smoking. In society at large, smoking among men was a common phenomenon and even an element of style and image. Smoking expensive tobacco brands carried a cache of prestige.

Since the Yava factory was based in Moscow and was one of the leaders in the tobacco industry, it was logical that the manufacture of the new products should begin there. However, the production facilities at the factory, as in the industry as a whole, were hopelessly outdated, and this might pose a problem when it came to renovate the plant and introducing new technologies. Voitsekhovich had foreseen all this and conceived the idea of erecting a new modern building on the factory's grounds. But there were a number of difficulties with this proposal. The construction of a new production building would require special permission from the Soviet government. Moscow had a special status, and the authorities were strict about maintaining a balance between the city's population size and its infrastructure capacity. Any decision to expand production sites that might increase the number of workers had to be made at government level. For this reason, it was decided to use a well-known scheme that provided a way around this stumbling block. First, permission was obtained to build a warehouse building, which was much easier. Then, at the right moment, it would be repurposed as a production building. In 1964, therefore, work began on the construction of a warehouse facility at the factory. The design parameters for the building (floor load, ceiling height, and so on) were set so that it could also be used for manufacturing. By the time I was appointed chief engineer, the shell was already in place, and construction work had been suspended. Now, a convenient moment had arisen to seek permission for repurposing.

The director was proved right. A decision was made right at the top for modern equipment to be purchased for the tobacco sector to enable the production of filter cigarettes. It should be noted that this was the first time Western technology had been purchased for the USSR's food industry, which gives some indication of how the authorities regarded smoking. At that time, as a result of a technical revolution, Western countries had begun producing highly sophisticated products of a completely different standard. Especially popular were king size cigarettes (85 mm in length with a 15 mm acetate filter). These products had a very good tobacco filling and were packaged twenty at a time in a triple-row pack. The cigarettes were wrapped first in foil, then in a pack, which in turn was shrink-wrapped in cellophane with a tear-off ribbon. It was an attractive product with good smoking properties, which was pleasant to take in your hands. The foil and cellophane film preserved the quality of the product during storage. This technology was used to manufacture international brand cigarettes. Compared with Soviet-made tobacco products, it seemed like a real leap forward. We were especially behind on packaging. Our products were packaged in grey, unattractive paper. Printing was carried out on old, outdated equipment. All in all, products made by Soviet factories were thoroughly behind the times in terms of both smoking properties and external appearance.

A contract for the purchase of equipment was signed in 1965. The British company Molins[1] undertook to supply fifty Mark 8 filter cigarette-making machines together with Hinge Lid packing machines for hard packs and Schmermund lines for soft packs. Even by international standards this was a huge contract. The amount of money involved – over five million British

---

1   The Molins Machine Company, founded in 1912.

pounds – was a very considerable figure for that time. The deal was handled at the highest level – by the USSR government. The purchase of the equipment meant that large quantities of filter cigarettes were now planned for production. This would inevitably affect the balance of consumption of tobacco products in the country as a whole. The question now was how the equipment should be distributed. This was by no means a simple matter. It stood to reason, of course, that the main bulk of the new cigarettes should be produced and sold in the capital city. At the same time, however, political considerations dictated that none of the Union republics that had a tobacco industry should be left out. The Yava factory, being based in the capital, was in a good position. Another factor in our favour was that the factory already had a new warehouse building that could be used to accommodate the new equipment. Voitsekhovich's authority and influence also played a significant role. Of the fifty cigarette machines, seventeen were allocated to Yava. That meant six lines. A line was composed as follows: three Mark 8 cigarette machines corresponded in capacity to two Hinge Lid or one Schmermund packing machine. The remaining machines were distributed among enterprises around the Soviet Union, but no more than one line per factory. This positioned the Yava factory as the chief enterprise for the manufacture of the new products and the assimilation of the imported equipment. It was at Yava that the contract negotiations had taken place, and to promote its wares Molins had set up a Mark 8 cigarette machine complete with a Hinge Lid packing machine at the factory even before the main agreement was signed. These subsequently became permanently labelled as the "promo machines". The appearance of the new line caused a great commotion, as everyone tried to get at least a peek at the marvellous machinery and its amazing cigarettes. It was practically the country's first foray into making consumer products conforming to international standards.

To ensure the security of the new products, Yava built a special glass-block facility, which attracted much attention from managers and distinguished visitors who came to the factory. This was probably why people wittily dubbed it the "crystal room". I will say more later about the cigarettes that were produced there. When the decision was made to install the bulk of the imported equipment at Yava, the factory's management was set the task of making products that the consumer would accept. This meant large production volumes and significant government expenditure. It was not an easy task, as filter cigarettes of this standard had never been sold on the domestic market before. The new products were classed as "premium-quality filter cigarettes". The pack price was much higher than for traditional tobacco products. To entice smokers over to the new products, it was essential to ensure a high standard of flavour attributes and external appearance, i.e. pack design. Getting the strength right was crucial, as this is the chief habit-forming factor. Our smokers were used to strong products, but the acetate filter lowered the nicotine content. The factory's chief technicians were asked for help in addressing these issues. We predicted that *papirosy* smokers could be persuaded over to filter cigarettes as long as the new products could be made more attractive while at the same time ensuring continuity in terms of taste and strength. Hard-pack cigarettes were more expensive and were positioned as luxury products. The soft-pack variety, being more affordable, was for those who preferred their cigarettes strong. It was therefore decided to use an enhanced Kazbek blend for hard packs and Belomor for soft packs. In other words, the strength of the products would be kept the same, but the taste and aroma characteristics would be substantially improved. History proved these calculations correct. There were virtually no problems in encouraging people to take up the new, more progressive filter cigarettes.

Much importance was attached to pack design, in which respect we were greatly assisted by Finnish partners. Finland had extensive trade ties with the Soviet Union, particularly in the paper industry. The Soviet Union supplied timber, while Finland, being more industrially advanced, supplied paper and printed goods. Deals were made through the Exportles foreign trade association, which oversaw the export of timber and the procurement of paper products, including for the tobacco industry. Negotiations over supplies usually took place at Yava. Over time, a close personal relationship developed between our director and the representative of the Finnish side, Mr Toll. The latter had been involved in trade with the USSR for a long time and spoke good Russian. Mikhail Demyanovich, for his part, was a lively and sociable individual who was used to taking the initiative. He managed to persuade the Finnish side to design the packaging for the new products free of charge. Our designers lacked the required experience. For the Finns, it was a matter of prestige.

Firstly, a key decision was made to call the new cigarettes "Yava". I remember that we received dozens of different options for the pack design. There were quite a few that we liked, but the Union Ministry also had to be consulted. In the end, I think we came down on the right choice of design for Yava cigarettes, which became a sort of emblem of the times. The hard packet had a grid pattern on a white background with a deep-blue strip in the middle on which the Yava name was printed in gold. The soft pack was white with a red circle in the centre and "Yava" written in very stylish gold lettering. This design was used for a long time and became a symbol of the factory's products. The creation of new brands requires professionalism, but also luck and a favourable set of circumstances. We succeeded in catching the right wave. Yava filter cigarettes became the most popular tobacco products for many years to come, a solid favourite among smokers. They compared favourably with the nationally sold Stolichnyie and Orbita brands made by other factories that had received new equipment. When I was appointed chief engineer, the promo machines were already standing in the crystal room. Installation and set-up were carried out by field engineers from Molins, who also trained the factory's staff in using the equipment. The cigarettes produced really were of a high quality. State-of-the-art equipment imported materials and attractive packaging printed in Finland: it was a world apart from our usual products. It was expected that a large quantity of imported equipment would soon arrive and significant quantities of new cigarettes would be produced for sale. An arrangement was made at the very top for the factory to be visited by the USSR Vice-Premier, Kirill Trofimovich Mazurov.[1] I remember that day very well. Mazurov was accompanied by the USSR Food Industry Minister, Zotov, the RSFSR Vice-Premier, Shkolnikov, and the RSFSR Food Industry Minister, Klemenchuk. Mazurov was shown the factory, the new equipment and our crystal room. He agreed that it would be practically impossible for the imported equipment to be set up in the old blocks. But since there was a newly constructed warehouse building on the premises, which would be perfect for organising state-of-the-art production of filter cigarettes, it was only a question of obtaining permission to repurpose the building as a manufacturing facility. Within literally a month, the Council of Ministers granted permission. Very little time now remained before the equipment was due to arrive.

It was a real revolution. When the promo equipment was installed, the factory's engineers rushed to take a look at this "miracle of technology". I

---

1 Kirill Trofimovich Mazurov (1914–1989) – former First Secretary of the Central Committee of the Communist Party of Belorussia, leader of the partisan movement in Belorussia during the war.

remember the scene: two of our top technical managers from the production shop stood gazing at the machines as if they were space rockets. It was only then that it fully dawned on us how far behind we were in engineering. European countries had progressed to a completely new technological level, whereas we still produced goods using machinery dating from the beginning of the century.

It fell to me to oversee the conversion of the warehouse building into a manufacturing facility. The director did not involve himself much in this process. I have said a fair amount about my first director, who really was a remarkable individual. At the same time, he was somewhat naïve and unprepared for serious changes. I remember one particular episode that gives a good illustration of the sort of person Mikhail Demyanovich was. When we brought him the preliminary design for discussion, the first thing he asked was, "Where's the front staircase?" We had already designed in a fire escape staircase for evacuation and two passenger lifts for workshop staff. There was no way we could stretch to a front staircase as well. The building was large – around 12,000 m³. But when we started planning where the equipment would go, it turned out that it would only just fit, with barely an inch to spare. Our director was disappointed by this. His ideas about the changes that were taking place were a long way off the realities of the situation. It galled him to think that the new building that he had dreamed about for so long would be without a beautiful front staircase!

The factory was buzzing during that period. It was as if people had grown wings. A delivery of imported equipment was expected soon, and a new production building was under construction. It was clear that the factory was going places. The imported equipment standing in the crystal room was there for all to see and new products were being turned out which, for the first time in the USSR, were being packed in attractive blocks of ten packs. The new line was used to begin production of hard-pack Yava cigarettes. The first cigarettes came out in time for the regular Party Congress and were written about in *Pravda*, the central newspaper. Hard-pack Yavas became the cigarette of choice for many top officials, cultural figures and other well-known people, which immediately raised our profile and drew increased attention to the factory. The crystal room was kept under guard. It would have been difficult to smuggle anything out, and people would not have dared try in any case, for fear of losing their jobs.

It was around the same time that a series of misfortunes began. Firstly, a fire broke out at a tobacco warehouse. The factory had its own tobacco storage warehouses on the Dmitrovskoye highway, in Beskudnikovo. The warehouses were rather dilapidated single-storey wooden structures. As usually happens, the fire broke out at night. Some of the tobacco was burned. But that was not the worst of it. The firemen did not hold back with the water and the tobacco was drenched. And wet tobacco in bales begins to putrefy very quickly. As the temperature inside the bale rises, it is literally a matter of hours before putrefaction sets in and mould begins to form. Urgent action was needed. Everyone was scrambled into action. The tobacco had to be saved. It was very expensive stuff. Most of our raw material was imported. It accounted for up to 80 per cent of the manufacturing cost of our products. Losing tobacco would result in heavy financial losses. And if those losses were above a certain level, it would go to the courts. That would be a real disaster. Something had to be done right away. The dampened bales needed to be broken up, i.e. separated into leaves. And then what? Lay the leaves out inside somewhere and leave them to dry? But the air was damp. It was early spring and quite cold. And in any case, where would we find a place to lay out such a large quantity of tobacco? It was decided that we needed to somehow get hold of equipment designed to dry out products of a similar structure to tobacco, such as hay or grain. But where would we get it from? The problem was so out of the ordinary that I decided to deal with it personally. Nowadays, of course, you can get everything you need via the internet, but in those days you had to go out and find it. I went to the agricultural machinery pavilion at VDNKh.[1] There, on a display stand, I saw the sort of machine we needed – an ordinary grain dryer. I went to see the pavilion director and explained the situation to him. He gave me permission to take the equipment, asking me only for a letter of assurance. People treated each other differently in those days, with more basic decency. The machine was delivered to our still unfinished building. The grain dryer occupied an area of about 200 m². It was not a particularly complex contraption. Hot air from a diesel engine was blown through pipes into the enclosed space into which the tobacco leaves were dropped. The whole factory was involved in the operation to save the raw material. The damaged tobacco was loaded onto trucks and transported to the factory. The bales were broken up into leaves and dried in the grain dryer. But there was another problem: how to get the tobacco up to the

---

1   VDNKh – the Exhibition of Achievements of the National Economy, an exhibition centre in Moscow.

first floor. The lifts had not yet been installed, and there were builders working away everywhere. We talked to the crane operator, who passed the tobacco to us on pallets hoisted on his crane. This was extremely risky and went against all the safety rules. In the end, though, we managed to save the tobacco, and our losses were kept to a minimum.

But misfortunes never come alone, as they say. Very soon after that, Voitsekhovich found himself in extremely hot water. I have said before that he was a flamboyant character – and for people like that, the Soviet regime could be very dangerous. He would sometimes go too far. He did not always follow the rules of the time. For example, he would call the Finns on a direct line. This did not go unnoticed. Once, Mr Toll arrived with his wife, who was the owner of a paper factory in Finland. Mikhail Demyanovich invited the couple to his home. This was a flagrant violation of all spoken and unspoken rules. Any close contact with foreigners had to be approved in advance. The head of Yava's special department was summoned to the relevant authorities over this matter. This meant that our director was under suspicion. His absolute authority as head of the factory had evidently caused him to forget the strict taboos of the Soviet regime. Being an expansive fellow with a sharp tongue, Mikhail Demyanovich let loose some disparaging comments about how things were done in the country. When he was told not to engage in direct contact with representatives of foreign companies, he objected: "But why not, if I am doing it for the good of the business?" During the negotiations over the supply of the new equipment, meetings at the factory were often attended by managers from the Tekhnopromimport foreign trade association, which was responsible for the contract on the Soviet side. It was very noticeable that the general director of the association, V.N. Dashkevich, and his deputy, L.Ya. Seltsovsky, both of whom spent most of their time abroad, were at pains to adhere to the rules of conduct befitting a Soviet functionary. It was the only way to behave, especially when dealing with foreigners. Unfortunately, Mikhail Demyanovich failed to grasp this essential rule. He struck up a relationship with the owner of Molins, Desmond Molins, who came to Sochi on his private yacht before travelling up together with his business associates for talks in Moscow. It was probably his close association with these rich and free people that had sown unfavourable ideas about the Soviet order in his mind. And since he was an open and uninhibited sort of person, this spelled danger.

Molins was represented in the contract negotiations by an Austrian businessman, Mr Heinrich Leder, who had an intermediary firm in Vienna. Leder spoke Russian well and began making frequent visits to Yava on business. He became friends with our director. A colourful character – large, loud and fond of a joke – he quickly won the affection of anyone he came into contact with. He would always bring various toys and gifts. Our people were new to all these things, although they had begun taking a keen interest in modern contraptions and conveniences. Soviet appliances – cameras, television sets and refrigerators – were very outdated, and even then, most people could not afford them. The director drove around in his own Zhiguli, which was something other employees could only dream of. But Leder, during a small gathering, produced photographs of himself and his wife getting into a splendid white Mercedes outside their beautiful suburban house. I do not know whether he was deliberately provoking our director, but I personally heard him say, "Would you like me to send you a Mercedes?" He did not, thank goodness, send a Mercedes, but he planted some "bad thoughts" in our director's head.

The negotiations drew to a close and Leder went back to Vienna. The close rapport between him and the director lasted right up to the last moment. Then, suddenly, came the news that Mikhail Demyanovich was being dismissed. I had suspected that something was amiss from the perceptible decline in the director's level of activity. Whispers had begun to circulate at the factory that he was in big trouble and faced the axe. Various reasons were floated. Some said that he had illegally purchased some hard-to-obtain television sets at factory price for himself and his close friends. Others said that he had become "morally degenerate" and was having affairs at the factory. The entire workforce stood up for him. An action group was set up and a collective letter was prepared, signed by over a thousand people. People were worried. As far as the workers were concerned, it was nothing short of a tragedy. The assistant secretary of the Leningrad *raikom*, Comrade Paramonov, arrived at the factory. He had previously worked at the Second Watch Factory[1] before being transferred from the post of secretary of the Party organisation to the *raikom*. He gathered the factory's managerial personnel together in the director's office. Mikhail Demyanovich sat next to him at the director's table. All those present had come with the intention of defending the director. But the meeting took a quite

---

1 Maker of the popular Slava watches.

unexpected turn. Paramonov led the discussion very adroitly. He was extremely strict and frank. He began by saying that Mikhail Demyanovich was a very strong and highly regarded manager. When the *raikom* had received the order for his dismissal, they had objected and asked for an explanation. It emerged that Mikhail Demyanovich had made "ill-judged remarks about our system". The "comrades from the authorities" had played them a recording made in a restaurant where the director had met with representatives of a foreign firm. This was a very serious charge. We left the meeting in complete dejection. If "the authorities" themselves had got involved, there was nothing more the factory could do for its director. The minister signed an order dismissing Voitsekhovich.

CHAPTER 4.

"THE DROWNING MAN MUST SAVE HIMSELF"

The factory found itself in a difficult position. It had just embarked on a full-scale overhaul involving the construction of a new production building and was expecting the arrival of new equipment from abroad. As things stood, the production building was no more than a shell, but the equipment was due to begin arriving at any moment. Unsurprisingly, our ministry was deeply concerned about the state of affairs at Yava. Until then, of course, the factory had been held together by Voitsekhovich. Klemenchuk, the minister, summoned the head of the chief directorate, Karakozov, with whom he had had a relationship of trust since they worked together in Leningrad, and told him, "Nikita Ivanovich, I am appointing you as acting director of the Yava factory. You will combine the roles of head of the chief directorate and director of Yava. It will be your job to find a new director". Of course, combining these two positions was practically impossible, and Nikita Ivanovich, acting at his own risk and peril, issued an order appointing me as acting director of Yava. A somewhat ambiguous situation thus arose. The factory's employees were informed of the chief directorate's order appointing me as acting director, whereas the ministry's order had appointed Karakazov. Luckily for Nikita Ivanovich, this "substitution" went undetected.

The factory was reeling from the loss of its director. And if that wasn't enough, a young chief engineer had now been put in the director's post at a critical moment. The new equipment was beginning to arrive, and there was nowhere to put it. The factory's technical department put together a temporary equipment layout plan. Every inch of available floor space was called into play, including, first and foremost, the already inadequate storage premises. Naturally, the crystal room had to be dismantled too. Every nook and cranny had to be utilised. It goes without saying that we had to adopt a layout that did not properly comply with the relevant technical standards. In a word, it was an enforced temporary arrangement. But there was a popular expression in the USSR: "There is nothing more permanent than a temporary fix".

However, despite the difficulties we faced in putting the equipment in place, the main problem was finding enough staff, and particularly mechanics. We would need around forty mechanics just to operate the seventeen cigarette machines in two shifts, and forty more to work the packing machines. The factory had managed to train five or six specialists since it had begun using the promo machines. But where would the rest come from? It was a very serious situation. An international contract had been signed for the supply of expensive imported equipment and was being directly monitored by the government and Party bodies. The delivery schedule was strictly laid down in the contract and, what was more, those "damned capitalists" were fulfilling their obligations to the letter. But we were nowhere near ready! The equipment began to arrive exactly on schedule. Three cigarette-making machines complete with packing units every two months. The ministry gave us another two months to install them and get them up and running. After that, there would be a production plan to fulfil. Allowances would be made in the first month, but after that the equipment had to be operating at 85 per cent of capacity, i.e. at full throttle. True, the contract did require the installation and set-up to be carried out by the manufacturer's specialists. It was they who were responsible for putting the equipment into service. But after that, it was up to us to ensure that targets were met. It took at least a year to train a mechanic, and experience showed that only around 30 per cent of trainees who were taken on actually managed to master the use of this complex equipment.

How could the factory have found itself in this situation of being wholly unprepared to use foreign equipment supplied under the close scrutiny of government agencies? I think there were a number of factors at play. Firstly, the decision to have such a large quantity of equipment supplied to one factory at such short notice proved foolhardy. It was hard to see where they expected to put the equipment when the new building was so far off completion. Decisions had been made at the very top without carrying out a professional expert review. It also turned out that little thought had gone into how the new equipment would be used in practical terms. Put simply, the industry was both technologically and organisationally unprepared to begin using it. For example, mechanics could have been sent for training at Molins' training centre. But the Soviet Union did not like to spend hard currency on so-called "non-productive expenses". What? Send ordinary workers to a capitalist country for training? What about our own much-lauded staff training system? Everything was left to chance.

Secondly, the standard of factory management was not adequate to handle the challenges that came with the supply of such a quantity of equipment. The shop and department managers were elderly people who had been raised on old technology and work methods. They had neither the expertise nor the internal resources required for the adoption of modern technology.

Thirdly, there was the business over the factory's director. In December 1966 Mikhail Demyanovich already knew that there was a threat dangling over him. For my part, I had not had enough time to get up to speed on everything that was happening. After the director was dismissed, I found myself on my own with serious problems and people who were unprepared for challenges of this nature. I remember, in this regard, a typical situation that arose at the time when I had just been appointed chief engineer. There were problems in the cigarette-making shop, which was finding it hard to keep up with its targets. The machines were old and worn out. Something needed to be done. I went over to the shop to find out what was happening and began talking to the workers. I always considered it more important to talk to the workers before the managers. They always spoke plainly about what needed to be done, what parts were lacking, and so on. I gathered information so as to discuss the situation with the shop foreman. I told him, "Let's sit down and decide what to do". To which he replied, "Well, what do you expect, the machines are old, there's nothing you or I can do about it". Rather than trying to solve the problems, he told me why it was impossible for anything to be done. It must be said that one of the major problems in the Soviet era was the lack of initiative shown by workers, and especially engineers and technicians. They were forever trying to avoid having to deal with problems, preferring to shift the responsibility onto others, meaning their co-workers. In Soviet times there was a popular saying derived from real life: "a good worker solves problems, while a bad worker looks for reasons why they can't be solved". I would say that the former kind were a rare exception, though I should add that there were very few incentives to work well: there was an active system of wage-levelling and an atmosphere of mutual cover-up among the majority of mediocre workers. It was in this extremely difficult set of circumstances, then, that we had to embark on a complete renovation of the factory and begin manufacturing sophisticated new-generation products. It did not take the managerial staff long to realise the gravity of the situation. The factory was at risk of failing to fulfil the plan, which would mean losing the quarterly bonus (the *progressivka*). So what happened? Most of them threw in the towel and began looking for people to blame. And it was easy enough to find the culprit: it was the young chief engineer, the acting director. Of course, if the old director had been in place, everything would have turned out differently. They hurled all sorts of accusations at me! First and foremost, however, they accused me of not being tough enough.

Of course, it was hard to get through those moments. Sometimes I felt at a loss. But the situation forced me to pull myself together, seize the initiative and often tackle problems "on the fly". I had to show the toughness that was mentioned. The first person I had to dismiss was the head of the technical department. Unfortunately, he had been my first immediate supervisor at the factory, the former head of the machine shop. The advent of the new machinery meant that the shop had a much broader role, and he had proved unable to adapt. Of course, in order to carry unpopular decisions into effect, I first had to obtain the support of the Party organisation. When things were going well, the plan was being fulfilled and the director was fully in control of the situation, the Party organisation played a nominal role: criticisms were directed at minor problems or against particular workers in relatively low positions. This meant that the manager could let the workforce get things off their chest while retaining control over the most important decisions. When things were going badly, however, the Party organisation would suddenly spring into action and the influence of the Party committee would rise dramatically. It was important in this case to steer its actions in the right direction. But this was not easy, as the workforce had a rather poor understanding of the problems faced. This made it essential to try to retain the initiative and work with the Party organisation to clarify the situation and the challenges that we had to address. Explaining matters to various levels of the workforce became a priority task during that period. But all that took time, while the situation we were dealing with was highly complex and demanded urgent measures. Firstly, there was the question of recruiting staff to operate the equipment. We decided to work with the military commissariats to help us find trainee mechanics. There was a ban on hiring people under eighteen years of age to work at factories with harmful working conditions. Besides, the job would require more mature workers. It made sense to recruit young people coming out of the army. They would be looking for a stable job after returning from service. Our representatives would sit at the commissariats and invite people being discharged from the army to come and work at the Yava factory as trainee mechanics. We also put announcements in Moscow newspapers (*Vechernaya Moskva* and *Moskovkskaya Pravda*). And people did come, because we set a wage of one hundred roubles per month for the training period. That was a very decent amount for a trainee. Many of those who came turned out not to have the required professional qualities. The equipment worked at a high speed, and mechanics needed to have quick reactions, mental agility and adequate technical skills. But there was no time to dwell on these matters: we put the new recruits straight onto machine training, reasoning that we could deal with the selection process later. Obviously, the trainees were not ready to work independently. But we had to find some way out of our quandary.

We assigned six crew foremen to a shift. Each foreman was in charge of three cigarette machines, which were operated by the trainees. The foremen were recruited from among our experienced mechanics. A trainee was not expected to carry out machine adjustment at first. He had to learn to set the machine running and carry out the most elementary operations. The main thing was not to interfere too much. The machines were equipped with automation systems, and many functions worked automatically. In case of serious aberrations, the foreman would get involved. It was the foremen who did the most essential work. They would flit from one machine to the next, correcting faults. It was only thanks to this manning system that we managed to get the equipment running despite the lack of trained staff. But even in a situation of such self-evident need, we had to overcome the resistance of the personnel department, which had always advocated a reduction in the number of foremen on the grounds that they did not directly produce anything. Yet here we were proposing not only to increase the number of foremen quite significantly, but to give them a pay rise as well. In other words, I came up against a total lack of understanding of the situation. And that was how it was with everything!

There were costs, of course. Breakages occurred owing to the trainees' lack of experience. But the main thing was that we had succeeded in putting the equipment into operation strictly on schedule! It then began to emerge that there had been no planning at national level over the question of maintaining and servicing this sophisticated equipment. At the time the equipment was delivered, not a single one of the component materials for the manufacture of cigarettes was produced either in the Soviet Union or in Comecon[1] countries. No thought at all had gone into the issue of manufacturing spare parts. How could it be that neither Gosplan nor the USSR Food Ministry had taken any real steps to provide for the maintenance of the expensive imported equipment?

The way in which the purchase of equipment for the tobacco industry was organised was a typical example of the style of administration that had begun to prevail in the country, i.e. a reckless approach to the making of important economic decisions. This was why, during the Brezhnev era, there was such a proliferation of imported equipment that remained unused. This became a real calamity for the country. It was local managers who took the rap for such things, but the real fault lay with the high-level officials who took decisions to buy equipment without considering the situation on the ground – or, more precisely, with the bureaucratic system itself through which decisions were made in the country. In our case, the first major problem was the manufacture of "labels", i.e. pack blanks used for the mechanised packaging of cigarettes. The labels were loaded into the packing machine, where they were manipulated to form packs of cigarettes. A six months' supply of them had been purchased in Finland. It was very high-quality packaging, beautifully printed and cut. A particular feature of the hard pack was the flip-up lid. No packaging of such complexity had ever been made in the USSR. Very soon, the need arose to organise the production of labels within the country. At first, the RSFSR Food Ministry assigned the task of making cigarette packaging to its principal container and packaging enterprise, the Moscow Cardboard and Printing Plant (the same *kartonazhka* as I mentioned before). When representatives from the *kartonazhka* brought samples of hard-pack labels to test on the Hinge Lid packing machines, we were horrified. The cut quality was hopeless: the flaps were not properly cut, the creasing was inadequate, and there was a burr along the edges. It was simply impossible to work with labels like these. The packing machine kept stopping, and we ended up with a lot of spoilage. All attempts to remedy the situation failed. And why did things turn out this way? It was because even the country's top enterprise worked with obsolete equipment. The cutting had been done with reciprocating mechanisms, whereas cutting the complex-shaped labels in the proper way required the use of rotary cutting machines. The Soviet Union did not have any of those.

---

1   Comecon – the Council for Mutual Economic Assistance, an economic union of Warsaw Pact countries.

The situation was dire: the lack of packaging labels could bring the expensive imported equipment grinding to a halt. As always, the well-known principle that "the drowning man must save himself" came into play. We were helped by a fortuity. During the discussions over the purchase of the equipment, someone had suggested including a sample machine for the cutting of hard-pack labels, which consisted of a rotary die, but in miniature form, for testing purposes. The machine only cut the labels. You loaded it with rectangular sheets of cardboard pre-printed with four labels. The machine passed the sheet of cardboard between two rotary rollers, which did the cutting. This meant that we could organise our own production of hard-pack labels "on the fly". The rectangular cardboard labels were printed at the printing shop, then cut on the sample machine. Since the loading was done by hand, the production rate was limited. The ministry ordered us to make labels for all factories in the country that had received the new equipment. To meet this task, we had to operate three shifts, working flat out. The machine proved surprisingly reliable and hardy. But it was, after all, a sample machine, not designed for industrial-scale production. It was a stopgap solution that allowed us to remain "true to our word" until modern printing lines made by the British firm Trissel were purchased (with rotary dies and gravure printing[1]). Those lines were installed at a cardboard and printing plant in Kursk, which kept the tobacco industry supplied with labels from then on. How that was arranged is another long story that illustrates the ministry's muddled thinking. The purchase of the Trissel machines was fast-tracked, but no thought was given to the question of where they should be sent. Once again, the matter had to be resolved without any serious pre-planning, so they decided on the first idea that came to mind, which was to install this bulky equipment on the ground floor of Yava's new production building. We were horrified, as this completely undercut our plans to use the building for the factory's manufacturing needs. After much hard wrangling, it was the firemen who came to our rescue. They wrote a report saying that equipment of that sort could not be installed in multi-storey buildings. Because the process involved the use of trinitrotoluene, it was classed as explosion-hazardous. And there ended the saga of the packaging labels. We had been saved by a little sample machine which had been purchased quite by chance, and which we used to the hilt. A paradoxical tale.

---

1   Gravure printing – a type of intaglio printing method that is widely used in making high-quality printed products.

Similar problems arose with other materials for the manufacture and packaging of cigarettes. The manufacturing process for cigarette and tipping ("cork") paper is so complicated that the idea of making it within the country was not even contemplated. There were well-known firms in France, Austria and Finland that made high-strength, slow-burning cigarette papers and were the world's main suppliers. The cardboard to make the hard-pack labels was bought in Finland, while the paper for the soft-pack labels was sourced from Sweden. Cigarette filters were wholly supplied by the British firm Filtrona. All this shows how far the USSR was lagging behind the West in terms of technology. Our country was a major exporter of timber, yet was hopelessly behind the times in terms of the processing and manufacture of paper, cardboard and other paper-based products.

The transition to modern cigarette production made the tobacco sector substantially dependent on supplies from abroad, which was a risky position to be in. The country had very limited supplies of foreign currency, its only significant source being from commodity exports, which were wholly dependent on global price levels. The task was set of developing an "import substitution" action plan, firstly with regard to labels and foil for cigarette packaging. The Moscow Non-Ferrous Metal Works was designated as the foil supplier for Yava. This was a small enterprise in the centre of Moscow which produced foil for the electrical engineering industry and domestic needs. Of course, it was a big step up to manufacture products with the technical parameters required for tobacco production. It was a small plant that lacked the necessary capacity. As a result, there were constant battles with deadlines. Things only improved a few years later after new capacities were brought on line at the Mikhailovsky Non-Ferrous Metal Works in the Sverdlovsk region. Another cigarette packing material is the cellophane wrapper. The only enterprise that manufactured cellophane film in the USSR was the Barnaul Chemical Works. The technology they used there was likewise very outdated. The film had large thickness variations, it was unevenly wound on the reel, and there were often visible splices on the material. It could not be used on such high-performance equipment.

And it was under these conditions, amid a complete lack of forethought about supporting the manufacturing process, that we faced the task of mastering the new equipment.

Nonetheless, within a year after the deliveries began, all the equipment had been set up and put into operation. A new team of workers had been built almost from scratch to man the filter cigarette production shop. That was around 200 employees. The shop and department managers had been gradually replaced, the old generation displaced by young people – former machine operators who had acquired a higher education through evening or correspondence courses. N.I. Karakozov, who was technically the acting director of the Yava factory, was keen to find a permanent director as soon as possible. Given the complex situation in which the factory had found itself, ministry officials hesitated to propose a candidate from outside. To avoid causing annoyance and keep the workforce united, it was thought better to appoint a director from within. The choice fell on the head of the *papirosy* production shop, Ivan Iosifovich Stepanenko. Only fifty years old, he was a war veteran who had come to the factory after his military discharge. He had worked as a mechanic and shown himself to be an active Communist. He had been elected secretary of the factory's Party organisation and had completed an evening course at the training college, after which he had been appointed head of the largest workshop. The only minus was that he did not have a higher education, but on the other hand he had a lot of experience of social and administrative work.

However, the factory was still in a difficult position. The trainee mechanics were not yet ready to run the equipment independently. As a result, the machines kept stopping, output was down, and targets were not being met. But the plan had to be fulfilled. There was a constant need to organise extra shifts on Saturdays and at nights.

To get a better idea of the problems the factory was up against in the process of manufacturing cigarettes, let us return for a while to the characteristics of the new products and the technology used to manufacture them. King size filter cigarettes are a unique product. An elegant item weighing only 1 gram, the cigarette is, at the same time, 85 mm long with a 7.8 mm diameter and consists of multiple components: tobacco, cigarette paper, a filter and tipping paper. During the manufacturing process these components undergo intricate manipulations, which are rendered several times more complicated by the high speed at which the equipment operates (2,000 cigarettes per minute, or over 30 per second) and by the highly complex physical and technical properties of the various materials used. First and foremost, there is the chief component: tobacco. Tobacco is a very unique and tricky (delicate to handle) product.

It possesses particular physical and technical characteristics which in turn depend on its moisture level. If the moisture level falls below 12 per cent the strength characteristics sharply decrease and the level of dust formation from mechanical treatment rises. Optimal strength properties occur in tobacco leaf with a moisture content of 15 to 16 per cent (up to 20 per cent) but at that level of moisture there is a risk of the tobacco "sticking". The tobacco becomes gummy, small fragments of the cut tobacco stick together, forming lumps, and the tobacco jams the works during processing. Ideally, therefore, leaf tobacco should have a moisture level of 18–20 per cent at the cutting stage, but 12–14 per cent in the process of manufacturing cigarettes. There are other important reasons, too. Since cigarettes are a long-life product (intended to last up to one year), a moisture level of over 14 per cent during storage may cause mould to form, in which case the products have to be destroyed. Internationally, ensuring that tobacco has the right properties at different stages of processing is achieved through a treatment process which involves a whole series of operations and a large quantity of equipment, and takes up the larger part of an enterprise's production space (more than 50 per cent). A key element of the production process is the rotary dryer, where hot air is used to help bring the moisture level of the tobacco down to the right level for feeding into the cigarette machine, i.e. 12–14 per cent. The drying process, as a highly important element of cigarette manufacture, incorporates a system for the automatic regulation of the moisture level of cut tobacco. Modern equipment simply cannot operate efficiently without this technology.

And what did we have at Yava at that time? Very rudimentary technology. The only advantage we had over other factories in the USSR was in having the vacuum units for the humidification of leaf tobacco. However, the lack of a process for drying cut tobacco made it impossible to get the leaf tobacco to the optimal moisture level. Our production unit had a very narrow adjustment range of 12–14 per cent. If the moisture content exceeded 15 per cent, the cigarette machines began to seize up, which could bring the whole workshop to a halt with the loss of large quantities of materials. This meant that the primary processing staff had to be constantly on the alert. Much depended on the moisture level of the tobacco when it was received in baled form. Sometimes the tobacco came to the factory with an already high moisture content (more than 15 per cent). In this case it could not be moistened in the vacuum units, resulting in a lower preparation quality. Decisions had to be made in each individual case about how exactly to proceed and what adjustments to make to the processing conditions. But there was very little room for manoeuvre. Any lapse in concentration, and the whole shop would begin to seize up, meaning that the machines had to be stopped and all their working elements had to be cleared of clogged tobacco before work could restart. An awful amount of working time, tobacco and materials was lost this way, and the losses had to be made up somehow. Alternatively, the tobacco would be too dry, which would be clearly reflected in the quality of the cigarettes, as you would get "loose ends", i.e. when tobacco crumbles from the end of a badly filled cigarette. This was not acceptable, and quality control would halt production. Again, there would be a mad rush and the same consequences as with damp tobacco. Unfortunately, situations like this arose on a daily basis. The process engineers did what they could to avoid these problems, but it was all a consequence of deficiencies in the manufacturing process. In this regard the factory proved wholly unprepared to work with the new equipment. I ought to add that similar situations also arose with *papirosy* production – but these were not quite so stressful. Making filter cigarettes involved a completely different process, different quality parameters and, most importantly, the use of high-performance equipment. It goes without saying that the quality requirements for the materials used were much more stringent.

Another manufacturing operation that caused a great many problems with machine adjustment was the process of bonding the filter to the cigarette. Because of the high speed at which the equipment operated, Molins recommended using a high strength adhesive for these purposes, namely polyvinyl acetate emulsion. Adhesive made by a British firm, Swift, had been purchased for the initial period of operation. The problems started after we switched to using an emulsion made by a Leningrad-based factory, Lakokraska, which was designated as the supplier of adhesive for tobacco enterprises. The factory produced emulsion for use in construction. Obviously, the quality requirements for that were much lower. It emerged that Swift's adhesive had a significantly higher degree of particle dispersion, and this is the main indicator of binding strength. Because of the inferior technology at the Leningrad factory, there were large variations in quality between different batches of adhesive. And what happened? The adhesive would suddenly start setting on the surface of the section of the machine where the attachment of the filter took place. The mechanics referred to this as "caking". What is more, it usually happened on all the machines at the same time when we had a bad batch of glue. And what did this mean? We had to stop the cigarette machines, wash out the adhesive flasks and clean the machine parts and the tubes through which the adhesive was fed. The process engineers, together with the crew foremen, would search the batches of adhesive to find some that would work properly. They often used mixtures (combinations) of adhesive from different batches. Experience gradually taught them how to deal with this problem. But these emergencies were disruptive and made it very difficult to fulfil the plan. Other problems arose, too, such as defects in the adhesion of the tipping paper to the filter, which the workers succinctly referred to as "flags" and "corners". Flags occurred when the paper was badly glued down along the whole length of the filter, and corners when just the end of the tipping paper was poorly glued and came away towards the tip of the filter.

Smokers found it very irritating when filters broke off while they were smoking. Defects of this sort caused endless problems for the support staff. There were times when the mechanics were unable to get a machine working for a whole shift, which likewise had a severe impact on our ability to deliver on plan targets. Gradually, though, the mechanics learned to deal with these problems more quickly.

Of course, operational problems took an hourly toll on performance. The factory was in a constant state of agitation. If the plan was not met, an inquiry would begin. People would be summoned to the ministry and the *raikom*. It was impossible to make the equipment work at the rate assumed in the plan. As a result, we would always be three to four million cigarettes short of the daily output target of eighteen million sticks. Over a month, that came to seventy to eighty million, which was the production volume for four or more full working days. The only way to make up the deficit was through overtime. Mobilisation of the work crews would begin right at the start of the month. Everyone understood that the payment of the *progressivka* to the engineers and technicians, bonuses to operators and the "thirteenth salary" to the entire workforce was entirely dependent on the plan being fulfilled. Fulfilling the plan was a question of survival. But people grew tired of this schedule. After the evening shift there would be another six hours of work at night – a total of fourteen consecutive hours without a break. Having to work at weekends meant that they could not rest properly or spend time with their families after a hard week. The only solution was to offer additional incentives for overtime work. Work at weekends and on night shifts was paid at higher rates. Things got especially frantic right at the end of the month. Night shifts had to be organised, and people refused. Desperate times called for desperate measures, so we would take the risk of paying those who agreed to work overtime an extra ten roubles. That was a decent sum in those days. Doing this was illegal, as people were only allowed to be paid for what they produced. But there was no other way out. One month ended, another began, and it was the same thing all over again. Another struggle to fulfil the plan. There would be a slowdown at the start for people to catch their breath. But the management knew only too well that a new storm would soon begin, and they had to begin planning for it right from the start of the month.

Even if we produced the required output, however, we still could not be sure of fulfilling the state plan. The factory was stretched to its limits with nothing in reserve. But having a "carry-over" was essential to ensuring the steady fulfilment of the plan. We had to sell the entire month's output. This was practically impossible, especially as the process of getting finished products out to market had become even more arduous: production volumes had increased, while storage space had decreased, thus aggravating an already difficult situation. And no measures had been taken in this regard. Glavmosavtotrans was the organisation in charge of picking up goods from the factory. It may have been in charge, but it was utterly unreliable. As a result, we would usually have three days' worth of production piling up on the shop floors. This made it simply impossible to work in the shops. There were situations when the factory was on the point of grinding to a halt. On the first day of each month there would be a frantic rush. We had to submit reports for the preceding month. We had strained every sinew to deliver on output, but a lot of it was lying in the workshops, which meant that the key plan target, volume of sales, had not been met! This was evidently a situation that was often encountered by enterprises, and the Trade Ministry had accordingly issued an instruction that allowed enterprises to hand over any unshipped products into the "custody" of its commercial contractor and draw up documents to the effect that the sales plan had been fulfilled.

Since there was no problem in selling tobacco products in the trade network, the factory could get the required documents signed at the Rosbakaleya Moscow office. However, according to the instruction, all the outstanding output had to be put together in an enclosed space, i.e. a stockroom, which then had to be sealed and the keys handed to the trade representatives. This was because the documents transferred ownership of the goods over to Rosbakaleya. There was a lot of stock involved, but we did not have any such facility at the factory. Therefore, after collecting all the stock together in spare spaces in the workshops as best we could, we would set about handing it over to the trade system. I would take the documents along to the Rosbakaleya office on Novokuznetskaya Street. The managers of the office were also placed in a difficult position. It was risky for them to accept products without proper observance of the rules set out in the instruction. On the other hand, they did not want to create problems either. No one higher up had any interest in a conflict. Almost every month we found ourselves in the position of having to persuade the Rosbakaleya managers to accept our goods. It was extremely humiliating, because the law was on their side and we had to act as suppliants. Back at the factory, meanwhile, the planning department and the accounting office would be awaiting the results of the negotiations. They had to report to the Central Statistical Office as soon as possible. After a lot of stalling, a favourable order would usually arrive from Rosbakaleya, the shipping personnel would count the boxes again, and the documents would at last be signed. This was a good outcome, but not without risks. Anyone suspected of fiddling reports could end up in court. But it was the realities of life that put us in that position. We had to shoulder the responsibility and take the risk. It was impossible to keep working like that for long.

As we saw it, a possible way out of the situation was to offer material incentives to the work crews. When materials fall short of requirements, the only thing that can salvage the situation is having skilled and highly motivated staff. It is rightly said that real ingenuity is born of adversity. The mechanics at the Yava factory had certainly found themselves up against adverse conditions, and many of them had gradually learned how to resolve difficulties through subtle machine adjustments. Operating high-performance equipment was stressful and physically demanding. We had to make it worthwhile for the mechanics to go above and beyond to fulfil the plan. It was only thanks to Kosygin's economic reforms that we were able to do this. Most of the material incentive fund was used to encourage crews to fulfil and overfulfil the plan targets, but there was a particular focus on incentivising the machine adjusters, on whom the factory's performance was most heavily dependent. It was a very effective incentive system. In fact, I think it was one of the main achievements of the factory's management. The best machine adjusters could earn over 500 roubles a month. Advanced workers earned more than the factory director and the shop foremen. It was a measure that we were forced to take. One might say that we simply "bought" the commitment of the crews to fulfilling the plan, which caused a certain amount of disgruntlement within the workforce. But it was the right decision, as there was no other way for us to get the plan fulfilled.

CHAPTER 5.

AFTER THE INITIAL SHOCK

When I first came to the factory, the management system was fairly primitive. People worked according to the old ways. Production processes essentially consisted of a series of daily-repeated operations in which the workers were well versed. This meant that the shop staff could cope well enough on their own with the day-to-day core production work. The factory's technical divisions were not directly involved in the management of production activities. Criticisms about this state of affairs were occasionally raised at Party and trade union meetings, but never went any further. An objective had been set of making department regulations more focused on the achievement of production targets, but nothing had actually been done about integrating the technical divisions into production.

After I was appointed chief engineer, I became greatly concerned about this issue and realised that the problem lay not in job descriptions or the motivation of the engineering staff, but in the shop-based management system itself. There was simply no mechanism for the involvement of engineers and technicians in production management. In truth, there was no real need for it either. The shop system was symptomatic of the profound technical and technological backwardness of industrial enterprises in the USSR. But the installation of modern, high-technology equipment at Yava triggered an urgent need for a complete revision of how things were run.

The main change was that production operations had become much more dynamic and difficult to manage. The technology itself was now much more complex, there were more factors affecting the production process, and getting everything right demanded closer collaboration between different kinds of specialists. The high-speed machines had placed a higher price on operating time, and there were more than enough potential reasons for the machines to stop working. With equipment maintenance becoming a top priority, integrating the engineering personnel into the production process was now a matter of vital importance. It was a complex task, of course. It meant changing the mentality of the workers so that they properly understood their functions and the importance of working together with other divisions. It was all about production! Maximum concentration was needed to prevent stoppages or, if they did occur, to analyse the causes and take appropriate action. We wanted each division to take steps to improve efficiency and reduce downtime. This defined the rhythm of work for all the factory's units. The material incentive system was based first and foremost on operating results. Indicators measuring the contribution of employees to operating performance were developed for each department.

The structure of management at the enterprise also had to change. In this regard we came up against major obstacles. In the command economy, everything was strictly regulated. There was a government-approved staffing chart that was hopelessly out of date. This dogmatic document prescribed the staffing structure that enterprises had to use for their divisions and departments, with no allowance made for real circumstances, as well as pay bands that made no provision for rewarding good workers. We were at least helped by the fact that Yava was classed as a Category 1 enterprise. A lot of work was needed to bring the staffing chart into line with our objectives. Once again, we were under pressure to go down the route of pay levelling. We needed to bring in new workers and incentivise our staff. We were able to reward the most skilled and efficient employees with pay supplements from the material incentive fund. There was a need for fundamentally different approaches to handling the organisation of production processes. A system was introduced to provide incentives to piecework crews operating the cigarette machines.

In the USSR, the main criterion for evaluating the performance of pieceworkers was the fulfilment of output quotas. The director of an enterprise would issue an order informing the workers of the quotas, which effectively amounted to a state production target for the work crews. Each month, the performance of the crews would be reviewed and worked out as a percentage of the assigned level. To ensure that they got the "standard wage level", the crew had to at least fulfil the monthly output quota. To earn more, they had to overfulfil it. State agencies strictly monitored pay at the enterprises for which they were responsible, so the fulfilment of output quotas was one of the most important indicators. At the factory, this indicator was under the watchful eye of the labour and pay department, which calculated output quotas for all categories of pieceworkers and effectively regulated pay at the enterprise. There was an inevitable streak of formalism in these processes. As a result of the bureaucratisation of state administration, the indicator began to lose its motivational role. As far as the authorities were concerned, the optimal level of fulfilment of output quotas was around 103–105 per cent. Some work crews could achieve as much as 108–110 per cent. Figures of this sort demonstrated that the enterprise in question had set reasonably challenging production targets and organised production activity in an appropriate manner. If quotas were substantially overfulfilled (more than 110 per cent), this was considered as an indication that the enterprise was not doing a good job of setting targets, i.e. it was setting them too low. The actual result of work was less important than the formal figure for it. As soon as crews or individual pieceworkers began performing significantly above the output quotas, the labour department would propose bumping up the quotas. This took away the employees' motivation. Priority was placed on preventing any unplanned increases in labour costs.

Effective motivation was needed for the workers tasked with mastering the use of the imported equipment. How was this to be achieved? Once again, it was the economic reforms that came to our aid. Under the reforms, bonuses from the material incentive fund were added to normal pay in recognition of superior performance. This was wholly in keeping with the objectives of pay reform at the Yava factory. Consequently, the "Regulations on the Granting of Direct Incentives for Increased Output from the Material Incentive Fund" were drawn up. Each crew was set a monthly cigarette production target in millions of units. No adjustments could be made to the targets. The payment of a bonus from the material incentive fund was conditional on the target being fulfilled. Work crews were given an impetus to achieve higher output levels through the award of progressive piece-rates for every additional million cigarettes produced above the target. The process of drawing up and implementing the new regulations was by no means easy, of course, given that the new system gave rise to substantial pay differences between high-performing and low-performing crews. There were highly successful crews that managed to produce up to five or six million extra cigarettes, allowing them to receive a very high wage. Those additional millions were very important in enabling the factory to fulfil its plan. The use of the material incentive fund encouraged high-performing crews to work even harder and low-performing crews to pull their socks up and improve their skills. The machine adjusters took to the new system straight away. It opened new opportunities for them. Their performance would now be judged on the basis of actual output.

Another important task was to develop a new system for maintaining equipment. The existing maintenance system at Yava was completely outdated: equipment was allowed to run flat out until it broke down. When the factory received modern equipment, it became clear that the maintenance and repair system was in need of a radical overhaul. Regular preventive maintenance had long since become normal practice all over the world. We designed schedules for shutting down equipment for preventive maintenance, taking as our basis the routine maintenance schedules recommended by Molins for various parts of the cigarette-making and packing machines. One of the first difficulties I encountered was the failure of shop and department managers to grasp the need for strict observance of the maintenance schedule. This was natural, given the factory's lack of experience in using such complex modern equipment. After the installation of the Molins equipment, not only did we have to devise a system for carrying out preventive maintenance operations, but, more importantly, we had to get it through to the workers that the maintenance schedule was law whatever the circumstances. When plan deadlines loomed, it was obviously very tempting for shop managers to cancel or postpone the shutdown of equipment for routine maintenance. How could one think of shutting down a perfectly functional machine when another one or even more were undergoing essential repair and every million cigarettes counted? Many found this impossible to understand. We did, however, aim to keep the downtime to a minimum. Gradually, the workers began to understand that timely and thorough preventive maintenance was key to keeping the equipment in good working order. The mechanics themselves made sure that routine maintenance was properly prepared for and efficiently carried out. After all, their pay was wholly dependent on the technical condition of the equipment.

Serious issues began to arise over the procurement of spare parts. The Molins equipment had been built using state-of-the-art design solutions. For example, the surfaces of some of the working elements of the cigarette-making machine were made of hard alloys, with graphite, plastics and other modern materials used in many cases. Orders to make these had to be placed with specialised engineering or defence enterprises. For some reason, our ministry simply pretended that the problem did not exist and shifted all the responsibility onto the factories. For all the materials, quotas were allocated, a specific supplier was designated, and the delivery specifications were worked out. In the Soviet economy, these were essential steps in getting anything supplied. With spare parts, the problem was even more complex. Because there was a large range of parts requiring different manufacturing technologies, a number of different suppliers had to be used, and in some cases a single part had to be manufactured in stages at different plants. For this purpose, we needed a Gosplan decision ordering the engineering ministries to find an integrated solution to the problem of manufacturing components for the tobacco industry's new imported equipment. Evidently, securing that decision was beyond the capability of the Ministry of Food Industry, and so they decided to let things take their own course. It was Yava that had the greatest problems, since we had the lion's share of the equipment. Plus, we were best placed to resolve the issues, since there were enterprises in Moscow that had the technologies needed. This is why Yava effectively became the coordinator in this matter. Unfortunately, in the command economy these matters could only be dealt with by unofficial means.

It must be said that we often came across real specialists who were attracted not so much by material gain as by the professional challenge. When problems arose with hard alloy parts, I sought advice from my teacher at the institute, the head of the metallurgy faculty, Alexei Alexeyevich Abinder. As a professional, he was greatly enthused by what he saw, but could only sympathise when he realised the complexity of the challenges we faced. He introduced me to a student of his, a leading specialist at the Moscow Hard Alloy Works. The latter helped us a great deal with the manufacture of various hard alloy parts and coatings. But there were problems that we could not resolve within the country. For instance, the cylindrical hard-alloy filter-cutting knife was impossible to make owing to its microscopic thickness combined with a fairly large diameter. On Abinder's advice we contacted the Kiev Hard Alloy Institute, the leading institute in its field in the country, and received the reply that the institute would be willing to conduct an experiment to "bake" a hard alloy blank of the part in question. This was the kind of highly complex problem we were dealing with.

Before long, we faced the threat of production being shut down for lack of what appeared to be a simple part: perforated plastic bands. Once again, the ministry left it to the factories to tackle the problem. This rapidly wearing part performed an important function in that it conveyed cut lengths of cigarettes to the filter assembly unit where the attachment of the filter tip took place. Cigarettes were held to the surface of the band by the suction created through the perforation holes. The service life of the band was one shift of the cigarette-making machine. If things went badly, a mechanic might use three or four bands in a shift. Very soon we began to run out of these parts. The threat of having to halt production hung heavy. To monitor their use, we introduced a system whereby a mechanic could only receive a new part after handing over a spent one. We made use of any opportunities to replenish stocks. For example, representatives from Molins, aware of the problem, tried to bring as many as they could with them when visiting Yava. But we could not operate like that forever. We urgently began to look into the issue of manufacturing them ourselves. The band had to be sufficiently strong and elastic and have the right thickness. The most suitable material was found to be Lavsan, a thermoplastic polymer, but it twisted out of shape when worked and there were problems with gluing it together. What was to be done? It was yet another unusual problem for Yava to solve. I was advised that living in an apartment building belonging to the factory was a man called Korobov, an inventor and natural genius who had worked in the aviation industry his whole life. His exceptional abilities had earned him the nickname "the wizard" among his neighbours. He was retired by now and lived with his wife. One of their rooms had been equipped as a workshop with small turning and milling machines and a space for fitting work. He was a unique and very talented person. He took the problem of making the perforated bands in hand and came up with a solution. He developed a method of working Lavsan, adapting an old Kinap motion picture camera to perforate a Lavsan band wound onto a spool-like film tape. The tape from the spool was then cut into sections of the right length and spliced together on a special contraption. The resulting perforated band worked just as well as its imported counterpart. This was a major triumph. Yava began making perforated bands not only for itself, but for the entire industry. We managed to ensure that Korobov was rewarded with what was a rather handsome sum in those days: 4,000 roubles.[1] As we parted, he suggested, "Maybe I could design you a control system for the front desk, so that not a single worker would get past with so much as a pack of cigarettes". Then he hesitated and added, "On second thoughts, better not. We might both end

---

1 By way of comparison, the 1970 price for a VAZ-2101 Zhiguli was 5,600 roubles.

up getting murdered". He had a point, though: theft had become a ubiquitous problem in the country at that time.

Overcoming problems required concerted efforts on the part of the staff, and not everything went well in this regard. The entrenched prejudice against the technical divisions did not help. When operating performance was discussed at supervisors' meetings, the shop foremen usually blamed non-fulfilment of the plan on poorly functioning equipment and the lack of spare parts. They somehow felt that it was nothing at all to do with them. Of course, the proper functioning of equipment did depend to a large extent on the technical divisions in terms of maintenance and the supply of spare parts. However, there were other factors that were just as important, such as production management, labour and process discipline, working conditions and material incentives, and staff training. All these components were the responsibility of the enterprise as a whole. It goes without saying that, things being what they were, the factory was coming up short in many areas, and this was the main reason why it was failing to meet production targets.

To raise efficiency, the shop foremen and technical managers needed not to apportion problems between them, but to work side by side. Rather than making generalisations about this or that issue, they had to start analysing the problems to identify the causes. Bringing about this change in approach was not easy. It meant changing the mentality of the workers. The factory faced very serious challenges. Unfortunately, it was increasingly obvious that the factory director, Stepanenko, was ill-suited to meet these challenges. His lack of education, vision and culture was beginning to show. The situation at the factory was undoubtedly a difficult one, with the fulfilment of the plan under constant threat. Yava was gaining a firm reputation as an unstable, unreliable enterprise. And ultimately, the buck stopped with the director. This was very hard. But I think that Ivan Iosifovich's limitations made it difficult for him to see that the peak of the decline had passed, and things had begun to move forward. Grasping this required an inside understanding of the processes occurring at the factory.

And we had problems up to our ears. The factory had been working under provisional arrangements for over three years. The equipment had been installed in a way that disregarded the most basic requirements for maintaining it. This exacerbated the harsh working conditions in the shops, pushing them to a critical level. The workspace was piled high with finished products and production waste. Materials were stored there too. And it was in these dire conditions that people had to work day in, day out. It was easy to understand how they felt. The only small compensation for these dreadful conditions was the chance to earn money. The factory was constantly monitored by public health, fire safety and environmental inspectorates. There were more than enough grounds for non-compliance notices, with violations left, right and centre. We were unable to remedy most of them. All we could do was write formal replies. The inspectorates were reluctant to shut us down without instructions from above, but they issued regular fines to the managers. That was how the system was constructed: everyone understood how things were, but each did whatever his authority allowed. It was only by relocating the equipment to the new production building that the situation could be improved to any significant degree, but this proved to be a protracted process.

Construction was poorly organised in the Soviet Union. Projects were not completed on time, and the construction process placed colossal demands on the project owner. Many enterprise managers lost their jobs for failing to ensure that new facilities were completed on time, which is why directors were generally in no hurry to get involved in renovation projects. Under the rules of the day, virtually all the responsibility for construction and commissioning was shouldered by the project owner. We were responsible for design decisions, the supply of equipment, dealings with administrative authorities and even delays in construction – despite the fact that there was a general contractor. It was as if the main functions had been specially divided in this way between the contractor and the project owner so as to deflect blame away from the builders if delays occurred. Unfortunately, this kind of arrangement had become the norm in the Soviet Union, and construction organisations did an excellent job of taking advantage. Problems began right from the planning stage. The planning standards were hopelessly outdated. Conflicts arose with the chief designer. For example, why were the lavatories in the shops so small? It turned out that the regulations only required one toilet per fifty workers. Only a recirculation-based ventilation system was allowed even though the air in the shops was full of dust. It was mind-boggling. Things were no better when it came to planning production processes. It was normal to use outdated production methods: the spirit of innovation was completely absent, and even considered dangerous (since you never knew what would come of it). It was another example of the one-size-fits-all principle that permeated the entire system. Every week, there would be construction meetings at the factory, presided over by managers of the construction trust. They would review the progress of construction and set deadlines for completing work. At subsequent meetings it would be observed that many tasks had not been completed. The builders were adept at showing that it was all because of failings on the part of the project owner. In fact, the reason why schedules were never met was because of the appalling way in which work was managed on construction sites. The main burden of the construction project was borne by factory staff: the chief engineer and technical supervisors. It was extremely difficult to supervise factory work and the construction of the new production building all at once. A food industry enterprise did not have a capital construction department as standard, which in itself is difficult to fathom: what differences could there be between food enterprises and Group A enterprises as far as monitoring construction work was concerned?

And what about our superiors – the ministry and the chief directorate? Did they realise what a difficult situation the factory was in and what the reasons for its predicament were? I think they did. But the state system required imported equipment bought with hard currency to yield a full return. Accordingly, Gosplan had worked out a plan based on maximum utilisation. This meant that shutdowns (whether for operational or maintenance reasons) had to take up no more than 15 per cent of total working time. Given the standard of production support, this was unachievable. But who was going to admit that? That would mean admitting that the whole business of purchasing the expensive equipment had been ill-thought-out and poorly planned, and that serious mistakes had been made in the process. Such things were not forgiven! There would be an investigation by the Party Control Committee of the CPSU, which was not known for its sense of humour. It was much easier to let the factory's managers and workforce shoulder all the responsibility for the fulfilment of the impossible plan.

The production plan for the factory was set by Rosglavtabak. Naturally, when the targets were being discussed we would argue that the plan was unrealistic, present calculations and point out the different reasons why the equipment sometimes had to be shut down. It was not in the interests of the chief directorate to have a well-known Moscow factory falling short of its production targets. But they could not lower the production plan to any significant degree:

Yava accounted for too big a proportion of total filter cigarette production (30 per cent of the total quantity produced in the country). This meant that the factory would have to factor in a large number of overtime hours. The engineering staff might not get their *progressivka*, which would be a heavy blow to their household finances. The factory managers would have the economic and Party bodies breathing down their necks. Right up to the end of the year, enterprise managers and workers worked under colossal strain. And at the end of December (usually on the 31st) the plans would usually be adjusted to reflect the figures actually achieved. On paper, therefore, the plan would be 100 per cent fulfilled. For purely ideological reasons, the Party leadership could not let it be said that the country's enterprises and organisations had failed to fulfil their annual plans. Their logic went like this: we have squeezed everything we could out of the enterprises – now we just have to make sure the figures are in order. The final decision was taken by the CPSU Central Committee. Economic and political factors were taken into account. Right up to the last moment, we did not know whether our enterprise's plan would be adjusted or whether we had been chosen as a scapegoat. In the latter case, a change of management would be a certainty. But even if an adjustment was made, there would still be a post-mortem on the year's results.

It must be said that intelligent, professional people and strong personal relationships did have a positive role to play in that harsh, overregulated system. I owe a great debt of gratitude to the head of the Union-level chief directorate (Glavtabak), Vladimir Alexandrovich Kholostov. He became head of the directorate after the war and was made deputy chairman of the Moscow *sovnarkhoz* (economic council) during the *sovnarkhoz* period; then, after the restoration of the ministries, he returned to the role of head of Glavtabak in the USSR Ministry of Food. Fairly advanced in years by this time, he was an imposing figure and very highly regarded among the top brass of Union-level government bodies. Where something could not be resolved at an official level in the Party-state system, the only recourse was to go through professionals like him, who knew how to cut corners and, as they used to say, "deceive the Soviet government for the good of the Soviet government". The man responsible for the tobacco industry within Gosplan was Vladimir Ivanovich Komarov. A war veteran who had lost one of his legs, he was a very serious, level-headed person. I know for a fact that he and Kholostov did a great deal in their quiet, measured way to bring cigarette production targets for the tobacco industry down to a more realistic level. This was very difficult, of course, but they called upon their contacts, choosing the right moment to act. All this was done for the general good. Of course, the targets were still very tough, but the industry had a fighting chance of fulfilling them. All in all, life was a never-ending battle. The hardest thing was not being able to call things by their names and having to mask one's real intentions. Other problems faced by the tobacco industry were dealt with in more or less the same way. Of these, the most significant was obtaining foreign currency, since the industry could not function without supplies from abroad. And foreign currency was always in short supply in the country. That is why Gosplan insisted on our switching to domestically produced materials and components. This made for lower quality cigarettes and reduced the productivity of the equipment. It was in the interests of the industry to try to source as much material as possible from abroad. On the other hand, political considerations dictated that it was important to show an interest in working with domestic suppliers. There were many moments when one had to strike a delicate balance between defending the interests of the industry and showing a willingness to honour the interests of the state.

The administration of industry was structured so that enterprises only performed the functions of producing goods and managing staff. All the necessary resources were allocated by the state through the chief directorates, while product distribution was handled by divisions of the Trade Ministry. Because goods were in short supply, there was no problem with sales, and prices were set by the state. But our dependence on resources was complete and absolute. Acetate filters, cigarette and tipping paper, cellophane, and cardboard to make packs were all purchased abroad. We were sorely in need of polyvinyl acetate emulsion and spare parts from Britain. It was a good thing that the industry had a stable supply of raw tobacco in that period. Thanks to the favourable status of foreign trade ties with India, Greece and Turkey, tobacco from those countries, as traditional suppliers of raw tobacco, was supplied to the USSR under barter arrangements. This was high-quality tobacco. We also received large quantities of tobacco from Bulgaria under Comecon agreements and, of course, from Union republics in Central Asia and Transcaucasia. The intensive development of tobacco cultivation in Moldavia also began during this period. The growth in cigarette production created an increasing need for tobacco. The way things were organised meant that the factory depended on the ministry and the chief directorate for solutions to most of its problems. Targets and material resources – all that was handed down from above. This meant that working with the chief directorate was a top priority for the factory's management.

As we have seen, the economy was still being steered by command methods with the aid of manual control. But what about Kosygin's reforms? These were successfully buried by the ministries at the order of the CPSU Central Committee. Enterprises had greeted the reforms with great hope. Back in 1965, when the reforms were still at their planning stage, the director M.D. Voitsekhovich had created a new position of "economist" in the staffing chart of the economic planning department, with a job description of preparing for the factory's transition to planning under the new conditions. This meant calculating the percentages of profits ("norms") that could be allocated to the production development and material incentive funds, thirteenth salary payments, and so on. The idea of the reforms was that ministries would use the calculations submitted by enterprises themselves to set long-term target norms for them. Enterprises hoped that, by finding internal reserves from which to boost productivity, they would be able to allocate substantial amounts to the development and incentive funds. The purpose of this was obvious enough. I remember the enthusiasm with which we prepared the calculations for the ministry. And what actually happened? The Yava factory is a very good illustration in this regard. The factory's economic results had increased substantially as a result of manufacturing high-cost products in the form of filter cigarettes. It naturally followed that, if the norms stayed the same, we could count on a significant increase in allocations to the enterprise's funds. And what did the people at the ministry do? They revised the norms downwards. Their explanation for this was simple: "You can't take the credit for this. You received new equipment from the state, and that is why the factory's economic performance has risen". But it had been down to us to master the use of the equipment. It was to the enterprise's credit that the equipment had been put into operation on time in the most difficult of circumstances. To keep it functioning, we had had to find emergency solutions to a whole range of technical and organisational problems. We regarded the ministry's decision as deeply unfair, although it was fully in keeping with state policy throughout the Soviet era. This sort of malpractice in setting norms happened across the board, and the norms were a key instrument of the economic reforms. In effect, therefore, the reforms never really happened. This came as a great blow to the most able and progressive managers and professionals, who had started to believe in the possibility of change. All that remained of the reforms were the development and incentive funds, which were monitored by the ministry. At least we could use these to give incentives to the machine operators and engineering staff. But in a situation where everything was dictated by the Party, there could be no question of any sort of independence.

Something had to be done, however. By that time, the inefficiency of the Soviet economy was being increasingly laid bare. The country was lagging far behind Western Europe and the USA in labour and resource productivity. Nor could there be any doubt that we were greatly behind in terms of the use of new technologies. The situation at the Yava factory served as eloquent proof of this fact. The new cigarette lines that appeared at the factory had found themselves in an unfamiliar environment of technological backwardness. This chasm could only be partly overcome with the aid of foreign purchases and the efforts of the factory's workforce as it battled for its own survival.

Having laid the economic reforms to rest, the authorities set course for a new method of raising efficiency with the introduction of the scientific organisation of labour (SOL). The relevant decree was issued by the CPSU Central Committee and the USSR Council of Ministers. Of course, the idea itself was a constructive one. Raising labour productivity and improving product quality depended in large measure on correct workplace organisation and the timely delivery of materials. These were real weaknesses in the Soviet Union. There was a lot to be done in this regard. To help implement the decree, sectoral and territorial SOL centres were set up all over the place. The All-Union SOL Centre issued guidelines on all areas of activity. Research institutes were enlisted to help develop recommendations for industry. The latest advances in the then very fashionable science of ergonomics were used to address workplace organisation: what a workplace should be like in terms of lighting, tools and appliances for workers, containers for materials, and so on. All this had to serve the purpose of raising labour productivity and product quality. Within a short time, a ramified institutional network had been set up to manage this process, employing an entire army of specialists and managers. But this good idea came crashing down. It turned out that there was no demand for the scientific organisation of labour.

With no market, and no real motivation for enterprises to increase productivity, the whole project turned into just another top-down formal exercise. Directors were too preoccupied with the immediate problems of fulfilling the plan to concern themselves with nebulous theories about raising efficiency through workplace organisation. The SOL centres developed prototypes of business equipment for workplace organisation. But the equipment was never made because enterprises saw no real benefit in it. And so the entire campaign was reduced to token measures. A series of exhibitions of achievements of foreign companies in the area of business machinery were organised in Moscow at around that time. The computer age had not yet arrived, and business machinery was an important way of enhancing production management. We gazed at the exhibits with rapture and envy. Particularly impressive were the products made by the Italian company Olivetti. But this was not for us: this was tomorrow's world, and we still lived in yesterday's.

Nonetheless, the country was changing profoundly. The Khrushchev thaw of the 1960s had caused a shift in people's worldviews, especially among young people. The winds of change had blown, and we had ceased to be a totally closed society. For the first time since the USSR was formed, government policy had begun to turn towards the interests of real people. As they swapped *kommunalka* rooms for individual apartments, people acquired a sense of the priority of family values over public interests. Although the old Party dogma began to be revived when Brezhnev took over, the people and the country had changed. Party influence affected bosses and functionaries, but the general public increasingly lived outside the sphere of Party ideology. I got a good sense of how people's mentality had changed from the processes that occurred within our workforce. When the factory received the new equipment, a lot of young people arrived. This was a completely different generation – much better educated, with a broader outlook and a greater sense of individuality. The things that meant most to them were family, personal life and fulfilling work. Since membership of the CPSU was an essential condition of climbing the career ladder, those who wanted to make a career in government service or in industry tried to join the Party. Manual workers had no reason to join the Party: there was no advantage to be gained from it at a time when there was a labour shortage. Besides, members of the CPSU had to pay quite hefty membership fees. What was the point? The majority of the population had long since lost faith in Communist ideals. As a result, there was a danger of the CPSU being transformed from a party of workers and peasants into a party of bureaucrats, functionaries and careerists. That is why it became an unspoken rule for Party organisations at enterprises that in order for an engineer to be admitted to the Party, three manual workers had to be admitted first. An engineer wishing to join the Party had to "persuade" three machine operators who worked under him to submit applications. This was what was impressed on him by the enterprise's Party bureau. But there was also a hard and fast rule that was strictly observed: no manager could be a non-Party person. Because how could a non-Party person be subjected to Party discipline?

The bureaucratisation of the Party was unstoppable. The main problem that hampered the reform of the Party was Party dogmatism. People's lifestyles were ever-changing, but Marxist-Leninist ideology remained immutable. Life took its own course, while Party ideology existed in and for itself like a "sacred cow" that had to be worshipped and constantly extolled. Everything that happened in the country, up to and including the rising of the sun, did so by virtue of the wise guidance of the CPSU Central Committee. In time, the gulf between what was actually happening in society and Party ideology would be stretched to breaking point, eventually resulting in a massive systemic crisis and the collapse of the USSR.

The Yava factory's Party organisation was part of the Frunzensky *raikom* (district Party committee). This very important division of the Moscow city Party committee controlled the central part of Moscow. The Frunzensky district was home to such highly important government bodies as USSR Gosplan and a multitude of Union ministries and departments (including the Food Ministry of the RSFSR). It also included leading aviation enterprises, such as the Banner of Labour factory, which was in charge of making the famous MiG fighter planes, the Sukhoi Design Bureau (Su fighter planes), the Ilyushin Design Bureau (Il civil aircraft), and the Institute of Biomedical Problems, which was involved in space research. All these organisations were systemically important, playing an essential strategic role in the country's development, and any matters concerning their activities were dealt with by the CPSU Central Committee. But even they had to reckon with the Frunzensky *raikom*. *Raikoms* were responsible for the proper functioning of the area under their control: the safety of people and facilities, the education and training of children and young people, social infrastructure (hospitals, clinics and other social institutions), the service sector (shops, canteens, cafés, restaurants), public transport, etc. Plus, of course, the observance of Party discipline in all spheres of life. It was an essential part of their functions to monitor the work of industrial enterprises, promote industrial growth and ensure that plan targets were being fulfilled by the district's enterprises. Technically, supervision was exercised through primary Party organisations, but in fact, managers of enterprises and organisations were wholly accountable to the *raikom*. The ministry could only appoint or dismiss the director and chief engineer of an enterprise after consulting with the *raikom*, and the director had to be a member of the enterprise's Party bureau. This symbolised support for the director from the factory's Party organisation and rank-and-file Communists.

Under the Constitution, all power in local areas was handed to councils (soviets) of people's deputies and their executive body – the executive committee of the district council. The chairman of the executive committee was elected by the congress of people's deputies of the district council and had to be a member of the *raikom* bureau. This meant that he was wholly subject to the decisions of the *raikom*. In effect, executive committees carried out the day-to-day administration of their districts under the supervision of local Party bodies.

The man elected first secretary of the Frunzensky *raikom* was Boris Alexandrovich Gryaznov, a strong-willed, authoritarian leader. Prior to this appointment he had worked as an instructor in the CPSU Central Committee, overseeing the Moscow city Party organisation and successfully absorbing the style and methods of Party leadership in the work of the highest body of the Party bureaucracy. As the head of the Party organisation of Moscow's central district, he was the only *raikom* first secretary to be admitted as a member of the bureau of the city Party committee. All this conferred a special status upon him and enabled him to establish a rigid Party-council hierarchy in the Frunzensky district. Heaven help any "transgressor" who found himself before a meeting of the *raikom* bureau: its judgments were most severe. Boris Alexandrovich emphasised his position as the real boss of his domain with external trappings, occupying a splendid office and reception area on the fourth and top floor of the *raikom* building on Gotvald Street. A separate lift had been installed for him which only he used.

Since matters concerned with the development of aviation enterprises were dealt with by the CPSU Central Committee, the *raikom*'s main criticisms and reprimands were directed at three large civilian enterprises: the Second Moscow Watch Factory and two enterprises of the food industry: the Bolshevik sweet factory and the Yava tobacco factory. Yava got it in the neck most of all, especially as it really did have serious problems. In almost every *raikom* resolution the factory's work was criticised on various fronts: erratic fulfilment of plan targets, violations of labour discipline, theft of finished products by workers, and so on.

The *raikom* usually saw the reasons for these failings as residing in the "weakening of ideological and educational work among the enterprise's labour collective". This was a standard formula for Party resolutions. In fact, all the criticism was purely formal in nature, while the sole underlying cause of the criticism was the factory's erratic performance in fulfilling plan targets. The *raikom* was, after all, responsible for the fulfilment of production plans by the enterprises under its control. The Yava factory was spoiling the district's performance figures and creating unnecessary problems – which is why it became a permanent target of criticism across the board. It was dangerous and pointless to discuss the real reasons for the non-fulfilment of the plan with the *raikom*, since these had their source in decision-making by the upper echelons of the country's planning and administration system. And who was going to take a swing at the inner sanctum? On top of that, the *raikom* apparatus was made up of workers of "elite" aviation enterprises, who were contemptuous of the problems faced by enterprises of the food industry. I remember that once, finding myself in a desperate situation, in my naïveté I came to seek advice from a *raikom* instructor. I had scarcely begun to speak when I sensed a complete detachment and even a hint of alarm in his gaze, as if he feared being dragged into some unpleasant and dangerous business. The *raikom* was unwilling to acknowledge that the Yava factory, having been supplied with modern equipment, had a genuine need for comprehensive state assistance. That is why, even in such a narrow matter as the manufacture of spare parts, we were not given any help, although there were plenty of aviation enterprises in the district that had the necessary technologies and capacities. What was to be done in this situation? The important thing was to play by the rules set by the *raikom*: to pretend that we took the criticism seriously and even welcomed it, laying stress on the importance of the instructions received. This was the natural way to survive. There was a good reason why people of experience, when attempting to gauge the soundness of an enterprise director's position, always began by asking him "What is your relationship with the *raikom* like?"

But what was happening in the tobacco industry overall? Socio-economic developments in the country had reshaped the structure of consumption of tobacco products. Young people preferred to smoke cigarettes, while *papirosy* continued to be favoured by older people and the rural population. Consequently, there was an increase in the consumption of cigarettes, and particularly non-filter cigarettes. Filter cigarettes were too expensive for the majority of smokers, and many preferred the stronger, unfiltered kind in any case. This trend suited the state, as the mass production of filter cigarettes demanded a lot of currency resources and was too much of a burden on the economy. At that time, the Soviet tobacco industry produced around 400 billion units of tobacco products a year, 80 per cent of which were *papirosy*. Meeting the demand for cigarettes would require the large-scale re-equipment of the industry.

The country did not have the funds needed to purchase equipment from leading manufacturers. And in any case, the Western world had almost entirely moved over to filter cigarettes. It was the Council for Mutual Economic Assistance that helped us out of our predicament. A cooperation deal was struck among Comecon member states for the supply of 400 DKET machines for the manufacture of unfiltered cigarettes to be supplied from East Germany. The job of manufacturing the equipment was given to Tabak-Uni, a firm that had specialised in the tobacco industry since before the war. Obviously, equipment manufactured in East Germany would be inferior to that made by well-known international manufacturers, but concluding a contract under the Comecon clearing system was the only solution. The supplies took place over the period 1969–1971. The combined production capacity of the machinery amounted to 150 billion cigarettes. Cigarettes were packed into single-layer packs using PUCh *papirosy* packing machines, which were upgraded by the tobacco factories themselves. Overall, therefore, the equipment was secured at minimal cost.

The DKET-PUCh lines were installed at all tobacco factories in the USSR. It was a revolution for the industry. The deployment of the new machines proceeded more organically than in the case of the Western equipment. In terms of design they were more in tune with the level of the domestic tobacco industry. They allowed unfiltered cigarettes to be manufactured using home-grown materials, with only cigarette paper having to be imported. In practice, however, things proved not so simple. The same old problems started to crop up: frequent shutdowns as a result of divergences in technology, and a dearth of spare parts. What is more, there were a lot of design faults. The factories had quite an ordeal using the equipment until they had taken the most problematic components in hand and remade them in their own way! No wonder the Russians dubbed the machines the "DK...bangs". Despite this, the authorities demanded more effective use of the equipment and set unreasonable targets for the factories. As always in such situations, operational deficiencies had to be countered with worker enthusiasm. Given that the DKET machines had an actual output rate of 800,000–850,000 cigarettes per shift, a drive was announced to get this up to a million. This gave rise to so-called "million-stick mechanics". All in all, obtaining the DKET machines did prove to be an affordable way of re-equipping the industry and fulfilling the state's objective of supplying the market with unfiltered cigarettes.

CHAPTER 6.

THE RENOVATION OF YAVA – THE ROAD TO CALVARY

Meanwhile, a momentous event occurred at the Yava factory: the construction of the new production building was completed at last. The work had been going on for six long years and was finally completed in January 1972. Now came the task of moving the equipment into the new building and raising cigarette production to a more sophisticated, better organised level. But this could not be achieved without imports. The first question to consider was how to feed the machines with cut tobacco. It did not make sense to move old machinery into the new building. The ministry understood this. In response to a call put out by Glavtabak, a number of international firms presented proposals to supply their machinery. The cost of this equipment was considerable, averaging around two million dollars. Nevertheless, the ministry did not give up on the intention of buying the new machinery. It was a question of waiting for the right moment. This was the USSR's first experience of creating some semblance of a modern tobacco enterprise. Unsurprisingly, we came up against serious problems from the very start. The new production building did not meet the required parameters for modern enterprises. A standard factory in other countries would be housed in single-storey buildings with a ceiling height of at least five to six metres. These were the building parameters on which Western companies based their designs. Our design institute, Gipropishcheprom-2, the only one that specialised in the tobacco industry, had absolutely no experience of dealing with the comprehensive renovation and design of tobacco enterprises. The institute mainly designed tobacco fermentation plants for Union republics. The Yava factory became the first renovation project in the tobacco industry. It was not possible for imported equipment to be factored into the design: Gosplan did not tend to make decisions about the allocation of hard currency on a planned basis, so planning imports at the design stage was out of the question. As in many other cases, we were heading towards a dead end. To obtain permission to move the cigarette machines, we had to get a finished renovation plan approved by the appropriate state authorities, but there was no final clarity about what the plan should contain. Once again, therefore, we were compelled, with the ministry's consent, to resort to a bit of trickery. We decided on the following course of action. We would draw up a renovation plan incorporating possible solutions supplied by Gipropishcheprom-2, get the plan approved and begin moving the equipment to the new production building. Then, as funds became available, we would bring in foreign machinery through separate projects. Thus, we obtained a working design for the renovation of the factory in which a number of important elements were completely unsuitable. But this enabled us to get the design approved and begin moving the cigarette-making machines to the new building. Typically, the ministry did not lower our production targets for the time required to get the equipment moved, as there was still an acute shortage of cigarettes on the market. As usual in these situations, we were told to "seek out internal reserves".

Production continued while the renovation was carried out. As I have said, various temporary fixes had to be found to keep things running. The most difficult issue was keeping the machines supplied with tobacco. There was much dithering over the decision on the primary processing section, but we could not put off moving the machines any longer. A compromise solution was therefore adopted whereby, for the time being, tobacco would be fed by a pneumatic conveyor system from the existing processing facility to the new building. The mechanics were already fully familiar with the equipment itself, i.e. the cigarette-making and packing machines. We only allotted two working days to move one machine to the new building. This required the technical departments to be fully mobilised, well organised and efficient. And of course, this sort of task could only be accomplished by a professional workforce with clear coordination between the various departments. For many workers, weekends ceased to exist, because this was the best time to iron out many of the problems involved in preparing to move the equipment. Despite the considerable difficulties, the mood among the workers was high. People had glimpsed the future: at last they would have decent working conditions. The improvements in the organisation of production would make it much easier to work. When the old buildings were vacated, I looked around those dismal premises, now standing empty, and could scarcely believe that we had been running highly sophisticated machinery for around six years in these dreadful conditions, somehow fulfilling the state plan.

All in all, the process of setting up production in the new building served as a real test of maturity for Yava's staff.

It so happened that, just as we were transferring operations to the new building, we received an unexpected opportunity to begin building a tobacco storage warehouse in Moscow. This is an interesting and instructive story about how construction issues were resolved in the country. Having facilities in which to store tobacco is very important for tobacco enterprises. In effect, the warehouse is the starting point of the production process.

At most factories in the Soviet Union, tobacco was stored in crude wooden facilities. Quite often, it would be stored outside under canvas, as a result of which it would arrive at the factory unprepared and damp. Since it went straight from the delivery trucks into production, this had an adverse effect on the quality of tobacco products, leading to additional losses and lowering the productivity of the equipment. Every year there would be fires at tobacco warehouses. It still amazes me that funds were never allocated to build proper storage facilities despite the advantages being so glaringly obvious. It was not as if hard currency was needed to build them. Most likely, it was the "shortage economy" at play. Gosplan would only allocate funds to increase production volumes: efficiency and quality were not important enough. In my view, this was the height of unprofessionalism.

The tobacco storage situation at Yava was complicated. Total stock generally averaged 3,000–3,500 tonnes. This required significant storage space – around 12,000 m². However, the factory did not have its own space. It had to rent warehouses next to goods yards belonging to the railway. The warehouses were scattered around different areas of Moscow. This made it difficult to manage our stocks of raw material effectively. The technical condition of the facilities left much to be desired. We had not lost hope of getting the funds needed to build our own warehouse building, especially as Yava owned a sizable area of land – around two and a half hectares – in the Dmitrovskoye Highway district. The land had been allocated after 1945, when that district was still in the outskirts of Moscow. In 1970 we received a classified decree issued by the Moscow city committee of the CPSU stating that the greater part of the land was to be given over to the construction of buildings for a research institute concerned with national defence problems. Yava could consider itself fortunate to have been left a parcel of 0.8 hectares. If things were delayed any further, they could easily take that away from us too. It was no good taking a building application to the ministry. It was very difficult to get approval for something like a raw material warehouse. As I mentioned earlier, preference was always given to production buildings.

What was to be done? As in many other cases, we were helped by personal contacts and a certain element of luck. I decided to seek the advice of Deputy Minister B.P. Volodin, who was in charge of the tobacco industry. The crux of the problem was that Yava was in danger of losing land suitable for the construction of a tobacco warehouse situated only twenty minutes' drive away from the factory itself. This would be a grievous loss. Boris Pavlovich called a fellow countryman of his from Gorky (now Nizhny Novgorod) who held the post of deputy chairman of USSR Stroibank (Construction Bank). It was the Stroibanks that controlled funds allocated by the state for capital construction projects. We were in luck. This high-level official turned out to be an understanding person with a statesmanlike way of thinking. He took an interest in the matter. Stroibank had powers to redistribute funds over the course of a calendar year with a view to achieving the most efficient possible use of state resources. At a meeting which took place in Stroibank's grandiose building on Tverskoy Boulevard, we were offered a way to resolve the problem. Stroibank would include the building of a tobacco warehouse for the Yava factory in the list of approved construction projects for the current year, to be completed the following year. However, this could only be done if there were guarantees from the project owner that the funds allocated for the current year would be fully utilised. This was an extremely tall order, as it was now July 1971 and as yet we had no design, no contractor and no resources. We did, on the other hand, have experience of building our new production facility and a few contacts in the construction world in Moscow. We took the risk and gave our agreement. To meet our obligations, we would have until the end of the year to carry out the foundation work for the warehouse building. After weighing up the options, we concluded that, given the limited time available, the only solution was to construct a pile foundation, which was a more efficient and less labour-intensive process. Again using personal contacts, we were put in touch with Moscow's primary pile foundation contractor, Mosfundamentstroi. They were very understanding and agreed to help. For them, given their annual volume of work, driving 400 piles (which was how many were needed by the end of the year) was really not a problem. Gipropishcheprom-2 was again called upon to work out the design. To save time, it was decided to adapt a ready-made standard design for a warehouse on a pile foundation. Once the design was ready, the next question was where to get the piles, since these were centrally allocated products. Mosfundamentstroi gave us a list of building sites where there were surplus piles. "As soon as you have the right number, we'll start work". We went to collect the piles at weekends, since the crane was in use elsewhere during the week. In December, just before New Year, we invited the managers of Mosfundamentstroi to a restaurant to celebrate the completion of the work. Subsequent work was carried out by our contractor, Rospishchestroimontazh.

In June 1973, the tobacco warehouse on the Dmitrovskoye Highway was put into service. It was in this roundabout way, after overcoming bureaucratic barriers, that we ended up with the new, modern warehouse that the factory had so desperately needed. The project proved highly efficient for the state. The funds allocated for the construction had effectively been going to waste, since they had not been utilised on another project; the piles had been lying aimlessly on a building site, and the contractor carried out the work without detriment to other projects. The experience revealed that Moscow had powerful construction enterprises led by strong and highly professional people. They had ample reserves that were constrained by the central planning system. If the enterprises had been given incentives, they could have achieved much more. That was the way things were: the system stifled growth.

1972 proved a very important year for the Yava factory. It was when the process began of moving equipment into the new production building. Negotiations were held with foreign firms about the first ever delivery to the USSR of primary processing equipment. The building of the tobacco warehouse was underway. The numerous issues that needed to be resolved required a high degree of professionalism and sometimes a creative approach. I think the ministry and the *raikom* were well aware that Stepanenko, the factory's director, was not up to the tasks that were faced. However, custom dictated that, for someone to be dismissed, a specific pretext had to be found, some serious dereliction of duty. But Yava had begun to fulfil the plan, the factory was operating on an even keel, and the workforce was going from strength to strength. Nonetheless, a pretext duly appeared. One night after the evening shift, a deflagration of tobacco dust occurred in the area where unfiltered cigarettes were produced. The damage was minimal, but, as always, the firemen who attended the scene generously drenched the whole premises, including boxes of finished products. The clean-up was done within a day, but news of the incident went right up the chain to the city Party committee. Fires and deflagrations were regarded as major lapses. As a result, Stepanenko was dismissed. I think he was actually rather relieved, as he realised that he was out of his depth in the face of ever more complicated challenges. To his credit, he opted to stay at the factory and was appointed production manager. Casting aside directorial vanity, he embraced this new role, which also had its challenges but to which he was wholly suited.

I was appointed acting director again, but this time by order of the ministry. At that time, I had no directorial aspirations and was more than satisfied with my role as chief engineer. There was less of the administrative and political work that I found boring. I was excited at the prospect of organising production in the new building. In effect, a new, modern enterprise was in the process of being created. This was the chief engineer's area of responsibility. The higher-ups were perfectly happy with this stance, and the personnel office looked for a director among ministry staff. The situation was the exact opposite of what it had been in 1967, with the Yava factory having plenty to recommend it. It was a leading enterprise with excellent prospects and a reasonable level of stability, turning out modern products that were in high demand on the Moscow market. All the country's top officials smoked mainly Yava cigarettes. In fact, our cigarettes had virtually no competition. The position of director of Yava was therefore rather an attractive proposition, especially as the frequent ministry reshuffles made ministerial employees nervous about their futures. Manufacturing, on the other hand, especially in the context of product shortages, offered a high degree of stability. That is why people used to say, "Hold on to the chimney!" In other words, hold onto your manufacturing job, it is more reliable. In any case, some ministerial officials were simply fed up with paper-pushing bureaucratic work and longed to be posted to an enterprise, where there was real, meaningful work and much more freedom. The appearance of the director vacancy at the Yava factory caused a considerable stir among staff at the ministry.

I do not know how candidates for the post were selected or what factors played a deciding role. The personnel office was the ministry's most secretive division and had its own specific decision-making mechanisms. However it came about, we were presently introduced to our new director, Nikolai Sergeyevich Kashtanov. Jumping ahead a little, I will say that in the four years plus that he worked at the factory, he played an important role in unifying the workforce. Yava's standing in the halls of power rose significantly during his tenure. He was a Russian to his core. Energetic, with a high sense of responsibility. Exuding positive energy, he knew how to engage with people, which was an important quality in a director. As a young man he had earned his living as a boilerman. After graduating from the Moscow Institute of the Food Industry, he had worked for a short time at the Ducat tobacco factory as foreman of the processing section. At the time of his appointment to Yava, he was head of a key department in the ministry's equipment and supply administration. Presumably, as an ambitious man, Kashtanov had been keen to get away from the bureaucratic environment. He had succeeded. We were the same age. Unlike me, with my relatively comfortable upbringing in a secure family environment, he had had to learn early on to fight for his survival, especially as he already had a family of his own with two sons. As a person who had experienced much in his life, Nikolai Sergeyevich was initially wary of his new surroundings, and in particular of the chief engineer who had worked at the factory for about ten years. Despite his experience at Ducat, his knowledge of the tobacco industry was fairly superficial. At first, he expected some sort of mischief on our part with a view to making a fool of him. Very soon, however, he became reassured of the sincerity of my intentions, and from that point we worked together in an atmosphere of mutual trust. Nikolai Sergeyevich had full confidence in me as a specialist and always supported me in every undertaking.

The main problem that remained at that time was moving the cigarette-making machines and setting up production in the new building. Since it had been necessary to make temporary arrangements for some production processes, problems arose with the regulatory authorities. Naturally, in those areas where temporary arrangements were made, we were unable to guarantee full compliance with current sanitary and fire safety rules. As a result, violation notices began to rain down on us, some of them of a categorical nature. We tried to explain the situation and offer guarantees, but the inspectors stuck to the letter of the law. The inspectorates had real power and could have sealed off the master switch feeding power to any vital unit, which would have been tantamount to shutting down production. This made everyone very jittery. Something had to be done. We had already moved most of the cigarette-making equipment into the new building, but the hard currency needed to buy foreign machinery had still not been allocated. There were a number of important operational decisions that could not be put off any longer. We decided that the solution lay in developing support systems using Soviet-made equipment. The entire workload was shouldered by the factory's technical divisions. I will talk here about two key projects.

One of the most important issues was the creation of a reliable system for ensuring the prompt supply of finished products to market. The project design envisaged the construction of an intermediate warehouse next to Rosbakaleya's (the distribution division of the Trade Ministry) shipping room. In foreign factories, finished products were usually moved around by a system of belt conveyors that collected boxes from each packing machine and then delivered them to collector conveyors and onwards to the finished product storage area. Nothing complicated about that, it would seem – but there was no one who could design and build even this fairly simple kind of conveyor system. In the 1970s the country lost the last of its product development bureaus with their small production units for the manufacture of custom equipment. The system did not encourage the development of such enterprises. It is quite possible that there were organisations in the defence industry or the machine-building sector that would have been capable of designing or making such equipment, but the way in which the command economy worked meant that it was not in their interest to get involved.

At the same time, we were aware of foreign firms that specialised in manufacturing such equipment. Their designs were of a very high standard. At the instigation of the ministry we received a proposal from the well-known Italian company SASIB, a manufacturer of cigarette-making and packing machinery. The Italians offered a solution that would completely transform the process by which products were packed and delivered to the shipping room. Automated cigarette-packing machines would be set up in the cigarette-making shop and the packs would be conveyed through light metal structures to a packing room located next to the finished product warehouse. In the packing room, the packs would be placed into boxes on a special production line. The proposal had a whole host of advantages. It meant that around thirty low-skilled workers could be let go. And moving the whole process of packing products into boxes to a separate facility outside the cigarette production shop would greatly increase the area available for organising workspace, thus improving conditions for the workers. I hardly need say that we were extremely keen on the project. It would move us to a higher level in terms of the organisation of production and labour. Unfortunately, as with many other projects, the funds could not be found. Consequently, we had to go back to the inefficient system of using trolleys to transport boxes of finished products within the shop. On the plus side, the newly created intermediate warehouse was a great help. It enabled us to move boxes out of the shop in a prompt manner and prevent it getting cluttered with stock. The decision to use a suspended cradle conveyor to move boxes from the cigarette shop to the warehouse turned out to be a good idea. We had looked at numerous options. The conveyor we chose was one of the most recent designs. It had a number of important advantages. Movement was affected by a roller chain on metal guides. The rollers were made from a special plastic. The very low friction afforded smooth movement and high manoeuvrability. Because of this, the conveyor track took up minimal space. Conditions in the factory being what they were, this was very important. By that time, we had managed to instil a taste for modern solutions in the factory's technical specialists, although our resources were extremely limited.

Another pressing issue in setting up operations in the new building was the installation of air cleaning systems. The problem of cleansing exhaust air of tobacco dust was an environmental issue, and one that was especially acute for enterprises located inside cities close to civil buildings. The Yava factory was in a complicated position. Built in the nineteenth century in what used to be Moscow's outskirts, by the latter half of the twentieth century it was virtually in the city centre. In the 1930s, residential buildings had been constructed near to the factory. At that time, no one conceived of such a thing as a "sanitary protection zone" around an enterprise, within which residential construction would be prohibited. In the sixties, the residents began writing complaints to government authorities about the high dust content of the air in their apartments and the areas around the apartment buildings. But there was virtually nothing we could do about it. The issue of air cleaning in Soviet tobacco factories had been wholly neglected. Our industry did not make equipment for the removal of tobacco dust. Enterprises used outdated equipment known as "cyclones", which had been manufactured since times immemorial by small-scale tinkerers. A cyclone had an efficiency rate of around 60 per cent. Over 40 per cent of tobacco dust was expelled into the environment. It was impossible to comply with dust control regulations using that sort of system. In fact, most tobacco factories in the USSR were located inside cities in close proximity to residential buildings. You could tell that there was a tobacco factory in the vicinity by the smell and feel of tobacco dust in the air. It was a major problem, and everyone realised that it was practically impossible to solve it. Up to now, local government authorities and inspectorates had chosen to turn a blind eye to the issue.

With the transfer of operations to the new building, expectations on the part of the authorities grew more stringent. We understood that we would have to meet much higher environmental requirements. Drastic changes were needed. There were a number of companies in Europe that designed cleaning systems. They produced high-specification ventilators and filters with up to 99 per cent cleaning efficiency. There were no funds to buy foreign equipment, and the choice of products on the domestic market was limited. In the end we decided on sleeve filters made by a machine-building plant in Shebekino in the Belgorod region. Air was cleaned as it passed through sleeves made from a special filtering material. Units of this kind were used in various industries, including metallurgy and consumer goods manufacturing. It was bulky equipment, but there was enough room to install it in the new production building. To increase cleaning efficiency, we decided to use the sleeve filters in conjunction with the cyclones. Each pneumatic conveyor system was fitted with its own individual air cleaning unit. The cyclone caught the large particles, while the filter dealt with the finer dust. It was not a bad solution, but we had a devil of a time using it. The design of the working elements was imperfect, to put it mildly, but the way they had been made was simply horrendous. I never visited the plant in question, but I imagine it had very outdated technology and facilities. We suffered large losses due to forced machine shutdowns. But what could we have done? It was the only plant in the country that made such equipment. Gradually, the factory's technicians managed to adapt the equipment to make it more workable. Needless to say, our domestically produced air cleaning system did not have the efficiency or operating characteristics of foreign equipment, but it was definitely a step forward. For all the problems they gave us, those units would enable Yava to continue operating in the centre of Moscow for a long time to come.

The main problem that remained was the primary processing section. While we had somehow managed to improvise our way through the previous projects, when it came to equipment for the primary section there was no option but to buy from abroad. At the ministry's instigation we were presented with three proposals from globally known companies – Hauni (West Germany), Comas (Italy) and Dickinson (Britain). The classic set-up of the primary process in tobacco production was well known and had been finely honed by all the manufacturers, so the proposals were of a high standard and differed only in a few minor details. Choosing between them was simply a question of market conditions. But time went on, and still no decision had been made. The factory struggled on with a makeshift set-up for feeding cut tobacco to the machines. Quite unexpectedly, it was again the Council for Mutual Economic Assistance that came to our aid. Under a Comecon cooperation arrangement, the People's Republic of Bulgaria undertook to manufacture primary processing equipment for the USSR. Close ties had been formed between the Soviet and Bulgarian tobacco industries. Bulgarian cigarettes and tobacco accounted for a large proportion of the trade balance between the two countries. The Bulgartabak association was one of the country's biggest exporters to the USSR. In the early seventies, many international design patents for tobacco primary processing equipment expired, and Bulgartabak decided to take advantage of this and start making the equipment. It was a logical move given the huge potential market in the USSR: over forty tobacco factories, all with obsolete equipment. As a first step, the Bulgarian side was willing to supply a full set of processing equipment for the Yava factory. The negotiator for the Soviet side was the Tekhnoimport foreign trade association. There were, of course, some doubts: Bulgaria was an agrarian country with very little machine-building experience, but primary processing equipment was the simplest kind of equipment in the tobacco industry. The commitment shown by the Bulgarian side suggested that the project was feasible. The supply of equipment to the Yava factory was its first experience with this kind of order. This became plainly obvious during the assembly process. A group of ten people came to the factory as installation supervisors. They worked in a very different way from Western specialists. Western firms supplied machines that were wholly ready for use. The Bulgarians sent engineers that had been involved in designing the equipment. When it came to connect it up, it was found that the parts did not fit together. Adjustments to the design and modifications to the equipment had to be made as the installation was carried out. The work dragged on for months. The Soviet side should at least have raised claims against the supplier for punitive damages. But we were dealing with a friendly country that had effectively come to our rescue. If it had not been for that project, the factory would have been in a dreadful situation. The factory's own specialists gradually joined in with the installation effort. It might be said that it ended up as a Bulgarian-Soviet joint project. Of course, the quality of the equipment was not as good as Western equivalents, but it did the job of processing tobacco. Setting up the primary processing section was a great step forward that enabled us to improve the quality of our cigarettes and raise our efficiency.

Chapter 7.

Yava in Front Again

When the new primary section came on line in 1974, the renovation of the factory was complete. Yava now had an end-to-end manufacturing cycle that began with the proper storage of tobacco in a modern warehouse. The workshops had air conditioners and centrally controlled pneumatic conveyor systems. The premises vacated as a result of the relocation of equipment into the new building were converted into storage areas, which enabled the factory to keep an adequate stock of materials on site. There were even positive changes in the factory's external appearance. Fronting 3 Yamskovo Polya Street now was the façade of a five-storey production building with a modern entrance area. Particular progress had been made in the quality of our cigarettes. One long-standing flaw in our tobacco products had been that they were too densely filled, making them difficult to smoke. This resulted from using tobacco that was either too moist or too dry. Experienced smokers would dry the packs on domestic radiators before using them. If the tobacco was dry, they would knead the cigarette to squeeze out the excess tobacco. Cigarettes like this were called "pencils". These were the most common defects, which negated all the efforts made by enterprises to improve the quality of tobacco products. The Yava factory was the first to overcome these problems. The quality of Yava cigarettes had risen to a new level, making them the undisputed leader on the Soviet Union's tobacco market.

The renovation process at Yava had showed the industry to be technically and organisationally unprepared for modernisation. The authorities were keenly aware of the huge importance of keeping the population supplied with tobacco products. All efforts were focused on increasing production volume, while quality remained a secondary issue. As the industry shifted towards the production of cigarettes proper, the task became more challenging. Equipment and most materials had to be purchased abroad. There was particular difficulty in organising the production of premium-quality filter cigarettes. The state was not up to the task. There could be no question of bringing in new primary processing systems, as this required factories to be refurbished, involving substantial capital outlays. This is why the authorities pursued a policy of increasing production of unfiltered cigarettes, which were easier to make and supply. Filter cigarettes were a prestigious product, and local Party bodies were keen for them to be manufactured and sold in their regions. Provincial factories tried to organise production of the cigarettes themselves, contriving to adapt outdated equipment for this purpose. They would use LUS machines produced by Lenmashazavod to pack the cigarettes. Achieving good quality on that sort of equipment was practically impossible. The cigarettes were so densely filled that they were difficult to get going and gave a bitter taste when smoked. The paper filter would quickly go soggy in the mouth and peel off. The packaging was awful. There would often be small particles of tobacco between the pack surface and the cellophane.

There were really only two enterprises on the Soviet market that made products conforming to international standards: Yava and Bulgartabak. Smokers tended to prefer Yava cigarettes, but Yava produced around six billion premium-quality filter cigarettes per year, and that was only enough to cover Moscow's needs.

Yes, it was a great honour to be the chief supplier of products for the capital city. Yava cigarettes were smoked by Party and industry bosses all over the country. The factory's products were supplied through so-called "special shipments" to the "special canteens" of Union republic central committees and regional Party committees for local Party and administrative officials. In Moscow, supplies to the top brass went through special depots 201 and 508. People visiting Moscow from other parts of the country would take the opportunity to buy Yava cigarettes to take home with them. It was around this time that gifts began to play a large role in people's dealings with each other. At clinics, hospitals, schools, shops and even government institutions, gifts were a very effective way of establishing connections and resolving various issues. Yava designed proposals for the production of gift sets in attractive boxes containing ten packs each. The idea was supported by the ministry, and arrangements were made for the boxes and pack labels to be printed in Finland. We had great success with our Rossiiskiye gift cigarettes, presented in an attractive pack with a bright, colourful design in the style of *Khokhloma* folk painting. The idea of creating cigarette gift sets was seized on by foreign trade associations, which began ordering special batches of cigarettes for promotional use at international exhibitions and auctions. The original design was commissioned by the associations, and the packs were made using top-quality imported materials purchased at the customer's expense. All this boosted the image of Yava products and of the factory itself. The gift sets were produced in small batches and were hard to obtain.

This was a rosy period for Yava. Yava cigarettes were in slightly short supply, i.e. it was possible to buy them, but it took a bit of effort. And in the Soviet Union, producing something that was in short supply raised an enterprise's prestige. The factory's economic performance was much higher than that of other enterprises in the sector. It displayed all the attributes of a successful Soviet enterprise. Morale within the enterprise improved, with its managers now working as a team. Nikolai Sergeyevich Kashtanov and I were adherents of openness in management coupled with strict allocation of powers and responsibilities. As managers, we had to demonstrate our commitment to these principles by personal example. The director had complete confidence in me as far as technical policy and production management were concerned. For his part, he busied himself enthusiastically with social policy, relations with civic organisations and the creation of a positive climate within the workforce, as well as, very importantly, liaising and promoting the factory's image with external institutions, such as the ministry and the city and district Party committees. New figures were elected to the posts of secretary of the factory's Party organisation and chairman of the trade union committee. The new Party secretary was a young man from among our new recruits, Alexander Vasilyevich Vikhrov, a pragmatic fellow with modern views.

As the only Soviet enterprise that was well-known in the international tobacco industry, Yava became a testing ground for the latest foreign materials and equipment. The factory's standing with government agencies was also growing. The authorities understood Yava's importance in keeping the Moscow region supplied with tobacco products. Party bodies began issuing resolutions giving positive assessments of various aspects of the factory's activities. Thanks to the popularity of its eponymous filter cigarettes, Yava became a nationwide brand, rivalled only by brands of the Red October confectionery factory, the Moscow Distillery and the AvtoVAZ plant in Togliatti, which made the famous Zhiguli cars. Yava was a household name. For that reason, the factory's representatives were treated very attentively – I would even say respectfully – by officials at all levels. And if they were given gift sets of cigarettes "as a souvenir", matters could be resolved in double-quick time. This was very useful.

CHAPTER 8.

BACK TO THE COMMAND ECONOMY

THE FAILINGS OF CENTRAL PLANNING

Ten years had passed since Brezhnev came to power. The rigid vertical structure of administration of the economy had been restored. The reforms designed to improve management methods had been killed off in their infancy. Administration of the national economy had been wholly transferred to the centre, restoring the command system. The Soviet Union was losing more and more ground to the West in terms of economic efficiency. Achievements in the space, nuclear and other defence sectors had been made possible by the inordinate concentration of the country's resources in those areas. Group B industry continued to lag behind in development. Home-grown consumer goods no longer satisfied the population's needs. This became especially clear after people began to have some access to foreign goods as a result of developments in foreign trade. Demand for imported goods created a "shortage within a shortage". Public spending power had grown, and the state was keen to increase production of higher-quality consumer goods (including in the food industry).

The CPSU Central Committee tasked the government with shrinking the quality gap between domestic and imported goods and produce. There was even an official term for this: "the achievement of international quality standards". Leading enterprises were identified in each sector of industry. In the Food Ministry's system these were the Red October confectionery factory, the Moscow Distillery (the future Kristall), Mospishchekombinat (the Moscow Food Plant), and the Yava tobacco factory. They had to demonstrate the successes achieved by the country in the economy and act as a sort of showcase of achievements in their sector. Each of them produced nationally popular brands. The leading enterprises were set the task of making products that met international standards. Modern imported equipment and materials were purchased for these purposes. The products produced by these enterprises were vastly superior in quality to their mass-market counterparts, but the quantities made were not sufficient even to meet the needs of Moscow's population. Evidently, the main purpose of implementing new technologies at leading enterprises was to bring about a gradual expansion of the production of high-quality goods at other enterprises of the food sector. Our minister, Klemenchuk, a very experienced and energetic leader with a subtle feel for developments in state policy, organised a "product display centre". It was located right in the centre of Moscow in a grand old house on the site of the Moscow Champagne Plant. Exhibited in its fine rooms, in large display cabinets, were specimens of the best foreign products alongside corresponding brands produced by enterprises of the Russian food industry. The Russian products really were of a good quality, but most of them could never be spotted on the shelves of Moscow shops. Our minister was very proud of the display centre. He would use it as a venue in which to greet foreign visitors and high-ranking Soviet officials and host enlarged ministry meetings. Time went on, but the main objective had not been achieved: Soviet-produced modern products had not become widely available. That would require enterprises and their suppliers to be rebuilt and fitted out with modern production facilities. But the funds to do this were simply not available. Not only that, but the political system was not conducive to the modernisation of the economy. As a result, a good idea turned into little more than a propaganda exercise, just to be able to say that we were capable of producing goods on a par with those of other countries.

Even favourable external factors did not help much. In the 1970s global oil prices were high, and since Brezhnev came to power oil production had increased as a result of the exploitation of fields in western Siberia. This brought in additional hard currency, meaning that foreign equipment and technologies could be procured for the food and consumer goods industries. But the funds were used extremely inefficiently. Priority was given to procuring imported equipment for factories in the process of construction or renovation, but many of these projects did not meet their completion deadlines and turned into semi-permanent construction sites. It came down to inefficient economic planning and administration. The country ended up with a large quantity of imported equipment lying idle. The system had proved unable to cope with the challenges posed, and the state budget incurred irreparable losses.

I will give an example. At around that time, a decision was made to increase beer production with the aim of reducing vodka consumption. A large quantity of brewery equipment was purchased. The collegium of the Food Ministry of the RSFSR was constantly discussing the unsatisfactory progress being made in upgrading the breweries and the problems they were having in putting the imported equipment into operation. No amount of punitive measures against the managers seemed to help. It was not long before the head of the brewery directorate (Rosprivprom), a very hard-working fellow, was removed from his post. Evidently, there were deeper underlying issues which the industry leaders were unable to change. Otherwise they would have done something, if only for their own self-preservation. Also of little help were the Public Oversight Committees, which carried out regular investigations into delays in the commissioning of imported equipment. The explanation was simply that the absence of real incentives for economic development perpetuated the poor standard of production and labour organisation. Construction deadlines were routinely missed, and the quality of project planning and management lagged behind the requirements of the times.

The cause of this glaring inefficiency was the excessive centralisation of economic administration. Decisions on production expansion in the USSR were made by central policy-making bodies. Each year, the government and Gosplan (the State Planning Commission) made decisions about investing public funds based on the interests of the state as they perceived them. Key performance targets and resource distribution levels for the various sectors were drawn up by Gosplan and sent out to the ministries. Materials and equipment were centrally allocated, with supply quotas being communicated to enterprises together with their output targets. This period saw the beginning of major breakdowns in the planning system at the highest level of economic administration. The struggle for resources grew particularly intense. Resources were not bought on the market, but strictly distributed. The objective of enterprise managers, sectoral directorates and ministries was to secure a greater amount of resources to make it easier for state targets to be fulfilled. Gosplan's objective was to cut industry requirements and ensure that plans were fulfilled despite the shortage of resources. Obviously enough, these aims were diametrically opposed, locking the ministries and Gosplan in conflict with each other. The ministries "defended" their calculations to Gosplan, while Gosplan looked for ways to reduce the demands being made. Each side tried to hog the blanket. As a result, the quotas granted by Gosplan to the ministries were often woefully short of actual requirements. Next to join the game was the State Supply Committee,

Gossnab, which organised the realisation of the allocated quotas. It was a sort of state within a state, controlling all the country's resources. Structurally, Gossnab consisted of large divisions known as *soyuzglavsbyty* (chief supply administrations), each of which was responsible for a particular type of resource. For example, one commodity that was in especially short supply was cement. The Gossnab agency in charge of the supply of cement was Soyuzglavtsement. Its role included ensuring that suppliers – cement factories – made supplies corresponding to the allocated quotas. If difficulties arose with the fulfilment of the supply plan, Soyuzglavtsement would call on the Ministry of Industry and Building Materials to take appropriate action and would get the local Party authorities involved. Sometimes it would reassign particularly important supplies from one enterprise to another. The supply system was controlled by the administrative triangle of Gossnab – ministry – local Party bodies. Things worked in much the same way for other types of resources. The Yava factory went through Soyuzglavtsvetmet for supplies of aluminium foil, Soyuzglavbum for paper and Soyuzglavtara for packaging materials. If problems arose with supplies, we would contact those agencies and they would usually help us out. Gossnab had a lot of power. This was all very well, but in real life there were numerous ways in which things could go awry. In such a vast country, it was impossible for the needs of the economy to be micro-managed from the centre: such an approach was disastrous for the efficiency of industrial enterprises. To resolve things, government bodies started distributing some resources manually.

I will give an example of how the system worked in the context of the Food Ministry of the RSFSR. The ministry received quotas for building materials, electrical equipment, plumbing fixtures and general plant equipment. Up to around 40 per cent of resources for the scarcest items was assigned to the so-called reserve fund, the use of which was supervised by the minister himself. Materials allocated from this fund were used to "put out fires" resulting from planning mistakes. Resources of the reserve fund were mostly allocated on the basis of individual letters. Klemenchuk would receive requests from Party and economic officials of autonomous republics and regions to allocate materials for the construction of industrial or social facilities. Owing to the critical shortage of centralised investment, regional authorities had begun organising many smaller building projects independently. But the resources needed for construction still had to be obtained through the ministries. The minister paid great attention to requests from local officials and made every effort to achieve a positive outcome. No doubt a similar system for the allocation of scarce materials existed in other ministries and higher up the government chain. Our minister simply acted in accordance with the rules of the game as they were at the time. Those in charge of distributing scarce resources gained increasing power. Materials for local construction projects had become too precious a commodity. There was no one who could resolve things locally, but the Minister could fix everything with one stroke of his pen. However, "a solution could easily be found". The system "adapted" to the changed situation in the planning of economic activity. These practices demonstrated the weakening of the central planning system and the acknowledgement of real trends towards greater initiative at local level.

State institutions were becoming less effective. Enterprises lacked incentives to perform, and the state planning system made them very wary of revealing any reserve capacity. The authorities had stopped setting long-term targets. At the same time, the planning approach based on past performance meant that the state expected enterprises to deliver growth year after year. Plan targets were set at above 100 per cent of the preceding year's results. Since, in the real world, this was not always achievable, experienced managers were very careful, when submitting their draft plans to the sectoral directorate and the ministry, not to "overstate the base", i.e. to leave enough slack for growth in future years. They had to learn to present the case to the ministry that there was no spare capacity and the performance figures submitted by the enterprise had been achieved at full stretch. The ministries made a similar "defence" of the industry's plans before Gosplan. The people at Gosplan probably had little inkling of how things really stood in the regions. Nor did they give much credence to the figures presented by the ministries. As a result, planning became less and less fact-based. Gosplan's primary focus was on satisfying demand. And since actual need was generally above what industry could supply, the only way to cover demand was through tough targets. The same applied when it came to setting plans for the tobacco industry.

Around September-October, Rosglavtabak would receive target figures for the following year from Gosplan and begin assigning them to factories. This was a crucial period. Each factory would do its utmost to ward off high targets. Party bodies would get involved in the process. After a long period of wrangling and lobbying, adjustments would be made to the draft plans of the enterprises concerned. However, one cardinal rule was always observed: the total production volume set by Gosplan for the industry as a whole could not be reduced.

The Yava factory was a special case. It performed the very important task of supplying tobacco products to the Moscow region. The complication lay in the particular nature of tobacco consumption. Cigarettes are a product that is consumed on a regular, everyday basis. Habit inclines the smoker to derive satisfaction only from the regular consumption of one particular brand of tobacco. In Moscow, Yava cigarettes were the most popular brand, and the factory therefore had a duty to keep the city's shops supplied with them on a daily basis. Any interruptions in the supply of cigarettes could have unpredictable social consequences. Later, we would come up against real tobacco crises and see how overwhelming and dangerous they could be for the country. It was not feasible for a shortage of Yava cigarettes to be compensated by products made by other enterprises. For this reason, Gosplan made the production target for the Yava factory a separate item in the overall plan for the industry. The requirement for Yava cigarettes was very high, and the production plan was set based on the maximum capacity of the factory's equipment, yet the factory was expected to increase production year on year. This could only be achieved by increasing the productivity of the cigarette-making machines, but there was virtually no reserve capacity.

Over the previous ten years there had been little improvement in the quality of Soviet-made materials. This was a reflection of the stagnation in the manufacturing sector. At foreign factories, cigarette-making machines were overhauled every seven to eight years by companies created specifically for that purpose. The equipment at our factory had been running for an even longer period of time. There was a need to set up a centralised repair base of a fundamentally new kind. Enterprises could not cope with this problem on their own. Senior government bodies were made aware of the problems in the tobacco sector. The matter of "supporting cigarette production" was reviewed on more than one occasion at various high levels. But the problem could not be resolved by purely administrative methods. It was the factory workers who shouldered the burden of fulfilling the unrealistic plans. We understood that, for the enterprise to survive, all of its internal resources would have to be brought to bear. We would need to give the workers a greater stake in performance, a say on management issues and a reason to be interested in resolving the factory's problems.

THE NEW MANAGEMENT CULTURE AT YAVA: RESULTS AND CONCLUSIONS

In developing the management system at the Yava factory we put our faith in people. We had to raise their independence, their proactiveness and their sense of responsibility. It was important for every employee to be given the opportunity to exhibit their best qualities and capabilities. The first step was to build a system of delegation of authority. This was essential to ensure that every worker was fully and independently responsible for the area of work assigned to him. Performance evaluations of division managers and their subordinates were based on their professionalism and ability to weigh up risks and take measures to address possible aberrations in the production process. Introducing this approach to management required a change of culture within the workforce. It began to be based on respect for employees and encouragement of their independence and right to their own opinion. Implementing this style of management at the Yava factory was a long and difficult process. Previous directors had been authoritarian leaders brought up on the command style of management. Voitsekhovich, during his tenure as director, had possessed unlimited power. That sort of centralisation was by no means always helpful. The role played by deputy directors was undervalued, and horizontal relationships between different specialists were liable to break down. Management became less efficient, with each manager attempting to resolve his own department's issues with orders signed by the director.

When I was appointed chief engineer, I had no experience of managing a large workforce. As head of the machine shop, I had mostly dealt with technical issues. So I had to find my own style of management and interaction with subordinates as I went along. My store of life experience was not huge either, but it was precisely what had made me the person I was. I had been brought up on the example of my parents, who were responsible, decent people. Veterinarians by profession, they had worked at the USSR Ministry of Agriculture, and like all people of their generation they had had a hard life. Their "non-proletarian origins" had barred them from choosing a higher education institution. They were not bitter about this, but always treated others with compassion and tried to give help to those who needed it. In our family we did not discriminate between people of different social backgrounds and were respectful of working folk. My early views on life were idealistic. As a student in senior school and at the institute, I believed that a person's fate depended on him alone, on his hard work, self-discipline and professional aptitude. I did not yet realise that much also depended on the nature of the state and society in which one lived. The notion of looking beyond oneself for the causes of failure was alien to me. But this served as a positive stimulus that disposed me to overcome difficulties by my own efforts. At the institute, I had shown an inclination towards scientific work, and through that work I developed a taste for the objective analysis of processes. This was the baggage of experience I had brought with me to the machine shop at Yava. After studying serious engineering disciplines, I had expected to be involved in modern manufacturing, but it was as if I had landed in the last century: dim, shabby buildings, primitive workplace organisation and worker facilities that were beneath criticism, machines made before the war and problems with tools. My first impression had been dreadful. And yet, before long, I began to find the work interesting. The machinery used to produce cigarettes and *papirosy* turned out to be complex, even unique. The machine shop had to meet some tricky challenges. I found the workers very interesting. They were all different people with their own complicated backgrounds, all professionals, all masters of their trade. I gradually came to understand these people, and a good working relationship developed between us. They acknowledged me as a leader. An unfortunate tendency had developed at the factory to treat the machine shop as a sort of "fire brigade". This made the workers tense and it had become impossible to establish a sound pre-production process and to work to a schedule. I set about correcting these practices. At the same time, I tried to help the workshops organise regular statistical records of the consumption of key machine parts. Little by little, the situation with regard to spare parts began to improve. The main thing was that it had become more transparent and there were now clear rules governing the machine shop's relationship with the production departments.

I was a great believer in the clear division of powers and responsibilities and a consistent approach to the resolution of operational issues. I began insisting on more thorough draughting work from the design and technical departments. This went against the family traditions that had built up among people at the factory over many years of working together. To bring about real change, it was necessary to show character and fall out with co-workers. I think that my initiatives were noticed by our director. He understood that the imminent renovation of the factory and arrival of the new equipment would require a significant amount of hard work and expertise. Appointing a young man with little experience under his belt as chief engineer was a somewhat risky move on his part. He was evidently counting on my proven ability to implement changes, which would be needed at the factory in the very near future. Besides, it may be said that youth lends itself to mastering new equipment and technology more quickly. Combined with Mikhail Demyanovich's experience, that could prove a great advantage.

I was appointed acting chief engineer in June 1966 and was confirmed in the post by the ministry in August. The equipment was due to arrive in the first quarter of 1967. Little more than a year remained, and there was virtually nowhere to put the equipment, the staff had not been trained and many issues surrounding the arrangements for the manufacture of a completely new product remained unresolved. The engineering staff consisted mainly of practical workers with narrow vision. Mikhail Demyanovich himself, though undoubtedly a bright and talented person, had never had to deal with problems on this scale. I think that the ministry and the chief directorate likewise had a very superficial grasp of the problems that lay ahead with the new equipment. They evidently thought that, as always, everything would sort itself out. When I took the position of chief engineer, I did not fully appreciate how fraught with danger this situation was. I did not sense the great anxiety among the managers about the situation we were in. Everything appeared to be going according to plan. The promo line was in operation, and beautifully packaged, international-standard cigarettes were being produced in the USSR for the very first time. Top officials had taken to smoking these cigarettes with great relish. The image and influence of Yava's management had been greatly boosted. There was a rule that whoever produced goods that were in short supply got access to people at the very top. And this was very important in the Soviet Union, as it was only people in high places who could help resolve important issues and secure the favours that were needed.

All the euphoria obscured the problems that arose when the factory embarked on the mass production of cigarettes. A few mechanics had been trained to use the promo line, but this was a drop in the ocean. It later turned out that our suppliers were not in a position to keep the factory supplied with high-quality materials. In the summer, the government authorised the conversion of the unfinished warehouse into a production facility. But several long years would pass before the building was ready for the equipment to be installed. I am now trying to work out why the factory was so inadequately prepared. Of course, 1966 was a very important year. It was the last year before the equipment arrived and an extremely difficult one for Yava. The factory had been without a chief engineer since the start of the year. Even after I was appointed, it took me a little while to get into the swing of things, and I was obviously lacking in experience. Then there was the fire at the tobacco warehouse. And to cap it all off, there was the dismissal of the director – the factory's leader and the man who had inspired the project. But where were our superiors in the ministry? They of all people should have understood the predicament that we were in, especially as this was a major industrial project of national significance, not something that could be ignored. The challenges were significantly broader than the capabilities of the Yava factory itself. Keeping production going would require input from various industries and the involvement of other ministries. In the Soviet economy this could only be organised through decisions of the government and Gosplan. And yet, as far as I know, no one had even drawn up a plan of measures needed to support the operation of the imported cigarette-making equipment. I feel sure that the manner in which this project was handled perfectly encapsulates the wrong-headed style and methods of industrial administration in the Soviet Union. Having purchased ultra-modern equipment, the ministry underestimated the complexity of the tasks that were set and the ability of Yava's management to cope with them on its own. This was due to the existence of the same old vertical structure of management in the upper echelons of power. Decisions were made by senior officials without seeking advice from specialists. There was no expert community. Sectoral research institutions led a wretched existence, and no one was interested in their opinion.

The Yava factory was a strong enterprise, but the management system that was in place at the factory at that time was completely unsuited to the magnitude of the challenges associated with the introduction of the new equipment. The command style of management worked well enough in the context of a long-established, well-mastered production process. Mikhail Demyanovich had always relied on trusted old-timers among the staff (which made his decision to appoint me as chief engineer doubly surprising). The lack of preparedness for the arrival of the equipment was a consequence of that style of management. If Voitsekhovich had remained director, he would not have been able to manage production using the old methods. New ways of working were needed.

When I was appointed acting director, I found myself feverishly searching for ways to survive. The command style of management was alien to me. It was insulting to the staff and prevented them from showing initiative. Where could I find support? Instinctively, I went to see the workers. After all, the problems that the mechanics were dealing with every minute of the day on the shop floor were the very problems that had to be addressed on a factory-wide scale. And the most experienced of them were capable of analysing a situation and drawing conclusions. I spent a lot of time in the workshops, chatting with the workers. It was from them, first and foremost, that I gathered the information that I discussed with department and shop managers. This was the way in which plans to reorganise the production process and optimise the performance of equipment were put together. In the course of our discussions the engineers developed a professional approach to designing solutions, a sense of responsibility and an understanding of their role in the overall system of production management at the factory.

This people-oriented management style was not understood by the most influential managers from the old team. The way they saw it, the chief engineer was effectively showing weakness and wasting a lot of time discussing matters with staff. Instead of showing firm management, he was being too soft. Mikhail Demyanovich would have been banging his fist on the table and forcing everyone to work properly. They failed to appreciate that the factory was facing a whole different level of problems. At that time, I myself did not have clearly formulated ideas about restructuring the management system at the factory. Rather, it was the process of meeting the highly complex challenges posed by the implementation of a fundamentally new manufacturing process that led me to a realisation of the need to change the style of interaction between management and workers. Serious problems could only be addressed by professional workers who understood their tasks and were motivated to carry them out. My opponents could not understand why this was necessary. After all, Mikhail Demyanovich had successfully run the factory using purely top-down management methods. In my view, it was the choice of the future direction and methods of management of the factory at that critical time that determined whether the enterprise would survive and cope with the task of assimilating the imported equipment. The supporters of conservative methods were considerably greater in number. The director, Stepanenko, had no intention of making any changes. Furthermore, he had nothing like the administrative charisma of Voitsekhovich. Because of his limited education and his age, he was incapable of studying and understanding the new production process in any detail. Accordingly, his management approach was vague and ineffectual. The secretary of the Party organisation, Zinaida Petrovna Alexandrovskaya, was an active – I would even say militant – advocate of conservative, Party-based management. As an honest and principled person, she sincerely believed in the effectiveness of hardline administrative methods conducted under Party control. Clearly, then, advocates of change were on shaky ground. However, it was at this time that the factory was beginning to experience a significant influx of new blood in its workforce. Many young men joined to work as trainee mechanics on the imported equipment. Gradually, the less committed recruits were weeded out, leaving those who were suited to the requirements of the job. These were young people, educated, with more modern, liberal views. Many of them had been through several changes of occupation and workplace before coming to the factory. What attracted them to Yava was the opportunity to earn decent money and learn how to use ultra-modern equipment. Indeed, it would have been difficult to find any other enterprise in Moscow that was offering these opportunities. As a result, the factory found itself with a sizable complement of young employees – people with aspirations, who knew what they wanted and were keen to make a good living. Gradually, as they became aware of the importance of their role in the fulfilment of the state plan, they became bolder about pressuring the administration to make improvements in the methods and organisation of production and labour. In these new mechanics, the factory's administration faced employees who held strong views and were prepared to stand up for their interests. This was a new force, which demanded to be reckoned with and encouraged change.

A new reality had dawned at the factory, leaving the old-guard management confounded. As managers retired, they were gradually replaced by young engineers. At first, these were factory employees who were on the reserve list for promotion, including workers who had gained a higher or intermediate technical education. Later, we began hiring staff from outside, primarily graduates of the Moscow Technological Institute of the Food Industry. Many of them were attracted on a professional level by the problems involved in the assimilation of modern imported equipment and the building and renovation of the factory. At the overwhelming majority of food industry enterprises, outdated production technology was still being used and there was no prospect of their being renovated or upgraded. For a genuine aspiring engineer, therefore, working at Yava was a great privilege. The young specialists gradually developed into a force that would help steer the enterprise out of a major crisis.

Molins cigarette-making lines were used in countries all over the world, but I feel certain that it was only in the Soviet Union that this expensive equipment was purchased without adequate preparation. We at the factory had to reorganise production, set everything up and fulfil the state plan on the fly in the most difficult conditions. Yava was regularly visited by specialists from foreign firms, who brought advanced materials for trial use and showed us the latest models of manufacturing equipment. This direct contact with specialists from abroad helped to develop the skills and broaden the outlook of Yava employees. The workers saw how superior the quality of foreign equipment and materials was. Particularly striking was the difference in packaging – the high-quality imported variety compared with the dreadful kind that was supplied by our own enterprises. You would think that we could at least organise decent packaging! Asking why things had turned out this way aided the self-development of the enterprise's employees. Closer contact with foreign achievements gave them a picture of what the standard of modern manufacturing should be. It is tough to be a manager at an enterprise where the workers are professional, educated people with a shrewd perception of all that is going on. However, it is only a workforce of this kind that is capable of coping with complex tasks. As the employees' insights grew, so did their expectations of the factory's administration. The administration had no option but to accept the challenge. This became the chief driving force for the changes that were so vital to the development of the enterprise.

There gradually emerged a group of highly competent workers with whom relationships of trust were built. After all, if you want to persuade someone to speak openly, you have to win him over, earn his trust. The workers had to feel that it would help bring about real changes in the workplace, which would make it easier for them to do their work and improve their conditions. At meetings, the workers asked frank and often hard-hitting questions. It was important not to be afraid of this, but to enter into honest debate and find the right solutions. It was through the development of these rudiments of openness that the best qualities of the Yava factory's workforce took shape.

CHAPTER 9.

THE CONTRADICTORY REALITY OF THE SEVENTIES

COMMUNIST IDEOLOGY STALLS

The formation of the new management culture at the Yava factory took place under the influence of cardinal changes in the structure of Soviet society. The country had changed too deeply to go back to Stalinism. People had begun to throw off the shackles of Party dogma. There was more freedom in choosing an occupation and place of work and greater opportunity to determine one's own path in life. Ties with foreign countries were developing, with the Soviet leadership keen to expand foreign trade. Respect for democratic principles and human rights in the Soviet Union had become a major topic of discussion at international level, which did much to advance the liberalisation of the internal climate in the country and the reframing of the relationship between people and government. Closer attention was paid to the mood of the people and ensuring that they were not unhappy with government policy. Regular press reports about local-level abuses of the law or human rights were usually followed up with thorough inspections, and the public would be informed of the findings and resulting measures.

The technological boom in the West forced the Soviet Union to respond by developing new areas of industry, primarily precision engineering, electronics, and the chemical industry. New factories were built, and existing enterprises re-equipped. This changed the situation on the labour market as demand for new occupations arose. Rather than a shortage of jobs, there was now a shortage of labour. Filling vacancies became a major problem in Moscow. The population of the capital was rising. Its growing needs forced the authorities to increase food production and improve the quality of what was produced. For example, supplying Muscovites with cold beverages and beer had become a serious problem. As always, there was a lack of coordination. In the winter, factories that produced soft drinks and beer stood idle as demand fell, while in the summer these products were in desperately short supply. The issue was constantly being discussed by government and Party bodies. To address the problem, a number of enterprises of the so-called "liquid group" were built in the Ochakovo district, and existing enterprises were expanded.

In Moscow, notices appeared by the entrances to industrial enterprises, research institutes and other organisations with job offers for manual workers and engineers of all descriptions. In an effort to counter the labour shortage, it was decided to bring workers in from neighbouring regions. To regulate this process, the authorities issued special quotas, or "limits", for the importation of workers from those areas. These workers were referred to locally as *limitchiki*, a disparaging term that reflected the negative feeling towards them among Muscovites. The number of *limitchiki* kept growing, so much so that they soon became a conspicuous part of the population. An especially large number of workers brought in under the limit system took jobs at large enterprises, in workshops with arduous conditions and at large construction sites, for which it was difficult to recruit people from the local population. Enterprises of the food industry tended to be short of women machinists. These jobs were filled by *limitchiki*. The authorities would give them various kinds of assistance and allocate hostel rooms for them. The number of women workers imported to work in Moscow's confectionery factories averaged 300–400 at each enterprise. They had to be accommodated, kept in order, kept safe. But these were young people without families and with disorderly lifestyles. Dealing with the *limitchiki* was a big headache for enterprise managers.

At the Yava factory, too, cigarette and *papirosy*-making machines were beginning to stand idle because of a shortage of women operators. Organising an official hostel and obtaining quotas was rather a long process, so we decided to tackle the problem in a different way, especially as our requirement for additional labour was relatively small. We made an arrangement with the director of a food industry college in Moldavia whereby students would come to work at Yava, and it would be classed as a work experience placement. This was in everyone's interests, giving the students the opportunity to spend some time in Moscow and earn some money. Every enterprise dealt with labour supply issues in their own way.

These changes were dictated by life itself. With the acceleration of industrial development, new jobs were created, new skills were needed, and workers began to move from one place to another. The formation of workforces along patriarchal lines was no longer viable. So-called "factory patriotism" was on the wane. Now, people were always on the lookout for a better job. Their priorities were now professional growth, earnings, and good working conditions. In effect, a proper labour market had begun to take shape in the Soviet Union, in which enterprises had to compete to attract workers.

In the real economy, reliance had to be placed not on the "public spirit and deep patriotism of Soviet people", but on giving employees a material stake in the results of their labour. Life had begun to offer new opportunities, and people strove for a better life, a higher material standard of living. Scarce goods began to be imported. Foreign-made household appliances, furniture and clothes began to appear in the shops. There was intensive construction of apartment buildings and whole residential areas. Many families received new apartments, allowing them to fashion a relatively cosy domestic life and furnish their new living space according to their taste. Young people looked for better housing conditions in order to start their own family, get away from their parents and start living independently. The waiting lists at district executive committees for the allocation of free housing were long. However, it became possible to buy a flat in so-called cooperative buildings, so people set about saving up money to buy a cooperative flat. The AvtoVAZ factory in Togliatti began making Zhiguli cars. It cost what seemed an inconceivable amount of money, but it was impossible to buy one on the open market. Like other scarce goods, cars were sold through enterprises and organisations to "high achievers". Accordingly, if and when the chance came, money was borrowed from friends and relatives so as not to let the opportunity slip away. Possessing one's own personal car conferred prestige and signified a totally different quality of life. People's priorities changed. After their long ideological imprisonment and the endless promises of a bright Communist future, they wanted to take full advantage of what life had to offer in the here and now.

Life now revolved around family, health and the raising of children. It became possible, mainly through one's workplace, to receive a plot of land outside Moscow and build a dacha or summer house. The authorities tried to make sure that people were not "turning bourgeois": the plot would be of a standard size (600 m^2), and the house had to be constructed from wood, for summer use, with strict limitations on floor area. During the summer, families would flock out of the city and happily spend time working on their plots.

However, the new opportunities for a better life were wholly inaccessible at existing wage levels. This gave rise to imbalances in society. Those who had the determination went all out to secure a better standard of living for themselves. When someone managed to buy a car, furnish his flat or build himself a summer house, people would say of him that he "knew how to live". Realistically, it was difficult to do these things on an official wage. People even used to say, when wishing someone ill, "May you live on nothing but your wage!" This mentality gradually turned into a way of life in the Soviet Union. The greatest opportunities for living "beyond one's means" went to people working in trade and anyone who had access to scarce goods and services. The deepening shortages in the country were the main driver of "under-the-counter" earnings. But what about the rest? They found different ways. The most common was petty theft at work, which became rife. As Arkady Raikin[1] once said in a stand-up routine, "Go into a person's home and you'll have a fair idea of where he works". The powers-that-be were well aware of this serious problem, but they preferred to turn a blind eye. It was said that a guest of Brezhnev's daughter, Galina, asked Leonid Ilyich how it was possible for people to live on 120 roubles a month. To which Brezhnev replied, in all sincerity, "Don't worry, everyone steals what they can, when they can. When I was a student, I used to get jobs unloading freight wagons, and I certainly didn't have to live on my stipend alone."

The country's leadership made no response to the changes afoot in the country. This destroyed people's motivation and their trust in the state. During Brezhnev's reign, people used to say "They [the state] pretend to pay us, and we pretend to work".

The pay-levelling system had an especially detrimental impact on the quality of work produced by research and design institutes. The Soviet Union lagged far behind in creating technologies for civilian industries. Even when they bought foreign technology, industrial concerns struggled to adapt it to work in a particular facility. This led to a growth in the number of unskilled manual jobs, particularly in areas such as terminal operations, intra-factory transport and haulage. Goods were transported in bulk form using low-tonnage trucks. Unloading was done manually, requiring a large number of workers. What was required to address this critical problem was for the country's entire transport

---

1 Arkady Isaakovich Raikin (1911–1987) – a popular stage actor, director and stand-up comedian known for his humorous and satirical monologues.

infrastructure to be overhauled, for factories to begin shipping finished products in packaged form and for transport organisations to start using large-capacity trucks. There was a need for modern handling equipment and labour-saving tools. But the equipment required to carry out these operations was not produced in the Soviet Union. Production and storage facilities needed to be enlarged to facilitate the transportation, storage and handling of pallets of finished products. The Soviet system proved incapable of such large-scale modernisation. At railway stations, transport organisations and industrial enterprises there was a growing number of loading hands toiling in dismal conditions. These people, having no real prospects in life, would gradually drink themselves to ruin and become a potential danger to society. The workers stopped valuing their jobs, since they could easily find employment elsewhere. Coming to work drunk became normal practice. Even having it noted in their employment record that they had been fired for "violation of work discipline" did not stop them. To avoid this sort of situation, we began employing workers in this category under temporary arrangements so that their contracts could be terminated at short notice.

There was a growing gulf between the ideological narrative of the Communist Party on the one hand and people's real lives and needs on the other. The pressure from above had eased significantly. People had shaken off their fear, but they had not received in exchange the incentives that could bring the population together and make things work for the benefit of the country and society. It is fair to say that the policies pursued by the state frustrated the development of a new social framework. Many things that defied common sense gradually became a normal part of life. I came up against this phenomenon from the moment I began working at the factory.

"TOTAL SHORTAGES" STEER THE ECONOMY

Formalism became a dominant feature of the authorities' approach to tackling important state problems. Imagine a young specialist who has just graduated from an institute where he studied engineering disciplines under the guidance of experienced teachers. When he comes to work at a factory, he is greeted by a scene that says: all that was just theory, forget it!

This was the situation I found myself in from the first day I worked at Yava.

The first thing that struck me was that components that were designed to be made out of special or construction steel were being cut from plain carbon steel, "St3". It was easy enough to see that the components were defective from the outset. They had low wear resistance and a short service life, meaning that the machines had to be stopped more often for repair. The increased downtime meant more losses for the enterprise. The machine shop had to work harder to make more components than was provided for under the regulations. I looked into this matter. After talking to the chief mechanic and the head of the supply department, I found that Gosplan did not allocate quotas for special steels to enterprises of the food industry, and there was nothing that could be done about it. This went against all common sense, but everyone went along with it. The country produced sufficient quantities of these metals: defence enterprises even had surpluses of them. But no one sitting in Gosplan's offices could know that the little Yava factory also had a great need for small quantities of this material. In the Soviet Union, there were things that no one could explain, but that were firmly ingrained in everyday life. People got used to this strange way of living. For professional people such as those working in the machine shop, it was demeaning. They were effectively being forced do shoddy work, as they said themselves. Their labour was devalued. I remember exactly how the workers put it: "It's a crime, nobody gives a damn". Later, as chief engineer, I found that this example was symptomatic of a wider trend in the country's economic development.

When Brezhnev came to power, production planning tumbled even further downhill. A vicious circle arose. The more the state attempted to combat shortages, the more ineluctable they became. Because enterprises lacked any incentives to increase efficiency, production stagnated. The quality of output did not rise, but losses of materials remained high. This made production increasingly material-intensive, thus exacerbating shortages of material resources. At Yava, supplies of low-quality materials resulted in lower productivity, high losses and great problems in maintaining the quality of cigarettes. From a common sense perspective, it would have been more economical to invest in modernising the supplier enterprises. The saving made from reducing losses in the tobacco industry alone would have more than covered the state's investment. But instead of real modernisation, decisions were made at the top, ordering the respective ministries to take steps to improve the quality of output at the enterprises for which they were responsible. Needless to say, those decisions remained on paper only.

Yava produced cigarettes from low-quality materials. In effect, it did "shoddy work". The workers felt let down: they were expected to achieve high results without being given the wherewithal to do so. But how could this be explained to people? After all, in their minds the Soviet Union was a great power, a leader in space technology. Surely Soviet industry was capable of producing good-quality foil, cellophane and glue to make cigarettes?

Procurement became the chief problem for industry. Shortages were an inherent feature of the Soviet economy, but it was under Brezhnev that the problem reached its apogee. Industry was developing, new enterprises were being built, technology was growing more sophisticated and the range of products was expanding. It was impossible to manage the economy efficiently through centralised methods. Under the system that existed in the Soviet Union, all resources for enterprises were allocated in the form of quotas through a chain of state agencies: Gosplan, Gossnab, and the ministries. Regional supply administrations were part of the centralised distribution system. They sold resources to enterprises within the quotas allocated by Gossnab. The centralised supply system was constructed in such a way that enterprises did not have free access to material resources, but neither were government agencies, for their part, in a position to supply the needs of a particular facility. This was one of the main reasons behind the country's persistent shortage of materials. The state continued, albeit at a substantial cost, to provide enterprises with quotas for key materials. Gosplan calculated the needs of individual sectors based on approved standard quantities of materials per unit of output. Gossnab assigned supply orders to specific suppliers and communicated them to industry in the form of quotas. When it came to engineering supplies, however, the situation was much worse. The Yava factory needed hundreds of different electrical components, complex ball bearings and special types of metal to make spare parts. The quantity of each item was relatively small, but the range was very varied. It was impossible for these needs to be met directly via Gossnab. What was needed, therefore, was to reform the distribution system, decentralise the state supply system and bring it closer to the actual consumer. But the system under Brezhnev was incredibly cumbersome. Group B enterprises received supplies of technical resources according to the "residual principle", i.e. after the needs of higher-priority enterprises had been met. Ball bearings were planned by quantity of pieces, metal by the tonne. The specific types of these products were not indicated. Even the Moscow city supply committee, Mosgorsnab, which was very influential, was unable to meet all the Yava factory's needs. We had to choose from what was available.

Since official channels did not work, the human element grew increasingly important. A need arose for capable supply agents, skilful operators who could use their personal contacts to conjure up scarce items out of nowhere. These qualities were coming to be valued more than anything in our society. People were starting to live by the principle of "you scratch my back, I'll scratch yours". This corrupted minds and distorted normal social relationships. Anyone who directly controlled resources wielded special power. Soviet people got used to the idea that there were some things that had to be obtained rather than bought. Various food products, imported furniture, domestic appliances and fashionable clothing could only be acquired through contacts. The shortages gave birth to a whole new class of people known as dealers or speculators. This illegal activity was very profitable. Over time, the dealers bonded with employees of state agencies that had access to scarce goods. An intermediary system began to emerge. People grew accustomed to this state of affairs and did not even judge it very harshly. The society that formed during the Brezhnev era was of a particular kind, unlike anywhere else in the world. Most countries had a free market economy built on natural human stimuli, first and foremost that of competition. The Soviet Union had a command-style, artificial economy. The principal instrument of economic regulation was the profoundly bureaucratic, unviable system of central planning and allocation of resources. A colossal number of people were involved in the central planning process. But it was impossible for the real needs of enterprises to be addressed from the centre. A lot of muddles occurred. Since the only way to resolve supply problems was through the central government authorities, all kinds of managers and officials would head to Moscow from all over the country. They would camp out on the doorsteps of high-level offices in an effort to find resolutions for essential issues facing their region or enterprise. Even local Party bodies would get involved in this process.

As a way out of this, enterprises began to develop their own horizontal supply lines and help each other. In Moscow, there were active arrangements among enterprises of the food industry. The Yava factory worked with the Ducat factory and other tobacco enterprises. Before long, this became normal day-to-

127

day practice. In the early morning, the Yava factory's supply department would turn into an "emergency headquarters". All the staff sat manning the telephones and making arrangements with their counterparts at other enterprises where a particular material was available to be borrowed or exchanged. Then they would be straight onto the transport department, telling them where to send our limited factory vehicles, sometimes on long journeys to other regions. These emergencies occurred on virtually a daily basis, and all of the efforts of the enterprises' staff were geared towards dealing with them.

The "stability" of the Brezhnev years came at a heavy price for the country's economy. For the sake of preserving the "sacred cow" of the central planning system, all levels of economic administration were compelled to perform functions that were not really theirs, straining every sinew to find manual workarounds to problems that were created by the government system itself. This gave rise to a popular expression: "We make problems for ourselves so that we can overcome them". A dead-end situation formed which would gradually lead the country to economic collapse.

As I mentioned before, our factory was often visited by specialists from foreign firms during that period. For the Western workers, production discipline was paramount. They had never encountered the concept of "shortages". They could not understand why the factory did not buy spare parts from their firm and instead put up with the higher losses caused by the reduced productivity of the equipment. As they watched the Yava mechanics struggle to adjust the machines properly, they could not understand it from a common sense perspective. They came to have great admiration for the professionalism and patience of the factory's workers. They felt sympathy for them, and whenever they visited the factory, they would bring along a few of the most hard-to-get parts in order to ease their plight a little.

Of course, everyone worked to earn, but people often performed miracles "above and beyond" purely out of a sense of responsibility and love for their craft. I think that any skilled worker at a Western company would be at a loss if he were faced with such problems. Today, looking back, I feel more and more appreciation for the contribution the workers made to the common cause. It was only thanks to their efforts that the factory managed to survive the most arduous period of its development. Among those specialists, there were genuinely talented, original people who have imprinted themselves on my memory.

THE "MOBILISATION OF WORKFORCES" IN RESPONSE TO GOSPLAN'S UNREALISTIC PLANS

The state authorities tried to tackle the shortages in the most primitive possible way. Gosplan doled out wildly high, unrealistic targets. How could they be fulfilled? The answer from above was to "seek out internal reserves". The main task of management was to organise employees and spur them to fulfil the production plan. This was officially referred to in military language as "mobilising the workforce to fulfil the plan". The same wording was normally used against the director of an enterprise that had not met its targets – "He failed to mobilise the workforce to fulfil the plan".

The authorities attached great importance to the way in which enterprises handled their personnel. The state system was arranged so that the management of an enterprise was responsible not only for production figures, but also for the moral character of employees and their behaviour in everyday life. To this end, the management would hold essential levers of influence on people in the form of the ability to grant social benefits.

Party bodies set the following goals: raise discipline and standards in labour collectives, and at the same time show concern for people's welfare and improve their working and living conditions.

This was how the system of Party control over "educational work" operated. Every time a public order offence occurred and a court judgment was issued, the law enforcement authorities would send information to the offender's place of work so that appropriate measures could be taken. On the basis of that information, local Party bodies drew conclusions about the "standard of educational and ideological work among the workforce" (as it was phrased in bureaucratic language). There were tough expectations. The factory would take punitive action against the offenders, depriving them of bonuses and other benefits. It created a "public atmosphere of intolerance towards violators of discipline" (that was the official wording). This was all very well, but there were many important issues affecting people's moral conduct that it was beyond the capacity of enterprises to influence. The lives of simple citizens remained very hard. Housing conditions were, in the main, still poor. Men tended to drink, and marital conflicts were a common occurrence. Moscow was becoming a hard place to live. New residential areas were being built, workers were being brought in from elsewhere, and the population was swelling. It became more difficult and took longer to get to work, buy food and take the children to school. The factory's workers now came in from different parts of Moscow and even from outside the city. Since their shift started at 6:45am, they would have to get up before five in the morning. The evening shift ended at 11:45pm. That only left time to get changed and run to catch the metro or electric train. It was especially hard for women. It was they, after all, who were burdened with most of the household concerns. Mothers had to ensure that their children were cared for. It was lucky if they had parents who could help out with the housework and look after the grandchildren.

Working conditions at the factory also drained people's strength. Most workers were on a piece-rate system, which kept them in a constant state of tension. A certain level of output had to be achieved every day in order to meet the monthly target. If something went awry, the crew would find itself behind schedule, and everyone would be on edge. No one wanted to lose pay. Every rouble was precious. Women mostly worked as machine operators on the lines. This was physically demanding work. The shift would last eight hours fifteen minutes. The rhythm of work on a high-speed line required great concentration from the crew members for the whole duration of the shift.

It used to beat me how these people ever got any rest. Work – home – work, all at a frenetic pace. That was why many of them were nervous and irritable. They would usually air their grievances in raised voices. Some were especially loud-mouthed. The biggest conflicts arose when the line wasn't working properly. Or there would be grievances about working conditions or the quality of materials. Life had taught them to fight their corner. In this context, the factory's management saw its main role as ensuring that the workers were motivated and had the stimuli they needed in their work and, therefore, in their lives. First and foremost, this meant a stable wage. Apart from that, it was considered important to show concern for the workers and give them help in resolving their day-to-day problems.

The social support system was also managed through the workplace. This was mainly achieved through the development of the so-called "social sphere". Whether an enterprise had a well-organised social support system for its workers came to be regarded as one of the major deciding factors when people were choosing a place to work.

The main thing was childcare. Under the law, mothers were entitled to paid leave for a year after childbirth. Most women workers could not afford to sit at home with their children without pay, so they usually tried to send them to nurseries and kindergartens. There were not enough places in municipal children's institutions, and making childcare arrangements became a problem. The factory had two kindergartens of its own, one next to the factory itself, which was very convenient as children could be dropped off on the way to work and picked up in the evening. It also had a creche for very small children. In the 1960s a second kindergarten was built in lovely green surroundings in the Oktyabrskoye Polye area. This one also provided all-week groups. People who had a long way to travel to their homes could pick up their children just for the weekends. The administration devoted much attention to ensuring that the kindergartens were working properly and covered a large proportion of their costs out of its own budget. The kindergarten staff were members of the Yava workforce who knew the parents well and treated the children as their own. They tried to create a pleasant, home-like environment for them, which was reassuring for the parents.

A pioneer camp was built just outside Moscow to provide recreation in the summertime during the school holidays. Children were taken there straight after school broke up at the beginning of June. Work on getting the camp ready after the winter hibernation would begin as early as the beginning of March.

Another important issue was the provision of meals during shifts. The work schedule was very tight. To allow the evening shift time to catch public transport when returning home after work, the lunchbreak was kept to a minimum: half an hour for the day shift and twenty minutes for the evening shift. But for the workers to stay healthy, they needed to have a proper lunch and a hot dinner every day. It was a race against time. The workers were not allowed to return to work late after the lunchbreak, as every minute of working time was precious. Consequently, some workers began bringing sandwiches from home to have with tea during their break. In response, we decided to provide extra motivation to use the canteen. Every worker became entitled to a full daily meal, free of charge, on both day and evening shifts. This made the workers determined to use the canteen, as they felt that otherwise they were wasting money, which for them was unthinkable. It must be said that the administration paid much attention to the quality of the meals. The menus even catered for special dietary needs. Recognising the difficult conditions in which the workers lived, efforts were made to bring scarce food products and various kinds of baked goods into the canteen so that people did not have to spend so much time shopping. Especially as the list of scarce products had grown substantially by that time.

The factory had a medical station which operated as a sort of small polyclinic. There were two general physicians and a dental surgery working full-time, and appointments could be made to see specialist doctors such as a gynaecologist, a surgeon or an ear, nose and throat specialist. During the evening shift an experienced nurse would be on duty to provide first aid. There was an on-site laboratory where it was possible to do blood tests and administer injections on doctors' orders. The administration devoted much attention to the work of the medical station, recognising that the workers did not have time to visit city clinics.

When the economic reforms were introduced, enterprises acquired greater scope to diversify the forms of social assistance offered to the workers. Money allocated to the Social Development Fund could be used by enterprises at their own discretion. Yava was attentive to its employees' problems. If they were facing hardships, financial assistance would be provided.

Great attention was paid to organising recreation for the workers during their regular annual leave. The chief trade union body in the Soviet Union[1] had an extensive network of spas and recreation centres. The factory's trade union committee would put in an application for vacation vouchers to the senior trade union organisation. Trade union vacation vouchers were usually allocated to enterprises at a discount of up to 70 per cent of their total value. They were called "thirty-percenters". The factory paid the remainder out of its own money, and the employee received the voucher free of charge. It was no wonder that the USSR was referred to everywhere as having one of the most effective social welfare systems. It was a conscious policy on the part of the state. Wages were low, but substantial amounts were distributed through social funds. This increased a person's dependence on the state. These factors served as real levers which the factory's administration used to raise the motivation, labour discipline and moral conduct of the workers. They were used as a means to "mobilise the workforce for the fulfilment of the plan". People understood, after all, that the incentive funds were tied to the fulfilment of plan targets, while the distribution of benefits to individual workers depended on performance appraisals carried out by the factory administration.

---

1 The All-Union Central Council of Trade Unions (VTsSPS).

The most problematic issue in the Soviet Union was housing provision. There was widespread construction in Moscow, yet the waiting list for new apartments never diminished. The state exercised strict control over the distribution of housing space. These functions were carried out by district executive committees via housing distribution departments. A whole system was created whereby housing space was allocated in turn to families placed on the district waiting list. These were families that really were living in grim conditions, with no more than 3 m^2 of area per inhabitant. But what about the rest of the population? Most lived in conditions that were already cramped to start with, but then they would start a family, and the children would grow. Many were in need of improved housing but did not quite fit the criteria for the district waiting list. Nor could they afford to buy a cooperative flat. In this case they would seek to resolve their housing dilemma through their workplace. People searching for a place to work would favour those enterprises and organisations where there was some hope of receiving an apartment. Some were even willing to accept harsh working conditions if there was a guarantee of receiving housing after a certain period of employment. People like this were said to be "working for an apartment".

During my time as director of the factory, two apartment buildings were built. This made it possible to improve housing conditions for many families. The process of building them was a headache for the administration, but it was worth the trouble. For many of the factory's workers, this was a critical issue. On the whole, the authorities tried to keep in mind the interests of the population and the principle of social fairness in allocating housing space. Since everyone was living in cramped conditions, it would not do to provoke discontent in society through excessively conspicuous extravagance. This was why, even in the so-called "superior design" buildings inhabited by members of the CPSU Central Committee and top enterprise managers, standard regulations were generally observed in the construction and allocation of living space. In the mid-1970s we witnessed a curious incident. As part of the programme for the reconstruction of Gorky Street, an elite residential building was constructed between Mayakovsky Square and Belorussky Station. It later became known as the "Pugacheva building"[1] owing to the fact that the prima donna herself received a flat there. It really was a unique building – I don't remember any

---

1 Alla Borisovna Pugacheva (b. 1949) – a very famous Soviet (and later Russian) pop singer.

other quite like it being built in Moscow during that period. The flats had already been allocated to high-level government officials and generals when the country's leaders suddenly grew annoyed and began barking complaints at the Moscow authorities: "Why is there no working class? Where is the principle of social fairness?" Most likely, they just wanted to cover themselves and soften the response of the general public. After that, events moved very fast. The Frunzensky *raikom* sent out an urgent instruction to a number of enterprises in the district to nominate workers who were in severe need of living space. As a result, Alla Pugacheva's neighbours came to include not only generals, but also factory workers, including two from Yava: a grinder from the machine shop, father to five children, and a machine adjuster from the *papirosy*-making shop.

LATE SOVIET REALITY: PILFERING AND DRUNKENNESS AT WORK

Theft of inventory occurred at virtually all enterprises in the country and became a real scourge. The nature and scale depended primarily on how readily the stolen items could be sold. At car factories it was common for car parts to go missing. Our neighbour opposite, the Bolshevik confectionery factory, produced various kinds of biscuits, pastries and cakes. Since selling biscuits was rather problematic, people tended to pinch production ingredients such as butter, chocolate and cognac.

At the Yava factory, the theft of cigarettes was a serious problem. Yava cigarettes were in high demand and selling them was as easy as could be. Cigarettes were sold through tobacco kiosks, and it was a simple matter to come to an arrangement with a kiosk keeper, who would take the dodgy items and sell them. Since the volume of cigarette sales was very high, it was almost impossible to detect the sale of illicit goods through a kiosk. The temptation was great. People took the risk in the hope of making a bit extra.

There had been thieving at Yava before, but not on such a mass scale. When we began producing filter cigarettes, the temptation to steal products grew much higher, while penalties had become less severe. The authorities had begun currying favour with the public, which led to a decline in discipline and responsibility. When I started work, it was officially considered that every worker had the right to take thirty *papirosy* or cigarettes out of the factory. This allowance, known as the *raskurka*, had its own history. In the pre-war years, it had been officially permitted for each smoking worker to be given thirty defective *papirosy* each day (thirty being the daily norm for smoking). This was specifically for personal consumption, to deter employees from taking *papirosy* from the conveyor. The law was very strictly enforced. Under Stalin, anyone caught stealing would find himself behind bars in no time. Before leaving the factory, therefore, the workers would place what remained of their daily *raskurka* in cigarette cases, which were fashionable at the time.

In the sixties, things changed in the country at large and, consequently, in people's mentality. Workers leaving the factory with a weighty bundle of loose *papirosy* would protest if a security worker tried to confiscate them: "I'm entitled to a *raskurka*. Why can't I take a few extra? Are you actually going to count them?" In fact, the confiscated bundles sometimes contained unseemly quantities (200–300 *papirosy* or more). Psychologically, this behaviour was no doubt influenced by the fact that the factory produced over sixty million tobacco units every day. Of these, 2–3 per cent were defective items, from which the tobacco was recovered for re-use. So what harm was there in taking a little bundle of *papirosy*? The state was hardly going to go broke because of that. A gradual change was occurring in society's attitude to state property. People were beginning to understand that the preservation of that property did nothing to improve the life of an individual person. They saw evidence all around them of the state's own wasteful, shoddy approach to the management of the nation's assets. This being so, they saw it as no disgrace if they, too, happened to grab what they could. And so, stealing from the state was no longer regarded as anything shameful. This made it difficult for the administration to combat the problem. The mindset of society as a whole affected the attitudes of individual people, including those whose job it was to stop thefts from taking place. Society became reconciled to the culture of mass thievery. A softer approach developed to dealing with offenders. Now, only people caught stealing large quantities of merchandise would face punitive measures.

When the promo line for the production of filter cigarettes was installed at the factory, Mikhail Demyanovich understood that the new products had to be protected against theft. As we already know, it was he who ordered the building of the crystal room, where all the workers were under strict supervision. When the factory began the mass production of premium-quality filter cigarettes, however, the security issue became much more challenging. Now it was a large workshop spread over two floors with over 200 workers, all of whom had direct access to finished products. Good luck patrolling that! Especially as it was as easy as anything for people to hide packets of cigarettes under their overalls. Of course, the issue of protecting the new products became one of the top priorities for the administration. But given the general situation in the country, it was impossible to avoid large-scale theft. Realistically, the best we could do was to keep it within limits. Unfortunately, the authorities did not accept this. They refused to acknowledge that there were systemic problems in the country and society which were responsible for the mass theft of socialist property.[1] This was why no measures were taken at a nationwide level. It was considered that if thefts occurred at enterprises, it was due to slack work on the part of the local management and poor organisation of educational and ideological work among the workforce. This was the easiest solution for the authorities, but it was an utterly fallacious position.

Detecting thefts was the job of the militia and its special subdivision, the OBKhSS (the Department for Combating Theft of Socialist Property). They would carry out spot inspections, often in the evening and at night. To avoid alerting people to these operations, workers leaving the factory would be arrested at a certain distance from the factory, on their way to Belorussky Station, which is where the nearest metro and railway station were. I never actually witnessed anyone being arrested, but I know that it was a deeply degrading process. People tried to run away and dump their stolen cigarettes. The detainees would then be taken to the police station to be searched. News of the inspection would quickly reach the factory, and a great commotion would ensue. Workers would quickly get rid of any stashed items, and security would take appropriate measures. The factory management would find out about the incident the following morning. OBKhSS officers would then bring the stolen goods to the factory, and the accounting office would count them and work out their value. The decision regarding the punishment of detainees was made by the militia and the public prosecution office. In most cases, it was left to the factory to take punitive measures. The offenders would forfeit their bonuses. If it happened more than once, more severe action would be taken, up to and including dismissal. If the theft was on a large scale (200–300 packs), the case would be referred to court. The culprits were usually ordered to pay damages to the state out of their

---

1   Socialist property" – a term used in the USSR for state property.

wages, as well as forfeiting bonuses for the current month and at the end of the year. Altogether, this amounted to a serious blow. In arriving at a decision, the authorities took into consideration the interests of the offender's family and the impact it might have on their children. On the whole, therefore, the decisions handed out by the courts tended to be fairly lenient.

The main route through which products were stolen from the workshop during working hours were the goods elevators, which were used to hoist materials into the workshop and take out production waste. Deliveries of materials were handled by loaders in the shipping department. If they conspired with workers in the cigarette-making shop, it was possible for finished products to be smuggled out of the workshop via the lift, for example by packing them into cardboard boxes concealed by a covering of rubbish. There were other ways of stealing, too. Usually, the lift operators would be involved in these arrangements. The administration was aware of these shenanigans. For this reason, the lifts were only opened to transport goods in the presence of a designated workshop employee. Inspections were made of production waste being taken out of the workshop. Boxes of rubbish were prodded with special skewers to make sure there were no finished goods inside. But the other side had tricks of its own, and it was not always possible to prevent thefts from taking place. Since such schemes involved the use of trucks to get the stolen items out of the factory grounds, security workers would inspect trucks leaving the factory. Usually, the cigarettes would be found hidden under the driver's seat or nestled among goods being taken out for delivery. Those suspected of attempting to smuggle out finished products would be sacked. Lift operators were regularly reassigned from one lift to another in an effort to prevent the formation of established groups of workers involved in the theft of finished products.

After the end of a shift, the workers would form a queue by the turnstiles at the entrance, where they would be searched before leaving the factory premises. This would involve having their bags checked and being frisked. If any suspicion arose, they would be invited into a special room for a body search. The security officers would also be accountable if anyone was detained by the OBKhSS after being inspected on leaving the factory. It might seem from all this that we were well placed to prevent theft. In reality, however, there were other factors at play. The factory workers had close ties with one another, and there were undoubtedly informal connections between security officers and individual workers, meaning that each officer had his "own people", whom he would let through if he thought it was safe. There was a sort of alert system in operation, so that workers about to leave the factory knew who was on security duty that day. The inspectors would check whether the coast was clear outside the factory. People took the risk. But the OBKhSS officers also operated professionally. They had a very good understanding of how factory theft was organised. At Yava they put together a group of informants so that they knew in advance about planned thefts. The performance of the OBKhSS was measured based on the number of arrests made for stealing. It was a situation in which everyone knew how things worked and each party pursued its own goals: the workers to earn a bit extra, the administration to keep thefts to a minimum, and the OBKhSS to hold things in tension and keep everyone on their toes. They had their own plan to fulfil – by making enough arrests.

More than anything else, this thieving behaviour was highly detrimental to the moral state of Soviet society. The thieves were not malicious plunderers. They were ordinary Soviet people. It was a phenomenon that was peculiar to our country and was a consequence of the Soviet ideological and economic system. The state was morally responsible for the hardships that drove people to this point. People had lost their sense of dignity. At the time, we often discussed this problem amongst ourselves. Witnesses recounted that during a visit to a foreign tobacco factory, members of the Soviet delegation were surprised to see a cigarette vending machine in the workshop. They asked, "Why do you have that?" After all, there was a conveyor full of finished products right next to it. A woman who worked there answered proudly, "We earn enough not to take from our master". Two worlds, two completely different mentalities.

Yava products continued to get stolen even outside the factory's premises. The culprits in this case were the truck workers who transported goods from the factory to warehouses or directly to sales outlets. Finished products were transported in boxes. One box contained over 500 packs. A completely filled box was sealed up by a special process with self-adhesive tape to ensure the products were protected during transportation and storage. Everything seemed to have been thought through. But Yava cigarettes were much too attractive. In order to steal the cigarettes, people worked out a "counter-process" to the factory's process for protecting the boxes. It went like this: the factory tape would be carefully removed with the aid of steam and one block of hard-pack cigarettes or two blocks of soft packs would be taken out of the box. The resulting empty space would be stuffed with paper. Then the boxes would be carefully resealed. An ordinary electric kettle would be used to generate the steam. All this would be done quite professionally, so that the tampered-with box did not arouse suspicion when the trade people took delivery. The theft would be discovered when the boxes were opened at a sales outlet. The trade people tried to deflect responsibility by claiming that the boxes were "underpacked" when they left the factory. But the factory staff were armed with a convincing defence. The thieves did an ingenious job, but the only thing they could not do was fully replicate the factory's process of sealing boxes. I do not know how these losses were written off, or, who they "hung" them on, as they used to say in Soviet times, but it was a big problem all over Moscow. Transit theft was something that never went away. It was difficult to do anything about this pervasive phenomenon, since it was practised by established groups of people who had turned their criminal activity into a steady, profitable business.

Another serious problem was drunkenness in the workplace. Before I came to the factory, I had never imagined that this phenomenon existed on such a tragic scale. The machine shop, where I first worked, was probably out in front on this score. Since it was an auxiliary rather than a core department, less attention was paid to it, making it easier to violate discipline. Metalworkers were regarded as the vanguard of the working class. Becoming a skilled turner or miller took at least five to ten years of working on machines, which was why there was a palpable shortage of people in those occupations even back then. The machine workers at Yava were proud people who were excellent at what they did and knew their worth. The things they had to say about life's problems were interesting and even profound. But it was just terrible how much they drank. It was a genuine illness. They could not function without a glass of vodka, so they used all sorts of ruses to nab a drink during working hours, to "put one away" or "take a glass", as they would put it. What was the reason for this mass sickness? People say it is a Russian tradition. But this "tradition" was first and foremost a product of the conditions in which ordinary people had to live. Throughout the ages, life had been hard and, worst of all, devoid of hope. And so things had remained under Soviet power. To a large extent, it was a generation crippled by life. People who were gifted with intelligence at birth felt let down; they had stopped believing in the possibility of change or a better life. These were the kinds of individuals I came across in the machine shop. They were not generally members of the Party. Outwardly they affected indifference to politics, but inwardly they were opposed to the regime. The life and fate of this generation was preordained at birth. On coming to the workshop as adolescent trainees, they had found themselves in a drinking environment. After the end of the first day of work, they would usually be given a tumbler of vodka: "Drink up, this is how you get enrolled, it's a tradition. Otherwise, what sort of man are you?" The new recruit would immediately be turned into "one of them". Then his adult life would begin. Poor living conditions, no prospects, disillusionment with life. The only comfort was in vodka. This was how people gradually lost themselves in drink and turned into alcoholics. What is surprising is that, despite all this, the people I am writing about somehow managed to preserve their human and moral qualities. They all departed this life early, before reaching retirement. No organism can withstand that amount of abuse.

After the death of Stalin, the country's leaders realised, on the whole, that things had to change. Something had to be done about drunkenness. They at least needed to acknowledge publicly that the consumption of alcohol was a national tradition and introduce more civilised frameworks for pursuing it, as was done in many other countries. In our country, there was no way for people to get together and have a drink in a proper setting. As a result, people would drink "on the go", somewhere in the shadows, or "round the corner", pouring a bottle out into glasses and quickly gulping it down, often without any food to go with it. This was a direct path to alcoholism. In order to wean people off this terrible practice and cultivate a taste for the civilised consumption of vodka, it was decided to open a network of special drinking establishments in Moscow, known as *ryumochnyie*, or vodka bars. Every customer could buy a shot glass (*ryumka*) of vodka, which had to be taken together with an open sandwich. There was no limit on how many times one could get served. People took to visiting these establishments. Of course, not everyone found it easy to make the transition from tumblers to shot glasses. Some, it was said, poured the shot glasses into a tumbler, and put the extra sandwiches into stacks. Nonetheless, it was a big step forward, providing an opportunity for a gradual transition to more civilised drinking habits.

Of course, the reforms begun by Khrushchev changed the condition of Soviet society. People began to sense that better days lay ahead. However, the situation with alcohol consumption remained much the same. This ruinous phenomenon was too deeply ingrained. But even the *ryumochnyie* started gradually closing down: it was said that they were not profitable enough. When Brezhnev came to power, virtually nothing at all was done to eradicate the causes of alcoholism. Worse still, the relaxation of discipline requirements made the problem of workplace drunkenness even worse. The state only tackled the outward effects of alcoholism. A network of "sobering-up stations", or drunk tanks, sprang up across the country. The police would pick up inebriated people on the streets and take them to the drunk tanks. Spending a night in one of those establishments was a degrading experience. Relevant documents would be sent to your workplace in order for measures to be taken. Since quite a large sum of money had to be paid for a stay in a drunk tank, people tried not to end up there. But many could not control themselves and were taken there in an unconscious state. This was a sign that the illness had got really bad. People like that would be sent – by order of the courts – for compulsory treatment at specially created rehabilitation centres.

TALENTED PEOPLE. DAMAGED LIVES

There were many interesting, talented people at Yava. Some were acknowledged leaders. One of the first who comes to mind is Gennady Mikhailovich Denisov. He descended from a line of Yava workers. His grandmother had worked at the factory as a simple worker before the Revolution. His mother, Maria Yakovlevna, had achieved a lot, becoming head of the packing shop back before the *papirosy* machines were aggregated into assembly lines. Although she had retired, her name was spoken with great respect. Gennady was a talented boy, did well at school, practised sports, and I heard that in his youth he dreamed of being an aviator. But a terrible thing happened. He was seriously injured while playing hockey and lost an eye. He had to forget about aviation. Following in his parents' footsteps, he went to work at the factory as a mechanic on the cigarette machines. He mastered the job perfectly. When the imported equipment arrived at the factory, it was he, as the best specialist, who was put in charge of organising the assimilation and maintenance of the new cigarette machines. Gennady's talent and organisational abilities were brought out to the full when he took on this highly complex work. Possessing an analytical mind, he studied in great detail all the intricacies of the machine parts, and in some especially complex cases he was the only person who was capable of diagnosing and fixing a fault. If something wasn't right, the mechanics would call for Geshka, as he was fondly known in the workshop. Gradually, he became an undisputed authority among the workers in the cigarette-making shop. He was appointed chief foreman for the cigarette machines. As you and I will recall, this was a difficult period. The fulfilment of the plan was constantly under threat. It was during this time that Denisov's strengths as an organiser came to the fore. When urgent action was needed to meet the plan, he personally went around speaking to the mechanics, and usually all of them would agree to do overtime. Geshka was so highly respected that no one dared refuse. What is more, Gennady himself set an example for the others. If necessary, he would work two or three shifts in a row to help get the factory out of trouble. He was an uncompromising, intelligent person. He was not afraid to speak his mind to anyone. Effectively the administration's right-hand man in the workforce, he was also an authoritative critic of deficiencies in the factory's work. And he had every right to be. Whenever difficulties arose, the first person I would call on was Geshka Denisov in the workshop. He was the only one capable of laying things out in an objective – albeit also highly emotional – manner. After speaking to him, a lot of things would become clear. Quite often, he expressed opinions that were not pleasant for the management to hear, but the points he made were always fair and relevant. In time, he became a highly principled, civic-minded leader, the foremost representative of the workers.

Another leading figure in the workforce was Vladimir Lvovich Protopopov, the electronics foreman. I have already mentioned the great problems faced by the factory in maintaining the complex electronic systems with which the cigarette-making lines were fitted. The factory had no previous experience of working with such equipment. We effectively needed to create a new division – but had no specialists to fill it. Good electronics engineers were worth their weight in gold, and since they usually worked at defence plants, luring them over to Yava was nigh on impossible. When Nikolai Sergeyevich Kashtanov took over at the factory, setting up an electronics group was one of the most pressing issues. He suggested inviting Vladimir Lvovich Protopopov, whom he knew from working at the Ducat factory, to organise the new division. Vladimir turned out to be a unique person in all respects. He had a lively mind, extraordinary energy and, I would say, a particular nimbleness and agility, with a keen focus on new ideas and advanced solutions. He was a born specialist with brilliant organisational abilities. He had not graduated from any institutes, but had taught himself everything he knew. His past was somewhat hazy. It was said that he had done time in his youth on account of some political jokes, but no one knew any details. He was around forty when he started at the factory. Living with his wife Tamara, who looked after him like a child, he collected books, kept fish, and fed birds from the window sill. He was manically devoted to his work. It did not take him long at all to gather together a team of young, capable lads. This was how, in place of elderly electricians, Yava came to have its crew of "young hairies", all as obsessed with electronics as their boss. This front-line team soon began to be referred to simply as "Protopopov's team". Its scope of activities was very broad. The team serviced all the electronics systems in the new production building – and that was all of five storeys, linked together in a single production chain.

By nature, he was an innovator and a natural leader in the workplace. Many designs made under his guidance were patented and received medals when put on display at VDNKh (the Exhibition of Achievements of the National Economy). With Protopopov by our side, we could handle any ultra-modern technology. He gave the prime of his career to Yava, working for us for the remainder of his life – over twenty years. Possessing excellent teaching abilities, he nurtured a whole group of specialists who went on to provide the factory with a high standard of electronic support services.

Among the engineering staff I would like to single out Valery Andreyevich Bykov. He had studied in the mechanical faculty of the Moscow Technological Institute of the Food Industry together with Kashtanov. When the director and I were having one of our regular discussions about problems at the factory, he said, "I tell you what, I'll invite Valery Bykov over for a chat. He's a very decent and clever fellow". The man who came to talk to us was a diffident figure with a slight nervous stammer. I liked him straight away, and we decided to offer him the position of head of the technical department. He soon became a leader among the technical supervisors. I respected these people for their talent and dedication. I valued the contribution that each of them made to the factory's performance. It therefore came as a great shock to me to learn that every one of them suffered from periodic alcoholism. I have done a lot of thinking about the causes of that terrible evil that afflicted so many talented people endowed with leadership qualities. I feel certain that each of them suffered serious emotional traumas in their lives and felt frustration at being unable to realise their potential. We understood that we were dealing with a serious social malady that was almost impossible to cure.

Chapter 10.

THE REALITIES OF THE "BREZHNEV STAGNATION"

SOYUZ-APOLLO CIGARETTES. A FITTING TRIBUTE TO THE INTERNATIONAL SPACE PROJECT

Meanwhile, the Soviet economy was becoming more and more integrated into the international trade system. International tobacco companies were eyeing the Soviet tobacco market with great interest. It was a vast market, with over 400 billion sticks produced yearly. A distinct class of smokers was emerging with a willingness to pay more for high-quality cigarettes. Furthermore, internal changes in the country made it possible for foreign companies to enter into dialogue with the Soviet government about cooperation and the creation of joint projects.

The first to seize the initiative was Philip Morris, the largest international tobacco company. Owner of the highly successful Marlboro cigarette brand, which had become the company's signature product, it had gained a reputation as the most aggressive player on the global tobacco market. Executives from the firm had been making regular visits to Moscow since the early 1970s. Their aim, in a word, was to "build bridges". Developing personal contacts with government officials had begun to play a crucial role in the advancement of major projects. It was not long before an ideal opportunity presented itself to make the first practical steps.

The first Soviet-American space project, the joint launch and docking in space of the Soviet Soyuz and American Apollo spacecraft, took place in 1975. This event had huge international resonance and symbolised strengthening cooperation between the two powers. And it was decided to mark this epoch-making occasion with nothing less than the launch of a special Soyuz-Apollo joint Soviet-American cigarette brand. In the USSR, decisions of this kind were made at the very top of the Party apparatus. Moreover, political considerations were paramount. The fact that cigarettes were chosen as a companion product for this landmark project is an indication of the high popularity of smoking in the USSR.

"Joint" meant that Philip Morris (PM) would be in charge of the design, the tobacco blend and the supply of materials, while the Soviet side would make the cigarettes at the Yava factory using the Molins equipment. There was absolutely no doubt as to the choice of Yava as partner for the renowned Philip Morris. The planned production volume was 500 million cigarettes. Most were intended for sale in the USSR, while fifty million would go to the American market. Since Yava's own tobacco processing equipment did not meet the company's standards, it was agreed that Philip Morris would deliver ready-cut tobacco from its main facility in Richmond, USA. News of the imminent launch of this grand project spread fast around Moscow, arousing almost more excitement than the launch of the spacecraft themselves. For Philip Morris, this was an unmissable chance to promote its product to the Soviet market.

The unique nature of the project meant that the eyes of the international tobacco world were upon it, and Philip Morris approached it with a great sense of responsibility. The pack design was simple and elegant. It depicted the docking of the spacecraft against the background of the Earth. The name was written in Russian on one side of the hard pack and in English on the other. The same went for information about the manufacturers. This emphasised the international nature of the product. All the products were packaged in attractive cartons. The taste qualities of the cigarettes are remembered by many smokers to this day with the utmost delight. Needless to say, participation in a project of this kind was highly prestigious for the Yava factory. It presented a unique opportunity to produce international brand cigarettes, since the Soyuz-Apollo cigarettes had to be wholly compliant with the quality standards required of Philip Morris products.

Preparations for the project began. Working with PM gave us a clear insight into why it was the market leader. The thing that stood out most was rigorous adherence to process. For example, the materials specifications laid out not only technical parameters, but specific manufacturers. No deviations were permitted.

Specialists from PM began visiting the factory to assess the standard of production. Of course, they were surprised, to say the least, by much of what they saw. After all, it was process discipline that was the weakest aspect of manufacturing in the Soviet Union. What most concerned them was the condition of the cigarette-making equipment, which by then had been in use for around ten years. Among the first to visit the factory, I recall, was a group of engineers. After a preliminary discussion in my office we proceeded to the workshop to inspect the equipment. Naturally, I invited Gennady Denisov, the chief expert on Yava's cigarette machines, to accompany us. When the foreigners saw the equipment, their faces fell in front of our eyes. The first reaction of the firm's specialists, who were used to working to strict standards, was that it would be impossible to manufacture Soyuz-Apollo cigarettes on equipment like that. Naïve souls that they were, they knew nothing about the quirks of our reality. Our government operated according to a completely different logic: if everything were arranged according to standards, what need would there be for enterprise managers? Given these conditions, we had been forced to adapt. Yava's mechanics had learned how to produce good-quality cigarettes on the equipment. I clearly remember Geshka Denisov firmly reassuring the doubting foreigners: "Don't worry, we'll be able to produce high-quality cigarettes". And we did – albeit with a bit of help from Philip Morris. It was agreed that the firm would supply sets of spare parts to replace worn-out components which directly affected the quality of cigarettes. But this was far from being the only problem. For instance, Philip Morris organised quality control differently from the way it was done in the Soviet tobacco industry. To resolve this, the firm supplied additional testing equipment and trained Yava staff in carrying out quality control according to PM standards. To produce the joint brand, a lot of work had to go into harmonising PM standards with Yava production practices.

Overall, the firm's experts were pleased by the professionalism of our engineers and operators. It was very important to establish a good working relationship between the specialists so that they could work as a team once production was underway. We noticed that where PM was concerned, there was no such thing as "minor details" as we would call them. Everything counted. For example, they saw that our mechanics were using primitive tools. This was actually a major problem in the USSR. Toolmaking was not a forte of Soviet industry. It was considered unimportant. But this affected the standard of equipment maintenance, making it difficult for mechanics to do their job. Our machine adjusters were delighted to receive lovely new tools in special, convenient containers from Philip Morris itself. After all, the results of the project would be largely dependent on the mood of the workers.

With all the fundamental issues resolved, preparations began for the production work itself. It was decided that the Soyuz-Apollo cigarettes would be produced using three Mark 8 cigarette machines and two Hinge Lid packing machines. Based on the planned volume – 500 million units – production was scheduled to take place over approximately six months. The level of excitement was huge. The sense of responsibility was very high. Since every worker dreamed of getting his hands on at least one pack of cigarettes, securing the products against theft was a chief concern. We had to go back to M.D. Voitsekhovich's ingenious idea and create another crystal room by organising a segregated production area in the cigarette-making shop. The administration established extremely strict control over the manufacture of these unique cigarettes. Materials and packaging labels were issued to the crews by the piece. Every pack had to be accounted for.

At last, everything was in place for production to begin. The equipment was ready, and all the materials and tobacco were now at the factory. The prepared tobacco made in Richmond had been delivered by ship from New York in special packages of 200 kg each. These were very sturdy boxes made of hardboard. Inside, the tobacco had been sealed in polyethylene film to prevent it from taking on moisture during the journey across the ocean. One is reminded of Gogol's government inspector, Khlestakov, and his tall tale about soup delivered directly from Paris: "You open the lid, and it's still steaming". Only in this case, it was real. You opened the lid, and there lay the loveliest tobacco of dark-tinted gold, dressed with a special flavouring. And you breathed in the wonderful aroma. Just fabulous!

Under the terms of the contract, production took place under the supervision of Philip Morris. A group of specialists from the company came to check that everything was ready. Then the project supervisor, a representative from PM's Lausanne office, Mr Werner, gave the command to start work. This elegant and always very punctual gentleman, with whom we worked closely throughout the duration of the project, was courtesy itself. His favourite word was "exactly". Where business was concerned, however, he was extremely strict and allowed no deviations.

We learned a lot from working with the firm's specialists, particularly in terms of precision in work and strict observance of process discipline. It was the only way to achieve good results. The Yava staff proved very receptive to new ideas. We proved through our work that we could work alongside employees of Philip Morris itself as equals, as partners! The cigarettes that we made were of excellent quality. The Yava-made Soyuz-Apollo cigarettes received a high score under PM's own points-based quality evaluation system.

Smokers were in raptures. These were proper "full-flavoured" cigarettes. The taste and strength properties favoured by Soviet smokers had been fully catered for while observing international quality standards. Not since then have I come across more aromatic and tasty cigarettes. Of course, it was Philip Morris's manufacturing process and supreme-quality tobacco materials, but the labour was ours. And that counts for a lot.

An incredible frenzy erupted around these cigarettes. The response from the public exceeded all expectations. The political games started straight away. It was very important at that time to ensure that successes were promptly reported to top officials. It was on such things that the authority of managers was largely built. The first specimens of cigarettes were immediately delivered to our minister, Klemenchuk, and he took them to people "up top". It was a more than worthy occasion. The Soviet tobacco industry had made international standard cigarettes in conjunction with the world's top tobacco company, Philip Morris. It was essential to make full use of this momentous event, especially as Leonid Brezhnev himself was an inveterate smoker.

It was decided to produce special gift sets for top officials. The design for these consisted of a flat box containing ten packs. On the surface of the box, on both sides, were fragments of a picture by the cosmonaut and Soyuz commander Alexei Leonov and the artist Sokolov depicting the docking in space of the Soyuz and Apollo spacecraft. The box was wrapped in cellophane and looked very attractive. PM supplied Yava with special equipment for packing cigarette packs into the boxes.

Alexei Petrovich Klemenchuk was a highly creative sort of official with a knack for presenting the industry's achievements in the best light. On his instruction I took a trip to Star City, where Alexei Arkhipovich Leonov put his autograph on fifteen boxes. I expect that these unique boxes were intended for the country's very top leaders. Philip Morris likewise tried to capitalise on its success. During visits to Moscow the company's vice-present, Mr Gembler, had audiences with high-placed officials and made generous gifts of specially made souvenirs symbolising the achievements of the two great powers in space. Everyone realised that this was only the first step in cooperation. The door had been opened just a little.

We sent the finished cigarettes to Rosbakaleya's Moscow office. How the cigarettes were then distributed in the trade sector, we had no idea. That was the Trade Ministry's job. I have little doubt that the trade people took the opportunity to line their pockets. In any case, Soyuz-Apollo cigarettes were not freely available and ended up in the category of extremely scarce goods. Since it was impossible to buy them, people would use various connections to obtain them. The state set an official price of sixty kopecks per pack. In reality, however, as with anything in short supply, the price was determined by completely different factors. Naturally, many people tried to obtain the cigarettes through Yava's managers. They would approach us directly. Under an arrangement with officials at Rosbakaleya, the director and I had been granted permission to order cigarettes released to market under a specified name, and we were inundated with calls. I realised then what it meant to be one of those people who have access to extremely scarce goods. In Moscow, it was a privileged caste. Of course, the secretary would put through calls from people of a certain status. My wife and I began to receive invitations to the biggest theatre premieres and pre-release shows and private screenings of the best foreign films at Goskino (at the famous building on Gnezdikovsky Lane), where we found ourselves sitting in a small auditorium alongside generals and important personages in civilian dress. But the most astonishing thing I saw was in the inner sanctums of our glorious trade sector – the notorious basements of "privileged" stores. There, concealed from the eyes of ordinary customers, was an abundance of scarce imported goods! And the principal patrons were OBKhSS officers, the very people whose job it was to stop transgressions against the "rules of Soviet trade". I was particularly amazed by the basement rooms at Moscow's central grocery store, the Novoarbatsky Gastronom on the New Arbat. It was a store within a store. Its clients were VIPs, who would be handed ready-made bundles of scarce food items. Here, in the land of socialism and equal opportunity, was a group of people who lived on an entirely different level from the majority of the population.

Kashtanov and I found ourselves in a difficult position. We had to take cigarettes on visits to "higher-ups". If we needed to go to our bosses to ask for something, how could we turn up without a block of Soyuz-Apollo? They wouldn't understand it. We would often get a call from our superiors asking us to "grab a few blocks and come around". They had their own obligations to the people ranked above them. But security in the crystal room was so tight that even the director could not simply come along and take a block of cigarettes. Besides which, we did not want to set the workers talking more than necessary. To resolve this, a system was established whereby quality control would officially set aside "test samples" from the daily output for the director and the chief engineer.

All in all, the project provided a further boost to the already high reputation of Yava products among the public. Various celebrities of the age came to the factory to see how cigarettes were made. There were also one or two curious incidents. Once, I received a call from someone with a very distinctive deep voice: "Hello, you probably know me, it's Kokkinaki here.[1] I have a request to make..." There were very few people at that time who did not know the famous test pilot and Hero of the Soviet Union! Almost without thinking, I said, "You are probably enquiring about our Soyuz-Apollo cigarettes?" To which I received a reply that I will never forget for as long as I live: "What would I need that crap for, I smoke ordinary Pamirs". The problem was that these ultra-strong cigarettes, once popular, had been removed from sale in the retail network. The tobacco industry had continued making them as back-up for the State Reserve system in case of an emergency. Now, the famous test pilot had been left without his accustomed cigarettes and found it impossible to switch to a lighter brand. Of course, we agreed to help him. In return, being a sociable fellow, he regaled us with lots of stories from his highly eventful life. This incident etched itself on my memory as an example of what a physiologically and psychologically complex thing smoking can be. It was a problem that the country would come up against again on more than one occasion.

The Soyuz-Apollo production project greatly lifted the mood among the Yava staff. The factory workers felt very proud that the products that they made were so familiar and so highly rated throughout the nation. Not only that, but they were also making cigarettes for export to America itself. Few Soviet workers could lay claim to such an honour. Moreover, and very importantly, these were not what were infamously known as "export version" products, i.e. superior-quality products made specifically for export, as was done in the Soviet Union. What was unique in our case was that there was no difference in quality between Soyuz-Apollo cigarettes supplied directly to our own retail network and those shipped to the USA. There was only one distinguishing feature. In

---

1 Vladimir Konstantinovich Kokkinaki (1904–1985) – eminent test-pilot who set twenty-two world records.

America, the cigarettes were subject to an excise tax. Every pack had an excise stamp glued to it. It was interesting to learn that every American state had its own rate of excise tax and, of course, its own individual stamp. The American side supplied sets of excise stamps from the different states, and we had to make individual batches of cigarettes for each state.

THE TOBACCO CRISIS AND THE POLITBURO

But all this was really just Kremlin games, putting on a façade of prosperity and progress. It was important for the country's leaders to create an illusion of things being achieved in various areas of activity. In most cases this bore no relation to the real state of affairs in the economy. In reality, the tobacco industry was in a grave condition. Most of the population was still smoking low-quality products, i.e. unfiltered cigarettes. Particular problems with the availability of smoking products had arisen in the Russian Federation. Demand for tobacco products was growing. Cigarettes were one of the few ways for the country's male population to relax. Smoking gave people a sense of freedom and independence at least for a short time. That is why people were so fond of smoking breaks. It was good to be able to say to each other, "Let's have a smoke". The state supported this tendency. The manufacture of tobacco products had become one of the main sources of government revenue. No information was given out about the harmful effects of smoking. Statistics show that over the period from 1970 to the 1980s, demand for tobacco products in the country rose by 50 billion units from 375 billion to 425 billion in 1980. However, the industry had not increased its capacity. Its machinery was outdated, and no hard currency was made available to buy new equipment. The DKET machines used to make unfiltered cigarettes, which accounted for the bulk of the industry's manufacturing capacity, were starting to break down. The Molins equipment was also outdated, but clung on thanks to its high durability. Only the *papirosy* lines rattled on unabated. The ingeniously simple design of the machines meant that they could go on operating practically ad infinitum.

Difficulties arising in the trade system led to a persistent shortage of cigarettes. This was especially acute in the summertime. It is a proven fact that people smoke more in the summer. The days are longer, and the warm weather encourages more frequent smoking in the street. And this is where another big problem came into the picture. There was a good reason why output of tobacco products fell in the summer season. According to a system introduced back in the pre-war period, every tobacco factory had to stop working for one month in the summer of every year to undergo planned maintenance. Most of the workers went on vacation. Only the maintenance divisions remained. There were, of course, many advantages to this practice. Given the high dust levels involved in tobacco production, it was essential to carry out regular preventive maintenance procedures. Apart from that, there was the business of renovating factory-wide systems, cleaning, painting and whitewashing the workshop interiors and restoring the workshop floors. In short, this was when we could do the jobs that could not be done while work was going on. The workers were happy about it, too. This guaranteed summer vacation was part of the benefits package provided in the tobacco industry. Trade union committees tried to provide vouchers for spas and recreation centres for those who wished to spend their vacations there.

All well and good. But the problem was that the tobacco industry produced no output for a whole month, and this seriously hampered the maintenance of a positive balance between production and consumption. Every year, therefore, there would be shortages in the summertime, with smokers nervously rushing around in search of cigarettes. Especially serious problems would arise when the local factory shut for maintenance. Knowing the potential consequences, the authorities would make preparations for this period. The schedule of factory shutdowns was arranged for a year in advance. Stocks of cigarettes were built up in the trade network. But because of the limited resources, they would first try to cover the needs of Moscow and other major cities. It was unacceptable to have serious shortages arising in the capital. By tradition, the Yava and Ducat factories in Moscow took it in turns to stop for maintenance in June and August. After one of the factories stopped working in June, both factories would work in July to build up stocks in the trade network before the other factory stopped in August. It was an issue that so preyed on the public's mind that the majority of smoking Muscovites knew when Yava was due to stop work in a given year and would prepare accordingly. Yava cigarettes would vanish from the kiosks in the first few days after the factory shut, but heavy smokers would stock up on their favourite cigarettes in advance to see them through the maintenance period. In Moscow, Bulgarian cigarettes would be imported to prevent any palpable shortage from developing, but serious difficulties would arise in a number of regions of the Russian Federation. Somehow, though, people got by. They got used to this state of affairs and learned to deal with it. In time, the factories would start up again after their maintenance and the situation would gradually settle down.

The first crack of thunder sounded in 1976. Unrest broke out in a number of Russian regions, with a particularly serious situation developing in the Kuzbass mining area. The only local factory, in Prokopyevsk, was unable to supply the region's needs. Nor, apparently, was it possible to bring in reserve stocks from elsewhere. The local leaders tried, as usual, to ride the situation out until the factory resumed operation. But the miners, as the most active contingent of the working class, kicked up a fuss. The CPSU Central Committee was bombarded with letters, which were reported to Mikhail Suslov, Politburo member and chief Party ideologist.[1] We were shown representative extracts from the letters. I remember one in particular – a cry for help from a miner's wife: "My husband comes home in a foul mood after his shift. He sends me out to buy cigarettes. In the morning he wakes up, and if he doesn't find cigarettes, there's a terrible scene at home. I understand that there isn't enough meat or butter… We're used to that. But surely it's not hard to provide cigarettes…"

Judging by the reaction of officials of the USSR Ministry of the Food Industry, the CPSU Central Committee took this matter very seriously. They understood what an important issue the availability of cigarettes was for the public at large, and what terrible consequences could ensue from any shortage of them. Everyone was aware of how salt, matches and pasta would fly off the shelves whenever there was some sort of panic. And if a shortage was actually allowed to develop, it then became very difficult to overcome it. This took large amounts of additional resources.

The danger posed by potential tobacco crises forced the government and Gosplan to allocate government funds to help develop the tobacco industry. The first task was to update production facilities. Since it was still not feasible for the Soviet economy to increase production of filter cigarettes, it was decided to focus on producing more of the unfiltered kind. A deal was made with

---

1 Mikhail Andreyevich Suslov (1902–1982) – a member of the Politburo of the CPSU Central Committee, the highest authority in the USSR. He was the state's chief ideologist in the Brezhnev era.

Molins for the supply of a large number of the more up-to-date Mark 9 – Schmermund lines to replace the obsolete DKET machines. The lines were specially developed for supply to the Soviet Union based on the firm's standard design. Over the period 1977–1979, over 200 cigarette-making lines were supplied, which greatly alleviated the plight of the country's tobacco factories.

Another serious problem for the sector was the supply of raw tobacco. To increase the domestic supply of raw material, it was decided to develop tobacco cultivation in Moldavia, which already specialised in growing tobacco. The result exceeded all expectations. Moldtabakprom became one of the ministry's most successful projects. Over a short period, the quantity of tobacco grown in the republic tripled to 140,000 tonnes. Moldavia became the chief supplier of tobacco for the country's tobacco industry. People started calling it the "tobacco republic". Cigarette production also began to develop in Moldavia. The sole small factory in Kishinev also became part of the Moldtabakprom association. Evidently as a bonus for its great success in developing tobacco cultivation, funds were allocated for the refurbishment of the factory. The Kishinev Tobacco Plant (as the factory became known after the association took it over) became one of the leading enterprises in the industry, and the best equipped. It was there, for the first time in the country, that equipment was installed for the processing of tobacco for the manufacture of American-type cigarettes – "American blend". The plant produced the USSR's only American blend cigarettes, called Temp. The establishment of the Moldtabakprom association was a successful example of the comprehensive development of the tobacco industry in an individual region of the country.

UNION REPUBLICS UNDER THE CENTRAL COMMITTEE'S WING

In other Union republics, too, efforts to develop tobacco enterprises were stepped up. And although the local elite preferred to smoke Yava cigarettes, factories in the republics began to produce their own decent quality "national brands". Worst off were enterprises in the RSFSR, which were not upgraded and continued to produce low-quality output. There were various reasons for this, one of the main ones being the state's federal policy. Under Stalin, the centre had pursued a tough line in relation to the Union republics. Russians living there had held the top jobs and enjoyed a somewhat privileged status. State regional policy, like everything else, had rested on fear. Even Stalin's comrades-in-arms among the Georgian elite had not been spared repression. When Brezhnev came to power, the Union republics breathed more freely. The local populations felt a renewed sense of identity. New national elites arose which were no longer weighed down by fear of the centre. Federal policy underwent a fundamental transformation, gradually shifting away from fear and rigid discipline towards a tactic of cosying up to the Union republics.

Economic targets and production and development plans were dictated from Moscow. The central government expected the leaders of the republics to fulfil those targets without fail. However, there was much weaker control over all areas of their activity. Although the local elites were not happy about the fact that all serious matters had to be decided in Moscow, they gradually found ways of arranging things so that dealings with the centre were made at the least loss to themselves. For its part, Moscow was ready to make compromises for the sake of preserving peace and keeping the republics loyal. Matters to do with the development and fulfilment of plan targets were usually decided at the top level of the Party. The Party central committee of a Union republic would present a proposal or request to the Central Committee of the CPSU. The latter would "carefully consider" whatever it was and advise the government to give it the "utmost attention". In especially important cases, a republic's Party leader might take the matter to the Politburo. Needless to say, once they received instructions from Old Square,[1] the government and Gosplan would in most cases snap a salute. Aware of the potential consequences, the ministries took a cautious approach to setting targets for the Union republics and would usually dump any remaining quantities on enterprises in the Russian Federation. This caused disgruntlement in the Russian government. People said that this situation arose because the Russian Federation did not have its own supreme Party body. There were only regional Party committees, which did not carry the same weight as the central committees of the Union republics. The consequence of this was an ever-increasing amount of infighting between Union institutions and government bodies of the Russian Federation. We saw this happening in the case of relationships between the respective food ministries.

In 1970 the USSR Minister of the Food Industry, Vasily Petrovich Zotov,

---

1   A square in the centre of Moscow where the CPSU Central Committee was based.

retired. An associate of Anastas Ivanovich Mikoyan, he had been a career food official who had worked for many long years in the Union government. His successor was Voldemar Petrovich Lein, who had done a brief stint working at the Riga Confectionery Factory right at the beginning of his career. He had then moved on to Party work, in which he had climbed up the ranks before being appointed as minister from the post of secretary of the Latvian Central Committee. He was a strong, explosive character with a firm belief in tough management. It is said of such people that "a new broom sweeps clean". Whereas under Zotov, relationships had been based on respect and trust within the management team, under Lein they rested more on fear of the minister, who was fond of picking loud fights with members of the ministry's board. The First Deputy Minister Fyodor Stepanovich Kolomiets remained a key figure in the ministry. A career official who had worked with V.P. Zotov, and a Hero of Socialist Labour,[1] he commanded great authority within the CPSU Central Committee. But he, too, was a very complex person. I had seen him become seized with rage over the most mundane matters. His hands would shake, his eyes would turn black, and it was hard to imagine what sort of decisions he could make in that state. Not for nothing did people call him Fyodor the Bloody. With this sort of leadership there was not much hope of objective decision-making. For instance, Voldemar Petrovich was for some reason very fond of Zolotoye Runo (Golden Fleece) cigarettes, which had been developed at the Yava factory and were only made there. These unique cigarettes, which had very distinctive flavour qualities, had a limited customer base. The small quantities that Yava made were perfectly adequate. And yet, at a time when the tobacco industry was experiencing serious problems, the minister suddenly presented Glavtabak with an order to significantly increase production of Zolotoye Runo cigarettes and extend the Yava factory's experience in manufacturing those cigarettes to other factories in the Union. And he assumed tight control over this matter. All the professional staff knew what a hare-brained idea it was. It meant creating a problem out of thin air. Only Yava had the tobacco processing know-how for Zolotoye Runo cigarettes. All the operations were done manually, and their quality depended on the experience of the workers. The attempt to produce the cigarettes at other factories failed. More to the point, there was not even much

---

1   i.e. a Cavalier of the Order of the "Hero of Socialist Labour Star", which was awarded for civil merit.

demand for them. But the minister stuck to his guns. He was a very authoritarian leader. But I don't think he was the only one. That style of management was very popular in those days.

He did not get on well with our minister, Klemenchuk. Alexei Petrovich was well regarded and had also had his sights on the Union Minister position. After Lein's appointment, therefore, a bad atmosphere hung between them. This had an adverse impact on working relationships between the respective ministerial offices and led to conflicts. Klemenchuk would often call Lein to protest against the biased decisions of the Union Ministry.

The weakening of control over the activities of state enterprises in the republics inevitably affected the way things developed within the republics themselves. They understood what was demanded of them: the main thing was to fulfil their obligations to the centre. Apart from that, they were free to arrange things for their own benefit. People wanted to live better, and since you could not get very far on an official salary, the phenomenon of "entrepreneurial activity" began to take hold in the republics. In Soviet times, this was only possible by violating socialist law. Various schemes aimed at the theft of socialist property came into being. In the main, they involved producing goods without using the officially approved materials, allowing state resources to be illegally diverted for the production of unrecorded, illicit goods. More dangerously still, there was a gradual forging of partnerships in these wrongdoings between industry managers and officials of administrative and law enforcement agencies. It was well known, for instance, that illicit goods were produced at tobacco factories in Georgia. Moreover, the entire workforces of enterprises would be involved in this, including manual workers. The way it worked was that plan targets would be fulfilled early by working extra hours, and the time left over would be devoted to making the unrecorded goods. The equipment and labour needed for this were already in place, but there were problems getting hold of materials (especially imported kinds), since the state only supplied enough to cover the production plan. For this reason, representatives of Georgian tobacco factories would come to factories in the Russian Federation and try to make private deals to buy the materials they needed. They offered good terms. Aware of the potential consequences, we avoided contact with such visitors.

People from the Caucasus and Central Asia began coming to Moscow with large amounts of cash. They might treat the government officials they needed to a restaurant dinner or give them generous gifts of gratitude. For the same reasons, they became popular patients at Moscow clinics. These sorts of goings-on had destructive implications for the economic and social system, altering the established principles of relationships within society and affecting the moral state of Soviet people. There was a rise in the phenomenon of "unearned income", as it was called, which assumed all sorts of forms. For example, it was around that time that I had to have a fairly major repair done to my private Zhiguli. I found that even at the motor repair shop on Varshavskoye Highway I received an offer to pay for the work off the books. This cheating of the state was especially widespread in the area of consumer services. Payment for work would often be made unofficially, off the record. Many people working in this sector (and not only this one) made a lot of money to which they were not entitled. This had an impact on the state of the consumer market in the country. The authorities tried to curb the growth in the free flow of money among members of the public. There were strict controls on cash withdrawals from banks. But it became increasingly difficult to keep the situation under control. One potential solution was to boost production of superior-quality consumer goods.

MARLBORO – SYMBOL OF THE AMERICAN WAY OF LIFE – MAKES ITS DEBUT IN THE USSR

Philip Morris is not a company to let opportunities slip away. It plays by the rule of "striking while the iron's hot". Its proposal to produce the famous Marlboro cigarettes in the USSR quite clearly dovetailed with the needs of the Soviet economy. In 1976 an agreement was signed between PM and the foreign trade association Raznoexport, representing the Soviet government. Of course, the groundwork for the deal had been laid by the success of the project involving the production of Soyuz-Apollo cigarettes. The basic framework of the contract was the same. The American party supplied all the components and the cut tobacco, while the cigarettes would be assembled in factories of the Soviet Union. I do not know the exact financial details of the contract, but it was well known that the Soviet party supplied very expensive Abkhazian Samsun aromatic tobacco as partial compensation for the American side's costs. The planned production volume was much greater than in the case of the Soyuz-Apollo cigarettes. For this reason, it was decided to expand the geography of production. Besides Yava, which remained the main producer, the Uritsky factory in Leningrad, the Kishinev Tobacco Plant and factories in Baku and Sukhumi were also brought on board. The little Sukhumi factory, representing Georgia, was evidently chosen in view of the involvement in the contract of supplies of Abkhazian tobacco.

The main problem for the Soviet side was the lack of suitable equipment in the factories. Mark 8 machines were considered outdated and were no longer used in Philip Morris's factories. Furthermore, international companies had now adopted a different cigarette format with a cigarette length of 80 mm and a filter length of 18 mm. This was considered more user-friendly and economical. Philip Morris was one of the first companies to switch to the new format with its Marlboro cigarettes. Equipment installed in Soviet factories, meanwhile, was designed to produce king size cigarettes. Glavtabak looked into this problem in the course of preparations for the production of Marlboro cigarettes. Foreign machine-building companies had not stood still either and now supplied the next generation of cigarette production and packing equipment. They had made huge advances, too. Molins had stopped producing Mark 8 machines and replaced them with the new-generation Mark 9 machines, which had twice the output rate, producing 4,000 cigarettes per minute. In recognition of the fact that the USSR was a major buyer of equipment, the firm decided to supply a Mark 9 machine free of charge as a promotional offering. This was a commonly used marketing practice, especially as it was well known how purchasing decisions were made in the Soviet Union: it was desirable first to demonstrate the equipment "in the flesh" to high-placed officials. Glavtabak put the Yava factory in charge of learning how to operate the new machine. Of course, it was an entirely new piece of equipment in terms of both design and appearance. Our specialists again gazed upon it as a miracle of technology. Achieving such a high productivity rate had required the incorporation of multiple new design solutions. As a result, the new machine was considerably bulkier. It differed from the Mark 8 particularly in terms of the degree of automation. One button set it in operation, after which all the functions started up automatically. However, maintaining such complex machinery required a higher level of skill. The mechanics were rather disconcerted at first when they saw the multitude of flashing lights on the large control panel in the centre of the machine. Of course, we chose our best specialists for the task of mastering the new equipment.

The Mark 9 machine performed well. The quality of cigarettes produced was excellent. Over a million cigarettes were produced in a single shift. When it came to decide which equipment to use for the Marlboro cigarettes, therefore, we opted for Molins. The factory took receipt of a brand-new line for making cigarettes in hard packaging, consisting of a Mark 9 cigarette-making machine and a Hinge Lid 2 packing machine, connected by a very elegant Oscar hopper unit. The latter performed two functions: the automatic transfer of cigarettes from the cigarette-making machine to the packer and the creation of a buffer reserve of cigarettes. This made the line work more efficiently.

The Yava factory proved to be fully ready for the production of Marlboro cigarettes. The experience gained from making the Soyuz-Apollo cigarettes stood us in good stead for the new challenges. Our workers and specialists had more or less mastered the operating procedures of Philip Morris. To prevent the theft of the much sought-after cigarettes, we had to build yet another crystal room, the third in Yava's history, in the workshop. The fact that the makers were geographically dispersed made things much more difficult for PM. Process discipline was a weak point for factories in the southern Union republics, and the tendency towards so-called "entrepreneurial activity" was at odds with observance of that principle. The state price for Marlboro cigarettes was set at one rouble per pack. On the black market they cost significantly more. Measures were needed to deter any intention of producing illicit output and monitor production volumes to ensure that products did not reach the market by illegal routes.

The preparatory period took quite a long time. Every factory had to be supplied with all the necessary materials. On this occasion, the cut tobacco was supplied from one of Philip Morris's factories in Switzerland. To help monitor cigarette production, Philip Morris issued cigarette-printing dies only after authorisation was given to commence production. The idea was that it was impossible to make an exact copy of the die impression, so a forgery would not go unnoticed. There was a rather curious incident in this regard involving the general director of Moldavtabak, Nikolai Filippovich Verbitsky. It happened in all innocence – he told me the story himself after he got back from a business trip to America. He had been due to meet the president of PM there and decided that it would be fitting to present him with a block of Marlboro cigarettes made in Kishinev. The Kishinev plant had already received all the manufacturing materials and tobacco but had not yet been authorised to begin production. Consequently, it had not received a printing die. Having summoned the director of the factory, Nikolai Filippovich grew incensed that he was prevented by this small detail from making an important gift for the company president and ordered the factory to make its own die and produce the first cigarettes. When all is said and done, he reasoned, I am the "general" (as general directors were referred to) and can take the responsibility upon myself. Comrade Verbitsky flew to America on schedule, met the president, presented him with a block of Marlboros and was delighted at how the meeting had gone. What happened next we learned from the wry, softly spoken Mr Werner, our old partner from the Soyuz-Apollo project, who was now head of the Philip Morris team in charge of Marlboro. One night, Mr Werner received a telephone call at his home in Switzerland. At the other end of the line was a furious Philip Morris president, bellowing "What the hell is happening in Kishinev? What kind of cigarettes are you making there?" Not surprisingly, besides the shambolic printing job, he had found a host of other defects in the unauthorised cigarettes.

Of course, it was very difficult to make cigarettes meeting PM's quality standards. Its quality assurance system picked up on the tiniest defects that were simply passed over at Soviet factories. The quality of cigarettes was measured by a points system. Every defect was described in detail and accorded a certain number of points. The sum of all possible defects added up to 1,000 points. I am proud to say that we achieved very good scores at the Yava factory, on a par with European manufacturers. Defects found with cigarettes made at Yava were regularly measured at less than 200 points. The biggest problems were at the Baku factory, where it was rumoured that attempts were made to dilute the original tobacco with local sorts.

The production of Marlboro cigarettes was not only a great achievement for the Soviet tobacco industry, but also a landmark event in the country's social history. It is wrongly thought that the first project in the USSR symbolising the "American way of life" was the much-hyped opening of the McDonalds restaurant on Pushkin Square in Moscow in 1990.[1] In fact, it happened much

---

1   The first McDonald's restaurant in the USSR. Its appearance was a major event in Moscow's cultural life. For a long time it was the biggest in Europe.

earlier, when the tobacco industry began the joint production of Marlboro cigarettes with Philip Morris. It caused a great stir. If the cigarettes had become freely available, I think the queues would have been no smaller than the ones at McDonalds. But it was in the tradition of Soviet trade for goods in particularly short supply to be distributed "through private channels". Despite the fact that production volumes were increased, the cigarettes were not easy to obtain, and by no means everyone could afford them. Many smokers dreamed of trying Marlboros. For others, it was a question of prestige, even self-respect. Some would simply put local cigarettes into a Marlboro packet and proudly take them out of their pocket in front of others. The popularity of the cigarettes was so immense that it would have been difficult to think of a better gift. They were accepted with gratitude by smokers and non-smokers alike. Producing Marlboro cigarettes once again made us the focus of much attention. Thanks to Marlboro, many doors opened for us and we were able to get things done. At the same time, though, it also caused problems. Everyone expected us to bring them gifts. We could only brazen it out as best we could and try to maintain an appropriate balance. We made Marlboro in individual batches every year for five years.

Yava also became the Soviet Union's only producer of low-nicotine cigarettes. The factory had received this assignment in 1975 through Glavtabak. At that time, international companies had begun expanding their production of low-tar, low-nicotine cigarettes, otherwise known as "light" cigarettes. This was a response to a public backlash over the harmful effects of smoking on people's health. Production of light cigarettes had begun to grow across the world. In the Soviet Union, there was no obvious government or public concern about the risks to health from smoking. People preferred strong cigarettes. The state's attempts to produce low-nicotine cigarettes probably had more to do with politics. It was a way of saying that we offer our smokers lighter cigarettes too. There was another fundamental difference. International companies had achieved low tar and nicotine levels using technological innovations designed to provide enhanced ventilation, such as perforation of the tipping paper or the use of high-porosity cigarette paper. We were not able to do any of this. The only way to achieve a low nicotine content (less than 1 mg) was through the selection of an appropriate kind of tobacco. There was a limited quantity of low-nicotine varieties of tobacco. On the other hand, demand for such cigarettes was not high. We began to make two brands of low-nicotine cigarettes: Vecherniye (Evening) and Rus. These were cigarettes for gourmands. No other factory in the Soviet Union could boast such a wide range of tobacco products.

LENIN'S *SUBBOTNIKS* – THE SWANSONG OF COMMUNIST LABOUR

The government tried to counter the deteriorating state of the economy and the widespread apathy in the population with artificially created enthusiasm, laying stress on the development of socialist competition and other forms of so-called "Communist labour". In any case, it was time for the loyalty of the Soviet people to the ideals of Marxism-Leninism to be demonstrated on a larger scale. A fitting occasion was found: on 22 April 1970, the country celebrated the one hundredth anniversary of the birth of V.I. Lenin. In the lead-up to the celebrations, the CPSU Central Committee passed a decree ordering future birthdays of the leader of the world proletariat to be honoured with glorious labour by organising special workdays, known as Lenin's Communist *subbotniks* all over the country. Participation was voluntary and the work was unpaid, so the CPSU Central Committee called upon citizens to show their conscientiousness and ideological maturity and mark the glorious anniversary with Communist labour in the nationwide *subbotnik*. The prototype was the original *subbotnik*, in which Vladimir Ilyich himself had taken part. There was a textbook photograph of Lenin carrying a log together with other Party members in that first *subbotnik*. And so, every participant had to emulate this by doing work that involved physical exertion. To meet this condition, it was decided that factory workers would spend the *subbotnik* at their workplaces, while white-collar workers, i.e. researchers, planners, designers, etc., were invited to clean up city streets and squares. Pensioners and housewives could set about tidying up the areas outside the buildings in which they lived. To enable the participation of workers from both shifts at industrial enterprises and maximise efforts to clean up urban spaces, it was decided to hold *subbotniks* on two Saturdays in April. Responsibility for organising them was placed on the managers of enterprises and organisations. Party bodies were in charge of general supervision.

I remember the preparations for the first *subbotnik* in April 1970. Every enterprise formed *subbotnik* command units headed by their managers. The higher authorities attached great significance to the event. After all, it was about Communist labour: "free joyful work of freely gathered people". Labour should bring joy, become a celebration. Which meant that factory management had to be at its very best; everything had to be just right. Performance should be driven to record levels by full-scale socialist competition. It was decided that the higher authorities – personnel of ministries and departments – would also take part in the *subbotnik* by working at the enterprises of which they were in charge. This required a great deal of preparation. All the ministry's officials were assigned to various enterprises. Making arrangements for them to work as part of the *subbotnik* was a big headache. Fortunately, the ministry's senior officials – the deputy ministers – preferred working at distilleries, wineries and sweet factories. It was decided that all the staff of Glavtabak would do their *subbotnik* at Yava. We had to assign each of them a task that they could cope with. Some of the younger officials expressed the desire to work on the machines. Others were tasked with sorting out defective materials or tidying up the factory premises.

Of course, the biggest worry was over how the workers themselves would take to the idea. They were expected to do a shift without pay and produce record results to boot. How could they be won over? In an ever more materially minded society, there were definite doubts over this. But the experience of the first *subbotnik* dispelled any such fears. Despite the changes in their lives, people still retained, deep inside, a sense of collectivism and a competitive spirit – a gut instinct to go out and put on a selfless display of valour. Besides this, the administration commanded quite a lot of influence with the workers. We did our best to create a celebratory atmosphere on the day of the *subbotnik*. Just before the day began, at six in the morning, the factory managers and public leaders greeted the workers at the entrance. Each of them was given a red ribbon and a badge with a picture of Lenin – symbols of the *subbotnik* – which was attached to the top right-hand side of their outer clothes. A live wind orchestra played inspiring tunes. There was a popular march written especially for *subbotnik* participants with a refrain that went like this:

> *Today, we are not on parade,*
> *Towards Communism we are proceeding –*
> *In the Communist brigade,*
> *Lenin is with us, ever leading...*

The workers would pass by in a festive mood, exchanging greetings on the occasion. Some would measure their step and salute the managers. On the shop floor, a real competition would ensue. Every two hours, the *subbotnik* command unit would display the figures achieved by the best-performing crews. The managers did not sit in their offices, but spent the whole day on the shop floor, talking to people. It was essential to give the workers the best chance of achieving high performances by eliminating any technical mishaps or deviations from the production process. In honour of the *subbotnik* it was decided to provide the workers with free celebratory lunches. We made regular reports on the progress of our work to the Party committee of the Frunzensky district, where the district command unit was stationed. The results exceeded our most optimistic expectations. We had a 100 per cent turn-out and many crews achieved record productivity. There were no disciplinary incidents and the atmosphere was excellent all round.

The state derived great dividends from the first *subbotnik*. A record number of people took part in it. People showed how conscientious and organised they could be, and the authorities demonstrated the extent of its influence and control over society. It also meant that an extra day's output was gained across the economy, thus improving the country's overall economic performance. Everyone gave their labour for free.

Enterprises transferred the savings gained from unpaid wages to the *subbotnik* fund, which effectively meant the government's coffers. The official performance figures, in the form of a report produced by the State Statistics Committee, were printed in *Pravda*.[1] The report gave figures for how many people took part, how much iron and steel was smelted, how much equipment, consumer goods and foodstuffs were produced, and so on. On the anniversary day itself, 22 April 1970, a ceremonial meeting took place in the Kremlin Palace of Congresses, attended by Party and government leaders. The General Secretary of the Communist Party, Leonid Brezhnev, delivered a long speech in which he summarised the achievements of the glorious labour of the Soviet people in the Communist *subbotnik*. A decision was made to hold *subbotniks* on a yearly basis.

From that time on, over twenty nationwide Communist *subbotniks* were held, right up to the collapse of the USSR in December 1991. The level of

---

1 The newspaper of the CPSU Central Committee – the main official Soviet mass media publication.

enthusiasm gradually waned. *Subbotniks* began to take on a purely pragmatic character. Industry needed to produce additional output to go at least some way towards rectifying the country's increasingly grave economic situation. "Communist labour" became just words. Government officials stopped taking part in the *subbotniks*, even though their participation in the first one had carried important moral significance. People had felt on that day that everyone was equal, regardless of whether you were a big boss or a simple labourer. It is a pity that this factor was not properly appreciated at the top. In the first *subbotnik*, everything had been taken very seriously. Enterprises even took stock of the work performed by ministry officials and transferred their earnings to the budget too. As for white-collar workers sweeping the streets, the work required of them and the level of organisation became less and less exacting. They still took part in the *subbotniks*, but increasingly turned up for the sake of making small talk and having a drink in the fresh air. Only the industrial enterprises carried on the traditions of the first *subbotnik*. We were expected to turn out good figures, and the objective measure of labour was the quantity of output produced. And so the workers continued to put in a hard graft on the *subbotniks*, working at full throttle. On a countrywide level, participation in the *subbotniks* had turned into an extra form of national service. But strange as it may seem, workers needed this form of work organisation. It was important for them to feel noticed, to feel that their work was valued. Right to the last, until cardinal changes began occurring in the country, they would enthusiastically turn out to work for free. And the administration, for its part, did its best to keep their illusion alive.

CHAPTER II.

TOTAL IMPASSE

"PRESENTS" FOR BREZHNEV

Over the period from 1976 to 1981, the economic situation continued to deteriorate. There was a ubiquitous, chronic shortage of labour, and productivity was declining. Enterprise managers had to devote more and more time to resolving supply issues. The main thing was to avoid production coming to a halt. The authorities seemed to have no idea what to do. On the central streets of Moscow there appeared large posters showing Brezhnev addressing the people with the infamous phrase "The economy must be economical" – which was patently absurd and, more than anything else, revealed just how utterly helpless and lost the country's leaders had become. Official reports now spoke less about economic successes, preferring to dwell on the achievements made by the Politburo and General Secretary Brezhnev himself in the area of foreign policy and the preservation of peace and international stability. The General Secretary had begun to focus heavily on foreign policy, meeting with leaders of Western countries. His trips abroad were surrounded with much pomp, with extensive coverage in the press and on television. This was evidently a conscious strategy on the part of the CPSU Central Committee aimed at diverting the public's attention from the country's worsening economic plight. People were being sold the idea that "however hard things might be, the important thing is to keep a peaceful sky over our heads".

It so happened that the Yava factory was involved in the preparation of the gifts presented by Leonid Ilyich during his top-level meeting with the French president, Georges Pompidou, and Chancellor Helmut Schmidt of Germany. The Food Ministry of the RSFSR was put in charge of preparing gift sets comprising products made by Moscow enterprises. They included sweets from the Red October factory, the famous Stolichnaya vodka, and a pipe and Zolotoye Runo pipe tobacco produced by the Yava factory. Large, intricately designed presentation boxes with special compartments in which to place the contents were hand-made by the Moscow Cardboard Plant. The assignment was an honourable one, but also highly responsible. Our expert pipe carvers coped with it perfectly. We would receive a letter of thanks from the CPSU Central Committee after the end of each official visit. Once, we received an order to make a pipe with a gold ring implanted between the stem and the mouthpiece. We had to buy a gold ring in a jewellery shop. We sent the documents evidencing our expenditure on making the gifts to the Party Central Committee. To give them their due, they acted very properly. The money was immediately transferred to the factory's account. On the whole, though, it is fair to say that even the presents that Brezhnev made at these top-level meetings were nothing special. Unfortunately, the choice of products made by Soviet industry was extremely meagre.

THE ROMANOV ASSOCIATIONS. "IT SHOULD HAVE BEEN TESTED ON DOGS FIRST"

The Party was desperately searching for ways out of the economic crisis. Much attention was paid to the initiative put forward by the first secretary of the Leningrad regional Party committee, Grigory Vasilievich Romanov,[1] to reorganise industry into a system of production associations. Romanov was the youngest and most ambitious member of the Politburo. Leningrad historically possessed great industrial potential. The city was home to such major industrial associations as LOMO, Svetlana, Elektrosila, the Baltic Factory, and others. The efficiency of the associations derived from the fact that the chief enterprise, which produced sophisticated products, and its supplier factories were combined within a single structure. An even greater effect was achieved from creating research and production associations with integrated research and development and design institutes. However, evidently inspired by the success of the Leningrad organisations, Romanov then came up with the idea of combining enterprises into sectoral associations.

In the food sector, this swiftly led to the creation of associations such as Lenkonditer (confectionery plants), Lentabak, etc. Essentially, it amounted to

---

1 Grigory Vasilievich Romanov (1923–2008) – first secretary of the Leningrad Regional Committee of the CPSU in 1970–1993. Was a genuine contender for the post of General Secretary of the CPSU in 1983–1985, but lost out to M.S. Gorbachev. A man of extremely conservative and antiquated Communist convictions.

consolidation. Enterprises in the food industry were end-to-end manufacturers with nothing to gain from this amalgamation. The disadvantages were far greater. It meant lumping together competitors with distinct cultures which produced different-quality goods and had their own customers. The Leningrad initiative was roundly criticised by the professional community in Moscow. The Moscow city Party committee also took a negative view. But it was the CPSU Central Committee that would make the decision.

At the end of 1976, the managers of Yava and Ducat were invited to a meeting with the head of Rosglavtabak, Vadim Alexandrovich Grigoryev, who announced that it had been decided to form an association comprising the two Moscow factories under the provisional name of Mostabak. He asked us to prepare a feasibility study for the creation of the association. That was how things were done: ill-considered decisions would be made somewhere at the top, and it was left to the professionals to "calculate the economic benefit". We could be frank with Vadim Alexandrovich. We told him exactly what we thought about the idea. To which he replied: if there is no economic benefit, then paint one in. That was the phrase used at the time. No objections were possible. The deadline was already set.

Next came a crucial question for both factories: which would be the chief enterprise, and who would be in personal charge of the association. The choice was not as simple as it first seemed. Yava was, without doubt, the acknowledged leader in the tobacco industry. But Ducat was a factory with great traditions of its own and a well-run enterprise. If Yava was famed for its Belomor *papirosy*, Ducat had begun to specialise in producing cigarettes proper as early as the 1950s. The turning-point had come in 1966, when Yava began producing premium-quality Yava cigarettes, making it the top manufacturer of filter cigarettes. Ducat's problem was that its factory occupied a very small plot of land right in the centre of Moscow and had limited production space, making it impossible to carry out a major renovation of the factory and upgrade its tobacco processing facilities. This in turn caused it to lag behind Yava in terms of the quality of tobacco products. There was a joke that went around during that period. The directors of Yava and Ducat bump into each other. The director of Ducat says, "Listen, I just can't work out the secret behind the quality of your products. We seem to be doing everything the same. What is it that you put in your cigarettes?" The director of Yava starts rattling off a list:

"This, that, such and such… and a little more tobacco". "Ah, so you put tobacco in them?" The authors of the joke were right that the reason lay in the tobacco. The standard of tobacco processing really was significantly higher at Yava. But Ducat had a very orderly workforce and had achieved a great deal in terms of the organisation of production and labour. While Yava, after receiving the new equipment, had immense problems fulfilling the plan, Ducat was renowned for its stability. A particular claim to fame for the factory was that Ducat's Novost cigarettes were smoked by Leonid Ilyich Brezhnev himself. A major role in the factory's success had been played by the director, Vladimir Anatolievich Talalayev. He was an ambivalent character. A leader by nature, flamboyant, he had a way of making an impression on people with his unusual behaviour. He was treated with respect by his superiors, but his colleagues were a little afraid of him. He was quite capable of "dropping them in it" at some crucial moment. I heard that ministry officials referred to him behind his back as a "peacock". Which explains why, even in our chief directorate, people tended not to have much to do with him.

This, then, was the tricky foe with whom we had to "do battle" over the division of power in the new association. Our corner was fought by the director, Kashtanov. There was a lot of very tense behind-the-scenes wrangling before a final decision was made. The main arguments were on our side, but it was important not to let the matter be decided in a random fashion, which was no rare thing in Soviet times. Nikolai Sergeyevich handled the task admirably. At the beginning of 1977, the ministry issued an order establishing the Yava Moscow Production Association of the Tobacco Industry (based on the name of the chief enterprise). A compromise was reached over the top personnel. Talalayev was appointed general director, while I was made chief engineer of the association. Directors of an association were simultaneously directors of the chief enterprise. Kashtanov was reassigned to the post of head of Rostabakprom, which had been vacated just before the association was established. The head of Glavtabak, Kholostov, had retired, and his place had been taken by Grigoryev.

The biggest loser in all this was the Ducat factory. From an independent enterprise commanding respect and influence, it had turned into was what degradingly referred to as a "production unit" – and worse still, as part of an association named after its chief competitor on the Moscow market. Ducat had effectively been deprived of any legal status. It did not even have a bank account.

The association was structured so that all its economic and financial units and its accounting department were comprised in the chief enterprise. All decisions on production development, personnel management and social matters were made at Yava. Ducat was left with a skeleton staff of administrative workers, who passed accounting and other necessary documentation to the association's head office. Ducat's managers (the director and chief engineer) had none of the usual authority and effectively acted as production supervisors.

Talalayev appointed his close allies from Ducat to senior economic and accounting roles within the association, and they, too, came over to work at Yava. Talalayev's right-hand woman, Zinaida Ivanovna Sokolova, reputed to be his eyes and ears, was appointed as the association's chief economist. Thus, the creation of the association only caused a rearrangement of management staff rather than allowing reductions to be made. As with any reorganisation, it took a lot of time to restore broken connections. New managers had come over to Yava from Ducat, and management functions had changed. Staff at Ducat, having lost any independence, had become demoralised and bereft of motivation. All the managers, including the director, had left the factory and moved over to the association, depriving the remaining staff of essential support.

In this very difficult situation, when there was a need to create new incentives for employees and rebuild morale in the factories' workforces, Talalayev behaved exceedingly strangely. He came to Yava with the clear intention of undermining the operating style that had evolved over many years to suit his own agenda. He began indiscriminately criticising everything that had been done before him. He would summon employees, give them a ticking off and instruct them to "go over to Ducat and learn from how things are organised there". It got ridiculous. Evidently, he thought that, by behaving in this way, he was raising the prestige of the Ducat factory within the association. The staff at Yava, who were highly competent, professional people, could not take it seriously, and would laugh about it. It inevitably affected the way he was regarded by the Yava workers, who were accustomed to a quite different management style. Jumping ahead a little, I will say that Talalayev's behavioural style – arrogant, unpredictable, judgmental – never did get accepted at Yava. There was a petulance about him, which can be a dangerous trait in a director. At Ducat, too, feelings about him had greatly soured. The engineers who remained there felt abandoned and humiliated. They harboured a grudge against their director for having defected to Yava and taken the whole top management team with him. Especially sore were the shop foremen, who had worked at Ducat for a long time and had been close to the director. These were strong leaders with a great deal of influence. It was on them that the factory's performance and the mood of the workforce largely depended.

My own relationship with the director was also rather uneasy. Now that Yava's management had effectively been taken over by the team from Ducat, "outsiders" with a quite different management culture, my role consisted in keeping together the labour collective that we had spent so long building at Yava and in heading off any rash decisions that might be damaging to business. Naturally enough, Yava staff came to me when problems arose. I was constantly forced to have things out with the director, whose views differed from mine, and stand my ground. The discussion would often end in raised voices. On one such occasion the words we exchanged went along the following lines. He made a spiteful remark. "You and Kashtanov have run things to a pretty state, and now it's me who has to clear up". When I objected, "How can you say that? The higher-ups have always rated the factory's work very highly", he came back with, "You just bought all that by taking cigarettes to the people up top". After that, I had to put him in his place. "Yes, we did take them cigarettes, because the products we made were highly sought-after. Now that you are working at Yava, you'll be taking them cigarettes, too". And he did, of course, because it could not be any other way.

After Talalayev's move to Yava, the directorship of Ducat was taken over by its chief engineer, Valentin Filippovsky. Of course, we could not spend the whole time at daggers drawn. Both sides understood that. Compromises had to be found and bridges had to be built with the new management team. They were complicated people: just like their boss, people with a hidden agenda. They loved to plot and scheme. Outwardly, they might shower you with compliments, but what they were actually thinking, one could only guess. This was completely at odds with the workplace culture that had developed at Yava. I feel very grateful towards the factory's staff, who showed firm resolve and refused to bend under pressure. No division occurred in the workforce: everyone got on with their own business. The leaders of the factory's Party and trade union organisations, Alexander Vasilievich Vikhrov and Nina Nikolayevna Ivanova, maintained a principled stance. They always supported the interests of the workers. The director did not always receive support at Party bureau meetings. It was in this fraught atmosphere that the Yava Moscow Production Association of the Tobacco Industry came into being. No one in the Party or administrative bodies gave any of this a second thought. They made their report: the association has been established and everything is fine.

The tobacco industry came up against new problems during that period. Soon after the association was formed, the factory received a visit from Minister of the Food Industry Lein's deputy, Nikolai Vasilievich Oreshkin. He was the Union Ministry's official in charge of the tobacco industry. In a private conversation which took place in the director's office, he said that he had come to consult with us about certain matters. Gosplan had cut the amount of funds allocated to buy imported raw tobacco. The ministry had been tasked with working out how to make up for the expected shortfall of tobacco. There was a discussion about what to do, but no meaningful suggestions came up that would not involve investment. One thing was clear: there were difficult times ahead for the tobacco industry. Of course, it would have been possible to cut raw material costs by 15–20 per cent by bringing in modern technology, but this would require substantial investment. All that remained was the tried and tested method of bureaucratic management, consisting in a top-down order to cut the raw tobacco consumption rate under the guise of tightening control over production activity. What it really meant was: we are cutting your consumption rates "at random", and you will have to deal with it as best you can. There was another serious problem, too: a growing shortage of filter cigarettes in the retail system. In Moscow, smokers were wandering from kiosk to kiosk, spending large amounts of time trying to get hold of "their" brand of cigarettes. It was especially difficult to buy soft packs of Yava cigarettes. Special arrangements had developed between vendors and customers. Kiosk keepers would keep hold of Yava cigarettes and sell them to regular customers, by mutual agreement, at one rouble for three packs (ten kopecks on top of the official price). The difference might seem small, but all told, it added up to quite a tidy sum. The scale of the problem was understood at the top. Reining in the crisis over filter cigarettes would require a substantial infusion of new capacities. Since Gosplan would not allocate any hard currency, other ways of solving the problem were sought. Through Comecon, talks were held with Czechoslovakia, which had the most developed machine-building sector among the Communist countries. Two filter cigarette-making machines made by the Czech firm Škoda were delivered to the Yava factory for testing. Besides cars, this large, diversified company made various kinds of equipment for many different industries. If the tests went well, there was a real possibility of arranging the delivery of a large consignment of this equipment through Comecon. The factory was absolutely committed to giving the Škoda lines a chance. But by all measures, it was not so much yesterday's technology as the day before yesterday's – in terms of both operating efficiency and the quality of cigarettes. The idea of buying the Czech equipment had to be abandoned. There was only one thing for it: to squeeze the tobacco enterprises for every last ounce of productivity, and then some.

The authorities continued their attempts to kickstart the economy without serious investment. In 1977 the CPSU Central Committee issued a decree on the introduction in industry of a "comprehensive product quality control system". The idea was a good one. The programme was aimed at developing enterprise standards that would help optimise production processes and raise product quality. The standards even applied to products of suppliers. Party bodies attached a great deal of importance to this work, seeing the implementation of the new quality control system as a panacea to cure all ills. But it was impossible to achieve any substantial improvements. We were well aware of the enterprise's bottlenecks, but resolving them was only possible with serious investment. Setting quality standards for our suppliers' products did not mean that we could expect any real improvement in the quality of the materials they supplied. And so, like the "scientific organisation of labour", the quality control scheme became just another Party exercise.

Meanwhile, the country was entering a period in which the economy was sliding out of control. Many key processes were behaving chaotically, making it difficult to predict anything. There were worsening shortages of goods in shops and materials in factories. Problems would arise unexpectedly, meaning you had to be on your toes. It was a particularly dangerous time to be in a management role. Industry bosses were becoming hostages to the situation. They had to meet very tight targets while facing problems that were unpredictable and largely beyond the control of individual managers. It was more a question of hoping for the best. Things might turn out all right, or they might not. Wherever you turned, there would be some new crisis springing up. At one point, soap suddenly disappeared from shop shelves. This was a serious problem for the whole country. Soap was something essential to everyday life (at that time it was all there was in terms of personal hygiene products). It was manufactured by enterprises of the fats and oils industry, and the man in charge of that was Deputy Minister Volodin, who was also responsible for the tobacco industry. I recall that Boris Pavlovich changed beyond recognition during that time. It was awful just to look at him. As a responsible person, he was deeply distressed about this predicament. He made daily reports to the Party Central Committee about the situation in the factories. There, of course, they did not mess around. They "called him on the carpet" – and a very rough carpet at that. The crisis was dealt with somehow or other, but it ended tragically for Boris Pavlovich. He fell seriously ill on account of all the stress and was forced to retire while still very much of working age. I do not think that he was seriously at fault for what happened. He was a professional man who knew his industry well. As a young combat veteran, he had graduated from the Krasnodar Institute of the Food Industry, specialising in the fats and oils industry. He had climbed his way to the directorship of the Gorky Fats and Oils Plant, the largest such plant in the country, before being transferred to Moscow to take up the post of Deputy Minister in charge of the sector. What happened was part of a larger systemic problem in the condition of Soviet industry. Cracks could appear anywhere. It was just that there were certain sensitive goods, shortages of which tended to provoke panic among the population and a corresponding reaction from the authorities.

The tobacco industry was likewise something of a powder keg, and Nikolai Sergeyevich Kashtanov found himself in a similarly unenviable position. It was one thing to be responsible for a particular enterprise, but quite another to be in charge of a whole industry that was riddled with problems. With more than twenty factories, many of which were hopelessly behind the times, disaster could strike at any time. The tobacco market was constantly on the brink of sliding towards unmanageable shortages. The authorities tried everything to prevent this from happening, mobilising all possible resources. Eventually, they got as far as the Gosrezerv (State Reserve) system. It was well known how cautious the country's leaders were about using this secret organisation, whose function was to gather the resources that would be needed in the event of a war or major disaster. Woe betide anyone who failed to deliver goods to Gosrezerv on time! By decision of the Soviet government, several billion units of tobacco products were placed in that agency's storerooms every year. They were gradually replaced to maintain the quality of the products. In 1976, because of the shortages of cigarettes in the shops, it was decided to assign a corresponding quantity of baled leaf tobacco to the stores rather than tobacco products. And while cigarettes were actually stored in Gosrezerv's own facilities, tobacco was kept in segregated areas of factory warehouses. Every so often, officials from Gosrezerv would come along and check that it was in place. Of course, it was not a decision that was taken lightly, but it was forced by the grave shortage of cigarettes. Moreover, it was patently useless in terms of providing for essential needs in times of emergency. For that, you needed actual tobacco products, not tobacco to make them from. But the government's dread of cigarette shortages was so great that they technically turned a blind eye to an important state matter. Before long, however, as in a sad joke, problems over supplies of raw tobacco duly arose. Tobacco stocks at enterprises had started to dwindle. At the Yava factory they were reaching a critical level. Using the Gosrezerv stocks was the only way out of the situation. It was vital to get permission to use that tobacco. The USSR Food Ministry made a direct appeal to the Union government. The arguments were more than persuasive, and from the government's point of view, stopping production at Yava was out of the question. The decision was made in our favour. Yet another in a long line of sticking-plaster solutions.

Meanwhile, queues were forming at specialised tobacconists and tobacco sections of grocery stores. Kiosks quickly ran out of cigarettes, but larger deliveries were made to the shops. The CPSU Central Committee suddenly decided that cigarette packs had to bear a warning about the dangers of smoking. It was true that in the West there was already a serious campaign underway to reduce smoking. One of its chief aims was to ensure that people were duly warned of the harmful effects of smoking. This was why a warning had to be displayed on every pack of cigarettes. But what prompted the Central Committee's sudden interest in this issue?! After all, there had been not been the faintest hint of any anti-smoking propaganda in the Soviet Union up to that point. Most likely, they thought that displaying health warnings might help ease the chaos around cigarettes. As always, the Central Committee treaded cautiously in implementing this decision. They did not want to provoke hostility among smokers. It was therefore decided to start by placing the warnings on soft packs of Yavas, which were the most popular cigarettes and the hardest to come by. We would make a test batch and start selling them in trade outlets immediately after the completion of the factory's summer maintenance. The calculation was that smokers would be so desperate for their favourite cigarettes that they would not notice the changes at first. After the initial reaction, it would be easier to figure out how to proceed.

It was decided that the first batch of cigarettes with the warning message would be delivered to a grocery store in a working district close to Avtozavodskaya metro station. During the lunchbreak we (that is, the chief directorate instructor Anatoly Mikhailovich Usachev, head of Glavtabak Vadim Alexandrovich Grigoryev and the writer of these lines) met the store's director and talked about how the cigarettes would be sold. It was crucial that every customer should be made aware of the new inscription on the pack. Evidently, news of the delivery of Yava cigarettes had got around in the area, because a large crowd of customers had gathered at the entrance. The store opened. Only one block (twenty packs) was allowed per person, but no one took a single pack less. Everyone was duly informed that there was now a new warning message on the packs about the harm caused by smoking. Standing to one side, we observed people's reaction. There was quite a variety: "Just give me the damn things…", "We're well aware of all that…", "It's probably so they can put the price up…". But it was all said in a casual way. No one seemed to attach much importance to the information. Evidently, that was what was reported to the Central Committee. We received an order to print the warning on all packs of Yavas, and soon the words "The Ministry of Health warns that smoking is dangerous for your health" appeared on all tobacco products made in the USSR. However, the inscription made no serious difference to attitudes to smoking. Nor did it bring about any reduction in cigarette consumption. It merely served as material for various witticisms and jokes, inviting comparison with the well-known jibe of that era about the "139th Chinese warning" to American aggressors.

The problem of the shortage of Yavas remained. Granted, one effect of the formation of the association was that it increased our capacity to produce Yava cigarettes. Ducat also made filter cigarettes in soft packs under the name Orbita. But the Orbita brand was not very popular in Moscow. The logical decision was therefore made to make Yava cigarettes at Ducat instead of Orbitas. This was probably the only positive thing to come from the establishment of the association. However, smokers immediately noticed the difference in the quality of the cigarettes, and seasoned smokers continued to look for Yavas made at the

Yava factory. They became affectionately known as "Yavas from Yava". "Ducat Yavas" would do when the original wasn't available. In any case, they sold out quickly too.

In times of shortages, it was important to ensure the swift delivery of products to the trade network. Here again, problems arose because of poor organisation on the part of the transport agency, Mosgoravtotrans. However hard we fought, however many letters we wrote, they continued to be very erratic about picking up cigarettes. At times we amassed such large quantities of finished products that there was practically no space in the shops to work. The workers complained, "We are being asked to increase production, but they can't even pick up what we've already made. The country's a mess, nobody can be bothered with anything". No one could exert any influence on the transport monopoly Glavmosavtotrans, headed by the all-powerful Iosif Mikhailovich Goberman. And then came a first. The Deputy Chairman of the Union Government, Ziya Nuriyevich Nuriyev, who was responsible for the food industry, was holding a small group meeting about how to resolve the issue of the shortage of cigarettes in Moscow. The only people invited were a few senior officials from the food and trade ministries and Talalayev, the general director of the Moscow association. At some point in the discussion, it was Talalayev's turn to speak. And he, in his characteristic manner, abruptly changed the course of the discussion. "Here we are looking at ways to increase production, but even what we do produce on time is not getting out to market. Instead, it is lying around the factory's shops and paralysing our work". When Ziya Nuriyevich heard how much stock was lying uncollected at Yava, he was shocked. He telephoned Goberman. For some reason, this call had a powerful effect on Goberman. The response was immediate. We were told that pick-ups of cigarettes from the factory would be made around the clock until everything had been cleared. What happened next may be characterised as the actions of a "monopolist run amok". Day and night, the whole of 3 Yamskovo Polya Street was crammed with Glavmosavtotrans trucks. The line of vehicles stretched all the way to Pravda Street. Passers-by were taken aback by the sight, unable to fathom what was going on. The loading of the trucks carried on non-stop. The factory was cleared of finished stock within three days, with a total of 400 million cigarettes collected. Perhaps this was Goberman's way of demonstrating his might, as happened in other similar situations. But what was surprising was that no one in the Moscow government realised just how damaging this sort of frenzied activity was. The mobilisation of so many trucks to the Yava factory inflicted a great deal of harm on the city's economy. The trucks were taken away from other facilities, meaning that their finished stock remained uncollected for three days. The vehicles were parked in a long line, which was not an efficient way to use them. And all so that Comrade Goberman could report to Comrade Nuriyev that his instruction had been carried out.

There was a sequel to this story, but not a favourable one. Nothing changed after that in the way our goods were collected. At times, we would have large quantities of finished stock amassing in the workshop. Evidently, the transport workers were now busy putting out fires at other enterprises. But it was naïve to think that such a practised player of power games and such a self-important character as Goberman would let Talalayev's insult pass without a fitting response. In Soviet times there was a wealth of bureaucratic tricks ready to be used for these purposes. And the pretext used in this case was the failure to arrange the prompt unloading of freight cars during national holidays on the Moscow Railway, which happened to be Glavmosavtotrans's fiefdom. This was a matter that Party bodies took very seriously and regularly checked up on. The staff at Yava kept careful track of these things and always arranged for deliveries to be collected from the railway before the national holidays.

The May holidays arrived, and everything had been arranged in advance with the railway people. But somehow, the Yava factory found itself on the list of enterprises that were guilty of causing undue detention of freight cars. The relevant papers landed on the desk of the first secretary of the Moscow Party committee, Grishin. It was useless to plead innocence. Talalayev was summoned to a meeting of the secretariat of the Moscow Party committee and handed an official Party reprimand. Everyone threw up their hands, unable to understand how it had all come about. But we figured out that it was most likely Goberman getting his own back on Talalayev.

I will give another graphic example of the ugly forms the bureaucratic style of management could take. One day, at just past five o'clock in the afternoon, the telephone rang. The call was from Minister Lein's office: "You and the chief tobacco man are to come and see Voldemar Petrovich right away". As was proper, I immediately informed the chief engineer of Glavtabak, Kolesnikov. Yury Pavlovich turned out to be unaware of our summons to the ministry.

When we arrived, Kolesnikov was already waiting in the reception office. The minister was in a meeting with some bigwig. Every now and then, waitresses from the special canteen would glide noiselessly past with trays. When we were invited into the office, Lein did not even greet us, but got straight to the point. Addressing Kolesnikov, whom he evidently did not like very much, he immediately fired the main question: why were there no Zolotoye Runo cigarettes on sale in Moscow? Yury Pavlovich tried to present the facts as they were. Yes, it was true that the cigarettes were not on sale everywhere, but the production plan for Zolotoye Runo was being fulfilled. Most likely, the problem lay at the trade end. But the minister was in an aggressive mood, and it was useless to expect that he would listen to reason. "What sort of a Communist are you, if that's your reasoning? You look on calmly while these cigarettes are nowhere to be found. You have to get onto the trade people and tell them to get their act together. And anyway, why are you lying?! We'll go and check right now whether there are any Zolotoye Runo cigarettes on sale". He called his assistant and ordered, "Take my car, and you and the driver go around all the kiosks on Kalinin Avenue (the ministry was located on one of the book-like buildings on that street). Wherever you see Zolotoye Runo cigarettes, buy a pack, then bring them all to me".

While we waited for the assistant to return, Lein continued to lay into Yury Pavlovich, with occasional interruptions for telephone calls. We, meanwhile, acted as non-speaking extras. The minister did not ask me a single question during the entire time. It was unclear why he had invited us at all. Evidently so that we could witness the humiliation of our boss. "What sort of leader are you? It happens that I have a Cossack whip lying in the cupboard. I ought to give you a thrashing for your idleness". When the assistant returned without a single pack of cigarettes, Lein was triumphant. It was late in the evening by the time he let us go.

I returned home with a feeling of dejection. The minister had behaved disgracefully. He had set out to humiliate us as professionals. Having found the time to invite managers from the enterprise, he should have used the occasion to have a proper conversation and discuss the reasons behind the industry's problems. We, of course, would have been able to supply him with useful information. But Voldemar Petrovich instilled a sense of fear and uncertainty in those beneath him. I saw the way industry officials' faces changed when they were summoned by Lein. One never knew what to expect from him. This style of management crushed the initiative of professional people. On the other hand, Lein was in good standing with the country's leadership. He was a strong leader and a real authority figure in the industry.

Happily, I also had the good fortune to work with senior officials of a different kind: intelligent people who showed respect for the opinions of professionals. One such person was Klemenchuk's deputy, Vadim Artyemyevich Malyshko. After Volodin retired, Malyshko was appointed as supervisor of the tobacco industry in the Russian Federation. He was one of the ministry's stalwarts, having worked there since its foundation in 1966. He had been permanently in charge of very sensitive areas of operation: supply, distribution and transportation. He was not a food industry specialist by education, but had had an interesting life and career. As a young man, he had been through the war. I had a lot of admiration for that personable, decent fellow. Vadim Artyemyevich had a way of quickly getting a firm handle on tobacco matters. He knew how to listen to the experts and was receptive to their opinions. I feel certain that Kashtanov found it much easier to work with Vadim Artyemyevich as his direct superior.

New people appeared in the top posts at Glavtabak, the chief directorate for the tobacco industry within the USSR Food Ministry. Vadim Alexandrovich Grigoryev had died of cancer at the age of fifty. The man appointed to head the chief directorate was Illarion Ivanovich Zverev. His curriculum vitae was a case study in career progression. Having graduated from the Krasnodar Institute of the Food Industry, he had been sent as a young specialist to work at the Yaroslavl Tobacco Factory. After working his way through all the different stages of production, he had become the factory's chief engineer. Following the formation of the USSR Food Ministry, he had been transferred to the post of chief mechanic at Glavtabak, where he had acquired administrative experience. Next, he had been appointed head of the ministry's industrial safety department. This was a difficult and responsible role. The Soviet food industry comprised a huge number of enterprises. Serious accidents happened practically on a daily basis, many of them fatal and involving multiple victims. The job involved travelling to the sites at which accidents had occurred, finding out what had caused them and settling matters with the local Party and government authorities – after which reports had to be made to senior ministry officials. During the years he spent in this demanding role, Ilarion Ivanovich had displayed professionalism and acquired experience of working at the top end of the Soviet bureaucracy, which was a prerequisite for any leadership role. Zverev remained head of the chief directorate right up until the dissolution of the ministry. And it must be said that this was a difficult period for the tobacco industry. His leadership steered us through many tricky problems, not least helping to avert a very possible disaster over the shortage of raw tobacco. The post of chief engineer went to Alexander Samsonovich Apozyants, an intelligent man who was open to new ideas. A graduate of the Krasnodar institute, he had worked as chief engineer of the Tallinn Tobacco Factory before being appointed to Glavtabak.

In 1979, the era of Alexei Petrovich Klemenchuk came to an end. He retired at the age of seventy-two. It is safe to say that this talented man, a patriot of the food industry, had made his mark. Having headed the ministry since its formation, he knew all the industry's problems inside out. He had been a fount of ideas and the inspiration behind all major projects. He had given his all to his work. Every day at eight in the morning he would be running up the stairs to his office on the third floor of the ministry's administrative building. He would finish work late in the evening. His energy and focus might have been the envy of much younger men. Even his family life came second to his work. It was well known at the ministry that he had a very affectionate relationship with his wife, Maria Nikolayevna. They had no children. They lived modestly at a state dacha belonging to the RSFSR government. Often, at the end of the working day, his wife would be patiently waiting for him at the ministry entrance on the back seat of his personal Volga. Particular mention should be made of the way Alexei Petrovich treated people. He had practically created the administrative team at the ministry himself, but he was also well acquainted with regional staff and enterprise directors. Though he was a demanding leader, he treated the people he worked with as family. He stuck up for them and gave many of them help when they needed it. At the ministry he was affectionately known as "papa". He had given the prime of his career to serve as a food industry chief.

He was replaced by a man from outside, a civil servant from the top echelons of government, Stepan Ivanovich Chistoplyasov. Prior to his appointment as minister, he had held the lofty post of chairman of the Perm regional executive committee. He was a people's deputy and chairman of the industry committee of the Supreme Soviet of the RSFSR. It was rumoured that, as chairman of that committee, he had often criticised the work of the Food Ministry. And as if in retaliation, they made him minister – as if to say, there you go, sort it out yourself, then. At any rate, many people regarded Chistoplyasov's new appointment as a demotion. With his arrival, the ministry's working style changed drastically. Stepan Ivanovich knew precious little about the problems of the food industry. Not only that, but he seemed to look upon those problems in a condescending way, without respect. He conveyed a sense that he was forced to deal with these issues, as if he had been sent to the ministry on a temporary basis to put things in order. He behaved in a manner typical of a high-ranking government official. He put greater demands on the officials beneath him. The way he saw it, it was down to them to generate ideas and take full responsibility for development in the industry. His job, meanwhile, was to watch over and ensure the ministry kept working in the interests of the state. As a state-minded person who commanded authority, he had a proven ability to assume responsibility and make unpopular decisions. This was indeed very important. A tough character, he had a strict, aloof manner about him. One might even call it arrogance. He did not let anyone get close to him. As people used to say, he maintained a distance befitting his station. It was better not to trouble him with personal problems. One of the first results of his tough, principled style was a decision concerning the future fate of the Yava association.

Two years had passed since the association was formed, but no real changes had occurred. On the contrary, the sense of estrangement in the Ducat workforce had grown deeper. Attempts by association officials to get involved in the factory's affairs had met with stiff resistance. There was also Talalayev's wrong-headed sense of patriotism to contend with. He did everything possible to block attempts to make changes at Ducat. Evidently, he thought that this would help him maintain his authority at his old workplace. Part of the role of the association's management was to bring about the integration of the factories' production processes. First and foremost, this meant the divisions responsible for core manufacturing activity. Soon after the association was formed, we had worked with the food industry institute on analysing the factories' existing support departments and had drawn up proposals for integrating them. This included supply, transportation, storage facilities and machine shops. The proposals were reported to the director, but he found various pretexts for refusing to give them the go-ahead.

The director himself was increasingly losing touch with what was going on.

He spent a lot of time off sick. His absences started to go on for a very long time. It was I who had to shoulder most of the management burden. The way things developed, I gradually found myself having to devote a lot of time to running Yava, while Ducat carried on operating virtually independently, in the same spirit. We understood that this could not go on for long. There was always an uneasy feeling that something was about to happen, that the association management would be asked to produce a progress report. Our supervisors at the chief directorate knew about the situation within the association, but they had adopted a wait-and-see position, preferring not to get into a conflict with Talalayev. The Party officials were resting on their laurels as usual. Superficially, everything appeared fine, and no one was inclined to look too deeply into the reality of the situation. They did not sense that a conflict was brewing. Talalayev was too highly regarded in the Party bodies.

It was Ducat that lost patience first. Its shop foremen, the "strong middle managers", wrote a letter to the CPSU Central Committee. We did not know what the letter contained, but we had a good idea of what the gist must be. There was an uneasy pause as we waited to see what action the ministry would take. Normally, a commission would be set up to check the facts set out in the complaint. Then, the results would be reported to the people in charge. Quite unexpectedly, it was the minister himself who came to deal with the matter. A meeting took place in Ducat's conference room, in which Chistoplyasov sat down with the managers of the association and the factory representatives who had written the letter. Malyshko and Kashtanov also attended as representatives of the ministry. Chistoplyasov conducted the meeting in a pointedly restrained manner. There was a sense that he had already made a decision. First, he let the Ducat representatives have their say. They all spoke about the disastrous state in which the once distinguished factory had found itself. They criticised the work of the association. Rounding off the discussion, the minister gave a summing-up. Turning to Talalayev, he said impassively, "I can see what a mess you've made of managing this place". And he announced his decision. "Because of the situation that has arisen, the association is to be dissolved". None of the people present had expected this turn of events. Normally, this sort of investigation would end with general instructions to make changes to the way things were run – or, in the most complex cases, with "conclusions regarding personnel". But to dissolve an association that had been established on the initiative of the

CPSU Central Committee?! Granted, the management had not been up to the task, but this was also an indirect sign that the top Party bodies had pursued the wrong policy. Of course, the minister could not have made this decision without seeking approval first. But it was definitely his idea.

I think that it had become clear by that time that the hastily created associations were not working at all efficiently. Things were going awry at the Rot Front confectionery association and other similar artificial amalgamations. What happened at the Yava Moscow Production Association of the Tobacco Industry proved to be the first portent. It was not long before other such associations went the same way – and not only in Moscow, but in Leningrad too, the "cradle" of the associations. The ministry issued an order dissolving the Yava MPA and reinstating the Yava and Ducat factories as independent entities. Surprisingly, no punitive personnel decisions were made in relation to the managers of the association. Talalayev was appointed as director of the Yava factory, Sinelnikov as chief engineer. Filippovsky was approved as director of the Ducat factory.

This, then, was how the saga of the industrial associations met its inglorious end. As with other failed Party initiatives, no conclusions were drawn. It is difficult even to estimate what damage the idea did to the national economy. What Comrade Romanov thought about it all remains a mystery…

WHERE THERE IS SMOKE THERE MUST BE MIRRORS

The tobacco industry was presenting the authorities with serious problems. The chief issue was over the supply of raw tobacco. Some way had to be found of compensating for the reduction in quantities purchased from abroad. The Council of Ministers made two critically important decisions on this matter. The first involved significantly increasing supplies of tobacco from Kirghizia, while the second concerned the reclaiming of tobacco waste generated during the manufacture of tobacco products. These were large-scale projects requiring significant investment.

The West had developed ways of reclaiming tobacco waste (dust and stems) to produce material known as "reconstituted tobacco". Factories would send waste off to special plants, which would then send back the reconstituted product. There were a number of different technologies for doing this, which were the proprietary know-how of the firms that developed them. As well as tobacco waste, other ingredients were also used, on which the quality of the reconstituted tobacco largely depended. What resulted was not a purely tobacco product. Normally, tobacco factories would ensure that the amount added made up no more than 10 per cent of the total tobacco blend. The story of the purchase of equipment and the building of a reconstituted tobacco plant is yet another example of misguided practice in undertaking large-scale industrial projects using imported equipment. The purchase of the technology itself was arranged without a thorough analysis of the options available on the market. As a result, preference was given to a French company. It was clearly the wrong choice. Some people even suggested that the choice of supplier was motivated by political factors. A key component of the technology was a paper-making machine, except that tobacco stems were used instead of wood pulp to make the web. Then the web was impregnated with a special infusion made from tobacco waste, cut into wafers the size of tobacco leaves, and packed into corrugated boxes. This was how the tobacco arrived at the factories.

It was decided to build the plant in the town of Yelets, home to the Yelets Tobacco Factory. The process design was developed by the Gipropishcheprom-2 institute, while the building work was done by a local contractor. Responsibility for commissioning the plant lay with the Food Ministry of the RSFSR and Rosglavtabak. It was the start of an epic ordeal, a Road to Calvary.[1] The builders failed to meet their deadlines and all sorts of inconsistencies were found in the design. Rosglavtabak's chief engineer, Arkady Sergeyevich Dmitriev, who was directly responsible for the construction, kept having to travel to the site to sort out problems. Numerous meetings took place at various levels. The completion date was postponed again and again.

In terms of what was gained from the plant, it would have been difficult to imagine a more wasteful use of resources. The reconstituted tobacco made no noticeable contribution to tobacco production. But the amount of hard currency spent on the project was enormous. Around fifty million dollars had been spent on the equipment and know-how alone. That would have been enough to carry out a wholesale upgrade of the entire national tobacco industry. The quality of the reconstituted tobacco was mediocre. The added ingredients generated an unpleasant off-aroma. Only after the technology had been purchased

---

1 *The Road to Calvary* – a trilogy of novels by Alexei Tolstoy, set during the Civil War.

was it found that tobacco stems were the main element used in making the reconstituted tobacco, while tobacco dust was only needed in small quantities. There was clearly not enough stem material. The plant was constantly short of raw material and sometimes had to shut down, while the factories had yet another target to contend with in the form of shipments of tobacco stems. At Yava, we only used reconstituted tobacco as an additive for low-grade products. This highly expensive project had given the country's tobacco industry nothing but an additional headache.

The construction of the reconstituted tobacco plant proved a major ordeal for the people in charge of Rosglavtabak. Kashtanov and Dmitriev found themselves on the receiving end of many an earbashing.

Then there was a major fire at the tobacco warehouse of the Rostov Tobacco Factory. The investigation was conducted by central agencies from Moscow. The situation was exacerbated by the grave shortage of raw tobacco in the country. The prosecution agencies started working on the theory that the fire had been started deliberately in order to conceal the shortage of raw material in the warehouse, with the factory's director, Anatoly Ivanovich Chibisov, bearing the brunt of the accusations. They began a painstaking inspection of records of raw materials received and quantities used in production. But keeping accurate records of raw tobacco was a real problem. Figures in accounting documents often differed from actual quantities of raw material held in warehouses. The reason lay in the state system for planning the consumption of tobacco at enterprises. Tobacco, like food crops, has a wide variation of qualitative indicators. Its physical and mechanical properties depend on the grade of tobacco and the weather conditions at the time of vegetation. Even tobacco of the same grade can vary considerably in quality from one year to the next. Experts divided tobacco into heavy and light grades. The heavy grades had greater "filling capacity", meaning that a greater quantity of tobacco products could be produced from a unit of tobacco weight. But consumption allowances were averaged out, ignoring this factor. As a result, depending on what grades of tobacco were in an enterprise's warehouses, sometimes consumption would go over the limit, while at other times you would end up with a "saving". It did not pay at all to show the real state of affairs in reports. If you showed a significant saving, the ministry would immediately cut your consumption allowances. If you showed excess consumption, this would affect the enterprise's performance figures and incentive funds. The chief directorate was aware of this problem, but it was impossible to change the long-established, flawed planning system based on past performance. Through no fault of their own, enterprise managers ended up in a no-win situation. The only response was to use "smoke and mirrors". At their own risk and peril, they would hide any saving by keeping the surpluses in the warehouses as unrecorded stocks. Then, if the consumption rate began to go over the limit, they would start feeding those stocks into production without putting them through the books. At large factories, these unrecorded stocks would sometimes run to hundreds of tonnes of tobacco. And if there was suddenly an inspection, the matter would go to the courts. There was also the risk of being reported by "do-gooders" among one's co-workers. For that reason, the amounts of these differences were only known to a small circle of trusted people. The director and chief accountant took the responsibility upon themselves, risking their own skin, one might say. I am sure that similar such practices went on at the Rostov factory.

The trial went on for over a year, attracting a lot of attention. The investigative authorities eventually dug out discrepancies in the reporting of quantities of tobacco moved from the warehouse to the factory. It was a very difficult time for the people at Rostabakprom and the Rostov Tobacco Factory. Kashtanov and his deputy, Basnin, kept being summoned by the investigators, and they tried to defend the actions of the factory's managers. The Rostov trial damaged the reputation of the Food Ministry of the RSFSR. The pressure on Nikolai Sergeyevich intensified. The director of the factory, Chibisov, was an experienced manager and a true leader to the workers. Before his appointment as director he had been head of the factory's Party organisation. The court paid no regard to any of this and sentenced Anatoly Ivanovich to five years' imprisonment.

All told, Kashtanov was having a difficult time of things in Rosglavtabak. As we have seen, the industry faced serious problems. There was growing pressure from Gosplan and the ministry about increasing production of tobacco products. Besides that, he was hounded by misfortune: the Rostov fire, for example, need not have happened. There was always some new stressful situation arising. There is no doubt that he had all the necessary leadership qualities. He had acquired a great deal of experience as director of the country's largest tobacco factory. He knew how to get on with colleagues and was capable of putting anyone in their place and getting them to do what they were supposed to do. He was nobody's fool, as they say. He was a strong-willed person who knew how to show resolve when the situation demanded it.

But as time went on, he began to crave opportunities to let go – whether it was from the strain of work or simply that sides to his character that had not been on show while he worked at Yava were now rising to the surface. In Moscow he felt under constant stress: conferences, ministry meetings, having to deal with one unpleasant situation after another. So where could he really kick back and relax? As luck would have it, his work required him to travel to other regions to inspect factories there. The factory directors would make the most of this opportunity to try to build an informal relationship with the industry chief. They would receive him with full honours – sauna, lavish meals, trips into the countryside, everything that the provinces had to offer. Of course, Nikolai Sergeyevich knew how to maintain a distance in all this, but it set a certain tone that was not appropriate for a person in a leadership role. Outwardly, he continued to play the stern chief, but his subordinates sensed his tell-tale weakness. Private late evening drinking sessions began to take place in the personal office of the head of the chief directorate. For all the good will that people bore Nikolai Sergeyevich on a personal level, this could not but make its mark on the working and moral environment among the staff at Rosglavtabak. All the above was on particularly prominent display during chief directorate conventions. These took place twice a year, rotating around different provincial tobacco factories of the RSFSR. The agenda usually consisted of reviewing the sector's performance for the period just ended, discussing any crucial issues and making plans for the future. It was also an opportunity to meet fellow-workers. And since all the managers had a host of problems at their factories, they began to come to the conventions to unburden themselves. The meetings would gradually mutate into parties that went on into the late hours, and the next morning many people in the meeting room would be nursing headaches from the previous day's excesses. Information about the unhealthy state of affairs at Rosglavtabak began to filter through to the ministry.

The decline in standards of discipline and responsibility among people in high positions became a general trend during the late Brezhnev period. People had lost any belief in the possibility of change for the better. A state of total depression had set in, which was reflected, above all, in the discipline of people in management roles. There was a noticeable deterioration in the cultural level of the directorial stratum. At the beginning of my career, I was fortunate enough to encounter a different breed of manager: responsible people, people of consequence, whom one could look to as role models. Kashtanov, on the other hand, proved unable to cope with a difficult situation and took setbacks too hard. Having accepted the role of a high-ranking official, he continued to behave like a jovial, spontaneous fellow. And those things were incompatible. Simply put, Nikolai Sergeyevich proved to be lacking in political skills.

In Moscow, smokers were still struggling to find cigarettes. The situation changed only briefly during the XXII Olympic Games, which took place in July/August 1980. The country's leadership took the preparations for this landmark event very seriously. Large numbers of athletes and tourists were expected to arrive from various countries. It was essential to ensure that foreign visitors had a comfortable stay and to acquaint them with the best traditions of Soviet culture and everyday life and the diverse cuisine of the peoples of the Soviet Union. It was generally agreed, however, that the foreigners would be reluctant to swap their usual international brands of cigarettes and soft drinks for Soviet or Bulgarian cigarettes, Zhigulyovskoye beer or Buratino soda. For this reason, contracts were signed with Finland, our closest partner in the capitalist world, to supply the USSR with ten billion cigarettes of popular international brands and large quantities of Fanta, Coca-Cola and well-known types of beer. But then disaster struck. In response to the Soviet Union's military intervention in Afghanistan, the USA declared a boycott of the Olympics. It was supported by over fifty countries. Far fewer athletes and tourists arrived than had been expected. The Moscow authorities overdid things, too. By way of precautions to ensure safety and public order, they took a whole range of preventive measures. They restricted entry to Moscow for people from other towns and put a blanket ban on business trips there. People with criminal records and so-called "anti-social elements" were forcibly removed beyond the outer boundary of the Moscow region – the "101st kilometre". Many parents left town with their children for the summer holidays. Simple Muscovites were psychologically inclined to keep away from Olympic events – to stay out of trouble, as people said. Quite unexpectedly, Moscow became a ghost town. Of course, there were crowds of people at the event venues themselves, but in other areas (especially outlying districts) it was eerily quiet. I observed a strange picture on my frequent travels about the city: empty, tidy streets, and on the pavement a lone kiosk with

Marlboro, Kent, Camel and Salem cigarettes displayed in the window. In the ordinary context of Soviet reality, this was a highly improbable scene, rather as if multiple international brands of cigarettes had suddenly appeared on Mars. Perhaps I felt this especially keenly because I understood how unrealistic this temporarily created situation was. Such a large quantity of foreign cigarettes had been bought that they had been delivered to practically every kiosk in the city. Not many people bought them at first. After all, they were priced at a rouble per pack. Traders even grew a little anxious. But it was not too long before life in Moscow returned to normal. And when it did, all these cigarettes swiftly vanished from the kiosk windows.

Talalayev did not change after the dissolution of the association. He was mortified by the treachery of the Ducat staff, but at Yava, too, he never became the director in the true sense of the word. He was never seen on the shop floor, never talked to people. He remained aloof. From time to time, he would express open irritation at the way things were organised at Yava. He fell into a depression. He would sit for long hours at his office desk with a detached air. The Yava managers tried to avoid getting into conversation with him, giving his office a wide berth. The director's relationship with the Party secretary, Vikhrov, was growing increasingly strained. I doubt that the *raikom* was unaware of this, but they didn't say anything. The authorities took no action, and now it was the turn of the Yava staff to lose patience.

The first bombshell came after a regular Party review and re-election meeting, when the director was not elected to the factory's Party bureau. This was an unprecedented event, delivering a major blow to the reputation of the *raikom*, and especially the first secretary, Boris Alexandrovich Gryaznov. It implied that the *raikom* was out of touch with the state of affairs at the factory and had failed to respond promptly to moods within the Party organisation. It was hard to imagine a worse indictment – especially given the lofty ambitions of the first secretary. Gryaznov's reaction was swift and firm. The secretary of the factory's Party organisation was immediately summoned to give an explanation. Gryaznov himself met with Talalayev and, evidently, got his version of events. A decision was made to arrange a meeting between *raikom* leaders and the chief members of Yava's Party organisation. The meeting took place at the factory, chaired by the *raikom* secretary for ideological and organisational work. Talalayev arrived in a formal suit, to which he had pointedly pinned his government orders and medals.

The factory's managers traditionally came from within. Young workers who graduated from the factory-and-works college and were later promoted to senior positions. Front row, from left to right: Fyodor Trifonov became foreman of the cigarette-making department, Mikhail Voitsekhovich became director, and Kuzma Zhukov became chief mechanic. Photograph from the early 1930s

A group of women machinists in the papirosy-making department. Maria
Khakhulina (furthest left in the front row) became one of the top production
managers. Late 1950s

Working conditions on the papirosy production lines were very hard. Tobacco
factories had to keep the population of a vast country supplied with papirosy
using this outdated equipment. Early 1960s

People at the factory took official events very seriously. During lunchbreak, a meeting in the primary processing department with a delegation from Libya visiting the factory under the auspices of the International Friendship Centre. The photograph was taken by Yakov Khalipov, a well-known journalist for *Pravda* and the *Sovietsky Soyuz* magazine. Early 1960s

A group of machine workers at the entrance to the machine shop. Mid-1960s

Yava employees at the Revolution Day workers' demonstration march, in the column representing the Leningradsky district of Moscow. People marched to Red Square with great enthusiasm. Late 1950s

In the 1970s the workers' demonstrations turned into strictly regulated party events. In the Frunzensky district's column on Gorky Street. In the centre is the factory's party secretary, Alexander Vikhrov

A meeting in the director's office to discuss the manufacture of packaging labels for Yava cigarettes. Representatives from Molins and Tekhnopromimport are in attendance. At the director's table is Mikhail Voitsekhovich, at the work table (third from left) is Mr Leder, and next to him is a supervisor from the Lubyanka. Meetings of this kind took place under the scrutiny of the KGB. Photograph by Yakov Khalip, 1966

After the renovation, the factory took on the appearance of a modern enterprise. Main entrance to the new production building from 3rd Yamskovo Polya Street

The pioneer camp was staffed by factory employees. The close-knit family of the "Kosmos" pioneer camp. 1988

We had great fun at the camp. Here we are cheering on at a volleyball match. Next to me is the head of the camp, Romanenkova

After a meeting. In the centre is the chief economist of the Yava Moscow Production Association of the Tobacco Industry, Zinaida Sokolova. On the left is the head of the technical department, Valery Bykov, an irreplaceable specialist who wore that threadbare denim jacket for the entire time that he worked at the factory. 1980

At Yava we always looked for new forms of labour organisation that would encourage employees to show initiative. A meeting in the director's office with the newly formed young people's creative team of electronic engineers. Seated at the table (from right to left) are: L. Sinelnikov, cigarette production manager M. Khakhulina, party secretary A. Vikhrov, and electronic engineering foreman V. Protopopov, whose idea it was to establish the creative team. 1982

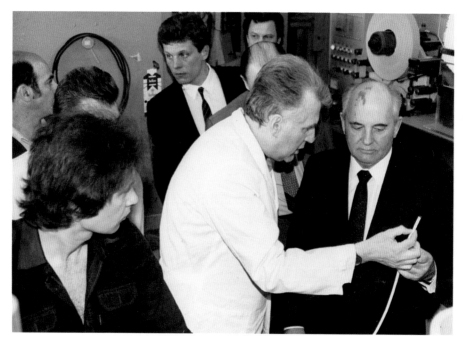

Mikhail Gorbachev's visit to the factory demonstrated the new relationship between government and society. During a tour of the cigarette production department. 1989

In New York at a reception organised by Philip Morris in honour of the Soviet delegation. Furthest left is the president of Philip Morris; on the right is Mr Gembler, head of the company's European division. 1991

Visit by a Yava factory delegation to Filtrona in a suburban district of London. Furthest right in the second row is the "mutinous foreman", Gennady Denisov. 1992

Signing of the "Letter of Intent" between BAT, the Moscow Government and the Yava factory. From left to right: president of BAT, Sir Patrick Sheehy, first vice-premier of the Moscow Government, Iosif Ordzhonikidze, and general director of Yava, Leonid Sinelnikov. 1992

After the signing: animated round-table conversation

Negotiating the foundation of the joint stock company was a long and difficult process. One of several visits to Moscow made by BAT executive director Martin Broughton (centre right). 1993

After completing our discussions, we usually had our picture taken in front of an antique carved cabinet in which samples of the factory's products were displayed. From left to right: Leonid Sinelnikov, Martin Broughton, Yury Trifonov, Nick Brookes, and the manager of the London head office, Alexander Lyuty

With the BAT directors after the establishment of BAT-Russia. From left to right: Richard Howe, Jim Green, Leonid Sinelnikov, Yury Trifonov, and Mario Chacon. It is hard to believe from these beaming faces that there were serious divisions in the management team. 1995

Russian business underwent fundamental changes in the 1990s. Presentation of the relaunch of Yava cigarettes to mark the 30th anniversary of the creation of the brand. 1996

If the tobacco is properly processed, the cigarettes are sure to be of a good quality. Richard Howe, Mario Chacon and I inspect the new tobacco processing line. 1996

After BAT-Yava JSC was founded, the factory's equipment was completely replaced, and new technologies introduced. With BAT executives in the cigarette production shop. From left to right: Ben Stevens, Martin Broughton, Berndt Schweitzer, and Leonid Sinelnikov. 1997

BAT executives demonstrate partnership relations with staff. According to the motto, "We all share a common purpose, and every employee, regardless of position, plays a valuable role". The company's general manager, Martin Broughton, has a friendly chat with a cigarette machine engineer. 1997

Martin Broughton (centre) discusses quality issues relating to Yava cigarettes with production staff

Modern cigarette-making lines require an intelligent approach to process management

Press launch for Yava Gold cigarettes at the National Hotel. From right to left: corporate relations director Vladimir Aksyonov, Leonid Sinelnikov, BAT-Russia general director Ben Stevens. In the background is the famous advertisement for the new cigarettes with the "Counterstrike" tagline. 1997

At a meeting of the Board of Directors of Rostabakprom. Seated are the general director of Donskoy Tabak JSC, Ivan Savvidi, and Leonid Sinelnikov. Standing next to them is Vasily Terevtsov. In the foreground is the general director of Nevo-Tabak CJSC, Yury Smirnov

During a break at a meeting of the Intergovernmental Negotiating Body for the development of the Framework Convention on Tobacco Control in Geneva. The Russian delegation. Furthest right is the well-known oncologist, Nikolai Pavlovich Napalkov. June 2003

He sat through the entire meeting with a stony, impenetrable expression on his face. Various workers with a high standing in the workforce, seasoned Party members, said their piece. They all said that the director neglected problems, was disrespectful to workers and shunned his colleagues.

I do not know what the *raikom* had expected from this meeting. It failed to find a compromise with the Yava workforce. Talalayev's fate was sealed. The ministry issued an order dismissing him from his post and transferring him to the design department at Ducat. Yet again, I was appointed acting director. Sometime later I was invited to see Malyshko. Vadim Artyemyevich told me that he had obtained approval from the ministry to nominate me for the post of director of the factory. We discussed the current state of affairs and the immediate challenges. I must admit that by that time I definitely had directorial ambitions. I felt that I had the abilities and the strength to take charge of the factory. In line with procedure, the minister sent a letter recommending my appointment to the Frunzensky *raikom* for Gryaznov's approval. However, no reply was received within the set timeframe. In the language of bureaucracy this signified a rejection. It became clear that Gryaznov was harbouring a deep grudge, convinced that the chief engineer and the Party secretary had set the director up, that they had been behind the protest vote at the Party meeting. Unfortunately, even after all that had happened, the *raikom* refused to accept the real causes of the conflict at the factory. One might feel sympathy for Talalayev on a human level, but the fact remained that a person with mental deficiencies had been installed as director, and he had completely squandered his time in the role. The *raikom*'s rejection of my candidacy meant that another person needed to be nominated. But Chistoplyasov was also a proud and ambitious leader who felt that his decisions ought to be respected. A little later, he resubmitted the recommendation to the *raikom*. Again, there was no reply.

For me, this was a difficult time emotionally. I had worked as chief engineer for over fifteen years. I had had a hand in practically all the major changes that the factory had been through, in building its professional staff and establishing a sound relationship with the workforce. I had seen four directors come and go. The question of promotion was of fundamental importance for me. When, after the *raikom*'s second rejection, Kashtanov summoned me and said that, shame though it was, there was nothing that could be done and we would have to find some other candidate for the director post, I seriously considered looking for a new job.

Meanwhile, the question over the appointment of the director hung in the air. I was also in the dark as to what measures the ministry was taking in this regard. About half a year had passed since I had been made acting director. I had not experienced any problems in my work. The workers looked upon me as the person in charge. Usually, the prolonged absence of an approved director would be regarded as a negative thing. But there was no sign of any imminent decision. Then, in September 1982, an order was received from the ministry approving Leonid Yakovlevich Sinelnikov as director of the Yava factory. Naturally, I was thrilled at receiving the order. It signalled the start of a complex and highly responsible phase in my career, the logical continuation of my personal and professional path. I did not yet know that Chistoplyasov had signed the order without the *raikom*'s agreement. This was an extremely bold move on his part, and an ambitious Party leader like Gryaznov could hardly let the minister's challenge go unanswered. I was soon to feel the full force of his response.

The following day, still in buoyant mood, I received a telephone message ordering me to go and see Boris Alexandrovich Gryaznov. In my innocence, I assumed that the first secretary wanted to talk to the newly appointed director about the challenges facing the enterprise and the problem of restoring the workers' trust in the management after the disastrous vote at the Party meeting. Having plenty to say, I went along to the meeting with great enthusiasm. What I could not have guessed was that I had become a pawn in what was now a conflict between the *raikom* and the ministry. I remember being taken aback, as I entered the large reception room, at the assortment of people waiting there: the deputy chairman of the executive committee, the head of the internal affairs department, the *raikom* instructor. After me came Vadim Artyemyevich Malyshko. We were quickly invited into the office, so there wasn't even time to exchange opinions. After a hastily delivered greeting, Boris Alexandrovich Gryaznov came straight to the point. Without a word about my appointment the previous day, he declared that, as a result of the inactivity of the administration and social organisations at the Yava factory, discipline had deteriorated and there were mass thefts of finished products. He cited figures supplied by the OBKhSS about the number of arrests made for stealing. The whole of this brief meeting took the form of a statement delivered by the first secretary. He did not ask anyone to comment. In conclusion, Gryaznov gave an instruction to the executive committee to form a commission together with the internal affairs department to inspect the factory's operations. The findings were then to be presented at a meeting of the *raikom* bureau. Addressing Vadim Artyemyevich, he asked for information about the meeting to be brought to the attention of Minister Chistoplyasov. I left the office completely shellshocked. Even in my worst nightmares I could not have imagined this turn of events. I will never forget the support that was shown to me in that difficult moment by the head of the internal affairs department, Colonel Gennady Ivanovich Kudryakov, with whom I was only superficially acquainted. He came up to me and uttered some very important words: "Don't worry, Leonid Yakovlevich. We will look at everything on its merits".

Gryaznov was an authoritarian leader, highly practised in the subtleties of Party management. He had chosen a counterpunch that could not miss. Every enterprise in the food industry had problems with theft. It could not have been simpler. This, then, was the second time in my career that I had been appointed to a senior position without the *raikom*'s prior approval: first as engineer, now as director. And while on the first occasion, Voitsekhovich had experienced a few rumblings of discontent, this time there was a more fundamental issue at stake: whether I would, or would not be, the director of the factory. After all, it would be no problem for the *raikom*, once the factory had been inspected, to prepare a recommendation to the ministry for the director to be removed for failing in his duties. By very subtly dangling me in this uncertain position, Boris Alexandrovich had sent a message to the minister that his order could easily be reversed. The situation was back in his hands. It was indeed the case that, in the Soviet system, it was impossible for a director to be appointed without the consent of Party bodies. By signing the order to appoint me, all the minister had done was to put the *raikom* in the position of having to make a decision – yes or no. This was the complex scenario in which I found myself immediately after being appointed director.

The *raikom* began acting in earnest. At the signal from the first secretary, the factory was effectively placed under siege. The commission set up by the executive committee began a thorough inspection, focusing chiefly on how things stood with the protection of socialist property, while the OBKhSS conducted daily raids. All the factory's workers knew what was going on. Most of my colleagues gave me their support. But for the part that they played, we would never have got through this difficult time. As the inspection carried on, the Party secretary and I were frequently summoned to the *raikom* to give explanations. I felt that I was being tested for reliability. After the meeting at Gryaznov's office, the ministry had also convened a board meeting to discuss the "deficiencies in administrative and disciplinary work among the Yava workforce". An official reprimand was issued to the director. Under the laws of bureaucratic administration, this was an essential step in order to try to deter punitive action through Party channels at the forthcoming *raikom* bureau meeting. It was a way of saying that the ministry had already taken action. This would be regarded as a mitigating factor. I understood that my fate rested entirely in Gryaznov's hands, and the only way of getting to be director was to pass through all the tests and prove my total reliability and willingness to obey.

It was time for the final examination. The first secretary handed me the task of conducting a show trial of three factory workers who had been arrested for stealing large quantities of cigarettes. It was evidently conceived as an educative exercise, which is why the factory was asked to arrange for the entire Yava workforce to attend the trial. The venue for the off-site hearing, the Large Hall in the building of the well-known Chkalov Club on Pravda Street, was shrewdly chosen. To fill the hall, all workers who were not on their shift had to be present at the hearing, meaning that it was easy to check the numbers from the quantity of empty seats in the hall. Organising this event presented us with some difficult challenges. While the engineers could simply be ordered to turn up, the machine operators had to be persuaded. It might have been their comrades who were being tried, but they all had their own things to do and were not at all keen on the idea of hanging around after work. This made for a lot of anxiety right up to the last minute. On the day of the trial I saw the workers filing to Pravda Street after the end of their shift. The hearing was conducted on the stage of the Large Hall. The accused were seated there too. Thankfully, the hall was full. This was a great victory for the administration, an indication of the influence it had over the workers. It was, of course, a rather degrading affair. But, to give Gryaznov his due, he had achieved his purpose in showing the recalcitrant factory who was boss. The trial made a great impression and sounded a warning to those present. The defendants received milder punishments than might have been expected, which was the authorities' way of showing their concern for the interests of working people. The purpose of the exercise had been to warn, not to punish.

The ensuing meeting of the *raikom* bureau played out according to a carefully scripted scenario. The issue on the table was "the serious deficiencies in the work of the administration and the Party organisation of the Yava factory in safeguarding socialist property". First, the report prepared by the executive committee's special commission was read out. It struck me that, although it contained serious criticisms, many of its concluding points had been somewhat toned down (at least in relative terms). It was noted that, in the course of the commission's activities and the *raikom's* inspections, the factory had taken certain measures to prevent the theft of finished products. It became clear that the *raikom* would not, after all, be seeking the removal of the director. Gryaznov gave his summing-up. By decision of the *raikom* bureau, an official Party reprimand was issued to the director, while the Party secretary and the deputy director in charge of the protection of socialist property received a stern reprimand apiece.

The *raikom* saga provided me with a great life lesson. I felt at first hand the huge significance that Party bodies had in the life of the country and of individual people. Why Gryaznov ultimately decided to let me remain as director is anybody's guess. After the difficulties I had passed through and the stresses I had endured, I had been, as it were, "sanded down" by the Party system and understood exactly what was required of me. Perhaps, in the end, Boris Alexandrovich realised this. But he still could not forgive the Party secretary's "treachery". The morning after the *raikom* bureau meeting, I received a call. Gryaznov had given an order for Party secretary Vikhrov to be transferred to production work with immediate effect. We conferred, and Alexander Vasilyevich was made foreman of the raw material section. It was impossible not to comply. The *raikom* never did understand, or simply did not want to understand, the real reasons behind Talalayev's removal from the director's post.

CHAPTER 12.
THE END OF THE BREZHNEV ERA.
THE DEATH THROES OF THE REGIME

SYSTEMIC PROBLEMS IN THE ECONOMY

1982 was the last year of Brezhnev's life. Seventeen years of stagnation had taken a grave toll. The General Secretary was seriously ill and in the grip of a complete mental decline. Hiding this from the public was becoming increasingly difficult. His public speeches became a source of widespread jokes. He even struggled to read out texts that had been written for him. His address at the Twenty-Sixth Party Congress went on for four and a half hours. To prevent Leonid Ilyich from getting muddled, a special official shuttled between the presidium and the rostrum, bringing him the next few pages of the speech. Every public appearance made by Leonid Ilyich was a further demonstration of the General Secretary's parlous state of health. In April I was invited to a ceremonial session at the Kremlin Palace of Congresses to mark the latest anniversary of Lenin's birth. There was the usual proposal to elect Politburo members, headed by the General Secretary, to the Presidium. The appearance of the members of the Presidium was greeted by those present with "vigorous and prolonged applause". In actual fact, it was a depressing spectacle. At the head of the group, moving laboriously with small, shuffling steps, came Leonid Ilyich. Following behind at a distance, adapting their pace to his, were the remaining members of the Presidium. It was obvious to everyone that Brezhnev was in no fit state to perform his duties. It was even said that Leonid Ilyich had put in several requests to resign, but the Politburo members, fearing any changes, had persuaded him to stay. The Politburo itself, an ultra-secret bureaucratic institution, reflected the views of the most conservative forces in society and had become the principal obstacle to positive development in the country. The decision made by the Party's top echelon in 1979 to send Soviet troops into Afghanistan was a tragic mistake that propelled the USSR towards political and economic collapse.

No longer able to control the situation in the Union republics, the centre resorted to purely ritualistic methods of preserving its influence. A particular style of relationship developed between the CPSU Central Committee and the central committees of the Union republics. The Politburo bestowed generous awards on the republican leaderships for their outstanding achievements. In return, the leaders of the republics expressed their profound gratitude to the Politburo and to the General Secretary, Comrade Brezhnev, himself. None of this reflected the real state of affairs. In September 1982 Leonid Ilyich visited Azerbaijan, then Georgia. Both republics were awarded orders of Lenin for their great achievements. The award ceremonies were grand, pompous affairs. In their acceptance speeches, the leaders of both republics, Aliyev and Shevardnadze,[1] went out of their way to sing the praises of the General Secretary. It was such a blatant exercise in flattery that journalists deliberated over who had done the best job. Leonid Ilyich himself was very fond of awards and gave them out generously to his fellow officials. This weakness of his was well known among leaders of other countries. The General Secretary's own breast had become a veritable iconostasis of orders, medals and other decorations.

The collective administration of the country had gradually veered towards "campaignism" – a reliance on sporadic bursts of activity rather than long-term planning. This style of management rubbed off onto regional governments, enterprises and organisations. The first systemic problem to affect the economy as a whole took the form of serious breakdowns in the country's transport network. The Soviet economy could no longer get by without substantial shipments of goods from abroad. Ensuring the timely flow of these supplies was of critical importance in keeping many industries running and supplying the population with essential food and goods. The bulk of import shipments came in by sea through western ports in Leningrad, Riga and Tallinn and from the south via Odessa and Nikolayev. The ports did not have adequate capacity or handling arrangements to enable cargoes to be processed and delivered to consumers on time. Vessels would stand waiting to be unloaded for weeks, sometimes even months. It was hugely damaging for the economy. When things reached a particularly critical point, telegrams would be fired off by the first deputy minister, Yury Leonidovich Brezhnev, the General Secretary's son. Funnily enough, it was said that this was the only effective measure. Anything

---

1 The future presidents of the independent republics of Azerbaijan and Georgia respectively.

signed "Brezhnev" was enough to get a shipment seen to in double quick time. Food supplies to the public were in a critical state. Despite substantial purchases from abroad, many food items were in chronic short supply. Most imports went to Moscow, but even in the capital there were long queues outside the shops. People from central regions of Russia would come to the capital to shop for food. I remember that people used to talk about the electric train from Yaroslavl. After doing their shopping in Moscow, the tired and hungry Yaroslavlians would settle on the train and reach for their bags of food. Children would hungrily gobble down raw sausages. There was a well-known joke about this: "What's green, long and smells of sausage? – It's the train going back from Moscow to Yaroslavl". In Yaroslavl itself, where I sometimes travelled to attend functions organised by Rosglavtabak, a visit to the shops was a dismal experience. Looking around at the empty shelves, it was hard to imagine how people got by. It was explained to us that, because of the shortages, the local authorities had switched to a so-called "regulated supply" system. Food orders were distributed through industrial enterprises. A similar picture was forming in other regions of the country. People were beginning to grow accustomed to the empty shelves. Scarce goods and foodstuffs were distributed through so-called private channels or obtained through contacts. The most persuasive way of declaring one's prosperity was to say, "my fridge is always full". No one was surprised that, despite the empty shops, people's tables were laden with myriad delicacies. Only foreigners were bamboozled by this mysterious paradox.

The bulk of scarce goods were distributed through Moscow's trade network, which became one of the main hubs of corruption in the country. Moscow trade chiefs began to operate in league with Party officials. There were widespread rumours about corruption in the highest echelons of power. A shadow fell upon the family of the General Secretary himself. Brezhnev had acted as patron to one of the chief crooks, the Interior Minister Shcholokov. And not, it seems, without motives of his own. Under Shcholokov's patronage, Leonid Ilyich's son-in-law, Churbanov, carved out a dizzying career for himself.[1] The General Secretary's daughter, Galina Brezhneva, was famed throughout the country for

---

1   Yury Mikhailovich Churbanov (1936–2013) – having married Galina Brezhnev in 1971, in the space of ten years he rose from colonel to colonel-general and deputy commander of the internal troops of the USSR Interior Ministry. In 1987 he was arrested on corruption charges in the so-called "Uzbek affair". He was convicted in 1988 and released in 1993. While in prison, he divorced Galina Brezhneva (at her request).

her great love of diamonds. Shcholokov helped satisfy that passion by presenting her with jewellery confiscated by the law enforcement authorities.

The symptoms of a profound crisis in the state system were plain for all to see. There was stagnation in every domain of the country's life. It was clear from outward signs. Even the centre of Moscow, especially in the evening, took on an unsightly appearance, plunged in gloom. People were starting to lose faith in any possibility of change, any hope of a better life. It was around this time that people began to talk about the strong, principled leader Yury Andropov, who was supposedly capable of restoring order. The KGB chairman, who possessed comprehensive information on all that was happening, understood that the country was facing serious danger. Under his leadership, the state security authorities began to unearth major abuses perpetrated by top officials in the Moscow trade system. Cases were brought against the director of the Yeliseyev Gastronom,[1] Sokolov, and the head of Moscow trade, Nikolai Tregubov. Needless to say, the trail of these crimes led to Moscow Party and municipal leaders. Clouds were also gathering over the head of the Interior Minister, Shcholokov. The trials attracted massive public interest and increased the authority of Yury Andropov. Many began to look upon him as the only person in the country's leadership who was capable of bringing the situation under control.

It was against this fraught background that I was appointed director of the factory. The responsibility was high. Amid the general decay in executive discipline there was a need to maintain a positive working climate among the factory's staff. Supply issues were beginning to play a critical role in the fulfilment of the state plan.

Gosplan was forced to allocate hard currency to buy new equipment. For the industry as a whole this was little more than a stopgap measure: far fewer cigarette-making machines were purchased than were actually needed. For us, however, the delivery of the new high-speed lines with Hauni Garant 4 cigarette-making machines meant that we could breathe more easily. The new equipment produced over 500,000 packs a day of our most sought-after cigarettes, soft-pack Yavas. Smokers noticed the difference straight away. And the completion of the tobacco

---

1 A food store founded by the wine trader and Petersburg merchant Grigory Yeliseyev in 1901 in the centre of Moscow. During the Soviet period it was known as Gastronom No. 1. The investigation into the so-called "Yeliseyevsky affair" in the period 1982–1984 resulted in the arrest, conviction and execution of the store's director, Yury Sokolov. A further 174 officials were arrested, and over 15,000 trade workers were prosecuted.

cultivation project in Kirghizia resolved the issue of raw material supply for the industry. Here, however, another problem arose. The republic wanted to sell the tobacco quickly, but the factories did not have the capacity to accept such large quantities in such a short amount of time. What was needed was a compromise that would allow deliveries to be spread out evenly over the year. But, as in other cases, the authorities did the bidding of the republican leadership. Glavtabak was forced to schedule deliveries in the autumn-winter period (immediately after the processing of the newly harvested tobacco). As a result, large quantities of tobacco wagons amassed on the railways. This became a colossal problem for the tobacco factories. Everyone was well aware of what lay behind it. But the authorities appeared incapable of making even the most elementary decisions.

Relations with the *raikom* had gradually eased since the momentous bureau meeting. Even Gryaznov had begun to show a measure of good will. Presently, we were informed that the factory was to receive a joint visit from the first secretary of the *raikom* and the Minister of the Food Industry. The visit had to be cancelled for technical reasons, but even the intention signalled a state of truce between the recent adversaries.

The large shipments of tobacco prompted an urgent need to find extra storage space. I made an appointment to see Gryaznov and asked for his assistance in this matter. After listening attentively to what I had to say, Boris Alexandrovich for some reason asked, "Are rats afraid of the smell of tobacco?" I did not really know, but without a trace of doubt in my voice I answered, "Of course". It turned out that some warehouse complexes were being built for the Frunzensky district on Zorge Street, but there had been a terrible problem with rats. I do not know exactly whether it was on account of my confident reply or because Gryaznov genuinely appreciated the seriousness of the problem, but Yava was allocated a site for the construction of a storage facility.

In the Brezhnev era of stagnation, the process of decision-making was highly subjective. It was often hard to fathom the real motives behind decisions that were made. Official procedures were effectively redundant, with decisions made directly in the offices of top officials. There was much dependence on personal contacts and even on quite random factors, such as the mood that a particular official happened to be in at the time. I encountered this in my own experience on a number of occasions. One example was a visit I made together with Gryaznov to the chairman of the Moscow City Council, Vladimir Fyodorovich Promyslov.[1] The background to the visit was as follows. When I was appointed director, the idea came up of building an administrative block on the factory's site. An old wooden house erected back in Gabay's time had been demolished during the factory's renovation, and our administrative offices were dispersed around the various production buildings. This was inconvenient. The construction of a new building would enable us to bring the administration together into one facility while simultaneously freeing up space that could be taken over for production use. In other words, the plan offered a twofold benefit. We had even had designs drawn up. But to get any further, we would need a construction permit. We knew very well that it would be practically impossible to obtain the authorisation we needed by going through official state channels. Matters of this kind could only be resolved by means of a well-prepared visit to the city's top men. I had decided to take a chance and approach Gryaznov, mindful of his influence. He was, after all, the only *raikom* First Secretary who sat on the bureau of the city Party committee. And that was the highest administrative body in Moscow. Unexpectedly, he came back to me and promised to help. It was he who arranged the meeting with Promyslov.

The trip served as a vivid demonstration of Gryaznov's lofty status. At the appointed time we left the *raikom* building on Gotvald Street in the first secretary's black Volga. As we reached Gorky Street,[2] the traffic police blocked the traffic so that we could carry on to the Moscow Soviet building unobstructed. At that time this was something that was done in exceptional cases. We made our way freely through the staff entrance and up to the third floor, where Promyslov had his office. On the way to the reception room, men in dark suits greeted Boris Alexandrovich respectfully. The secretary announced us, and we went straight through into the office. It was a strange sight that greeted me. In that vast room, at the furthest corner of a large conference table, sat a small man. He and Gryaznov embraced warmly, and Gryaznov briefly introduced me. Without even asking what the purpose of our visit was, Vladimir Fyodorovich began holding forth with great enthusiasm about the thing that was really on his mind at that time: the publication of his memoirs. It turned out that none

---

1   Vladimir Fyodorovich Promyslov (1908–1993) – chairman of the executive committee of the Moscow Soviet, i.e. the administrative leader of Moscow, from 1963 to 1986. This is somewhat of a record for remaining in a post of that kind.
2   Now Tverskaya Street.

other than Leonid Ilyich Brezhnev himself had read them and given them his hearty approval. He immediately signed a copy of the book and respectfully handed it to Boris Alexandrovich. It was obvious that the seventy-four-year-old Moscow leader had long been out of touch with the real problems of the city. He did little more than sign documents prepared for him by his staff.

The country had been seized by an epidemic of this sort of thing. I feel sure that much the same atmosphere reigned in the CPSU Central Committee, where elderly Party bosses had lost their grip on the situation in the country but clung tenaciously to power. Once Vladimir Fyodorovich's fervour had died down, Boris Alexandrovich reminded him of why we had come and presented him with a letter from the Yava factory requesting permission for the construction of an administrative block. "Ah…" said Promyslov, and glancing quickly over the text, proceeded to sign it. "Permission granted". I found the visit a rather depressing experience. We joked for a long time afterwards about the way the decision had been made, but it was enough to get the matter resolved quickly. Granted, the new block never was built, as life forced us to adjust our plans.

THE KGB – THE LAST STRAW

Brezhnev died on 10 November 1982. The appointment of the new General Secretary was a process shrouded in mystery. The matter was decided by a close-knit group of Politburo members without any consideration of the opinion of ordinary Party members. It was well known that the Politburo wanted to nominate Brezhnev's close associate, Chernenko, so as to leave everything unchanged. But the situation in the country had grown so complicated that they were forced to approve Andropov's candidacy. The public became aware of this on the day before Andropov's official election, when he was appointed chairman of the governmental commission in charge of the funeral arrangements. This was standard bureaucratic procedure ahead of the appointment of a new General Secretary. Andropov immediately got to work on trying to restore order in the country. After Brezhnev's death, the Interior Minister Shcholokov resigned and, with the investigation drawing ever closer to his doorstep, committed suicide. The trials of the Moscow trade bosses came to a close. Sokolov, the director of the Yeliseyev Gastronom was executed, while the head of Moscow's chief trade office, Nikolai Tregubov, received a lengthy prison sentence. At Andropov's initiative, the investigation into the notorious "cotton affair" in Uzbekistan was intensified, forcing the leader of the republic, Rashidov, to quit his post.

As I have already said, discipline among medium-level managers and officials had fallen to a low ebb by this time. Many had started using working hours to see to their private affairs. It had become a sort of tradition to arrange meetings at the *banya*, or bathhouse, to discuss important matters with colleagues. Drinking sessions often took place in managerial offices. Andropov initiated a crackdown on such practices. Raids were carried out in shops, at consumer service enterprises or even on the streets of Moscow. Transgressors were arrested and punished. Tip-offs from so-called "well-wishers" would bring the police bursting into offices. They would make regular sweeps of hot spots such as the Sandunovsky and Central Baths. There was a lot of talk about a strong leader who was bringing order back to the country. At first, the public appeared to greet these measures with approval. People had grown fed up of the uncontrolled excesses of the Brezhnev era. As time went on, however, people ceased to take these roundups seriously. The country had moved on, and these primitive ways of imposing order were no longer effective. People had expected the new General Secretary to deliver serious change. There was an urgent need for fundamental reform of the entire system, starting with the Party itself and its Politburo. Since the Party had been hailed from high places as the "organising and directing force of Soviet society", it was only right that it should be held responsible for the stagnation that had enveloped the Soviet Union. But Andropov, though undoubtedly an intelligent and experienced statesman, was not cut out for this task. A glance at his career path should be enough to explain why. A Party worker since 1944, he had played a key role in the crushing of the Hungarian uprising as the Soviet envoy to that country. From 1967 to 1982 he had served as chairman of the KGB.

THE ROT SETS IN

The reshuffles at the top were having no impact at all on the state of the economy. The breakdowns in central planning and administration were exacting a heavy toll. The people learned from Andropov's address to a plenary session of the CPSU Central Committee that the last two five-year-plans had been fulfilled on paper only. Systemic problems were going from bad to worse. The crisis on the country's transport arteries had reached catastrophic proportions, bringing the economy to the brink of collapse. The authorities made no effort to tackle the real causes behind this state of affairs. They put all the blame on enterprise managers.

At first, directors were "called on the carpet" by local Party bodies and public oversight committees. But these standard Party chastisements were no longer effective. The problems had grown too severe, enveloping practically the entire country. Then they came up with the idea of the so-called nationwide "conference calls". These were conducted by government officials together with the USSR Railways Minister. More often than not, it would be the first deputy prime minister, Geidar Aliyev, and the secretary of the CPSU Central Committee, Yegor Kuzmich Ligachev. Local government leaders and enterprise directors who were at fault for the excess detention of freight wagons would be invited to goods stations. The situation on the railways as a whole and on each individual line was scrutinised. Entire trains carrying coal, cement, ballast and numerous other strategic goods stood idle with their loads. The most overloaded stations were contacted and ordered to give explanations. Tough deadlines were set to sort matters out. Reprimands were issued, and sometimes people would even be fired during a call. Time was too short to deal with things properly – it was a big country, after all – which meant that there was little hope of objective treatment. People went into a conference call with no idea of how it would end for them personally. They might end up in hot water through sheer bad luck. How could any of those bigwigs in Moscow have a clue what was really happening at some little railway station? If someone was put on the spot and grilled for explanations, it was known as "falling under the train". If they were not punished straight away, they would be put on probation and would have to meet the deadlines they were given. These nationwide conference calls were hardly likely to change anything in real terms: after all, the crisis was a systemic issue caused by serious deficiencies in the work of government authorities. Rather, it was an intimidation strategy. Nobody wanted to end up a hostage of circumstance. Moreover, it was extremely distressing to receive such a high-level dressing-down in the presence of a large audience – in front of the entire nation, one might say.

Once the Kirghizian tobacco-growing enterprises reached their planned capacity of 70,000 tonnes of raw material, tobacco factories found themselves facing a critical situation over the unloading of freight wagons. The Yava factory had up to 200 wagons standing idle, waiting to be unloaded. This was a disastrous state of affairs. We searched feverishly for a solution.

Our salvation came from an unexpected source in the form of the warehouses of the Lipetsk Procurement Office. This organisation had been established in pre-war times for the procurement of *makhorka* tobacco. Now part of Rosglavtabak, it owned storage facilities in the Lipetsk and Tambov regions. The office's job had been to buy raw *makhorka* from peasant farms, stockpile it, store it, and supply it to factories for processing. After *makhorka* production ended, it was left with the warehouses and a small service staff. In order to somehow get by and earn a crust, it stored random merchandise and various kinds of agricultural produce. The money earned from this was used to maintain the storage premises. Up to now it had seemed a pointless organisation and something of a millstone around the industry's neck.

When the problem over the tobacco deliveries reached a complete impasse, we remembered the Lipetsk Procurement Office, and it became a real lifesaver to the tobacco industry. The Yava factory signed a contract for the storage of raw tobacco, and freight wagons that had arrived in Moscow began to be redirected to the Lipetsk region. The warehouses were in a dreadful condition, with leaking roofs, but the main thing was that we had somewhere to send the tobacco. Then, together with the manager of the office, Alexander Semyonovich Kostin, we set about arranging repairs. This gave us some breathing space. But soon the warehouses were filled to capacity. After all, there were other factories besides Yava sending wagons of tobacco there. The office was refusing to take any more tobacco. Now what would we do?

Usually, the freight wagons would amass at the stations at weekends. The factory would be informed of their arrival on Monday morning. The loads had to be dealt with straight away if we were to avoid ending up on the Moscow-Oktyabrsky railway division's report on excess detention of wagons. The report would go to the city Party committee and the conference call organisers. In both cases the consequences could be very severe. The only thing we could do was persuade the management of the Lipetsk office to accept the cargo. This did not always work out. We had to turn to Kashtanov, the head of the chief directorate, for help. Kashtanov would contact Kostin personally. First, he would try to persuade him, then he would resort to giving orders. Kostin did not want to have freight wagons standing loaded and idle at his end either, but he would cave in under pressure from above. All this negotiating took a great toll on the nerves.

As a last resort, there was one other trick we could use. In especially difficult situations we could try to persuade the railway station management to conceal the arrival of the freight wagons by temporarily sending them to relief tracks about fifty to a hundred kilometres outside Moscow, making sure they were not too conspicuous. The railway referred to this as "laying them up". This way, the wagons did not get put into the report. The catch was that we had to drink far too much vodka with the station chiefs. We really had to go all out. The person in charge of taking delivery of goods at the station was our deputy director, Vladislav Alimurzayevich Khabliyev, a man with a well-developed gift for so-called Caucasian hospitality. He knew how to win people's favour, talk them round. And this was our only chance when it came to resolving issues with the transport agencies. Very often we found ourselves on the brink of major trouble. We acted according to the old adage that "it is up to the drowning man to save himself".

It soon became clear that it was impossible to get very far with dilapidated old wooden warehouses. We had to find more effective arrangements. After discussing things with Rostabakprom, we agreed on a new plan. The Yava factory would build a warehouse complex of easily erected metal structures on a site belonging to the Lipetsk office. There were major advantages when it came to building out in the provinces: as long as there was a site ready to be used, approval could be obtained in virtually no time. We chose the village of Pervomaisky in the Tambov region. We did the building work "in-house",[1] making use of quotas for building materials. As a result, we received a serious amount of new space. We could store over 1,000 more tonnes of tobacco there. Building the new storage premises had become a priority task for the factory's administration. We even sacrificed our own comfort. Instead of the administrative block, we built a modular warehouse facility to store materials.

The saga over the raw tobacco shipments was another bone of contention between the USSR and RSFSR Food ministries. The Russian side took the view that its Union counterpart was scheduling unreasonably high volumes of tobacco shipments. The latter countered that the crisis over the unloading of wagons was all the result of poor planning on the part of the Russian ministry.

---

1   In other words, using our own workers rather than hiring contractors.

With the two government bodies so polarised, there was scant hope of a consensus being reached. And yet the situation could hardly have been clearer. If large deliveries of tobacco were planned, then additional storage facilities would have to be built for the tobacco industry. Since the Soviet Union had a planned economy, it was up to both ministries (each acting within its respective powers) to address this issue head on by allocating financing and quotas for materials, equipment and construction work. Then, after all that was arranged, they could have made enterprise managers responsible for carrying these tasks out. But yet again, enterprises were left to deal with the consequences of government agencies failing to do their jobs because they were guided not by practical considerations, but by personal ambition and attempts to save face.

A good case in point was the meeting at the office of the first deputy minister of the USSR Food Ministry, Kolomiets. He started by hauling the Rosglavtabak chief engineer, Dmitriev, over the coals, demanding explanations as to why there was such a problem in Moscow over unloading tobacco wagons. He spoke rudely and accused Rosglavtabak of shirking its duties. It soon became obvious that Fyodor Stepanovich was not attempting to get to the bottom of things. The whole meeting was an exercise in box-ticking, so that he could say that the issue had been looked at and measures had been taken. Then Kolomiets picked on me. I had only just begun to say my piece when I was interrupted: "Go and write your explanation in written form". Soon after that, the director of Ducat, Filippovsky, also came out to write an explanation. Since it was an issue in need of urgent attention, I quickly wrote a detailed explanation. When we went back in, the meeting had already ended. Fyodor Stepanovich was sitting alone in his office. Silently taking our explanations, he leafed through them and, still without a word, dialled a number on his special government telephone. We realised that the person at the other end of the line was our minister, Chistoplyasov. I can recount what was said almost word for word. "Stepan Ivanovich, I have the directors of Yava and Ducat here with me in the office, and they say that the ministry of the Russian Federation is not providing enough help over the matter of unloading tobacco wagons". A brief pause ensued, then: "All right". And he hung up. Then, addressing us, he said, "Stepan Ivanovich will be expecting you by eight o'clock tomorrow morning", making clear that there was nothing more to be said. We left the office in a state of shock. Without even reading our explanations, Kolomiets had completely distorted their contents. He had, as they say, "passed the buck" to the Russian Food Ministry. The next morning, Valentin Alexeyevich and I were in Chistoplyasov's reception area. The secretary announced us, and a few minutes later Stepan Ivanovich appeared at the door of his office. Without inviting us in, he sent us packing in rather rude terms: "What are you doing here?! If you can't do your jobs, hand in your notice." That was the end of the conversation.

The government had effectively acknowledged its complete inability to tackle the problem head on. We understood this and therefore tried to deal with it in our own way. Increasingly, solutions depended on personal contacts. To avoid production coming to a halt, our people would travel to Leningrad to talk to people there about speeding up the unloading of steamboats and the delivery of imported materials to Moscow. Because of the confusion on the railways, we had to wander around stations ourselves looking for lost freight wagons, literally walking along the tracks. Many other issues had to be dealt with in the same sort of way. And all this went on in the context of what was purportedly a planned economy. The only things we could count on in this situation were our own strength, good production management and the initiative of our employees.

Amid the general dwindling of administrative competence in the country at large, we were more convinced than ever that our policy of putting faith in people was the right one. As before, the workers viewed Yava as their second home, and so if they noticed something amiss, they did not keep it to themselves but openly expressed their opinion and gave their suggestions on how things could be improved in particular areas of work. Their input was an invaluable help to the management and the driver of continuous change. Constructive feedback from the shop floor helped us assess the effectiveness of the activities of the factory's subdivisions. To make life easier for the workers, we decided to establish an Amenity Centre at the factory. Together with the Party secretary we resolved to make a serious effort to get this matter sorted. We went to see the chairman of the Frunzensky district executive committee, Anatoly Afanasyevich Tsybulsky, to seek his assistance. As a result, we were allocated the first two floors of a small building next to the factory grounds. The Centre soon became a lifesaver and a full-fledged subdivision of the factory. The district executive committee arranged for Yava to be registered with the best shops on Gorky Street: the Yeliseyevsky store and the fish and confectionery shops. Every week, each employee could obtain pre-packed assorted food orders through the

Amenity Centre. They could also hand in things to be dry-cleaned and arrange clothing and shoe repairs. The Centre operated for over ten years and protected the factory's employees when scarcities of food and goods were at their worst.

This was a highly productive period. There was a sense of complete mutual understanding among the factory's staff. The arrival of new equipment for the production of filter cigarettes allowed us to increase production and raise performance. Quite by chance, Yava received a very generous gift from the Ducat factory. Evidently to compensate it for the moral damage inflicted by the association, Ducat had been due to receive a new-generation line for the production and packaging of filter cigarettes. Literally at the last moment, just as the line was about to be shipped to Moscow, the Ducat management for some reason decided not to take it. We had no hesitation in accepting it, considering it a great stroke of luck. And the line really did prove to be state-of-the-art machinery in all respects. It was composed of equipment made by two top firms: a Protos cigarette-making machine made by the German firm Hauni and a hard-box packaging machine made by GD (an Italian firm). The line could produce 7,000 cigarettes, or 350 packs, per minute. It was later used by Yava to produce Marlboro cigarettes, and at the end of a successive batch would switch to making hard-pack Kosmos cigarettes. Up to five million cigarettes (250,000 packs) were produced in the course of a day. The line came to play a major part in the factory's overall performance.

In 1983 Yava was declared the winner of the All-Union Socialist Competition. It received top awards: the Transferable Red Banner and the Certificate of Honour of the CPSU Central Committee and the Council of Ministers of the USSR. The competition results were published in *Pravda*. This was a great achievement for the staff. The factory's outstanding results had been achieved thanks to the contribution made by every employee and reflected their initiative and resourcefulness. People at the factory were constantly looking for ways to improve performance. It sometimes happened that practical suggestions were at odds with formal regulations. For instance, installing the new Garant 4 cigarette-making machines meant that we had to decommission some old machines. We obtained permission to write off four Mark 8 machines that had long since reached the end of their useful life. The changeover meant that productivity was lost while the old machines were dismantled and the new ones put in. To help ease the transition, chief foreman Gennady Denisov suggested that two of the

211

written-off Mark 8 machines could be set up in the new location and produce additional output until we got the new lines up and running.

A little while later I was summoned to the USSR Public Oversight Committee. It turned out they had received a tip-off. Some "well-wishers" had signalled that the Yava factory was using written-off equipment to turn out products. This was an illegal way of achieving high production figures and securing awards, bonuses, etc. I had to write an explanation as to why this temporary measure had been necessary. It was fortunate that the Committee had brought Vasily Ivanovich Kopylov into this matter. Formerly an engineer at the Krasnodar Tobacco Factory, he understood how things worked in the industry, so he tried, as far as was possible in that deeply conservative body, to look at problems on their merits and find compromises. Before long, the matter was closed. But the investigation had been a demeaning experience. We were put in the position of having to defend ourselves for finding a way to produce extra output for which there was great demand among smokers. Common sense and practicality were sacrificed to ossified ideological considerations. I remember in this regard that, in 1977, the tobacco industry began producing soft-pack cigarettes with the brand name Iskra (Spark). Quite out of the blue, one of the Old Bolsheviks, i.e. the people who took part in the 1917 October Revolution, voiced his indignation about this. In his view, it was an insult to the memory of the famous eponymous Bolshevik newspaper of the revolutionary period. The CPSU Central Committee sympathised with the opinion of the distinguished veteran and ordered production of the brand to be stopped. Not a thought was given to the fact that a large quantity of materials created specifically for its production lay unused in factory warehouses. Of course, no one had the heart to destroy the specially made packaging labels.

At the beginning of 1984, Andropov died. During the last few months of his life he became seriously ill and had to spend most of the time in hospital. Over the short period in which he was in charge of the country, Andropov managed to open the window in the stuffy room of the Politburo just a crack. An extraordinary plenary session of the Party Central Committee supported the Politburo's proposal to appoint Konstantin Ustinovich Chernenko[1] as General Secretary of the Party. This appointment signified a return to the

---

1 Konstantin Ustinovich Chernenko (1911–1985) served as General Secretary of the CPSU for one year and twenty-five days.

Brezhnevian stagnation that had paralysed the country. Chernenko had never held any significant posts or proved himself in any way before being elected to the Politburo. The sole and decisive distinction in his career was his closeness to Brezhnev. His candidacy presented itself as the most convenient, and the elderly members of the country's highest administrative body were perfectly happy with it. Konstantin Ustinovich was a seriously ill man who possessed no ideas of his own and had not the faintest idea of how to run the country. His appointment reflected the final stage of decay in the highest echelons of power. The people were too tired to take any notice. They didn't even come up with any new jokes.

At a local level, however, Party bodies did not seem unduly anxious about the situation in the country. They carried on organising Party events in grand style. A good example of this was the Frunzensky district Party conference. District Party conferences took place once every four years. They would elect the district Party committee, the internal review committee, and delegates for the municipal Party conference. The Frunzensky district Party conference was scheduled for December 1984, and the *raikom* central office had made meticulous plans for it. The most important thing was to ensure that all production targets in the district were overfulfilled. It so happened that, for various reasons, Yava was struggling to fulfil its plan for November. A large amount of overtime work would be needed to get it fulfilled. We took the view that this was unwarranted: the factory had exceeded planned output in previous months, thus ensuring that the plan for the fourth quarter and the year would be fulfilled. From a management perspective, this decision was perfectly justified, but it was at odds with the parade mentality of the Party bodies. A call came from the *raikom*. "How are things going with the November plan?" I explained our position. The caller replied, "It is unacceptable for the plan not to be fulfilled just before the Party conference. Boris Alexandrovich would not understand you". There ended the conversation. Faced with this blatant threat, there was no option but to take urgent measures to fulfil the November plan, spending significant amounts of money on overtime work. Needless to say, the *raikom's* industrious efforts ensured that all plans were fulfilled and overfulfilled. I have no doubt that wherever the figures fell short, they came to an arrangement with the higher authorities about adjusting them. The high reputation of the Frunzensky district Party committee had to be preserved.

The conference took place in one of the most prestigious buildings in Moscow – the new Moscow Art Theatre (MKhAT) on Tverskoy Boulevard – and was organised with great pomp and ceremony. The Frunzensky district was home to all the central authorities, leading aviation and space firms, theatres and creative unions. The presidium therefore included a number of specially invited celebrities: ministers, marshals and generals, chief designers of air and spacecraft, and leading figures of the arts world. The chests of most of the presidium members seated on the theatre's stage gleamed with the gold stars of Hero of the Soviet Union and Hero of Socialist Labour medals. The conference delegates, chosen from the district's grassroots Party organisations, sat in the stalls. They had been driven to the MKhAT building in nice new imported coaches. During the interval, the same vehicles whisked the delegates off to lunch at the city centre's biggest restaurant – the Novoarbatsky. The numerous invited guests had seats in the balconies.

The conference sessions proceeded smoothly, in strict accordance with procedure. After the summary report read out by the *raikom* first secretary and a speech from the chairman of the internal review committee, the "debate" got underway. The speeches had all been prepared in advance. Throughout the entire duration of the conference, not a single spontaneous thought was aired, not a single topical local issue was raised, there were no differences of views and certainly nothing resembling a real debate. Viewed objectively, it was hard to see why the conference was being held at all. Sitting in the presidium were people ranked considerably above the level of the district Party organisation. They had not the foggiest idea about the problems of the Frunzensky district, and were simply going through the motions, as they say. The congress delegates were not capable of tackling the actual problems facing the district: they had no knowledge of how things really were, and in any case they had been raised in the spirit of unquestioning approval of the "decisions of Party and government". More than anything else, the conference resembled a badly staged show. It was designed to demonstrate the grandeur and power of the *raikom* and of the first secretary himself. Floating above the entire performance in a state of rapture was Boris Alexandrovich Gryaznov – director, scriptwriter, and leading man. This kind of ceremonial, bureaucratic style of administration was entrenched at all levels of the state Party system. Serious, relevant discussions of problems and solutions to the crisis were replaced by pompous events put on by the Party nomenclature. The representatives of the people were there as extras. As and when needed, at a command from the presidium, they would raise their hands or tickets as a sign of approval. The system of rule was further than ever removed from the realities of the country's situation.

In February 1985, Chernenko died. The country was burying its third General Secretary in little more than two years. Chernenko spent the last few months of his life in hospital. No longer able to take part in Politburo meetings, he did nothing more than sign documents. A truly farcical ceremony took place in which the first secretary of the Moscow city Party committee, Grishin, presented Chernenko with an identity card of a deputy of the Supreme Soviet of the RSFSR right there in his hospital ward. The television cameras showed the whole country a totally incapacitated General Secretary, who had to remain seated in his chair to accept the card and could not even put a few coherent words together. As they watched this scene, people did not even feel pity. Rather, they were overcome with a sense of bitterness and anger. How could a man in such a parlous state of health have been chosen as the leader of such an enormous country? Why had he himself agreed to it? The public finally lost all belief in the ability of the authorities to govern the country effectively.

CHAPTER 13.

GORBACHEV'S PERESTROIKA – THE LONG-AWAITED ERA OF CHANGE

Mikhail Sergeyevich Gorbachev was not an especially popular figure in the country at the time, but the appearance of a comparatively young man, a new face, presented at least some hope of change. No one, however, suspected that this appointment would end up turning the life of our vast nation upside down. This new era, which became known throughout the world as perestroika, may without exaggeration be called the brightest period in the history of the USSR. The man who instigated and inspired the sweeping changes was Gorbachev himself, who very accurately identified the primary targets of long-overdue reform. The policies of perestroika (restructuring) and glasnost (openness) were designed to put paid to the worst vices of the Brezhnev era: stagnation and the concealment from the people of the real state of the affairs in the country. The people enthusiastically supported the need for serious changes. If the country was to have any chance of overcoming its profound social and economic crisis, the Party-based, bureaucratic style of administration that had formed in the Brezhnev period would have to be cast aside. Gorbachev began from the very top of the Party. Literally before people's eyes, the Politburo was radically overhauled. One by one, members of the old guard began to shuffle into retirement. With Gorbachev's arrival, the old rule book was thrown out. The General Secretary's wife, Raisa Maximovna, began to appear at his side at official events. Unlike the wives of the previous leaders, she looked really quite modern. People began to talk of the USSR having a "first lady" just like in other countries throughout the world.

The extent to which bureaucratism had penetrated Party-state structures was revealed in the first few months of the perestroika policy. The first victim was the anti-drinking campaign announced by the new leadership. As I have already mentioned, the problem of drunkenness had taken a sharp turn for the worse during the Brezhnev years, and by now had turned into a national calamity. Per capita alcohol consumption had exceeded all previously set records. People drank all over the place: managers in their offices, workers on the shop floor. It was taking a devastating toll on work, demographics and family life. The CPSU Central Committee had been deluged with desperate letters from wives and mothers pleading for urgent measures to be taken, even if it meant introducing prohibition.

In May 1985, the Soviet government passed a decree "On Strengthening the Fight Against Drunkenness and Alcoholism and the Eradication of Moonshining". It brought in severe measures: restrictions on sales of alcoholic drinks, a gradual transition to the consumption of weaker drinks, such as beer and wine, stricter controls, and penalties for drunkenness in the workplace or in public places, as well as for moonshining. The government was willing to accept a drop in budget revenue to achieve its goal of reducing alcohol consumption. Of course, the programme was designed as a long-term strategy and required meticulous work on the part of local authorities with due consideration of regional factors. It was a highly complex problem that demanded coordinated action. However, the way in which it was handled showed the government's complete inability to carry out tasks of national importance. Measures taken to implement the decree amounted to superficial, short-term gestures. Authorities everywhere began closing shops and restricting trading hours, but it was all done so incompetently that it resulted in the formation of huge vodka queues, and the anger of the "afflicted" was directed entirely at the initiators of the anti-drinking campaign, Gorbachev and Ligachev, the secretary of the CPSU Central Committee. The whole thing descended into farce. Why they started laying waste to the vineyards in some of the country's wine-growing regions is a complete mystery. The government decree had spelled out in black and white that people should be encouraged to switch to wine and beer. Whether it was someone's cack-handed way of trying to advance their career, or they wanted to stitch up the people at the top, is impossible to say. The way it turned out was like in the proverb: "Make a fool pray, and he will split his forehead open". In most regions where they had stuck to prohibitive measures, there had already been reports of progress in combating alcoholism.

Despite the perestroika and glasnost policies announced by Gorbachev, Party bodies continued to operate in the same way. The behaviour of our Frunzensky *raikom* was a good case in point. Literally a few months after the decree was issued, Gryaznov decided to gather the top foremen of the district's major enterprises together in his office. It was supposed to be something to do with the campaign against alcoholism and how the situation at enterprises had changed as a result. Having consulted with the factory's Party secretary, we decided to send Gennady Denisov, our top specialist and a sensible fellow. The meeting took place at the end of the working day. The next morning, the entire *raikom* was up in arms. The calls came thick and fast. "Who was that you sent?" "That Yava again!" It turned out that what had happened was this. The meeting had been carefully planned by the central office as a feel-good conversation between the first secretary and the workers. The people who spoke said what Gryaznov wanted to hear. They reported that, since the decree had come out, people were more conscientious, discipline had improved, and no one drank anymore. Boris Alexandrovich was in a good, buoyant mood and listened very attentively. Evidently, he had planned after the meeting to report to the city committee on a job well done. The meeting was just coming to an end when Denisov, Yava's foreman, asked to speak. He turned to the first secretary: "Boris Alexandrovich, I've been listening to all this and feel astonished. You are a serious person. Surely you do not believe everything people have been telling you here? People in Russia have always drunk, still do, and always will." He left it at that. He had gone and spoiled the whole game, as they say. What had promised to be a triumphant meeting had suddenly ended on this flat, gloomy note. I can write about this with a note of humour now, but at the time, it was not funny at all. We expected retaliation from the *raikom*, but it never came. They let the incident slide. Evidently, the course set by the government towards openness had had its effect, and that was why the *raikom* decided not to take it any further. Later, I had a chat with Gennady Mikhailovich and tried to tick him off. He replied, "I'm fed up of all this lying. How much can we take?" There was nothing I could say. Of course, the mutinous foreman was an uncompromising person with a tendency to make harsh judgements. But in essence, he was right. There was no way that this dreadful national scourge could be defeated by some short-term Party campaign.

Major changes began to occur in the administration of the economy. The food industry was one of the first sectors to be affected. Gorbachev had been planning to rebuild the country's food supply system since his days as the Party's agriculture secretary. His approach had been as follows: to unite all food production industries under the command of one large agency. This would help eliminate the bureaucratic barriers that prevented general development problems from getting resolved. Day-to-day administration would be entrusted to local agencies, bringing it as close as possible to actual producers. Since the issue concerned the growing and processing of agricultural produce at local level, this made absolute sense. After becoming General Secretary, Mikhail Sergeyevich returned to this issue. In December 1985, the CPSU Central Committee and the Council of Ministers passed a decree "On the Further Improvement of the Administration of the Agro-Industrial Complex". This replaced the six ministries responsible for agriculture, the food industry, the meat and dairy industry, agricultural machine-building, land development and water supply with a Union-republican industrial committee known as Gosagroprom USSR. The man appointed chairman of the committee was Vsevolod Serafimovich Murakhovsky, the first secretary of the Stavropol regional committee, whom Gorbachev knew from his time working in the Stavropol region. The new agency was very large and had enormous significance for the country, and so the chairman of Gosagroprom was also vested with the status of a first deputy chairman of the government. The task of organising the committee, deciding on its structure and staffing it appropriately presented a colossal challenge.

We were somewhat alarmed when we heard about the creation of the committee. We remembered how things had gone with previous large-scale reorganisations.

Within Gosagroprom RSFSR, the Russian branch of the new committee, the agency responsible for the tobacco industry was Rosglavtabak. After Kashtanov fell seriously ill, chairmanship of the latter was taken over by Vasily Nikolayevich Terevtsev, who had previously been the director of a tobacco factory in Dushanbe, and then first deputy minister of the Food Industry in Tajikistan. Tobacco factories in the Russian Federation were effectively under dual control. Rosglavtabak set plans and allocated resources, while day-to-day management was in the hands of the regional *agroproms* (agro-industrial committees). The exceptions were enterprises in Moscow and Leningrad, which answered wholly to their respective city *agroproms*. Granted, quite a mess was made of setting up the Moscow *agroprom*. It was decided to appoint the former first secretary of the *raikom* of Moscow's Krasnopresnensky district, Fyodor Fyodorovich Kozyrev-Dal, as head of the city *agroprom*. When it came to it, he turned out to be a dyed-in-the-wool Party bureaucrat. Time went on, and the new body had not started working at all. Rumours went around that Fyodor Fyodorovich had surrounded himself with a team of lawyers who were drafting regulations and instructions. The silence went on for quite some time. It seemed that either the new chairman had decided to beaver away quietly in his offices until he had come up with instructions covering every possible eventuality, or he was so afraid of taking charge of matters he knew nothing about that he was creating a semblance of feverish activity. Whatever the truth of the matter, half a year had gone by, and the absence of a supervising body in Moscow could have had a severe impact on the running of enterprises.

Under the influence of the ideas of perestroika and glasnost, fundamental changes were occurring in government policies. First and foremost, these affected the relationship between the government and the people. Gorbachev called for people to be told the truth, for the needs of people to be put first and for the public to be brought into discussions about the country's problems. The press was beginning to play a central role in the country's renewal. After the Politburo passed a crucial decision to relax censorship, the central press was utterly transformed. A lot of hard-hitting, truthful information began to pour out, and the political speeches of the new Party leaders began to be printed in full. This led to a full-scale blossoming of public interest in various facets of the country's life. People would look forward to receiving the next editions of their favourite newspapers and magazines. Early in the morning, queues would form outside newspaper kiosks, and there would already be lively discussions about the latest news. The country was beginning to wake up after the long period of stagnation.

It was the Party nomenclature that stood to lose most from the policies of perestroika and glasnost. Many long years of holding a monopoly on power had led them to consider themselves the undisputed masters of their fiefdoms. After Chernenko's death they had supported Gorbachev's appointment, realising that the country needed change, but no one had expected such a radical turnabout in policy! Party bodies faced the threat of losing their unlimited power. The reaction in some areas of the country was to try to slow the progress of perestroika, while in others it was outright resistance. People inspired by the ideas of perestroika wrote to the Politburo to complain that nothing was happening in their regions, that the leaders there were still stifling criticism and rejecting any sort of dialogue with the public, pretending that everything was fine as it was.

Perestroika within the Party became the main priority. A leading role at national level was played by Moscow's Party organisation, the Moscow City Committee (MCC). In December 1985, Boris Nikolayevich Yeltsin was appointed first secretary of the MCC. He began work in his new post with a large-scale purge of personnel. The very next day, he ordered the chairman of the Moscow Soviet, Promyslov, into retirement. Within a month, he had replaced all the MCC's secretaries. The purge also spread to the committee's central office staff. In the second phase, it was the turn of the *raikom* first secretaries. The process went like this. The city committee set up commissions, which made thorough and aggressive inspections of the work of the *raikoms*, whereupon the findings were delivered to the city committee bureau. Just such an inspection took place in the Frunzensky district. There were rumours that dark clouds were gathering over Gryaznov's head. An article appeared in *Moskovskaya Pravda* (the official press organ of the MCC) criticising the working style of the *raikom* and its first secretary in particular. Gryaznov was accused of authoritarianism and bureaucratism. It was observed that, under his leadership, the *raikom* had cut itself off from the real problems of the people and lost touch with reality. Needless to say, these were distressing times for Gryaznov. The *raikom* itself scaled down its activities. While the inspection was going on and with so much uncertainty in the air, there was little appetite for regular Party work. I therefore found myself going to Gotvald Street a lot less frequently than before. It was quite by chance that, on one such visit, I found myself alone in a lift with Boris Alexandrovich. After all the accusations, it seemed that he was reluctant to use his private lift. I could not help uttering a few words of sympathy. And for the first time, I saw not a high-ranking, arrogant official, but a man in deep suffering. He replied, addressing me with the familiar pronoun for the first time, "You can't imagine what an ordeal this has been for me". By that time, his fate was sealed. Not long afterwards, the city committee bureau held a meeting in which it used identically worded accusations in serving Gryaznov with a strict Party reprimand. It was impossible for his Party career to continue. All that remained was the last stage in the process – the holding of a *raikom* plenary session to relieve the current first secretary of his post and elect a new one. The plenary session took place in the *raikom*'s Large Hall. Gryaznov gave an address. He looked fairly confident. Evidently, he had managed to pull himself together. His speech left me dumbfounded. I had never heard such brazen Party demagoguery.

It went something like this: "Fellow Communists! The city committee bureau has quite rightly made stern criticisms of my work. Yes, indeed, I went down the path of bureaucratism and grew out of touch with the people and real life. My style of leadership began to bear attributes of authoritarianism". Thus, he repeated word for word the accusations that had been levelled at him. Then, however, Boris Alexandrovich made an unexpected volte-face. "Yes, I fully acknowledge my mistakes, but I must declare that you, fellow Communists, are also to blame for what happened to me! You failed to point it out to me on time (?) and criticise me (?) for going in the wrong direction". And how, exactly, would that have worked? Never in my life had I encountered such elaborate self-righteousness. After the opening part of his speech, which had been the purpose of convening the plenary meeting, Gryaznov formally reported the results of the *raikom's* activities and requested his fellow Communists to relieve him of his post. The plenum unanimously granted his request and elected as their new leader Vyacheslav Ivanovich Terentyev, who had previously held the position of second secretary of the Frunzensky *raikom*.

The purge of Moscow officials won support among the public. It was certainly true that Muscovites had felt irritation at the Party bureaucrats with their lavish privileges, and a change of personnel was needed, but the methods by which it was carried out raised certain doubts. The majority of Moscow's *raikom* first secretaries were replaced. Some saw this as a former provincial leader wielding his axe against the big city Party elite. Yeltsin, people said, was "busting asses" in the old provincial Party style. Not everyone made it through this traumatic time. The head of the Kiev *raikom*, a highly cultured man by the name of Korovitsyn, committed suicide by hurling himself from the window of the *raikom* building.

Boris Nikolayevich immediately showed himself to be a tough, decisive leader. When it came to light that the process of the creation of the Moscow *agroprom* had been unreasonably delayed and this might lead to food supply problems in the capital, he fired the man responsible, Kozyrev-Dal. To set things back on the right track, he asked Yury Mikhailovich Luzhkov[1] to take over the new agency. At the time, Luzhkov had a high-ranking post as first deputy chairman of the Moscow Soviet (the city council). He had a wide range of responsibilities and was overburdened as it was. But he could not say no to Yeltsin, to whom he owed his position of power. After his appointment to Moscow Boris Nikolayevich

---

1 Yury Mikhailovich Luzhkov (1936–2019) – Mayor of Moscow from 1992 to 2010.

had been about to set off on a business trip and needed an expert chemist as part of his accompanying team. The Minister of the Chemical Industry, Kastandov, recommended Yury Mikhailovich Luzhkov, who was head of the ministry's science and technology department. Yury Mikhailovich must have made quite an impression on that short business trip. On returning to Moscow, Yeltsin had made him first deputy chairman of the Moscow Soviet. Luzhkov immediately got down to business. The *agroprom* was set up and began work in double quick time. Luzhkov showed exceptional capabilities from the very start: breathtaking efficiency, great alertness and an ability to identify where the main problems lay. He would personally drop in on the city's enterprises and other industrial facilities on a daily basis. His working day began early in the morning and ended late in the evening with hardly a break. The bureaucratic style of management was not his thing at all. Often, when he was unable to meet Mosagroprom [First mention of this – presumable this is the Moscow *agroprom*, but perhaps a definition is needed?] colleagues in person, he would go through the relevant paperwork in the late hours and dictate instructions into a tape recorder. In the morning, his deputies would listen to the recordings and begin work. He acquired a fine grasp of the problems of the food industry, which was a new field for him, and tackled them head on. This very quickly earned him the respect of directors of Moscow enterprises.

By this time, changes had started to occur in the methods of economic administration. Gorbachev was an advocate of decentralisation and the handing of greater independence over economic and industrial matters to local authorities and enterprises themselves. Restructuring the administration of the agro-industrial complex had been the first step in this direction. The next step in increasing independence was the passing of the law "On State Enterprises and Associations" at the June 1987 plenary session of the CPSU Central Committee. Under the new law, enterprises would begin operating according to three main principles: cost accounting, self-financing and self-management of the workforce. Cost accounting set clear rules regarding an enterprise's relationship with the state. Self-financing gave enterprises a greater motive to increase production and raise efficiency. All money earned after the payment of dues to the government and the bank could be put into developing production, paying salaries and meeting social needs. Moreover, the limits on the use of an enterprise's funds were largely removed. Self-management increased the role and responsibility of the enterprise's workforce and each individual worker. The quantity of targets set by the centre was reduced to a minimum. Gosplan and the ministries gave enterprises only one target figure – the "state order". This was the quantity of products that an enterprise was required to produce for the state. Aside from the state order, enterprises were free to enter into contracts with other customers and set prices for the goods they produced. This was a colossal change! The absence of such rights had previously held manufacturers back from showing initiative and using reserve potential to earn additional income. The customer-producer relationship was made much more flexible. As it happened, enterprise directors tended to favour high state orders, as it meant they had guaranteed supplies of material resources and a guaranteed market for their output, ensuring greater stability.

State policy also swung in favour of satisfying the needs of the population. Enterprises would now report the provision of paid services to the public in a separate line in their accounts. This was another complete about-turn. Previously, enterprises had not had the right to use their resources even to help their own employees. We had done this in extreme cases, resorting to all sorts of tricks. The authorities had been afraid of state resources being frittered away. It had got quite absurd. After the new law came out, the state actually encouraged the use of enterprises' spare resources to render services to the public, such as renovating apartments or hiring out vehicles for personal use. It made these activities legal. The volume of production of consumer goods was also reported separately in accounts. Under the new approach, the state began to encourage the production of consumer goods at enterprises for which this was not a core activity. Enterprises in various sectors began to look for ways to produce goods for the people using their know-how and reserves of time and material resources. For example, machine-building enterprises began making metal implements for housework, gardening and car maintenance, prefabricated garages, and so on. Various kinds of household products made of plastic began to appear. Figures for consumer goods and consumer services became important in assessing enterprises' performance and were monitored by Party bodies.

Workers were a handed a major role in the running of enterprises. The workers' meeting became the highest governing body. Under the law, the director of an enterprise was elected by the workers' meeting for a term of five years. This rule caused a lot of differences of opinion: could the workers be trusted to make the right decision based on practical considerations? Many people thought that this put enterprise directors in the undesirable position of being dependent on the opinion of employees. On the other hand, the candidate nominated by the meeting had to be approved by a higher organisation, meaning that a dialogue could then take place between the workers and the supervising government agency until a compromise was reached. At Yava, the law on state enterprises was greeted with enthusiasm. The workers were ready for the new working arrangements and for the changes in relationships both with state bodies and within the enterprise. The policy of developing the role of the workers and extending their influence over important decisions had already been pursued at the factory for quite some time. As a result, the enterprise already had mature team leaders who were ready for the new challenges.

With the country still suffering from shortages of tobacco products, maintaining adequate supplies of cigarettes remained one of the government's strategically important objectives. For this reason, the state order assigned to tobacco factories amounted to 100 per cent of the annual production plan. Naturally, it all went under the heading of "Consumer goods". The situation was much the same for the overwhelming majority of food enterprises. The challenges involved in keeping such a gigantic city supplied with food were complex and varied. A major problem arose over supplies of imported foodstuffs. Since the Moscow *agroprom* was responsible for all these issues, it did not have the time to micromanage individual enterprises. The director had to be relied on to keep things running. No one interfered in day-to-day operations unless, of course, major problems arose. Enterprises drew up their own plans and did whatever was necessary to implement them. Twice a year, the factory's performance was examined by Mosagroprom's review board. The board's decisions reflected its appraisal of the enterprise's work. As director, I also felt more secure. I was elected by the workers' meeting. Mosagroprom concluded a contract with me for five years. I enjoyed a respectful, business-like relationship with *agroprom* officials and there was a clearer division of power and responsibilities. The chief problem was over supplies of imported materials. The *agroprom* was responsive to our requests for assistance and immediately set about resolving the issue. If necessary, letters to higher authorities would be signed by Luzhkov as the first deputy chairman of the Moscow Soviet.

Generally speaking, that did the trick. All in all, the changes taking place in the way industry was managed were heading in the right direction and made for greater efficiency.

THE IDEAS OF PERESTROIKA FLY IN THE FACE OF PARTY POLICY

The country was going through cardinal changes in all areas of life. Sacred taboos that had been central to CPSU policy were crumbling. Gorbachev advanced new ideas about international relations, which he called "new thinking". This involved acknowledging that the world community was one and interrelated, rejecting ideological confrontation, and approving common human values. These principles were in complete contradiction to the international doctrine of the previous Soviet leadership about the inevitability of political and ideological confrontation between two global systems. In terms of specific steps to reduce international tensions, the Politburo made a very important decision to withdraw Soviet troops from Afghanistan and put an end to that senseless, unpopular and economically damaging war that had cost the lives of tens of thousands of young men. Talks began with the leaders of the United States and other major countries about specific steps to limit all kinds of weaponry.

Internally, the ideas of democracy and openness were evolving at pace. A key factor in the development of these important political trends was played by the decision to curb censorship. Fictional works and historical and philosophical literature that had previously been prohibited now began to be published. Books appeared that poured light on the abuses that had occurred during the period of Stalin's cult of personality and spoke the truth about collectivisation, the pre-war repressions and the tragedy of the Great Patriotic War. A revolution occurred in the most popular mass medium – television. People were literally glued to their screens when programmes such as *Vzglyad* (Outlook), *Before and After Midnight* and *600 Seconds* came on air, live and uncensored. Important decisions were made about giving citizens personal freedom and extending opportunities for individual enterprise. At the end of 1986, the law "On Individual Work Activity" was published. This allowed people to engage in private enterprise and establish cooperatives – things that had previously been treated as criminal offences. In the same year, the rules regarding private travel into and out of the USSR were relaxed. The change in foreign policy doctrine opened up new opportunities to expand forms of economic and technical cooperation with foreign countries. Laws were passed to back this up. First, by way of an experiment, a number of ministries and enterprises were permitted to enter the export market directly and form joint ventures. At the beginning of 1987, the Presidium of the Supreme Soviet issued an edict "On Matters Relating to the Establishment in the Territory of the USSR and Activities of Joint Ventures, International Associations and Organisations with the Participation of Foreign Organisations, Firms and Management Bodies". In effect, therefore, the three key pillars on which Soviet policy had once rested – total censorship, the prohibition of any kind of free enterprise and a monopoly on foreign trade – had begun to be toppled.

The democratisation of public life fostered the practice of open debate, even among members of the previously monolithic Politburo. This helped raise the standing of particular Party leaders among the population. Besides Gorbachev, these included Ryzhkov, Shevardnadze, Yakovlev and Ligachev. Yeltsin began to win more and more popularity. He actively called for the complete renunciation of Party privileges and for swift and decisive measures to reform the Party apparatus. These initiatives were supported by the public. Party privileges had become one of the thorniest issues of the day. The Party elite had literally set itself apart from the people, receiving supplies through special distributors, living at exclusive, fully serviced dachas, having their children educated at elite colleges, and being sent on trips abroad through the Foreign Affairs or Foreign Trade ministries. The situation was aptly summed up by a cartoon in a popular Western magazine, showing a trolleybus crammed with people, some even riding on the footplates, and alongside it a private Volga in which some big boss is lounging on the back seat. The caption read "Masters of the country and their servant".

Boris Nikolayevich Yeltsin pushed hard for the abolition of privileges for the Party apparatus. He made numerous visits to factories, talked to workers and became one of the most public politicians in the country. I remember a meeting in which Yeltsin addressed Moscow's industrial executives. It took place in the recently constructed building of the Political Education Centre of the Moscow Committee of the CPSU, situated on the corner of Tsvetnoy Boulevard and Trubnaya Square. The directors of Moscow's enterprises were interested in what

Boris Nikolayevich was doing, but also wary. They thought that he was crossing a line, winning artificial authority with populist rhetoric. Before the meeting, a rumour flew around that there had been an instruction to note down the numbers of directors' private cars in the car park next to the Political Education Centre. This was unlikely, of course. But what if...? There was no telling what the Party committee would do with the information. So everyone agreed to send their cars away as soon as they arrived. The subject of the meeting was "The Challenges for Moscow Industry". After a few inconsequential speeches, Yeltsin took the floor. His delivery was a far cry from the plodding, formulaic addresses of his predecessor, Grishin. He genuinely engaged with his audience, sometimes even in a rather eccentric way, which caused laughter and animation in the hall. The speech lasted around three hours. Boris Nikolayevich devoted a lot of time to the issue of restructuring the work of Party and administrative organs and, of course, to his favourite subject – the eradication of privileges. He said that he himself travelled to work on public transport, shopped at ordinary stores and wore Bolshevichki suits and shoes from the Skorokhod factory. At this point, he gracefully stuck out a foot, clad in a Soviet-made shoe, from behind the rostrum. He said nothing specific regarding the subject of the meeting. I only remember that everyone was very tired after sitting in the hall for over five hours. I left feeling somewhat uneasy. Yeltsin's speech had made an ambivalent impression. What he had said seemed fair enough as far as it went, but there had been little substance. There was no public transport running, so I walked briskly towards Sverdlov Square. I managed to call home from the vestibule of the metro station so as not to cause any worry. My wife was a little suspicious: meetings of that sort had never gone on so late before.

The liberalisation of legislation created opportunities for entrepreneurial activity. The law "On State Enterprises and Associations" permitted this. Besides the obligatory state order, resources could be used to produce additional output under direct contracts with customers. This especially affected engineering works. Their process structures meant that they had reserve capacity in certain departments. Implementing the new systems meant having to change the way production was organised and plans were formed. It required a gradual movement towards market relations and, most importantly, a change in the mentality of people who, over long years of Soviet rule, had been dispossessed of real initiative and were accustomed to acting only on instructions from above.

Management staff were completely unprepared for the new changes. They had all been brought up on the sanctity of the planned economy, and these crutches were not easy to give up. The distribution of material resources remained in the hands of state agencies, but the state only guaranteed the supplies needed to meet the state order. The government issued a decree on the development of wholesale trade, but the shortage of resources in the country meant that it had no real effect.

There is no doubt that the authorities supported the creation of cooperatives. In Moscow it was Luzhkov who looked after this area. His high status meant that he could give real assistance to would-be founders of cooperatives – or "cooperators", as they were known. It is well known that Yury Mikhailovich devoted much attention to this matter. He often received visitors until late at night and set many of the country's prominent businessmen on the road to success. It was something new, there were many doubts, and attitudes within society varied – sometimes wary, sometimes downright hostile. This form of activity went against the ideas that had been instilled in Soviet people from birth. But the cooperative system specifically attracted people who were psychologically prepared for entrepreneurial activity. It effectively gave rise to a new social group who lived by completely different principles. Yury Mikhailovich himself was a new kind of leader – a pragmatist, unblinkered by ideological taboos. He came to Mosagroprom with the intention of changing the system. His work in reorganising Moscow's vegetable warehouses achieved particular resonance. The story of these facilities was perhaps the most classic example of the formalistic, bureaucratic management style of Party bodies.

The supply of fruit and vegetables to Moscow's population was viewed as a political concern. Over a short period of time (two to three months), produce had to be delivered, processed and put into storage so that there would be enough until the next harvest. The problem was exacerbated by the critical state of the agricultural sector, which was no longer able to supply the country with good-quality produce. The authorities would not allow quantities supplied to the capital to fall below the planned levels, but they turned a blind eye to quality. Produce would in most cases arrive in a dreadful state, piled up any old how with no regard to standards. A lot of it had to be thrown away. The busy season would approach for the Moscow authorities. The way the work was organised, the limited permanent staff of the warehouses could not cope with the job of processing the produce received. Responsibility for this matter lay with the Party bodies, and their customary modus operandi was not to organise, but to mobilise. There were no problems in this regard. As they saw it, the city's enterprises, and especially the research and design institutes, had large reserves of workers. Even if some design institute had to close for a couple of months, it wouldn't really matter. And so the job of vegetable procurement was done en masse using labour drafted from enterprises and organisations. The number of workers mobilised each day ran into the thousands. This was a big problem for enterprise managers – but just try not to do as you were told!

The Frunzensky *raikom* was in charge of the Rostokino vegetable warehouse. We sent workers there every year, so we had a good idea of how things really were. A greater shambles would be hard to imagine! People stood sorting vegetables in cold, ill-equipped premises without any facilities. Labour efficiency was extremely low, the disregard for so-called state property was shocking, and the losses were colossal. It was as if the warehouse management was in no way responsible for organising the work. There was no supervision. The *raikom* took a narrow view of its own role: to provide the required quantity of people. Evidently, Party bodies in rural areas took a similar approach to the administration of agriculture. The losses in terms of squandered produce and wasted working hours of the people drafted in were incalculable. But what did any of that matter to the people in charge of the warehouses? The drafted workers even continued to be paid by the very enterprises who provided them. This meant there were no real incentives to ensure that work was organised efficiently. The lack of proper supervision meant that it was easy to conceal the huge losses and growing thefts of produce. As a result, the state incurred significant losses and people got used to seeing poor-quality vegetables in their shops. The conditions in which people were forced to work at the vegetable warehouses were extremely degrading. Just one look at how work was organised there was enough to inspire loathing towards the existing Party regime.

When Luzhkov declared that he would reorganise the system and end the practice of drafting people out to the vegetable warehouses within six months, people scoffed at first. To everyone's surprise, Yury Mikhailovich was as good as his word. The main problem was that the warehouse staff were not motivated to improve the results of their work. As always, the authorities kept stepping on the same rake. Yury Mikhailovich managed to get the Moscow city executive committee to set realistic spoilage allowances. All revenue from sales of produce saved from spoilage could be used to pay bonuses to the warehouse workers. Wages were significantly increased. This completely turned the situation around. While giving Yury Mikhailovich his due, it must be said that this bold solution was only made possible by the policies of perestroika. After all, it completely flew in the face of Party dogma. That is why the USSR Public Oversight Committee proceeded to accuse Luzhkov of acting illegally in changing the officially prescribed allowances. They seemed to think that the state making colossal losses on the vegetable bases was the way things should be. Times had changed, and nothing came of their complaints, but Yury Mikhailovich, a proud and ambitious man, always bore a grudge against the Oversight Committee.

Despite the profound changes occurring in the country and society, there was no visible breakthrough in the economy. There were objective reasons for this. Industry was still centrally managed by the same bureaucratic agencies: Gosplan and the ministries. Resource quotas were allocated by Gossnab. Enterprise managers and staff had been raised under the Soviet system of administration. A close look at the law "On State Enterprises and Associations" shows that managers and workers are given extensive powers to carry out restructuring, dispose of assets, prepare plans and expand the range of goods produced and types of activity carried out. But the commanding heights of industry administration remained in the hands of conservative ministries. After giving enterprises broader rights, what was then needed was to reform the entire system of economic administration on a countrywide scale. Moreover, to make such serious changes it was necessary to change people's mentality. And that took time – it was not something that could be achieved overnight. A series of adverse external circumstances pushed the economic situation in the USSR further into decline. The price of oil suddenly dropped to eight dollars a barrel, and oil revenue was the country's only significant source of hard currency. On 26 April 1986, a major manmade disaster occurred: the explosion and fire at the Chernobyl nuclear power plant. Besides the enormous psychological shock, dealing with its aftermath required substantial material and human resources and significant financial inputs. The impact of this was felt above all in the state of the consumer market. It became more difficult to buy food and goods from abroad. Meanwhile, people's spending power had, on the contrary, increased. In an effort to raise labour productivity, the government had lifted restrictions on wages. There were pay increases across the board, but this did not directly translate into increased production. More cooperatives and youth technology centres had begun to be set up. These new organisations received the right to cash out funds held in their accounts without restrictions, which further increased the amount of spare cash in public hands. All this aggravated the old problem of the shortage of goods available to buy. Because of the deteriorating foreign trade balance, the state placed restrictions on purchases of new technology and equipment from abroad. The government attempted to balance these substantial losses by declaring a conversion programme. The abatement of the arms race made it possible for defence enterprises to be partially converted to manufacturing equipment for civilian industries, and first and foremost for the food processing and meat and dairy industries, which worked entirely with imported equipment. The defence industries were the country's pride and joy. They were thought to be equal to any task. It turned out that the picture was a little more complicated. In actual fact, defence enterprises, like the rest of industry, were behind the West in terms of technology. Furthermore, food processing equipment had its own uniquely complex features. Western firms, with their many years of experience, had achieved a high level of sophistication in the design and manufacture of such machines. This was not something that could be copied in a flash. When a group of specialists from the Ministry of Medium Machine-Building came to visit the Yava factory, they took one look at the supreme sophistication of the cigarette-making equipment and just threw up their arms. And thank goodness! Because in those industries in which the conversion programme began to operate, a lot of time and effort was frittered away with no end result. All this dispelled the myth of the all-powerful Group A defence sector and the "primitive" Group B food industry.[1]

The June plenary session of the Central Committee, aimed at reforming the economy, laid bare the substantial differences of opinion in the highest echelons of power. Gorbachev took a more radical stance. He called for a decisive break with the command-administrative system and a gradual transition towards market mechanisms. The chairman of the government, Ryzhkov, was in favour of carrying out economic reforms within the framework of the Soviet system of administration. Ryzhkov's proposals were aimed at streamlining the Union

---

1 This does not contradict the fact that Soviet weaponry had excellent operational characteristics. It was just that it was manufactured at tremendous cost.

government, scaling down its functions in regulating enterprises and reducing the administrative levels involved in the running of industries. Only the core industries would remain under the direct control of the USSR government, while those industries that fulfilled social roles – consumer goods, the agro-industrial complex, and construction – would be administered at republic level. The number of ministries in the centre and in the republics would be reduced. As another step towards giving enterprises more independence, it was proposed that the chief directorates within the ministries should be abolished.

A fierce battle erupted within the Politburo and the Central Committee around these ideas. The public, too, was actively involved in the debate. Articles by commentators and eminent economists appeared in the central press. I remember an article by the academician Shatalin, who supported a decisive transition to the market. The introduction of market mechanisms was, of course, essential, but the idea of suddenly demolishing a colossal administrative system and leaving enterprises face-to-face with new market conditions was extremely dangerous. This was why, as Gorbachev later reasoned, a compromise decision was reached. The law on state enterprises and associations became a key document. On the matter of reforming the economic system, the more conservative proposals of the Soviet government were adopted. It was decided to carry out reforms gradually over 1988–1989. Of great importance was Gorbachev's instruction that Party committees should not interfere in the day-to-day running of enterprises. While opting for a relatively cautious approach to the reform of the state economy, the government at the same time decided to encourage enterprises in the cooperative movement, on which all restrictions were removed. In February 1987, the Council of Ministers issued a decree "On the Establishment of Cooperatives for the Production of Consumer Goods". This was followed in May 1988 by the adoption of the law "On Cooperative Societies in the USSR", which permitted cooperatives to engage in any kinds of activity, including trade.

POSITIVE CHANGES IN REAL LIFE AND THE FIRST SERIOUS PROBLEMS

Real life in the country was changing by the day. This was especially palpable in relationships between enterprises and government authorities. Our Frunzensky *raikom* had likewise changed its manner of dealing with enterprise managers: rather than giving them instructions, it invited them for discussions. The influence of Party organisations at enterprises had declined: workers' councils had now taken over the leading role. These tendencies were quickly picked up on by our foreign partners – suppliers of materials and equipment. The country was desperately short of hard currency. The purchase of equipment from abroad had all but ceased, and money to buy materials was allocated irregularly. Foreign trade associations were bereft of funds and unable to conclude contracts as and when required. Standard state procedures did not work. The Yava factory often found itself on the brink of having to stop work. We wrote letters to the government bearing Luzhkov's signature. The authorities feared that the shutdown of such a strategically important enterprise could spell disaster and usually allocated funds on a targeted basis. Consequently, foreign managers arriving in Moscow would now make Yava their first port of call, having realised that funding issues could be dealt with more quickly through the factory's management. Foreign firms, having already witnessed transitions from state-controlled to private economies in other countries, understood that the path that the Soviet Union had embarked on would sooner or later lead to denationalisation. They therefore began to focus heavily on developing contacts with industrial enterprises.

Luzhkov paid close attention to Moscow's tobacco factories. He understood how important it was to keep Moscow supplied with tobacco products. The situation was very precarious. There were times when a lack of materials made it difficult to avoid a shutdown of production. Supplies of our most popular product, soft-pack Yavas, were particularly acutely affected. We looked for all sorts of ways to increase production. The factory produced long cigarettes that had never really found regular buyers. In an effort to rectify the situation, we had done some experimenting. Alongside Yava-100 cigarettes we had launched new brands of long cigarettes (for example, with a mint flavour). The cigarettes did sell, of course, but they did not go far towards satisfying smoker demand. Then we had the idea of reconfiguring the line to produce 80 mm cigarettes so that we could start using it to counter the shortage of soft-pack Yavas. This involved replacing a large number of components in the cigarette-making and packing machines. We asked for a quotation, and Hauni replied that it would be prepared to supply the required components for 70,000 dollars. I took this offer to Luzhkov, who gave his approval. We decided to apply to the foreign trade bank, Vneshtorgbank, for a loan. The loan would be taken out by the factory, and Luzhkov would arrange for the Moscow Soviet executive committee to stand as guarantor. Of course, this was a revolutionary solution at that time. I do not know whether we were the first enterprise to apply to a state bank for a hard currency loan, but it was certainly a completely new practice. I remember taking Luzhkov's letter of approval to the all-powerful chairman of the Moscow Planning Committee (Gorplan), Bystrov. He and Luzhkov were rivals at the time. He put up a long fight against giving us the guarantee, thinking up reasons to refuse. In the end, however, we received the loan, and a few months later we were able to supply substantially greater quantities of soft-pack Yava cigarettes to the trade network. Of course, an arrangement of this kind, such a novelty for the Soviet economy, was only possible thanks to perestroika. The idea of an enterprise obtaining a hard currency loan by itself and signing a contract directly with a foreign firm would have been virtually inconceivable not long before. Perestroika had destroyed the old stereotypes. The loan proved highly effective, which was again in contrast to the practices of the stagnation era, when blundering decisions about multi-million-dollar projects would be made by people in the lofty reaches of the Party-state system.

Securing hard currency allocations was a major problem in that period. Luzhkov understood this and did what he could to help the factory. With the aim of bringing government agencies on board, he visited the factory together with the deputy chairman of the Union-level *agroprom*, Yury Alexeyevich Borisov, who oversaw the use of currency funds. Yury Alexeyevich was a heavy smoker who only smoked hard-pack Yava cigarettes. During his tour of the factory he showed a great interest in the workings of the manufacturing process. When we were inspecting the primary processing section, I pointed out to him that the lack of modern drying equipment worsened the quality of cigarettes and reduced efficiency. If we spent a million dollars or so on buying a drum dryer, the potential economic benefit would repay the investment several times over. Borisov, as a long-standing smoker, understood the problem well, but he responded by lamenting about the difficulties with hard currency. Since the atmosphere was benevolent, I decided to come out with a rebellious idea: to secure the hard currency through re-exports. Every year, the Yava factory received large quantities of Virginia tobacco from India. The tobacco was supplied on a compensation basis against India's debt to the Soviet Union. Indian tobacco was in high demand on the global market and could be sold for hard currency. So why not sell some of the Indian tobacco and use the hard currency proceeds to buy equipment? Under the right circumstances it would be possible to achieve a significant economic benefit from re-exports. In the Soviet Union, even raising such an idea was "politically immature". But times had changed. With Borisov's support we received official permission to sell 200 tonnes of raw tobacco and use the proceeds to buy equipment. It was an unexpected triumph. The right to arrange the deals was granted to the enterprise directly. We engaged the foreign trade associations Raznoexport and Soyuzplodimport to handle the export-import operations. Now, however, they acted not as state agencies, but as contractors for the Yava factory. Of course, there was a lot of hard, unfamiliar work for the Yava management to do before we received a spanking new drum dryer made by the British firm, Dickinson. I should add that, since it was eager to supply its equipment to Yava, Dickinson itself arranged for the Indian tobacco to be bought from the Soviet party by the major international tobacco supplier Standard Commercial. All that Raznoexport had to do, therefore, was agree on a few details and draw up a competently worded agreement. There were quite a few dramas during this process. I remember our chief tobacco specialist flying to Arkhangelsk at the very last stage. The physical handover of the tobacco to representatives of the foreign firm took place right there in the port, and the relevant documents were drawn up. That was when we knew that the deal was done. I am grateful to Yury Alexeyevich Borisov, an excellent fellow and a truly principled leader. We had cause to seek his assistance on a number of occasions after that, and he always gave us his support.

Of course, these changes in state policy were only made possible by perestroika. The interdictions of the state-Party system, along the lines of "that cannot be done because it can never be done", had been jettisoned. That approach had resulted in the total loss of rational economic thinking, which now had to be revived. On this occasion, by giving up 200 tonnes of tobacco (little more than 1 per cent of its annual requirement), the factory had improved the quality of its cigarettes and saved a significantly greater quantity of raw material.

The law "On State Enterprises" allowed more contributions to be made to enterprises' funds. This created much greater opportunities for granting incentives to workers and making use of social funds. The factory introduced new social schemes. For instance, interest-free loans would be issued for workers to buy housing, carry out home improvements, and so on. All these benefits would be linked to the performance of an individual employee and the workforce as a whole. The workers' council played a major role in decisions about the distribution of funds. It was important to ensure transparency and openness in the way that funds were used. These new schemes changed the mindset of our employees. They began to see that a lot depended on how well we worked, that we could make our own decisions about how to use the money we earned. People felt invested in the business, which is why, thanks to the initiative and professionalism of the workers, so much was achieved during that period in terms of improving production. New principles of enterprise management began to come into play. For the first time in many long years, people felt a renewed sense of self-identity and self-respect.

The cooperative movement provided real opportunities to show business initiative. People could establish a cooperative themselves or get a job in one. They carried on all kinds of activities. Cooperatives were given much greater freedom of operation and serious financial incentives, which the authorities hoped would boost the production of goods and the provision of consumer services. As a rule, however, the cooperatives did not have production facilities, and creating them required significant amounts of money and time. The law was then changed to allow state-owned enterprises to use cooperative forms of management, while cooperatives could rent premises and equipment from enterprises. These decisions helped expand opportunities for the development of cooperatives, but they also had certain negative consequences. Enterprise managers began artificially converting individual departments into cooperatives for the sole purpose of securing financial benefits. The activities of these cooperatives were wholly dependent on the managers of the enterprise. Conflicts of interest often arose over the leasing of equipment and premises to cooperatives.

After giving greater freedom to cooperative businesses, the state found itself facing a whole new set of problems. It became difficult to monitor how cooperatives used the money they earned. With the removal of restrictions on employment, earnings soared, which in turn swelled the spending power of the public. The state had to adapt to the new circumstances. Of course, it was much simpler to manage the economy through strict regulation, but the stagnation period had shown that this was a dead-end approach. Joint ventures had similar rights to use the proceeds of their activities, only they could do foreign trade deals as well. At first, joint ventures with foreign firms were set up by ministries and large industrial concerns under state control. They were designed to attract Western technology and investments into specific industries. Soon, however, this form of cooperation began to expand. Enterprising people started setting up joint ventures out of nothing. They would find partners abroad with a view to making advantageous financial deals. Often, they were insufficiently qualified to handle serious matters, but they fulfilled contracts without the foot-dragging that was typical of state institutions. For that reason, enterprises began to go through such firms to make purchases abroad with their own money. For example, enterprises were allowed to use their own funds to buy foreign appliances such as televisions and video cassette recorders as incentives for their workers. These things could not be bought domestically. The joint ventures turned their hands to all kinds of work. There were no administrative levers of control over their activities, while tax levers had yet to be created.

Granting freedom of enterprise had led to the state losing much of its control over the use of money. This gave the Party bureaucracy and conservative officials a pretext to identify Gorbachev's reforms as the cause of the crisis that had taken hold in the consumer goods market. In fact, the severe financial and economic crisis was a consequence of centralised methods of economic administration. Over the long years of the Brezhnev era of stagnation, the country had become uncompetitive, incapable of independent development and wholly dependent on foreign supplies. Engineering works that made equipment for the consumer goods, food processing and meat and dairy industries had fallen by the wayside. These industries now depended on imports for their equipment and most of their materials. Nothing had been done to develop domestic research in the area of new technology. As a result of the Party's ruinous agricultural policies, many agricultural commodities were purchased abroad, including grain, meat, butter and milk. During Brezhnev's reign the Soviet Union had become firmly hooked on foreign supplies. Only the decrepit Politburo had ventured to talk about the "progressive advance" of the Soviet economy. The truth was that the complete stagnation had resulted from the Communist Party's absolute monopoly on power in the country. On becoming General Secretary, Gorbachev, as a convinced Communist, had hoped to achieve results by reforming the Party. However, he soon came to understand that advanced countries had achieved their high level of development through democratic political systems and free market relations in their economies. Gorbachev was the first leader of the USSR to decide upon a course that had once seemed impossible: stepping over Party ideological dogma, he began the process of democratising the political system and liberalising the economy. At the January 1987 plenary session of the CPSU Central Committee, Gorbachev proposed the radical reform of the country's political system. Real power would be transferred to the soviets. The CPSU would abandon the executive functions that were not appropriate for a party and transform itself from a monopolistic state structure into a political party. A key turning point was the decision to hold alternative national elections to the local soviets, or Councils of People's Deputies. This deprived the Party of its monopoly and opened up a path to power for new people, talented and worthy individuals. Members of the CPSU would have to prove their right to remain in power through free elections. It was astonishing how Gorbachev managed to drive through decisions which effectively destroyed the basic pillars of Party policy. He was helped in this by the traditional Party approach to decision-making whereby proposals made from above were unanimously supported. That said, there was growing opposition among Central Committee members to the ideas of perestroika. Open criticism began to be directed at the General Secretary, and that, in the context of a rigid Party hierarchy, was dangerous.

The most vociferous support for perestroika came from the intelligentsia, for whom, after all, freedom had always been an essential condition of fruitful activity and the goal of spiritual endeavour. The policy of glasnost and freedom of the press had made it possible for the intelligentsia to express their thoughts and advance ideas in the public domain. We were surprised to find out how many bright, talented, intellectual people there were in our country. During the stagnation period they had sat quietly in institutes and libraries and discussed problems in kitchens. Some had written "for the desk drawer",[1] as people used to say, and were known only in professional circles. But during the perestroika period, they became symbols of the time. Their articles and speeches were lapped up by the thinking part of society. The historian Yury Afanasyev, the literary critic Yury Karyakin, the political scientist Fyodor Burlatsky, the writers Ales Adamovich and Grigory Baklanov, the journalists Yegor Yakovlev, Vitaly Korotich and Igor Golembiovsky, the economists Sergei Shatalin, Nikolai Shmelyov, Gavriil Popov, Leonid Abalkin, and others. These

---

1   A phrase denoting works that could not be published as they would not pass the censor.

figures, together with the academician Sakharov who had returned from his exile in Gorky, became generators of ideas and created the intellectual field for the advancement of the policy of perestroika. Relations between the intellectual elite and Mikhail Sergeyevich were not always smooth. They would often get into arguments with him, and he would respond by getting angry and shouting back at them. In fact, though, these people were his chief allies and supporters. Gorbachev had to be careful in expressing his thoughts, being bound by various obligations and compelled to make political compromises. The members of the intellectual elite were free to say what they pleased and openly expressed ideas that the General Secretary could not.

It was against this complex background that preparations were made for the Nineteenth All-Union Party Conference,[1] which was due to address the issue of the further reform of the country's political system. The turn towards democratisation was palpable in everything, including the nomination of delegates for the conference. It so happened that Mikhail Sergeyevich was nominated through the Frunzensky *raikom* – and specifically by the Party organisations of the Second Watch Factory and the Bolshevik and Yava factories. The choice of enterprises was unusual. Previously, the delegation of the General Secretary would have been entrusted to some industrial giant of no lesser magnitude than, for example, ZIL. But here were three enterprises that produced consumer goods. Another unusual factor was that Gorbachev had a rival candidate in the form of a self-nominated shop foreman from the watch factory. This meant that there had to be a debate. A plan was therefore made for the General Secretary to visit the watch factory, especially as this was a well-known, large enterprise. Its employees numbered over 10,000. The Second Watch Factory was our neighbour: we shared a fence. We did not notice any changes on the day of the visit. For Yava, it was an ordinary working day. At around six o'clock that evening the telephone rang: "The General Secretary will be visiting your enterprise tomorrow". They did not give a specific time. Usually, such visits were thoroughly prepared in advance, but in this case there was hardly any notice at all. It emerged that, after visiting our neighbour, Mikhail Sergeyevich had asked, "Why did we not schedule visits to the other two enterprises?" And he expressed the desire to do so the very next day, without delay. Since it was too late for anything to be done that day, I gave

---

1   The conference took place from 28 June to 1 July 1988.

an instruction for the shop supervisors to be put in the picture so that we could make preparations for the visit as early as possible the next morning.

I arrived at the factory early next morning to find that officers of the organs responsible for Gorbachev's security had already settled themselves in my office. They had inspected the facility and posted their people in positions around it. Even more surprised were the workers of the morning shift, who arrived at the factory by 6:30am, knowing nothing about the visit. Overnight, the whole of 3 Yamskovo Polya Street from the watch factory to Ulitsa Pravda (the route that Gorbachev would be taking) had been resurfaced. It had been done in such a hurry that they had even gone over the manhole covers. Even now, it was found necessary to build Potemkin villages. Word about Gorbachev's visit flew around the factory, and the workers were in buoyant mood. Mikhail Sergeyevich was a tremendously popular figure. Time flew very fast. Finally, we were warned that the General Secretary would be there within half an hour. Just in case, I went down to the foyer immediately to arrange the greeting. Of course, I felt very nervous. This was, after all, the first time that the factory had been visited by the leader of the country. And no less than Gorbachev himself. There were already a lot of people around. A number of journalists had turned up, as well as other people who were connected with the visit. Among the welcoming party was the second secretary of the Moscow Party committee, Yury Prokofiev. While waiting, we exchanged opinions. I winced at his openly disdainful remarks about Gorbachev. Unfortunately, such views were shared by Party workers of various levels. By the time Mikhail Sergeyevich arrived, the whole of the factory's foyer was crammed with people. At that moment, the main shops had just stopped for lunch, and everyone wanted to see Gorbachev in the flesh. It was true that he wielded some magical power over people around him. Standing next to Mikhail Sergeyevich, I felt that he radiated positive energy, composure and confidence. Gorbachev chatted to people in his customary manner and spoke briefly about the goals of perestroika and glasnost and why the Party had started these processes in the country. Then I suggested that we proceed to the director's office to wait out the lunchbreak. Accompanying the General Secretary were Ivan Timofeyevich Frolov, secretary of the Central Committee and editor-in-chief of *Pravda*, and the man who had become his virtual shadow, the security chief Medvedev.

Mikhail Sergeyevich conducted himself very modestly, very democratically.

He had never been a smoker himself and held a negative view of smoking. Knowing what a weight of responsibility lay on the General Secretary's shoulders, I felt that it would be inappropriate to burden him with the problems of the tobacco industry as well. Not that it wasn't tempting. There was a custom in our country of using visits by high officials to resolve burning issues. I told him briefly about the factory and its workers and showed him a Gorbachev-branded pack of cigarettes, made in Switzerland. Gorbachev had become a highly popular figure abroad by this time. But he reacted with obvious annoyance, commenting acidly, "That's my name they're bandying about for all sorts of nonsense". He was clearly very busy. In the course of the visit he was discussing various matters with Frolov, with whom he appeared to have a relationship of trust. The tour of the factory passed off very well. Mikhail Sergevevich showed a particular interest in the cigarette production and packing machines. The equipment really was quite unique. I still have a photograph in which I am explaining to Gorbachev the workings of our most modern line, the Protos. The workers were thrilled to see him. One of the mechanics even broke through the tight security, and Gorbachev signed his autograph for him on the back of a cigarette pack label. As if this was the normal routine in such situations. The spirit of the new age was Gorbachev himself, an inspiring individual who had overcome what appeared to be impossible obstacles and become a true leader of the country.

I felt greatly uplifted after the visit, buoyed by a sense of connection to the grand changes that were happening in the country. It was in the same celebratory mood that I attended Gorbachev's meeting with the Communists of the Frunzensky district that same evening in the Large Hall of the building of the *Izvestia* publishing house. Mikhail Sergeyevich gave a speech in which he talked about the further challenges of perestroika and the great difficulties that lay ahead. The audience listened very attentively to his speech. There was a sense that this was a gathering of Gorbachev supporters. The following day, the central press published detailed reports about the General Secretary's visits to two of Moscow's well-known food industry enterprises.

The perestroika policy restored people's sense of dignity. I remember, for instance, the demeaning processes that Soviet people had to go through when it came to business trips abroad. Decisions were made at the very top, by the CPSU Central Committee. Then groups would be formed and there would be an endless series of formalities and approvals. Would they let people go, or wouldn't they? In any case, next to nothing would be gained from such trips. With perestroika, however, the rules on going abroad were liberalised. Enterprise directors could make their own decisions about the purposes and timing of the trips. All they had to do was make arrangements with the host party and obtain from them an official invitation and a guarantee that expenses would be paid.

A process of democratisation began in public organisations and creative unions, which had turned into purely bureaucratic institutions under Brezhnev. Back in the early 1970s, in view of the need to expand trade relations between the USSR and the USA, a top-level decision had been made to establish the American-Soviet Trade and Economic Council (ASTEC). The USSR Chamber of Commerce founded the Soviet branch, and a corresponding body was set up in the USA. Under the charter, they were headed by the respective ASTEC co-chairmen. The Council organised annual meetings involving representatives of the business communities of both countries. The Yava factory had been a member of ASTEC since its creation – or rather it had been appointed as a member by an order from above. That was the way public organisations were created in the country. The purpose of the Council was to promote ties between Soviet enterprises and American business. But enterprises in the Soviet Union had limited rights, and the state exercised a monopoly over foreign relations. Since everything was decided by the ministries, it was government functionaries who sat on the Council. ASTEC effectively became a closed bureaucratic institution. Yava's membership was just a formality. We took no part in the Council's work and received no meaningful reports about its activities. All we did was regularly transfer fairly hefty sums of money by way of membership fees, which went on maintaining this bureaucratic organisation. In return, they would send a Council-branded New Year calendar together with a greetings card from the executive director. Even when the Yava factory had been involved in major projects with the American company Philip Morris for the joint production of cigarettes, there had been no reaction from ASTEC. Such was the bureaucracy-centred policy of the government in the stagnation era. When perestroika began, a business environment started to take shape and enterprises acquired greater independence. There was a drive to bring fresh forces into the administration of the economy, to tap the potential of Soviet society. This was also reflected in the work of ASTEC. There was more activity on the American side, too, now that relations between the two countries had significantly improved and an atmosphere of trust had appeared. The business community sensed that there were opportunities for real cooperation. On the wave of the cardinal changes, the ninth annual meeting of ASTEC members in April 1988 took place publicly for the first time. We were invited to take part in it. The meeting was organised as a top-level event and took place at the International Trade Centre on Krasnopresnenskaya Embankment. A large American delegation arrived in Moscow, including major officials and businessmen. The co-chairman on the American side was Mr Kendal, head of PepsiCo. The meeting went on for two days. Besides the plenary sessions, there were meetings of functional committees and a seminar on marketing and advertising on the US market. The event received great support from the leaders of the two countries. On the very first evening, "on the occasion of the holding of the ninth annual meeting of members of the ASTEC", the General Secretary of the CPSU Central Committee, M.S. Gorbachev, hosted a dinner in the Kremlin Palace of Congresses. All members were invited. It was a very grand reception. Gorbachev gave a welcome speech. It was clear that the General Secretary was highly committed to the development of relations between the two countries. The next day, I received an invitation for my wife and I to attend a reception organised by the US ambassador, Mr Jack F. Matlock, and his wife at Spaso House, the ambassador's residence. One sensed from the atmosphere of these official events that fundamental changes were happening in the country. It was clear that the country's leaders placed great hopes in us, while American business was watching what we were doing with interest. They viewed us as potential partners.

In April 1989 the next annual meeting took place, but this time in the USA. It was written in the charter that the two sides would take turns to host the event. To my surprise, I received an invitation to attend as part of the Soviet delegation. At that time, a trip to America was an exceptional event for Soviet citizens. The delegation had a high official status and consisted of approximately 150 people. It was headed by the co-chairman on the Soviet side, the chairman of the USSR Chamber of Commerce and Industry, V.L. Malkevich. Government officials and chairmen of foreign trade associations still made up the bulk of the delegation, but there were also some notable changes. The members now included directors of state-owned enterprises and joint ventures established under the state's patronage, and even the chairmen of several production cooperatives and a number of business cooperation associations from various regions. There were also representatives of the scientific community. Most significant, perhaps, was the broad geographical spread of the organisations represented – from Kaliningrad to Vladivostok, as people used to say. In terms of well-known figures, I remember the deputy minister of Foreign Economic Relations, N.I. Kachanov, the minister of Instrument-making and Automation Systems, M.S. Shkabardnya, the chairman of Gosplan RSFSR, N.I. Maslennikov, the chairman of Vnesheconombank (the Bank for Foreign Economic Relations), Yu.S. Moskovsky, the director of KAMAZ, N.I. Bekh, and the director of the First Watch Factory, A.S. Samsonov. I was the only representative of Moscow's food industry. Why did they choose me? I think that the Yava factory's long relationship with Philip Morris had something to do with it. To be fair, the organisers of the meeting put a lot of serious thought into selecting the delegation members. After the first few days of general meetings, the trip schedule allowed for individual programmes of visits to relevant firms to discuss business. The programmes were arranged in advance, before the trip began. Everything seemed to be ready, but we had to endure the usual mishaps and indignities. On the last day before the flight we had to assemble in the Chamber of Commerce building on Ilyinka, where we were given relevant instructions, but it was not until one o'clock at night that our foreign travel passports and visas were brought from the Interior Ministry. For the whole time until then, all those distinguished people, tired and hungry, could only sit and wait patiently. And they had a hard night ahead, too: the plane was due to leave at 7am. Surely these things could have been thought through?

We arrived in Washington on a special flight and set off in coaches for the town of McLean, where the meetings were to take place at the recently opened Hilton luxury hotel. Seeing America for the first time immediately plunged me into a state of shock. Literally everything seemed somehow unreal, and the overall impression was of landing in some completely different civilisation. The meetings were very grand and business-like. The US Trade Secretary spoke at the opening. The American delegation was large, with over 350 people: businessmen, bankers and officials. The Agriculture Secretary and a few American senators and governors were among the participants. There was a lot of interaction. Everyone was intrigued by the changes in the Soviet Union and the promising prospects for Soviet-American relations. The words "Gorbachev" and "perestroika" were constantly on the lips of the American delegates during private conversations. In the meetings there were discussions about the most promising areas for the development of cooperation. In the seminars, the Soviet delegates were introduced to the basic principles of the American market economy. The changes in the Soviet Union were reflected in the activities of the Committee on Small Business. Among the people attending the ASTEC meeting were representatives from Philip Morris: the head of the Moscow office, Robert Rosen, and Mr Evans, a manager from the company's European division in Lausanne, Switzerland. After all the plenary meetings had ended, the Soviet delegates were split up among representatives of American firms. My group, accompanied by representatives of Philip Morris, set off by car to Richmond to take a look at the company's headquarters.

At this period in time Philip Morris was in its heyday, one of the top ten companies in the world in turnover terms. It was evidently to demonstrate the company's achievements that they had built this spectacular factory, unlike any other in the world. Literally everything was impressive – the architecture, the vast spaces, the machinery, the volume of output. The factory worked three shifts, producing 220 billion cigarettes per year. That was more than all the tobacco enterprises in the Russian Federation put together. And what products! International brands of filter cigarettes – Marlboro, L&M, Philip Morris, and others. We were given a top-class reception. The managers had worked hard to organise a detailed professional tour. Evidently, they had received an instruction to this effect from head office. As we walked through the factory, I noticed how neatly the workplace was organised, how smoothly this enormous plant was run. The equipment was of the very latest kind. All the top engineering companies were eager to supply the first models of their new machines to Philip Morris, and especially to the Richmond factory. This was considered a great coup and a good advertisement for the new designs. We were accompanied on the tour by one of the high-level managers. In the way she talked with the workers I saw the characteristic features of the American way of life. All the workers tried to show their good spirits. They would smile broadly and do everything to show that all was well with them. When asked how they were, they would usually answer "Fine!" And indeed, a job at an enterprise of this kind was a good, prestigious position, even though the work was not at all easy, with the high-speed equipment and the high tempo of the three-shift schedule. One could not help noticing that most of the employees were dark-skinned – not only the workers, but the managers, too. Of course, I had a good idea of how difficult it was to get a huge plant working so efficiently. When we toured the workshops, the premises were so vast that I could not see where they ended. It was as if there was an infinite row of machines, all working smoothly and in unison. I am sure that underneath this outward well-being lay a lot of hard work at building mutual understanding among the workers, creating a good working environment and making sure the staff had the right motivation. But to the outside, everything seemed to go on effortlessly. As if someone had waved a magic wand over a splendid model and everything had started spinning and turning. Only the music was lacking. Electric buggies carrying tourists drove one after the other down the wide, specially equipped aisles. This was another element of the company's activities. People had to see and marvel at its achievements. The tourists came from many different countries, too. It was part of advertising for the company's global brand, a showcase. Philip Morris paid great attention to its image in the world, and this was another effective marketing device.

While in Richmond, I saw what a varied place America was – the vast contrast between the large, ultra-modern cities and the quiet, patriarchal provinces. We were put up in a superior hotel that wholly conformed to my ideas about the colonial times. It was as if nothing had changed since that period save for the enormous, splendid factory, which I would say was more reflective of some distant future than the present day. In the evening we were invited to dinner by the factory's director and production manager. On hearing that we were going to New York, they began to apologise for that city as a hotbed of the vices of modern civilisation which did not, in their view, reflect the true face of America. The next day, we flew to New York on the company's private plane. At the aerodrome it was clear what a special status Philip Morris held in the town: it had its own individual hangar. And not surprisingly! The company was a massive employer, attracted tourists and paid considerable sums to the local budget. This was vitally important for such a small town. During our stay in the US I was constantly amazed at the neatness and precision with which activities were organised for us. At the exact moment when we landed at the aerodrome for private planes, a limousine drove right up to the airstair to transport us to one of the best hotels in the centre of Manhattan – the Hyatt.

We were treated to a packed programme during our two days in New York. The next morning, I was received by the president of Philip Morris. The meeting took place in the company's central office in Manhattan. Most of all, he was interested to hear about the changes that were happening in our country and the opportunities they might bring for new forms of cooperation. In general, the changes taking place in the Soviet Union were the dominant theme of any meetings and discussions. Philip Morris did not only make cigarettes. It owned the food manufacturer, Kraft, one of whose products was the famous Miller beer, sold in cans. To develop its food production business the company was engaged in a joint project with the agrarian sector in Dnepropetrovsk (Ukraine). We were joined in New York by two people from Dnepropetrovsk, who were also members of the ASTEC delegation. One of them was the seemingly unremarkable Pavel Lazarenko, a representative of the Dnepropetrovsk agro-industrial committee. He and I later met at the next ASTEC meeting in 1991, by which time he was a representative of a farming company. Ten years later I was surprised to learn that "Pasha" (as his colleagues called him) had become prime minister of Ukraine with all the adventures that ensued.[1] The Lord really does work in mysterious ways.

In the evening, we were invited to dinner. The private club was on the sixty-sixth floor of the skyscraper in which the airline Pan American had its headquarters. It was all very unusual for us – the private club ambience, the exclusive service in a separate room, the highly sophisticated, exquisite style of the dishes and drinks. We poor Soviets looked upon all this as something bizarre and wondrous. The trip only lasted a week, but it left us with a multitude of new impressions. Compared with previous group trips, when our every step was monitored, we felt free. The only thing was, we had no money in our pockets. How could we return from America without presents for our nearest and dearest? All Soviet people who got sent on trips abroad made it a priority to bring home foreign electronic goods, such as televisions and video recorders. At that time, having a "video" was just about the foremost indicator of a well-to-do family,

---

1 Pavel Ivanovich Lazarenko (b. 1953) – Prime Minister of Ukraine 1996–1997. In 2006 he was convicted by an American court of financial crimes and spent a total of eight years in an American jail.

which is why the well-known "Russian" video technology store in New York was one of the city's main sights for Soviet citizens. All the wonders of Western life could be bought there at affordable prices. The shop was run by people from Georgia. A visit there was an absolute must. Also, the family of one my mother's schoolfriends, who had emigrated to the US in the 1970s, happened to live in New York. Now that there was nothing to fear from contacting emigrants, I called them. Our meeting after so many years apart was very warm indeed, and there was plenty to talk about.

The delegation members met up again at New York's airport before the flight back to Moscow. Everyone had bought up lots of video equipment, and suitcases were bulging, but unlike on our arrival, no one was there to send us off. The official part of the event was over, and coaches had been sent to the hotel to take us to the airport. It was quite funny to observe all these "official persons", who had not long ago been gliding grandly around New York in fabulous limousines, huffing and puffing over their luggage and wiping the sweat from their brows. Rather inevitably, we still lived up to the "Homo Sovieticus" label that had become firmly established abroad, but changes were already happening in all aspects of the country and society. This was reflected in the general resolution of the twelfth meeting of ASTEC directors and members, which stated as follows: "The Council notes the new prospects that are opening up for the development of Soviet-American trade and economic cooperation as a result of the perestroika processes occurring in the Soviet Union. Perestroika has given thousands of Soviet enterprises and organisations the opportunity to work directly with their Western partners, for the first time allowing direct contacts between sellers and individual consumers. The importance of these changes is underlined in particular by the composition and size of the Soviet delegation attending the twelfth annual meeting. It consists of directors of enterprises, foreign trade associations and scientific and industrial concerns, as well as heads of governmental organisations". I arrived in Moscow feeling inspired and full of plans. Historical events for the country and the world really were unfolding before our eyes.

It so happened that the Congress of People's Deputies of the USSR, the country's new supreme body, was holding its first session at this time. The creation of this body was a real revolution, signalling a definitive rejection of the command-administrative system and a transition to parliamentarism. The elections that had preceded its formation had been a real triumph of genuine democracy. There simply had not been any proper elections in the USSR before: only the rubber-stamping of candidates put forward by Party bodies. In the perestroika period there was real competition among candidates and people had a free choice. Since every citizen in the country had the right to nominate himself, there were a lot of candidates. People trusted Gorbachev. The results exceeded all expectations and showed how much more engaged the public had become. Preference was given to intelligent, educated, highly motivated people who supported change. Many members of the Party nomenclature, on the other hand, fell flat on their faces.

JOINT VENTURES – THE FIRST STEP TOWARDS DENATIONALISATION

The state was no longer capable of supporting the needs of the tobacco industry. It was now widely understood that the country was at the point of transition to a new economic system. Perestroika had made it possible to secure direct foreign investment by establishing joint ventures with foreign partners (JVs). It was there that we saw a way out of the crisis that had developed. The usual arrangement was for the Soviet party to provide production facilities, a ready-made workforce, infrastructure and access to the local market, while the foreign partner supplied new technology, equipment and materials, i.e. assumed all the hard currency costs. JVs of this kind had already been established in a number of branches of industry, but the process was not yet widespread. Foreign partners had begun to show interest and engage in discussions, but they held back from making a final decision. They took a cautious approach, sizing things up. The country was in a transitional state. Large amounts of investments would be involved, and many matters were still in the hands of the state, not least one of the most important elements of business – pricing. Before coming to any decision, it was essential to make a thorough assessment of the risks. The tobacco industry was perhaps one of the most ideally suited for the establishment of joint ventures. The market was enormous, there was a massive shortage of filter cigarettes, and there was broad integration with international production practice. The factories were familiar with foreign equipment and already had close ties with foreign firms, well-trained staff and experience of working with modern materials and new technologies. But it was essential for the interests of the contracting parties to coincide, and this was difficult to achieve.

The first people to approach us about setting up a joint venture were representatives from Reynolds. The company had recently become part of the newly created Nabisco industrial conglomerate, which included a number of large American food manufacturers (mainly confectionery and tobacco). The State Commission on Food and Procurements suggested that they look at two large enterprises – the Uritsky factory in Leningrad and Moscow's Yava. Reynolds was planning to set up a joint venture to manufacture the well-known Winston and Camel brands of cigarettes. It undertook to supply modern equipment, materials and ready-processed tobacco. The Russian side would organise production. It was a tempting offer that involved major investment, but Yava was unable to agree to the conditions. It involved installing a substantial quantity of new equipment, and the factory did not have enough spare space. We would have had to reduce output of our own popular Yava brand, and that was unacceptable. Besides, having two enterprises with different forms of ownership operating at the same production site would be unviable. For one thing, it might make effective workforce management an impossibility. The offer was more likely to suit the Uritsky factory in Leningrad, which was lagging badly behind in development and still mostly made *papirosy*. It had lost its influence on the market, and the people who ran the enterprise and the sector as a whole were anxious to upgrade the plant to produce cigarettes. That meant that there should be few barriers to installing new equipment in the existing production facilities. However, talks broke down there, too. The risks involved in making such large investments were still very great. We used the experience of the first proposal to formulate our position regarding the attraction of a foreign investor. It was set out in the international trade journal of the tobacco industry, *World Tobacco* (September 1989 issue), in an article entitled "Moscow cigarette factory seeks partners for joint venture". The factory made the most popular tobacco products in the USSR, so we were interested in attracting investment with a view to increasing output and improving the quality of Yava cigarettes. Those were the terms on which the factory was willing to work with foreign firms.

Our next negotiating partner was the West German firm Reemtsma, producer of the famous West cigarette brand. At first, we decided to develop cooperation on a gradual basis, beginning with the upgrading of the primary processing section as the most important step in improving quality. Reemtsma had some unused tobacco processing equipment at its disposal. We drew up a preliminary plan for the refurbishment of the primary section, and it was decided that the factory's specialists would visit the firm's plants in Germany. At that time, many people in European countries had taken to smoking roll-ups. Smokers used special devices to make hand-made cigarettes, and the tobacco factories had switched to producing rolling tobacco. This saved smokers a lot of money, because unlike cigarettes, those products were not subject to excise tax. We visited some factories that had converted to making rolling tobacco. Sure enough, some of their equipment had stopped being used, and we could have made use of it. The business trip went well, but for some reason the company changed its position. Different managers arrived and began insisting on the conclusion of an agreement to manufacture West cigarettes under licence at Yava. The renovation of the primary section was proposed as the second stage. This idea did not work for us and we decided to call a halt to the talks. It appeared that foreign firms were rather hesitant at this stage when it came to making serious decisions. They had a clear preference for licensed manufacturing arrangements. Meanwhile, we were building up negotiating experience and refining our position.

After the First Congress of People's Deputies there was an explosion of private enterprise. Intelligent, adventurous people began to go into business. It was now possible for people to free themselves from strictly regulated state-run institutions, set up their own businesses and start earning money. Back in the stagnation period there had been pragmatists in the highest echelons of power, in Party bodies and the KGB who understood that the Soviet political and economic systems were destined to fail. Outwardly these high-level officials had displayed their devotion to the Party, but all the while they had been casting glances at Western countries. They had been dissatisfied with the material side of life. These people began to lend various kinds of unofficial assistance to the new entrepreneurs. Yesterday's cooperatives and youth technology centres turned into major concerns. Commercial banks and commodity exchanges began to appear. Among the first of these was Inkombank, formed in 1988. Its main shareholders were foreign trade associations and large export enterprises. In 1989 Alexander Smolensky founded Stolichny Bank, and in 1990 Mikhail Khodorkovsky set up Menatep Bank. In October 1990, the

Russian Commodity Exchange was founded and German Sterligov established his private exchange, Alisa. The Moscow Commodity Exchange opened its doors. Vladimir Gusinky founded the Most group, followed a little later by Most Bank. The creation of such large commercial entities de facto amounted to a clarion call for a transition to market relations. Effectively, large dents had been made in the government's existing processes for running the economy. Significant quantities of goods and commodities began to change hands through commodity exchanges. New stores opened selling products made by cooperative businesses at commercial prices. The ground floors of buildings owned by large enterprises were dotted with signs advertising private concerns, and the rent received became a major source of income. By selling some of their output through cooperatives, state enterprises began to take advantage of the higher prices that private enterprises were permitted to charge. Even such tightly closed institutions as the facilities administrations of the CPSU Central Committee and the Council of Ministers were shifting to a commercial footing. Previously, the services of these organisations could only be obtained through government channels strictly according to ranking within the bureaucratic hierarchy. The use of "restricted" vacation retreats was permitted only to officials of the appropriate rank or, on occasion, to directors of major enterprises. Now, stays at such centres could be purchased at high commercial prices, and some of the "new cooperators" began to take advantage. A similar thing happened with motor vehicles. Governmental fleet depots had previously only served officials of the highest levels and released service vehicles strictly according to quotas for ministries and other governmental organisations. Now, cars could be ordered on a commercial basis. I was quite amazed when my new deputy ordered up two government Chaikas[1] to meet experts arriving from Philip Morris. He was not yet initiated in the Yava management style and got it soundly in the neck for such extravagance. But the mere fact that this had become possible spoke volumes. There were now rich people about – real, legitimate rouble millionaires. Before, millionaires had operated in the underground and were liable to prosecution. Everyone remembered the story of the deputy foreign trade minister, Sushkov. Being in charge of many large international projects, he had received expensive gifts from foreign partners. He was arrested in 1985 in the Kremlin, straight

---

1   Chaika – GAZ-13 or GAZ-14. Models of executive cars made by the Gorky Automobile Plant from 1959 to 1988.

after a dinner given in honour of participants in the annual meeting of ASTEC, which he attended as co-chairman on the Soviet side. It was said that a search of his home had led to the confiscation of jewellery and other valuable items worth a lot of money. Becoming rich in the Soviet Union was something that could only be achieved illegally through so-called unearned income. Such people ended up on the wrong side of the law and were roundly condemned by public opinion. It was a real shock, therefore, to learn that the chairman of the Tekhnika cooperative, Artyom Tarasov, and his deputy had made three million roubles each in January 1989 (the average wage was around 150 roubles). This fantastic sum had been earned by selling foreign computers on the domestic market, which was now regarded as a legal activity. It became hard not to notice the signs of wealthy people in the community. The first cooperative restaurants opened, and private security firms began to offer their services. On arriving at a government vacation retreat outside Moscow for a few days' holiday, I was taken aback to see armed men wearing camouflage. It transpired that they were guarding the wives and children of some new entrepreneurs. So far, all these things amounted to little more than specks on the existing landscape, but they were a sign of things to come. People's mentality was changing, but conservative forces were still in a strong position both in government and among the population. It was hard for a country raised on the laws of Soviet ideology to adapt to new principles of life. There were strong feelings of envy, and therefore hatred, towards people who had suddenly grown very rich.

New forms of activity were poorly protected by legislation at this stage, and regulatory bodies were dominated by forces that still operated in the old mould, as if nothing had changed. The liberalisation of economic relations afforded opportunities to "catch the odd fish" and show the customary zeal for the protection of public property. State price levels were for the most part out of date and did not reflect actual costs. This was plainly obvious, but the authorities were hesitant to proceed with major changes to price and tariff policies. Instead, they decided on a softly-softly approach. First, it was decided to stimulate activity by allowing the use of so-called "negotiated" prices when entering into arrangements with cooperatives and private firms. Under the new law, estimates were drawn up using state prices, but it was permitted to apply multipliers reflecting the complexity of the work involved. The amount of the multipliers was negotiable and was determined by agreement between the client and the contractor. It was also one of the points over which the inspection bodies commonly took issue, and for them the important thing was to have something to latch onto. Only clear-cut, unambiguous rules worked under the Soviet system. When it was a matter of choosing a particular option based on logical arguments, there could be big trouble. The existing system of management and control was based on naked administration, with no room for analytical approaches. Objectivity was out of the question. This represented a serious danger for burgeoning business relationships.

PUBLIC OVERSIGHT STILL LIVES!

In August 1989, the factory stopped work for a month for regular maintenance. A great deal of work had been planned. Usually we hired so-called "self-organising" brigades during the maintenance period. Most of these brigades had worked at Yava year after year and knew what was involved and what the client's requirements were. However, most of the workers had moved over to cooperatives, which offered them better working conditions and pay. This meant that we had to hire construction cooperatives to carry out the work. In September, the factory had just started work again when an inspection team suddenly descended on us. And not any old inspection team, but one from the most fearsome organisation of all – the USSR Public Oversight Committee. It began to appear that there were serious grounds for the inspection. Very soon, our fears were confirmed. The inspectors had discovered large overpayments to the cooperatives. There was also another problem, which I had not anticipated. One of the cooperatives used was Tandem-2, founded by Alexander Samsonovich Apozyants, who then occupied a high post in the State Commission on Food Resources as a chief specialist and head of the division for the tobacco industry. He was our colleague and technically our boss. Unfortunately, the chief engineer, Pozdnyakov, had omitted to run this matter by me – and Apozyants himself, an experienced official, had been rather careless. The situation could easily be construed as "collusion among officials or illegal use of official position for personal gain". And that is precisely what happened.

The inspection was completed, and the matter was put to a meeting of the Public Oversight Committee. The chief accountant and I were summoned to a drab, dark-grey building on Ilyinka to be shown the draft of the Committee's resolution. What was striking was that the document had been composed in the spirit of the most reactionary periods of Soviet history – as if, through the windows of this building, time had stood still and nothing had changed. Practically all the multipliers used in our estimates were declared unlawful. The amounts charged as a result of applying them were held to be overpayments. After all, they had to justify the purpose of the inspection and find abuses. It was as if there had never been any law "On Cooperation" or instructions on the application of multipliers. The Oversight Committee simply ignored the decisions of the USSR government. In actual fact, nothing much had changed as far as payment for the maintenance work was concerned. Previously, the factory had paid maintenance brigades according to a job order system. The rates of pay were high on account of the harsh working conditions, tight deadlines, and the fact that most of the workers worked overtime (evenings, and often nights as well). Effectively, the total payment had likewise amounted to a negotiated fee. And that had all been considered normal and above board. So what had changed? The only differences were that we had hired cooperatives instead of brigades and paid them through the bank rather than in the form of cash wages. This was a more civilised arrangement which was in keeping with the government's new policies. So why were we facing legal action?

Then we got to the really ludicrous part. There was no recognition at all of the changes happening in the country. The findings of the resolution read as follows: "In summary, owing to the absence of control, money held by the enterprise in non-cash form was turned into cash in the hands of the cooperatives, which contributed to a rise in inflation in the country". In short, we were accused of nothing less than aiding and abetting inflationary processes – although quite how on our own we could have had any palpable impact on inflation in such a large country was a mystery.

What this really amounted to was a direct condemnation of the actions of the new leadership in pursuing the liberalisation of the economy. On reading this charge sheet I could not help smiling, although it was by no means a laughing matter. Glimpsing my reaction, the official who had received us, a certain Comrade Nekitayev (imagine, I remember his name!), an obnoxious nonentity of a man, immediately piped up, "I wouldn't smile if I were you. A lot of defendants are carried out with a heart attack after our committee hearings". And he proceeded to give an example of one such recent case. We tried to present arguments in our defence, but to no avail. The inspection had been carried out in the old, time-honoured style: not to find out the true state of affairs, but to create a semblance of feverish efforts to protect state interests and single out people to blame for the country's ills.

While treating Yava as the principal case, the Public Oversight Committee decided to carry out a parallel inspection of the Rosbakaleya office in organising the supply of tobacco products to the Moscow trade sector. This was a very acute issue, with shortages of tobacco products reaching critical levels. There were long queues for cigarettes and instances of price abuse. The inspection was carried out in the usual tendentious style. Rather than examining the real causes of the crisis, i.e. the grave condition of the tobacco industry and the general shortages on the consumer market, the inspectors set about nit-picking. They accused the general director, Anatoly Veniaminovich Levi, of artificially engineering the shortage of tobacco products in Moscow. That was what they wrote. As in our case, the wording of the accusation was clearly political. This was nothing short of sabotage. It was 1937 all over again.[1] In the opinion of the inspectors, there were sufficient resources to keep Moscow continuously supplied, but Levi had failed to organise their timely delivery to the trade network and a large quantity of tobacco products had been diverted for various kinds of special measures and illegally shipped to other republics and regions of the RSFSR. No explanations were accepted, although all the proper documents were submitted containing instructions from the Trade Ministry. The shipments referred to were miniscule and could not have had any impact on the availability of tobacco products in the capital. But no one was interested in any of that. The Public Oversight Committee was created as a punitive body. A scapegoat had to be found, which was why the Committee's resolution was primarily about punishing the guilty. In earlier times, I think I would have been in serious danger of losing my job. But under the law on state enterprises, a director could only be dismissed with the consent of the workers. The draft resolution therefore proposed a strict reprimand for the director and chief accountant plus a fine equal to three months' pay for the damage inflicted on the state. Levi was to receive a reprimand. It was true that he had acted on the ministry's instructions, and he was not expected to face any harsher measures.

---

1 1937 was the peak of Stalin's repressions. The number of people executed on false political charges was in the hundreds of thousands.

Worst off was Apozyants. He had broken the cardinal rule that an official of a government institution had no right to engage in business activity. A decision was drafted to relieve Apozyants of his duties. The committee approved the decision.

The hearing took place on 22 January 1990. Members of the Public Oversight Committee were seated at a table in the large hall. Besides the main players in the case, representatives of relevant higher organisations had been invited to attend. There were journalists in the hall: the central press still published columns entitled "On the trail of Public Oversight decisions". The head of the consumer goods and food industry reported on the results of the inspection. We were called upon to give explanations, but this could not in any way affect the resolution prepared in advance. The bureaucratic system of decision-making was finely honed. Before a matter was put to a hearing, it was thoroughly worked through and agreed upon at every level. Quite unexpectedly, however, when the matter of Moscow's supplies of tobacco products was raised, one of the committee members came out with a hysterical speech, declaring, "Do you know what started the 1917 Revolution? There were no bread deliveries to Petersburg for two days. Which goes to show that Comrade Levi could have provoked a revolutionary situation in Moscow through his actions. I propose that he be dismissed from his post". The Committee members voted in favour of the proposal.

I left the hearing with a sunken feeling. I had been ready for the punishment imposed, realising that there was nothing that could be done about it, but what I had witnessed – the complete indifference and brainlessness reigning in that hall – had surpassed all expectations. Immediately after the hearing I decided to go and see Luzhkov. Despite the late hour, I hoped that Yury Mikhailovich would be in his office. It was my duty to give him an objective account and discuss our actions: his views, after all, carried a lot of weight. What saddened me most was the unexpected decision in relation to Levi. I felt that I bore some of the blame, since everything had started with the Yava inspection. Luzhkov was scathing about the Public Oversight Committee and had a lot of respect for Anatoly Veniaminovich. I know that he did what he could to get the decision changed. When that failed, he found Levi a position as head of department at Mosagroprom. As for myself, I had endured many unpleasant moments over the course of the inspection. The experience had left me with a deep sense of disgust and dejection. I felt the need to "cleanse myself" and pull myself together.

I was happy to get back to my job, back to my colleagues. I wanted to take some time to assess what had happened, dot the i's and obtain an expert evaluation of the charges that had been brought against us from the perspective of current legislation. We contacted the Institute of State and Law, which was the principal drafter of laws and the top source of legal expertise in the perestroika period. It found that our dealings with the cooperatives had been entirely lawful. After the Public Oversight hearing, *Pravda* had published a piece under the heading "Inspection by the Public Oversight Committee: Misappropriation of Funds at the Yava Tobacco Factory". The article was written in the stuffy, outmoded style of old, regurgitating phrases from the Committee's resolution. We decided to make a public response clarifying the issue from the angle of contemporary thinking. We contacted one of the most authoritative newspapers of the new school, *Moskovskiye Novosti* (Moscow News), headed by the famous Yegor Yakovlev. They arranged for me to meet their chief economics correspondent, Vladimir Guryevich. A small article was published. After a lead-in about the Committee hearing and its obstruction of perestroika processes, the author wrote approximately the following: "The democratisation of the economy has given enterprises new ways of developing their activities. The Yava factory has arranged a loan with Vnesheconombank, is developing relations with foreign firms and is in negotiations about the creation of a joint venture. We thought that all this was permitted by the new legislation. But it turns out that this is not the case. First we were supposed to seek the permission of the Public Oversight Committee!?"

Our contact with the Public Oversight Committee carried on in the form of this "duel by correspondence", but later we again clashed directly over the matter of the inspection. The Committee's resolution had directed that "Comrade Sinelnikov is ordered to report to the factory's workers about the misappropriation of funds and the measures taken to make restitution for the damage inflicted on the enterprise. The Consumer Goods and Food Industry Department is to take part in the preparation for and conduct of the meeting". For our part, of course, we had discussed the outcome of the inspection at a meeting of the workers' council without needing to be told to do so. About a month later I was called and asked to arrange a workers' meeting to be attended by representatives of the Committee. We agreed a date and began preparations. The day before the meeting a call came from the RSFSR Public Oversight

Committee. At that time, relations between Union and republican agencies had nosedived even further. A person whom I could trust warned me, "Leonid Yakovlevich, the Union committee is not satisfied. They are planning reprisals tomorrow. They have invited journalists. They want to stage a show trial and have it put on television. Think hard about whether you want to be there." I reflected on the situation. The Committee's officials were masters of provocation and used the most despicable methods to achieve their ends. It galled them that they had been unable to have me fired right there at the hearing. Perhaps they were also riled by my public attempt to defend my innocence. It really would be better to avoid such a confrontation. I had a meeting with the chairman of the workers' council, Gritsai, and the chairwoman of the trade union committee, Ivanova, and explained the situation. I said that I would not come into work tomorrow, as I did not want any part in that filthy spectacle. They could decide for themselves what they wanted to do.

I felt a sudden sense of relaxation, almost like an emptiness. How would it all end? I had effectively placed my fate in the hands of other people. They were people whom I trusted, but all the same… For perhaps the first time in all those years I found myself on the outside of a battle that would decide not only my own fate, but the future of the business that I had served. The next day, everything felt strange. I was at home with my family on a working day. For some reason, my son did not go to school. I did not call anyone, and no one called me. As usual, at nine o'clock in the evening we turned on the television to watch the news programme *Vremya*. And suddenly, at the end of the programme, there was a special report. Officials from the Public Oversight Committee had arrived at the Yava factory to take part in a workers' meeting. Journalists had also been invited, but the workers' council had passed a decision not to let them into the factory. They showed the main factory building and a group of visitors at the entrance, composed of officials from the Committee and a bunch of journalists carrying bulky equipment. The chairman of the council, Gritsai, came out to meet them. He explained in a very calm, dignified manner that the director was not at work today and the workers' council had decided not to go ahead with the meeting. He added, "We will deal with the matter ourselves". He ended it at that. Next, the deputy chairman of the Public Oversight Committee, Ilyenkov, appeared on the screen. He was asked to comment. Adopting a pointedly calm air, he tried to smooth over the Committee's defeat, declaring that what had happened was, on the contrary, a sign of real democracy being established in the country: "The workers' council is the rightful governing body at the enterprise. It is an elective body which represents the workforce. If that is what the members of the council have decided, we must bow to its authority". And this was broadcast to the entire nation. Literally a few minutes later my home telephone rang (we didn't have mobiles back then). It was Luzhkov. Without any preamble, he exclaimed, "Leonid, well done! You really sent them packing!" That call meant a lot to me.

The next day I went into work as usual. We did not even discuss the events of the previous day. I was grateful to my colleagues and proud that they had shown such independence, maturity and courage. They had come through a stern test and triumphed. I only found out some of the details. The factory's main Party members had gathered in the morning and decided not to hold the meeting and not to let the inspectors into the factory. In the end, though, we did have to hold a meeting: the people at Yava respected the law. We were used to complying with decisions of higher authorities, but we drew the line at holding a meeting at the bidding of the Public Oversight Committee. As for the Committee, it abandoned its previous aspirations and decided to put a tick against the matter: "measures taken".

By way of a postscript: a little more than a year later (in May 1991), the Public Oversight Committee was dissolved. That unique invention of the Soviet regime was reconstituted as the USSR Control Chamber. Apozyants met a tragic fate. Very shortly afterwards, he fell seriously ill with a terrible, incurable disease. It was as if Nekitayev's grim prediction about heart attacks had come true. Alexander Samsonovich was an intelligent man who fully understood the absurdity of the system by which the country was run. When perestroika began, he had enthusiastically set about adapting himself to the new trends. He was one of the first to learn to use a computer and to set up a cooperative. He was a profoundly decent person who lived by a code of honour, but he had made a mistake. Evidently, he had put too much faith in the changes that were happening and had lost sight of reality. This had been seized upon by the Public Oversight Committee. Of course, technically speaking, they were in their rights to dismiss him. His fate was typical of that of many talented, original people in the Soviet Union who found themselves unable to play by the rules. Mikhail Demyanovich Voitsekhovich had been another example.

People like that were rendered vulnerable by their incompatibility with the system under which they lived.

DEEPENING OF REFORMS. CATASTROPHIC SHORTAGES

Despite such reverses, the reform of the country's political system was progressing at full steam. In March 1990 there were elections to the soviets of the Union republics and autonomous regions of the RSFSR, as well as to local soviets. The elections were democratic and free, with multiple candidates to choose from.

After the elections to the soviets there was a need for swift action to establish new, professional administrative structures and strengthen executive power. It was to this end that the Supreme Soviet of the RSFSR decided to institute mayoral posts in the country's two main cities – Moscow and Leningrad. The elections took place on 13 June 1991, the same day as the election of the first president of the Russian Federation. Popov was elected mayor in Moscow, Sobchak in Leningrad. Luzhkov became Moscow's deputy mayor. Popov proposed a new administrative structure, replacing the Moscow city executive committee with a "government of Moscow". Luzhkov was appointed chairman of the government. Fundamental changes were made to the system of administration within the city. Instead of thirty-three *raions* (districts), Moscow was divided into ten administrative *okrugs* (areas), which were in turn subdivided into municipal *okrugs*. The administrative *okrugs* were governed by prefectures, the municipal *okrugs* by executive councils. Under this new system, the Frunzensky district was merged with the Timiryazevsky district to form the Northern Administrative *Okrug*. The Yava factory geographically came under the Begovaya Executive Council of the Northern Administrative *Okrug*. The prefecture of the *okrug* was headed by Mikhail Timofeyevich Dyomin, the former chairman of the Timiryazevsky executive committee.

The country was racked by severe shortages of goods at this time. There were restrictions on the sale of a number of essential products, with ration coupons issued to buy them. Rising inflation undermined confidence in the rouble. People started using scarce goods, including cigarettes, as a form of currency. There were huge queues in the shops. This critical situation led to a palpable deterioration in the standard of living and put the reformers at risk of losing public support. After all, it was over the period of Gorbachev's reforms that the shortages had reached this critical level. What was most surprising, however, was that people did not want to go back to the stagnation era. By and large, they continued to support the new political line. Indeed, they even accused the country's leadership of indecisiveness, of holding back restructuring processes. At demonstrations it was common to see people with placards reading "Mikhail Sergeyevich, be decisive!" This was a sign of the people's wisdom. They put freedom of choice and the possibility to influence government policy over temporary material hardships. A worrying development came with the strike movement in the Kuzbass. The strikes started over food supplies to the miners, but soon escalated into political demands. The strikers did not protest against perestroika, but demanded the resignation of the government, the nationalisation of the Communist Party's property and the closure of Party committees at enterprises. The miners' strikes soon began to have a significant impact on the political situation in the country. A so-called "rail war" broke out in which the strikers began to block important railway lines passing through coal-mining regions. A round-the-clock picket of the White House[1] was organised. It was an unusual experience to watch the miners sitting on Gorbaty Bridge, beating their hats against the ground in protest. Such a sight would have been simply unimaginable in times gone by.

The country's leaders understood that economic problems were threatening the progress of perestroika. The situation was growing desperate. Ways out of the economic crisis were hotly debated in sessions of the USSR Congress of People's Deputies. There was now open talk of a transition to a fully-fledged market economy. But it appeared that Gorbachev and other leaders did not fully appreciate the inevitable consequences of a delay in taking decisive steps. The introduction of free enterprise and the weakening of the Communist Party's influence had effectively undermined the Soviet centralised system of economic administration. The groundwork had been laid for a transition to market relations, but this had not been followed up with further reforms. A serious imbalance had arisen between the availability of goods and the spending power of the public. This could result in the collapse of the economy.

The person charged with developing the programme for the transition to

---

1 The White House is the unofficial name of the main office building of the Russian government in Moscow.

the market economy was the first deputy prime minister and well-known economist, academician Leonid Abalkin. The plans drawn up envisaged the gradual denationalisation of state property, the founding of joint stock companies and banks and the development of private enterprise. But all of these measures required time, and the situation was getting critical. The first thing that had to be done was to somehow rein in the surplus money supply that had amassed in private hands and restore faith in the rouble. As an urgent measure, therefore, it was proposed to reform the country's conservative pricing system – one of the chief causes of the shortages. Despite high inflation, prices remained stable. From the point of view of real economics, this was completely unacceptable, but in historical terms it was viewed as a crucial advantage of the Soviet system, perhaps the most important psychological factor in the relationship between the population and the government. It seemed that there was nothing for it but to allow prices to rise. But no sooner had Ryzhkov announced the government's intentions from the Congress rostrum than an almighty panic broke out among the population. In time-honoured tradition, stocks of so-called strategic products – flour, cereals, salt, vegetable oil and butter – were sold out within a day. A wave of protest demonstrations swept across the nation. The country's leaders lost their nerve, and the Congress ordered the government's plans to be revised.

THE 1990 TOBACCO CRISIS – A BAROMETER OF THE TIMES

Towards the end of the summer of 1990 the country found itself in the grip of an almighty tobacco crisis. Accounts about this being a deliberate plot to stoke up tensions in the country and force the government to allow foreign cigarettes onto the market are simply not true. The real causes of the crisis are easy to identify inadequate production capacity and the outdated technological infrastructure of the industry. In 1990 output decreased because of problems with supplies of materials. By the summer, stocks of cigarettes held in the trade sector were critically low. Tobacco factories began shutting for maintenance in June, and this time the authorities were completely powerless to prevent the crisis. The decentralisation of administration, with factories placed under the control of local *agroproms*, meant that there was limited scope for the mobilisation of resources. At first, however, the problems were confined to a local level.

The real, "nationwide" crisis came in August, when Moscow effectively ran out of cigarettes. Ducat had been the first factory to shut for maintenance, in June. June and July were ridden out somehow, but when August came and Yava shut down, the last stocks were exhausted. That was when the real disaster began. Huge queues formed at kiosks as people waited for cigarettes to be delivered – and when nothing turned up, they gave vent to their emotions by ransacking kiosks, smashing their windows. In outlying areas, local administrations looking for a way out of the situation gave factories permission to supply cut tobacco to the trade sector so that people could make roll-ups. There was no time to worry about standards – the important thing was to calm people down. It got to a point where old women began collecting cigarette butts and selling them for two roubles a jar. The situation had slid out of control, and the authorities were virtually powerless. The introduction of ration coupons, issued through local housing authorities, only intensified abuses. A belated response from the authorities came in the form of an edict signed by Gorbachev firing the chairman of the State Commission on Food and Resources, Nikitin. Many people thought he had been chosen as a scapegoat. It was certainly true that the agency of which he was in charge had little to do with the state of affairs in the tobacco industry and had no real levers of influence. Nikitin himself was blatantly clueless about the problem. When the crisis reached Moscow, he asked the general director of Rostabakprom, Terevtsov, to come and see him. As they discussed the situation, Vasily Nikolayevich said that one of the main causes of the crisis was the lack of funds to buy equipment from abroad. He was baffled when Vladlen Valentinovich replied by asking, "How much does a cigarette machine weigh?" After pausing to think, Terevtsov gave him a figure: "About one and a half tonnes". And he was even more disconcerted by the reply that followed: "Well then, can't we just make one ourselves? After all, we make combine harvesters that weigh several tonnes!" There was not much that could be said after that. Nikitin, after all, occupied the lofty post of first deputy chairman of the government.

Whatever was behind it, Gorbachev's edict showed that the Soviet leadership was gravely concerned about the situation regarding cigarette supplies. After Nikitin's removal, responsibility for dealing with the tobacco crisis was placed on another of Ryzhkov's first deputies, Voronin. Lev Alexandrovich was an experienced and proficient manager. He immediately called a meeting in his

Kremlin office to examine the situation and look for ways out of the crisis. The main problem lay in the fact that the industry was inadequately supplied with materials and equipment. He made a very favourable impression on me, conducting the meeting in a business-like manner and giving clear instructions. As an avid smoker of Marlboros, he understood the problems of smokers.

By now, everyone was waiting for the Yava factory to start work again. The only way for the supply problem in Moscow to be alleviated was for the factory to begin turning out products. And it was the Moscow crisis that worried the country's leaders most of all. It was our task, therefore, to start making full supplies of cigarettes to the trade network as soon as possible. Smokers, too, were yearning for the appearance of fresh Yava products like manna from heaven. Everyone knew that Yava was about to resume work, and hoped that as soon as that happened, cigarettes would immediately be back on sale again. Few realised that the crisis ran much deeper than that, that it had enveloped the whole country and was not just about Yava shutting down. There is a golden rule that to overcome shortages, you have to increase supplies of a product several times over until the market is saturated. After the maintenance ended, the factory had to get back up to speed, and that usually took up to ten days. Yava returned to work on time after the maintenance break. The administration made every possible effort to increase output, but changes in the retail situation happened very slowly. The tobacco crisis was just about the top story on news programmes. Every day the main television channels would beam pictures of enormous queues and enraged smokers attacking tobacco kiosks. Now, even members of the public were starting to blame the ongoing crisis on problems at the Yava factory. Ridiculous rumours were put around about the reasons why the factory was working so poorly, even accusing it of sabotage. I remember that I personally felt under immense pressure. Although I knew how absurd the accusations were, public opinion weighed heavily on my state of mind. But of course, who else would people blame but the Yava factory – Moscow's principal supplier of cigarettes? Even though it was scarcely a week since it had gone back to work.

Smokers were in militant mood. Once, we were informed that a group of people who had waited in vain for a cigarette delivery to show up were heading towards the factory to find out what was going on. When things got to that stage, there was no telling what might happen. It all had a negative psychological impact on the factory's staff. I was constantly having to explain the situation to all manner of people, to assure them that the factory was doing everything it could to increase production. Lev Alexandrovich Voronin was one of the few people who did not believe the rumours. He came to the factory in person, saw for himself how things were and gave his assistance. As an experienced, level-headed official, he understood when to make demands and when to give support. But the situation was becoming really quite grave. There was a danger of it escalating into a direct confrontation between incensed smokers and the government. The Yava factory was caught in the middle, and it was impossible to predict how it would all end.

The culmination and conclusion of events came quite suddenly, around the middle of September. The Soviet president, Gorbachev, and the Moscow mayor, Popov, were due back from vacation on more or less the same day. Their return was awaited by both sides of the conflict. Smokers had already set up a pressure group and were planning a special protest action: they intended to block Gorbachev's way to the Kremlin as he returned from his vacation to make him aware of the tobacco situation in Moscow. The new Moscow government realised that things could not go on like this, but they hesitated to take any major steps in the absence of the city chief. From that point, events began to unfold rapidly. The protestors tried, but failed, to prevent Gorbachev from reaching the Kremlin. However, a large crowd of people gathered on Red Square. They demanded a meeting with government officials. They were extremely determined and had no intention of dispersing. The first deputy chairman of the Moscow Soviet, the well-known politician Sergei Stankevich, came to negotiate with the demonstrators. His assurances that the Moscow authorities were doing everything in their power to overcome the crisis did nothing to appease the crowd. Then Stankevich suggested to the protestors that they elect trusted representatives, and he would go with them to the Yava factory to ensure that products were being manufactured and delivered to the trade network. Evidently, this was the best the Moscow authorities could come up with. And so it was that, at around six to seven o'clock in the evening, without any warning, Sergei Stankevich arrived at the factory together with a group of aggressively disposed representatives of the smoking community (I think there were four of them). During that period, I tended to be at the factory until late in the evening. I invited them into my office. Stankevich briefly outlined the reasons for the unexpected visit, and without further ado we decided to proceed into the works. Fortunately, the machinery was operating as normal and the workers were at their places. The overall impression was of a smoothly running operation. Cigarettes were being churned out and boxes of finished products were being sent to the shipping department. I don't know what the demonstrators' representatives had expected to see, but I noticed how the expressions on their faces gradually changed from hostile to perfectly normal and good-natured. Stankevich himself made an unpleasant impression on me. It was immediately obvious that he was terribly on edge, his eyes darting around and his whole manner oozing malevolence and arrogance. He had evidently made up his mind that we had made a mess of supplying Moscow with cigarettes and it fell to him, who had nothing do with it, to sort everything out. After looking around the works, we headed for the shipping department. There, likewise, the loaders were busy moving finished goods. Meanwhile, smokers in the city were waiting for cigarettes to be delivered to the kiosks. At Stankevich's instruction, the deputy head of the Rosbakaleya office, Dreitsen, was urgently summoned to the factory. Armed with information from the Moscow Soviet's operations unit, we sent trucks laden with cigarettes to the places where there was most unrest. It was just like the revolutionary headquarters in 1917, except that our aim was, on the contrary, to prevent a revolutionary situation from arising in the city. It was late in the evening by the time our work was done. I was happy to see how much the "parliamentarians" had changed in their manner. They were amiable and even grateful when we parted. A common useful endeavour always brings people closer. As it turned out, the only person who was not happy was Stankevich. I found this out when I received a call from Luzhkov the next day. I don't know what Stankevich reported to him about the visit to Yava, but this was the first time Luzhkov had addressed me in this tone. "Leonid Yakovlevich, what is going on at your place? Bear in mind, if things don't get straightened out, I will be forced to take tough measures". And he hung up. When it came to it, the "democrat" Stankevich turned out to be a commonplace careerist who was prepared to resort to mudslinging if he felt his career was under threat[1]. And the threat was real. A good idea of how rattled he was is conveyed in an article I

---

1 Sergei Borisovich Stankevich (b. 1954) – one of the leaders of the perestroika period. From 1995 to 1999 he was in emigration, fearing arrest. Since returning to Russia he has mostly been engaged in business pursuits.

happened to read in *Literaturnaya Gazeta* (the Literary Gazette), written by the well-known economist Nikolai Shmelyev. "We are sitting in Gorbachev's office discussing options for economic reform when Mikhail Sergeyevich is called to the telephone by his assistant. It is Stankevich calling on an urgent matter. Mikhail Sergeyevich comes back looking annoyed. 'Here we are discussing the fate of the country, and I have Stankevich calling to tell me that some smokers have assembled on Red Square to protest about the absence of cigarettes. What should I do, he asks? I told him – you're the Moscow authorities, you deal with it'". When a matter went right up to the top, they didn't delve into the niceties of who was in the right and who was in the wrong. Generally speaking, no punches were pulled, and it was bad luck for whoever happened to be in the firing line.

It was amid this tense atmosphere that a meeting was called at the office of the Moscow mayor, Popov. The latter conducted the meeting in a surprisingly calm, business-like manner, carefully piecing together the facts of the situation. As an experienced economist, Gavriil Kharitonovich took a completely different approach to the problem and identified the primary cause of the crisis. He understood that the Moscow cigarette factories had limited production capacity, and simply boosting output would not solve the problem. He therefore placed an emphasis on the use of purely economic measures. First and foremost, he was interested to learn how things stood in the trade network and how the panic-buying of cigarettes could be stemmed. He listened to the opinions of the Moscow trade directors who were at the meeting. He did not even call on us producers to say anything, but at the end of the meeting he gave a severe warning that if things did not get sorted out within the next ten days, heads would roll. The decision made by Popov after the meeting came as a complete surprise to everyone, but it was the right answer to the crisis at hand. The mayor issued a directive setting a new price for Kosmos cigarettes at three roubles per pack. The calculation was simple: raise the price for the most premium brand. After a severalfold price increase, Kosmos cigarettes immediately appeared in the kiosks. Now anyone who wanted to could buy cigarettes, and that was an important psychological factor in overcoming the crisis. For this and other reasons, the crisis began to subside. The factories had also started to operate more steadily, increasing the supply of cigarettes to the trade network. The mayor's wise decision played an important role, sparking an improvement in the situation. Popov himself, however, came in for flak rather than gratitude. Pricing policy was considered the prerogative of the Union government. Popov's actions were condemned as illegal, and the USSR Price Committee ordered the Moscow authorities to rescind the decision. When the authorities refused, the Price Committee filed a legal suit, but the mayor stood firm. Gavriil Kharitonovich was a brave politician, as he showed on a number of occasions during the perestroika period. But times had changed, too: the central government no longer had the influence that it had once had.

To help restore tobacco supplies to a normal level, the Moscow authorities tried to incentivise the workforce by giving them coupons to buy scarce goods, such as furniture, household appliances, foreign clothes and perfumes. The number of coupons was limited. The factory met its obligations, and the authorities then decided to give the workforce a gift that was literally fit for a king: they arranged a private visit for Yava employees to the most coveted foreign goods store, Leipzig. On the last Sunday of September, the huge store was closed to the public and placed entirely at the disposal of the factory's personnel. This was a truly grand event. Every Muscovite aspired to get into that store – and we were being offered nothing less than a private event. The workers prepared well in advance for the great day, storing up cash. Most of them came with their families. They were determined to make the most of this rare opportunity and take their place in the queue before the store opened so as not to miss the feast. The goods on offer really were of the scarcest kind – imported sheepskin and fur coats, jeans, and other things that people usually only dreamed of. It was a busy day for the managers of the enterprise, too: we were responsible for keeping order. Sometimes the most trivial things could get blown out of proportion, and the enterprise could end up earning itself a bad reputation that would stick like glue. Fortunately, everything passed off without incident. Everyone was happy and talked for a long time afterwards about how they had "stocked up" at Leipzig.

Philip Morris, meanwhile, managed to take advantage of the crisis by signing a contract with the USSR government to supply cigarettes. The supplies took place under a credit arrangement made with the firm on preferential terms. Realising that the Soviet market would inevitably open up to foreign goods, Philip Morris was determined to steal a march on its competitors.

CHAPTER 14.

HOW THE SOVIET UNION BROKE DOWN UNDER THE PERESTROIKA REFORMS

THE "PARADE OF SOVEREIGNTIES" OF THE UNION REPUBLICS

The political structure of the USSR had outlived itself. It was clinging on only by virtue of the Communist Party's monopoly on power. At the heart of the Party's power lay the so-called "principle of democratic centralism": strict Party discipline and unquestioning obedience to the decisions of the central authorities. This enabled the Union to be preserved at least in a formal sense, despite growing internal divergences between the republics and the centre. In the republics, the local elite wanted more independence, while the respective peoples craved the freedom to assert their national identity. Thus, there was a long overdue need to reshape relations within the Union in the direction of genuine federalism. But rather than making real changes, Brezhnev's government had preferred the policy of placating the republics. Perestroika opened the way for change. The leadership role of the Party was challenged. People were permitted to express their opinions and form social interest groups. This could hardly fail to provoke a swell of national movements in the Union republics. Popular fronts sprang up as exponents of national interests. In the vanguard of this movement were the Baltic republics and Moldavia. They maintained that their annexation by the USSR in 1940 had been an illegal, coercive act.

The first manifestation of change came when the Supreme Soviet of the Estonian Soviet Republic passed a Declaration of the Sovereignty of Estonia in November 1988. This was a completely unexpected event. I remember watching the Channel One television broadcast of the session of the USSR Supreme Soviet in which this matter was discussed. The chairman of the Estonian Supreme Soviet, Arnold Rüütel, who was present at the session, was ordered to rescind the resolution on the grounds that it was illegal. But he firmly stood his ground. This sort of thing would have been impossible even to imagine before. The USSR Supreme Soviet refused to recognise the declaration, and the matter was left hanging. But the very fact that the issue had been considered by the country's highest authority was of great psychological importance for the subsequent policy of the republican leadership and was indicative of the new political climate in the country.

The elections to the Councils of People's Deputies in 1990 meant that the republics now had legitimate organs of power. In a number of republics, the people elected as heads of the Supreme Soviets were new figures who favoured secession from the USSR: Landsbergis in Lithuania, Gamsakhurdia in Georgia and Yeltsin in the Russian Federation. The events triggered after this became known as the "parade of sovereignties". One by one, the Supreme Soviets of the Union republics began passing acts proclaiming sovereignty. The first to do so were the Baltic republics, Azerbaijan and Georgia. On 12 June 1990, the First Congress of People's Deputies of the RSFSR passed the Declaration of the State Sovereignty of the RSFSR. Despite the stated intention to create a democratic rule-of-law state as part of a renewed USSR, the declaration included a provision according the constitution and laws of the RSFSR priority over legislative acts of the USSR. The Russian parliament's sovereignty declaration dealt a mighty blow to the centre. The Russian Federation was the beating heart of the USSR. Moscow was home to both USSR and Russian government authorities. The assertion of the priority of Russian laws set a dangerous precedent that could affect the functioning of the Union government. After Russia declared itself sovereign, doubt was cast on the very existence of the Union as people knew it. This had a major psychological impact on the remaining Union republics, which also passed sovereignty declarations over the course of 1990. It was the first step towards the collapse of the USSR.

The reform of the Union was one of the most pressing issues for the country's leaders. It became the subject of a fierce battle between democrats and conservatives. Speaking at the First Congress of People's Deputies, the academician Andrei Sakharov[1] proposed a draft of a new treaty with the republics which would turn the USSR into a confederation. But these proposals

---

1 Andrei Dmitrievich Sakharov (1921–1989) – academician, one of the creators of the Soviet hydrogen bomb. The best-known Russian dissident of the 1970–80s. Winner of the 1975 Nobel Peace Prize. Subjected to repression by the authorities from the end of the 1970s until 1986.

were not supported by a majority of the Congress. The conservative wing of deputies opposed it. They rejected the idea of any changes in the structure of the Union and its relationship with the republics and viewed any relaxation in the policies of the centre as unacceptable capitulation and defeatism. The opponents of reform were driven by purely pragmatic as well as ideological considerations. The reform of the Union meant the loss of unlimited power and the shrinking of the colossal central apparatus and budget. But the reforms that had already started from below, in the republics themselves, had now gone too far to be stopped. By dithering, the centre had lost the initiative, and that could result in uncontrollable decisions being made by the new authorities in the republics. The situation boiled over after the parliament of the Lithuanian republic declared independence from the centre on 11 March 1990. Efforts to restore constitutional order by force came to nothing. The attempted storming of the Vilnius television tower by Riga OMON troops ended in failure. There were casualties among those defending the tower. It took a great effort to avoid further bloodshed. It was no longer possible to use force to resolve political matters.[1] But the political battle over the reform of the Union was intensifying. Article 6 of the USSR Constitution establishing the dominant role of the Communist Party was abolished, paving the way for a multi-party system. The General Secretary of the CPSU was no longer automatically head of state. To strengthen power, therefore, a new post of president of the USSR was created, for which Gorbachev was duly nominated and supported by a majority of the Congress.

It had now become impossible to ignore the changes in the relationship between the centre and the republics. This was an arduous time for Gorbachev. The Union was in urgent need of fundamental reform. But the consensus that would enable progress to be made could not be found. Tensions flared between the democratic wing of the Congress and conservatives in the "Soyuz" group of deputies. Taking advantage of the indecision at the centre, the republics began to renege on their obligations as members of the USSR. The Supreme Soviet of the RSFSR set the example for the other republics. Long-established industrial ties were disrupted and state discipline over supplies began to break down. Amid severe shortages, Russian regions even stopped supplying goods to each

---

1 The storming of the Vilnius television tower by OMON troops took place on the night of 12–13 January 1991. It was one of the key events of that time.

273

other. This had a devastating impact on the economic situation in the country. A pivotal role in the weakening of the centre's position was played by Boris Yeltsin. He had been Gorbachev's chief opponent throughout the perestroika period. He made constant efforts to inflame the situation, countering the General Secretary's compromise positions with radical solutions. A wilful leader, he went all out to win power, and was not shy of adopting a blatantly populist approach. On becoming chairman of the Supreme Soviet, and then president of the RSFSR, he effectively took charge of efforts to weaken the Union. On a visit to Ufa in August 1990 he made a sensational exhortation to the regional authorities: "Take as much sovereignty as you can swallow", which subsequently became a familiar refrain and rebounded against the interests of the Russian Federation itself. After this, all of Russia's constituent autonomous republics passed sovereignty declarations. Power in the Soviet Union had rested on rigid centralisation, and its economy on strict discipline in the fulfilment of state targets. And suddenly, with the republics declaring their sovereignty, that system of rule was rapidly disintegrating. The country faced a real threat of political and economic collapse. It was in this complex climate that the Fourth Congress of People's Deputies of the USSR took place in December 1990. The intensity of the discussions reached boiling point. Some radically minded deputies openly accused Gorbachev and his team of leading the country to this point. The question of Gorbachev's removal from the post of president of the USSR was raised at the Congress but did not receive a majority of votes. Once again, the central government delayed in arriving at a decision. The situation now had to be addressed as it actually presented itself. There was no other option but to construct a new relationship between the centre and the republics. The Congress passed a decree "On the Reform of the Union and the Reorganisation of the USSR as a Federation of Equal Sovereign States". Because the matter involved fundamental changes to the country's political structure, Gorbachev proposed that it be put to a national referendum.

The adoption of what was effectively a forced decision on the reform of the USSR intensified the political struggle in the country to a critical point. The top posts in the Communist Party had been taken over by functionaries who were young (by the Party's standards), pragmatic and reactionary. For them, preventing the loss of the USSR was the final frontier in the battle to preserve power and Communist ideology. Among the best-known were Yury Prokofiev in Moscow, Boris Gidaspov in Leningrad, Stanislav Gurenko in Ukraine, and Ivan Polozkov in the RSFSR. Unable to accept the changes that had occurred in the country and the Party, they hatched plans to remove Gorbachev from the post of General Secretary of the CPSU. The conspiracy among the new Party nomenclature was gathering pace. Furthermore, Gorbachev lost the support of his closest allies, the people who had supported him the most during the perestroika period. At the Fourth Congress of People's Deputies, the Foreign Minister Eduard Shevardnadze resigned. He condemned the hounding of Gorbachev and his associates and declared straight out that "Dictatorship is coming". His speech was broadcast to the entire nation and made a strong impression. Another to resign, in the wake of the economic woes and the government's failure to win support for its latest proposals, was Nikolai Ryzhkov, who had been at Gorbachev's side since perestroika began. Alexander Yakovlev, the chief architect of perestroika, quit his senior post in the CPSU. Before that, Vadim Bakatin had been moved from the Interior Minister post to another job. These figures were replaced by Party bureaucrats. The position of Chairman of the USSR Supreme Soviet was taken over by Anatoly Lukyanov, who had long worked within the apparatus of the CPSU Central Committee, and more recently in its most conservative arm, as head of the administrative bodies department. To the great surprise of everyone, an obscure trade union functionary, the national trade union council chairman Gennady Yanayev, as bland a figure as you could imagine, was elected to the post of vice president of the USSR. This appointment was greeted by many with utter bewilderment. Valentin Pavlov replaced Ryzhkov as head of government. A well-known financial expert, he had held high government posts in recent years as chairman of the State Price Committee, then USSR Minister of Finance. After a long time working within the government machinery, he was an advocate of centralised administration. There were serious doubts about whether he had it in him to carry out economic reforms.

These appointments were perceived by public opinion as a step backwards in the reform process. Why had Gorbachev let this happen? Perhaps he wanted to quell criticism from among the hardliners. As a result, however, his relationship with the democratically minded part of the Congress grew distinctly frostier. There was an increasing sense that at this difficult time, Gorbachev was stranded in an ideological no man's land.

ENTREPRENEURS BY NECESSITY

The changes in the political landscape affected the state of the economy. I remember it as a very strange period. A vacuum had formed in terms of the state's involvement in the running of industry. Party bodies no longer had any influence on our work. The economic authorities were all at sea. The loss of Party support had deprived them of their main lever of influence over enterprises. State discipline over supplies had begun to break down, and the government's control over the fulfilment of production plans was weakened. Imagine: in an economy built on central administration and the strict distribution of resources, the state's authority was in decline. The economic crisis and the devaluation of the rouble were sapping the motivation of manufacturers. This was a dangerous combination. The only state body to which the Yava factory answered, Mosagroprom, had gradually edged away from any real leadership of the food industry in Moscow. It had effectively become an association in which parties could discuss general matters relating to the development of the sector without making any firm commitments. I think that these trends in relationships between enterprises and state bodies were, to one extent or another, replicated in other industries too. In these circumstances, enterprise directors had no option but to assume full responsibility: to act independently and show initiative and enterprise. The main focus now was not fulfilling the state plan, but ensuring that work could continue, wages could be paid, and workers could be kept on. To avoid production being shut down, there was an urgent need to refashion relationships with suppliers, establish direct ties, make agreements. There was a rapid rise in the use of barter – the first sign of a weakening currency. There were also major disruptions in supplies of essential food and goods to the public. The most well-organised enterprises took it upon themselves to address this problem. Obtaining scarce products became an important element of their activity, in some ways even more important than paying wages. Generally speaking, however, these matters were handled through unofficial channels. The authority of an enterprise director came to depend on his ability to arrange supplies of goods for the workers. To this end, enterprises needed to have some resources of their own. Tobacco factories were blessed in this regard. Cigarettes were still one of the most sought-after products. During this period, we came to fully appreciate how timely the creation of the Amenity Centre had been. The factory's employees got through this difficult time relatively painlessly.

Many enterprises did not have these advantages and found themselves in serious difficulty. I remember one incident that seemed strange at the time. The director of a furniture factory in Noginsk came to see me. The enterprise was in a difficult financial position, and the workers' council was about to meet to elect the director. In an effort to win over the workers, he asked me to let him have just a few boxes of Yava cigarettes, which were hard to buy. It turned out that even a trivial thing like that could make a big difference in a crucial situation. A few years later I was happy to learn that the factory was producing good-quality, popular furniture under the same director. Since the adoption of the law "On State Enterprises", we had grown largely used to the idea of working independently.

The Yava factory sourced its materials from a very wide geographical area. But amid disintegration processes in the republics, supplies of raw tobacco from Moldavia, Kirghizia and Azerbaijan were disrupted. We continued to experience problems with supplies of cigarette filters from Armenia. It was then that we began seriously looking into the possibility of setting up a filter manufacturing joint venture in Moscow with the British firm Filtrona, a world leader in the field. Miraculous feats of resourcefulness were needed to keep things running. Personal contacts and direct arrangements between enterprises began to play an important role.

Cigarettes had a particularly high bargaining value, but at Yava we only used this resource in cases of extreme necessity. Tobacco products were still in short supply, and keeping Moscow supplied remained an important government priority. Supplies to the trade network were strictly monitored. But sometimes we found ourselves in a desperate situation. For many years Yava had been supplied with *papirosa* paper by the Arkhangelsk Pulp and Paper Plant.[1] Suddenly, however, the shipments stopped coming, and the supply agents asked me to speak to the director. When I asked about resuming supplies, the plant director explained, "We can't work because we've run out of pulp. That's because they've stopped supplying us with wood. The loggers have stopped cutting down trees". It was true that industries in which hard physical work was used were going through an especially difficult time. When I asked, "How can we resolve this?" he replied, "Either supply cigarettes for the loggers or pay

---

1 Founded in 1940 and located in Novodvinsk, to the south of Arkhangelsk, this pulp and paper plant specialised in wrapping and writing paper.

in hard currency" (it turned out that such things were possible by this time). After the fruitless discussion with the director we sought help from the chief authority for the pulp and paper industry, Soyuzglavbum, which held all the quota allocations for paper products. That once mighty organisation told us that they had lost all their levers of influence over suppliers and were unable to help. High-level government authorities were acknowledging their impotence. There was nothing for it but to send cigarettes. There were other examples of this kind. The whole supply chain was crumbling. It had come about because of the delays in pushing ahead with economic reforms. A system was needed in which consumers and suppliers could deal with each other on mutually beneficial terms. Much had already been done in that direction: the groundwork for the transition to market relations had been laid. All that was needed was to take the next steps. But time was running out. Gorbachev was forced to take emergency measures to preserve the USSR.

Importantly, the country had begun to develop an entrepreneurial environment – one of the key factors in the transition to a market economy. I saw this for myself when I attended the annual ASTEC meeting in May 1991 in New York. This time the Soviet delegation was very different in size and make-up from the last meeting, even though only two years had passed. More than 400 people had made the flight to New York. They were mostly young people from the new Soviet business world – managers of joint ventures, cooperatives, commercial banks and business associations. What had been a profoundly bureaucratic organisation had been transformed before our eyes into an association open to anyone who was interested in developing trade and economic ties with American business. Joining ASTEC had become a much simpler process with clear criteria. The general style of engagement between members of the Soviet and American delegations had also changed. Now, it was an atmosphere of free communication among interested buyers. As I observed this diverse group of new people and their free-and-easy behaviour (albeit it all stayed within the rules), I was struck by the scale of the changes that had happened in our country. In effect, this was my first encounter with representatives of the USSR's burgeoning business community. Of course, I had come across them before, but never in such a concentrated group. I became closely acquainted with budding businessmen who would later become leaders of the business community and play a substantial role in the political life of independent Russia. There was the highly affable, good-looking Leonid Nevzlin, a representative of the new, ambitious Menatep Bank. There was the founder of the Russian Commodities Exchange, Konstantin Borovoy, with his ironic manner and attempts to come across as a pragmatist. There was also the well-known entrepreneur and politician Mikhail Bocharov. He had been elected as a Union deputy, and as chairman of the RSFSR Supreme Soviet's Higher Economic Council, he had been one of the people behind the initiative to transfer construction organisations to lease-holding arrangements. He was often seen together with Vladimir Gusinsky, then still a slim, relatively young man. In business, however, he had already achieved a great deal, setting up first the Most construction cooperative, and then a corporate group and a commercial bank with the same name. He had also proved himself a successful lobbyist, securing major orders to renovate buildings in the centre of Moscow. All in all, it was remarkable to behold such a diverse mix of young, ambitious people, all eagerly eyeing the opportunities opening up before them.

Also in attendance were some of my industry peers: Mikhail Mikhailovich Leontiev, director of Mospischchekombinat (the Moscow food processing plant), and his counterpart at the Moscow Distillery, Vladimir Anatolievich Yamnikov. The latter's hotel room turned into a sort of headquarters for high-level members of the Soviet delegation. The distillery supplied products to a Soviet foreign trade firm in New York which sold the famous Stolichnaya vodka to the American market. It was from there that crates of vodka were brought to Yamnikov's room, and some of our senior officials would regularly pop in on him to down a quick glass on the sly. It was, unfortunately, an ineradicable disease. And what a tough job it was to be the director of a much beloved distillery! Always in sight. It offered great opportunities, but you had to be sure to regale the right people at the right time. The crucial thing was not to succumb to the bottle yourself. That took great skill. The previous director, Bachurin, had managed it. He had been a very influential figure. Even Klemenchuk, the minister, had frequently turned to him for help over this or that delicate matter. Unfortunately, Volodya Yamnikov, with whom I had studied at the institute, failed in this respect. He was still a relatively young man when he fell seriously ill and died of cirrhosis of the liver.

All in all, there was a palpable difference within the Soviet delegation between the old guard and the young entrepreneurs. This was quite clearly a completely new generation of people. We also met members of the Soviet UN staff, such as interpreters and other technical personnel. In the Soviet Union, those who had managed to get abroad were the most enterprising and pragmatic people. They had been quick to realise that this was one of the few ways of achieving a good standard of living. It was interesting to see how their outlook had changed. Previously, they had courted the favour of important government officials, whereas now, having sensed which way the wind was blowing, they sought contacts with business people, offering them their services. They would ask us, "Have you not opened an account in America yet? We can help you with that. Quite a few directors have already done it". The way in which this practical, proactive group of people had switched focus was a clear demonstration that influence in Soviet society was passing from government officials to business owners and managers. Even if they were directors of state-owned enterprises.

After the official part of the meeting had ended, all the participants dispersed to wherever they had been invited by American partners. On this occasion I had received an invitation from the major international tobacco company Reynolds. The company had two global signature brands: Winston and Camel. Camel had been the most popular cigarette brand during the Second World War. At the end of the 1970s the company had attracted attention with the development of so-called "smokeless" cigarettes. The key difference in the new product was that it was smoked without the tobacco or cigarette paper being burned, which was the main factor in the formation of unhealthy compounds in cigarette smoke. This was the first time that the idea of using thermal vaporisation of tobacco material to achieve a smoking effect was executed. A similar principle is used today in electronic cigarettes, although now it is a whole device of fairly sizable proportions. The difficulty in what Reynolds attempted to achieve lay in the fact that the smokeless cigarette had to have the same appearance and size as an ordinary filter cigarette. I have had the opportunity to try one of these cigarettes. To smoke it, one had to light to the tip of the cigarette, but it was designed so that it did not burn but only smouldered during smoking. Hot air passed through a capsule containing tobacco material located inside the cigarette. The heating of the tobacco generated an aerosol which could be inhaled by the smoker. It was effectively a completely new product. Costly new technology and equipment had to be made to manufacture it. Reynolds gambled a lot on the creation of the smokeless cigarette and promoted it extensively all over the world. Experts waited with interest to see how the project would turn out. But it ended in failure. The cigarettes were not accepted by the consumer. The flavour qualities were inferior, while the cost of production was higher. The project had to be shelved. The firm's losses ran to billions of dollars. The blow to the company's finances led to a series of top management resignations.

We took a scheduled flight from New York to Winston-Salem in North Carolina, where Reynolds had a huge complex of buildings, including the head office, the main production facility and a large research centre. A meeting with the vice-president in charge of research, Mr De Marco, was scheduled for the following day. A year earlier, he had visited Yava to inspect our work on the development of new filters. We greeted each other like old friends. What I saw exceeded all my expectations. The research being done there was of the highest order. In the world of international business, that was the only way to stay on top.

We returned via New York. Before the flight back to Moscow, Philip Morris organised a grand reception for ASTEC members. There were a lot of guests, but the company's president found the time to invite me for a chat. Everyone understood that fundamental changes were happening in the USSR and were anticipating the opening of the country's vast market to international business. At the end of our short conversation the president hinted enigmatically that Philip Morris was preparing another interesting proposal for Yava.

THE "NOVO-AGARYOVO PROCESS". GORBACHEV'S TRAGIC ISOLATION

I returned to Moscow in mid-May. One would never have imagined that in just three months' time we would have the so-called August putsch, which would put paid to the future existence of the USSR. In the March referendum, an overwhelming majority of the population had voted for the preservation of the Union.[1] The country's economic and financial crisis was worsening. By now the government had more pressing worries than economic reform. It had to resort to urgent measures to withdraw a large portion of the money supply from circulation. A pretext was found. It was announced that a lot of false banknotes

---

1 The referendum, which took place on 17 March 1991, was the one and only such vote in the history of the USSR.

of large denominations – fifty and one hundred roubles – had appeared. The confiscatory monetary reform was initiated by the prime minister, Pavlov. He had intended it as a way of stabilising the circulation of money in the country. But it did not remedy the situation.[1] The only thing the government's intervention achieved was to undermine the public's trust in the central authorities.

In Gorbachev's view, the key to resolving the serious problems faced by the country lay in signing a new Union treaty as soon as possible. On his initiative, a meeting at the presidential residence in Novo-Ogaryovo was convened on 23 April. Its participants comprised nine republics and the Union centre. The talks at Novo-Ogaryovo subsequently carried on in that "9+1" format. The country was in desperate need of political stabilisation, and the first meeting instilled hopes of positive changes. The talks ended with the adoption of a joint declaration.

The partocrats were categorically opposed to the signing of the Union treaty. Literally the next day, at a plenary session of the CPSU Central Committee in Smolensk, the most reactionary members of the Central Committee made an attempt to dislodge Gorbachev from the post of General Secretary. Misgivings about the talks over the conclusion of the Union treaty were felt even among the president's closest associates. The chairman of the USSR Supreme Soviet, Anatoly Lukyanov, was particularly instrumental in this process. It was the Supreme Soviet that had tried to block Gorbachev's negotiations with the heads of the republics. In June, Gorbachev presented the Supreme Soviet with a draft treaty on the creation of a Union of Sovereign States. With Lukyanov's support, Pavlov demanded to be given extraordinary powers that would limit the president's real authority. Speaking at a closed session of the Supreme Soviet, the heads of the Defence Ministry, the Interior Ministry and the KGB supported the prime minister's proposal. The KGB chairman, Kryuchkov, characterised the perestroika reforms as a CIA plot, stating plainly that "if we do not take extraordinary measures, our country will cease to exist". Yury Blokhin, leader of the influential Soyuz faction of deputies, declared that his faction would vote against every article of the Union treaty. Opposition to the treaty had reached its zenith.

---

1 This was the first confiscatory monetary reform since 1961. As a result, money supply was reduced by fourteen billion roubles – mostly accounted for by high-value banknotes outside the USSR which people did not have time to repatriate and exchange within the allotted three-day time limit. For the majority of Soviet citizens, the reform did nothing but cause them additional stress and further erode their already low confidence in the financial authorities and the national currency.

The profound differences in the respective positions of the centre and the republics made the negotiation of the Union treaty appear impracticable. I think this was why Gorbachev took the entire responsibility upon himself and conducted talks with the heads of the republics virtually single-handedly. The country followed the progress of the Novo-Ogaryovo talks on television until at last the meetings ended and a weary-looking Gorbachev led the republic leaders down the steps of the residence building, where they were awaited by journalists. It was obvious how tough the negotiations had been for the president. The upper hand had undoubtedly lain with the republics, which now stood to win more independence. Under the new treaty, many more powers would have passed into their hands, including the setting of the Union budget and the fate of the country's president. At that difficult, complex moment, Gorbachev had been forced to accept serious compromises. It was as if he had been battling all alone to save the situation, push through the Union treaty and preserve the state.

The centre's final attempt to halt the treaty process was made in July. The USSR Supreme Soviet passed a resolution "On the Draft Treaty on the Union of Sovereign States", setting up a plenipotentiary Union delegation to sign the treaty but at the same time ordering the text to be revised under the delegation's guidance. However, Gorbachev never once assembled the Union delegation.

Finally, work on drafting the new Union treaty was completed. A date was agreed with the leaders of the Union republics for the signing of the treaty: 20 August 1991. Having completed the negotiations, Gorbachev left for a vacation at his summer retreat in Foros, Crimea, intending to return in time to sign the treaty. The atmosphere was extremely tense. Effectively, only one step remained before the signing of a treaty that would fundamentally change the structure and spirit of the country. The *Sovietskaya Rossiya* newspaper, followed by a number of other "patriotic" press outlets, published the text of a letter entitled "A Word to the People", signed by the well-known writers Bondarev, Rasputin and Prokhanov, the generals Varennikov and Gromov, the singer Zykina, the sculptor Klykov, and others. The letter railed against the reform of the Union and called on people to "come together to stop the chain reaction of the disastrous collapse of the country, the economy, and the individual self". It was naïve to think that the future members of the "State Emergency Committee" would not make a last-ditch attempt to torpedo the signing of the treaty. We fully understood the complexity of the situation, but there was no sense of any serious danger. We thought that a return to the old ways was impossible.

THE PEOPLE STAND UP

I spent Sunday, 18 August with my family at a country apartment not far from the village of Iksha. Early on Monday morning I was about to set off for work as usual when there was a knock on the door. It was one of our neighbours at the country house, the well-known Moscow builder Vyacheslav Krymov. With a notable tremor in his voice, he said, "There's a military coup in Moscow. Troops have been sent in". I remember feeling an enormous wave of shock, as if something had snapped. I knew how military interventions ended in the USSR. The experience of past events left no room for hope. In a single instant, all our plans, everything that had kept us going in the last few years, had turned to dust. From that moment, everything carried on in a sort of haze. I don't remember how I got to work. I tried to get a grip on myself and keep busy, but I just couldn't get anything done. It was simply too awful, after all the changes we had been through, to think of going back to the Soviet cattle yard. Information about what was happening in the country was very scant. It was immediately reminiscent of the official news during the stagnation era. On the radio, the same announcements were broadcast over and over again from six in the morning: the imposition of a state of emergency in certain regions of the USSR, Vice President Yanayev's edict about his assumption of the duties of president of the USSR on account of Gorbachev's illness, the Soviet leadership's declaration of the establishment of the State Emergency Committee (the GKChP), the GKChP's appeal to the Soviet people. It was even worse on the television, where they repeated excerpts from the ballet *Swan Lake* on a loop the whole day long. It looked very much like the country had returned to the worst times. The activities of political parties, social organisations and mass movements were suspended. Many central newspapers were banned. At around three o'clock in the afternoon I received a telephone message from the new chairman of Mosagroprom, Yevgeny Alexeyevich Zotov, inviting me to attend a meeting of enterprise managers. That did nothing to improve my mood. What was I likely to hear now: that all state-owned enterprises were under the control of the GKChP? It was in that frame of mind that I set off for the meeting.

We drove from Belorussky Station along Gorky Street to Pushkin Square. The disruption to the ordinary life of Moscow's centre was plain to see. Instead of the usual crowds of people on bustling streets, there were just occasional figures hurrying to get somewhere. We passed a lot of soldiers in armoured cars. They were just keeping up a presence, not actually doing anything. The organisers had evidently planned this primarily as a visual statement of the imposition of a state of emergency in Moscow. All this was as one would expect. But before the turn-off from Suvorovsky Boulevard[1] onto Kalinin Avenue[2], something completely unexpected happened. Suddenly, I saw that the traffic on the lane towards the Ukraina Hotel had been blocked off, and the police were directing our car along with others onto the oncoming side, which was now being used by traffic travelling in both directions along Kalinin Avenue. The restriction of lanes had resulted in a traffic jam. As we proceeded towards the junction with the Ring Road, I was astonished to see that the entire right-hand side of the road was filled with people. We were moving slowly, so I got a good look at these people, even paying attention to their faces and the way they walked. They were proceeding in silence with a firm, resolute step, intensely focused, clearly united by a common purpose. Their faces were etched with resolve and readiness for action. This picture made such a strong impression on me that I remember it to this day in the minutest detail. I had never seen anything like it in my life. I did not know who these people were, where they were going or for what purpose, but their resoluteness at that difficult moment could not but transmit itself to those around them.

The situation at Mosagroprom was quite different from what I had expected. In Moscow and Leningrad, democratically minded citizens had refused to recognise the legality of the state of emergency. Resistance to the GKChP's actions was led by Boris Yeltsin. Early that morning, he and his closest associates had driven unhindered from his residence in Arkhangelskoye to the Russian Government House on Krasnopresnenskaya Embankment. From then on, that complex of buildings in the centre of Moscow had become the headquarters of the resistance to the illegal authority of the coup organisers. We were shown the address by the Russian leadership to the citizens of Russia and the edict signed by President Yeltsin. These were clear, bold declarations

---

1 Now Nikitsky Boulevard
2 Now New Arbat Street

that befitted the enormity of the situation: "The committee's announcement shall be deemed anti-constitutional and its actions shall be treated as a coup d'etat... All decisions adopted in the name of the so-called committee shall be deemed illegal and devoid of force in the territory of the RSFSR". Such open opposition to the strong-arm measures of the central authority in the USSR seemed incredible. After all, the GKChP was led by the heads of the most fearsome agencies – the KGB, the Defence Ministry and the Interior Ministry. I remember what a great impression this made on the directors who had gathered at the meeting. Everyone was seized with optimism and enthusiasm. We discussed Luzhkov's call to declare a general strike in Moscow, but decided that food enterprises should continue to operate to ensure that the population remained fed. I left Mosagroprom in a completely different mood. Events were moving in an unexpected direction. I felt ashamed that, at a time when Moscow had become the scene of dramatic events of momentous significance for the entire country, I had almost thrown in the towel. Of course, I had embraced perestroika wholeheartedly, associating it with changes in our lives that I had dreamed of seeing. And yet, it seemed that the old fear of the rigid state-Party system was still deeply lodged inside me. Life had now turned all those past conceptions on their head. There is no doubt that this turn of events stemmed from the perestroika policies and the profound democratic transformations in the country. Most importantly of all, "His Majesty the People" had changed. After all, without the support of the population, no resistance to the coup leaders would have been possible.

The chronicle of events on the first day of the coup ran as follows. Troops and armoured vehicles occupied strategic points on the main roads leading to the centre of Moscow and surrounded the area adjacent to the Kremlin. A few dozen tanks drove right up close to the White House – the residence of the RSFSR government. At around twelve o'clock several thousand people gathered on Manezhnaya Square. The demonstrators began to head towards the White House. Boris Yeltsin came out to meet the thousands of people who had assembled at the White House and stood on a tank to read out a statement to the Russian people. The people outside the White House began erecting improvised barricades. Thus began the three-day defence of the White House as the centre of resistance to the coup. Now I understood where the columns of people on Kalinin Avenue had been heading. They had been

White House defenders, answering the call of the heart, resolute and ready for battle. This was a different country and a different people. A people like this could not be vanquished. This fact had evidently dawned on the coup leaders themselves, who were unable to conceal their total disarray and indecisiveness. In the evening, a press conference held in the Foreign Ministry press centre was broadcast on television. The GKChP members looked demoralised. The entire nation saw Yanayev's hands trembling with nervousness as he read out the committee's statement.

Resistance to the illegal regime was growing. Events unfolded at an incredible speed. There was an urgent need to restore the supply of reliable information to the public. The editors of eleven independent newspapers gathered in the offices of *Moskovskiye Novosti* and agreed to put out a "Common Newspaper" (*Obshchaya Gazeta*), which was hastily registered with the Russian Press Ministry. The highly respected Yegor Yakovlev stepped in as editor-in-chief, and the newspaper came out the very next day. The "Echo of Moscow" radio station continued broadcasting directly from the White House. People would be listening to the radio the whole day through, never switching it off. The defiance in Moscow was supported in other major cities. A huge demonstration took place on Palace Square in Leningrad. Demonstrations in support of the Russian leadership took place in Nizhny Novgorod, Sverdlovsk, Novosibirsk and Tyumen. Despite the curfew declared in Moscow, people came out onto the streets, building barricades to stop the armoured vehicles from advancing. As I drove through the streets, I saw many elderly Muscovites talking in a fatherly fashion to the servicemen, urging them not to go against the will of the people. It was clear that the use of military force was unlikely. Over two thousand people had formed a human ring around the White House. They were ready to stand to the end to prevent the Government House from being taken and Yeltsin and his allies from being arrested. More than once, there were alarming rumours that the KGB's special Alpha and Vympel units were poised to storm the building. But seeing the determination of the people and fearing large numbers of casualties, the coup leaders hesitated to act. By this time, it was obvious that the coup had failed. Panic broke out among the GKChP members. Prime Minister Valentin Pavlov was taken to hospital with high blood pressure. Then the news came that the Defence Minister, Yazov, had resigned. He must have realised that military action against one's own people was a terrible crime. And yet, casualties were not avoided. On the night of 20–21 August, three young men – Dmitry Komar, Vladimir Usov and Ilya Krichevsky – were killed in a tunnel at the intersection of Tchaikovsky Street (renamed Novinsky Boulevard in 1994) and Kalinin Avenue (now the New Arbat). This tragic incident, resulting in civilian deaths, precipitated the culmination of the August events. On the morning of 21 August, the GkChP ceased to exist.

RUSSIA'S BLOODLESS REVOLUTION. THE COLLAPSE OF THE USSR

For the entire duration of the coup Gorbachev was detained in Foros under the guard of a KGB unit. His communications with the outside world were cut off. On the night of 21–22 August, he and his family returned to Moscow accompanied by a delegation of the RSFSR leadership. His return was broadcast on television. He cut a deeply traumatised, crushed figure as he descended the steps from the plane. Revolutionary changes had occurred in the country during his absence. The attempt by the GKChP to use force to erase the achievements of perestroika and take the country back to the Brezhnev era of stagnation had wholly discredited the central authorities. The anti-constitutional actions of the coup leaders had not only not been rejected by Union institutions, but had effectively proceeded with their blessing. Neither the USSR Supreme Soviet nor the chief Party body, the CPSU Central Committee, had spoken out against the imposition of the state of emergency. No attempt had been made to convene an extraordinary meeting of the Congress of People's Deputies. Gorbachev's plans to establish a renewed USSR and reform the CPSU lay in tatters. The fact that the GKChP included figures from the president's immediate circle cast a shadow over his own role in August's tragic events. Boris Yeltsin had become the country's undisputed leader.

It would be accurate to say that the August coup, whose aims had been to preserve the USSR as a unitary state and restore the complete supremacy of the Party nomenclature, actually triggered the revolutionary events that brought about the collapse of the USSR, the dissolution of the top Party bodies – the Politburo and the CPSU Central Committee – and the banning of the CPSU itself. The plans of the coup leaders had failed completely, and the outcome was the exact opposite of what they had intended. The architects of the revolution had been the people themselves, who for the first time in Soviet history had stood up for democratic gains. There was unbounded rejoicing.

I myself remember feeling enormously uplifted. We had all become participants in great events that no one could have predicted. The idea of the Communist order ever falling had been impossible even to imagine. My wife and I were invited to a celebratory evening at the Bolshoi Theatre dedicated to the victory of democracy and the memory of the three young White House defenders who had innocently lost their lives. In the auditorium there were some well-known people, members of the elite. Sitting in the government box were Gorbachev and Khasbulatov,[1] to whom everyone gave a rapturous greeting (for some reason Yeltsin was not there). You probably never forget moments like that. But the euphoria of victory could not eclipse for long the serious problems that became still more acute after the August coup.

Arguments over how the USSR could have been saved and who was to blame for its collapse rage on to this day. Some criticise Gorbachev for carrying out reforms without having a clear idea of what the ultimate goals were. Others accuse Yeltsin of adventurism and a craving for power. Even now, many people think that the destruction of the USSR was a tragic mistake that resulted in the loss of a great country. Yes, Gorbachev fought to the end for the preservation of the Union, while Yeltsin strove to make Russia an independent state. But the collapse of the USSR did not come down to the aims of particular individuals; rather, it was the result of objective historical processes. The Soviet Union was the product of a Party-state machine which was reliant on the absolute power of the CPSU. As a result of the August events, the CPSU was banned and the supreme Party organ – the Central Committee – was dissolved. The system of government on which the USSR depended for its survival had been overthrown. No one could have predicted that things would turn out this way – least of all Mikhail Gorbachev, a committed Communist whose whole conscious life had been bound up with the Party. Gorbachev did not plan the collapse of the CPSU, but the ideas of perestroika and glasnost which he set in motion were designed to root out bureaucratism and dogmatism, which were part and parcel of the way in which the Party operated. The new ideas narrowed the

---

1 Ruslan Imranovich Khasbulatov (b. 1942) was then acting chairman of the RSFSR Supreme Soviet.

CPSU's field of operation. The Party was at odds with the General Secretary on fundamental matters concerning the country's development.

Boris Yeltsin must be given credit for his bold and resolute actions. At that decisive moment he showed himself to be an outstanding politician who knew how to lead. The image of Yeltsin on a tank delivering his statement to the Russian citizens gathered outside the White House has become a symbol of the heroic resistance to the anti-constitutional actions.

The Soviet Union ceased to exist. It happened in quite a humdrum way, without any of the fanfare one might expect for such an event. It was as if that huge country had never been, as if it had vanished without trace over the four months that followed the August events. The people were chanting "Russia! Russia!". All that remained was President Gorbachev, who, surrounded by his closest aides, announced his resignation and made a short farewell speech to the nation. After that, he left his office in the Kremlin for good. The statement was shown on television. It was painful to watch. At that moment, Gorbachev looked like the loneliest man in the world.

THE LEGACY OF PERESTROIKA AND THE NEW RUSSIA

Gorbachev's contribution to the reform of Soviet society was immense. He launched democratic processes in a totalitarian country virtually on his own amid the total supremacy of the CPSU and the absence of any organised democratic forces. Several generations of Soviet people had lived in a state of unfreedom and complete oppression by the state. Society had been in a state of deep depression. Gorbachev instinctively spoke directly to the people. People responded to the calls for change and believed in the sincerity of the country's new leader. Gorbachev's reforms rested on humanistic, democratic values: freedom of speech, individual enterprise, respect for the law. The country changed in front of our eyes. Freedom of the press, the emergence of social movements, and later political parties, permission to engage in entrepreneurial activity, the liberalisation of foreign economic relations – these were all things that had been under a Party taboo in the USSR. For the first time, people felt that they had a real part to play in shaping the structures that governed them. It was a tremendously uplifting time for all. There were heated arguments about the path the country should take. Everyone followed the open debate between

Gorbachev and Sakharov and the pointed speeches of that fine orator, Anatoly Sobchak. Articles by Yury Afanasyev, Yury Karyakin, Fyodor Burlatsky, Nikolai Shmelyov and other writers were eagerly devoured. After the mind-numbing, nonsensical Party slogans, people were finally hearing real, meaningful words. The mood of the nation was utterly transformed.

The structure of Soviet society changed. The country was gradually liberated from Party oppression. A viable entrepreneurial environment began to take shape. Many charismatic figures entered politics thanks to free elections. This gave talented and educated people a chance to be useful to the country and society, to assume a role befitting their capabilities and social position. Tremendous changes took place in all spheres of life. New political forces came into being. By the end of the perestroika period, over fifteen parties were in operation, all with their own political agendas. Even in the economic sphere, in which the policy was judged to have failed, reforms were enacted which set the course for the evolution of market relations and the independence of enterprises. From today's perspective, the law "On State Enterprises and Associations" is seen as affording extensive opportunities. Only we did not yet have the experience and knowledge to take full advantage of them.

Sovereign, democratic Russia became the successor to the USSR. The former republics became independent states and set off on their own paths. And these momentous changes occurred without major bloodshed. This was probably the best outcome that could have been imagined. The legacy left by the perestroika reforms had huge geopolitical significance. The military and political confrontation between East and West was ended for a long time to come. The Berlin Wall – one of the most odious symbols of the Cold War – was torn down. The countries of Eastern Europe gained their freedom. There was a surge of mutual understanding, allowing Russia's integration into broader European and global processes. And yet – such is the fate of the reformer in Russia! – Gorbachev hastily departed from the Kremlin without receiving a word of gratitude. Not only that, but he stands accused of starting perestroika without anticipating the consequences that led to the collapse of the USSR. I think these accusations are unfair. The country needed reforms like fresh air. And the transition from totalitarianism to democracy is such a hugely complex process that it is impossible for anyone to predict what the consequences will be.

The key to understanding the origins of the unprecedented response of the people must without doubt be sought in the personal freedom that was granted them by the perestroika policies. Freedom to receive information, choose an occupation and hold political views. Freedom to choose a place to live, travel around the country and go abroad. The chance to have a say by voting in honest, transparent elections at all levels of government. These changes helped people to form their self-identity, gave them a greater sense of dignity, made them feel that their opinion had to be respected. I remember noticing how the workers at the factory were suddenly transformed. Gone was their indifference, replaced by a sense of investment in a common cause. They were not afraid of speaking their mind, regardless of their rank.

The Communist regime ruined the lives of many millions of people. The ideological principles on which it operated claimed to be progressive, but in reality were inhumane and mendacious. People's lives were placed in the service of mythical state interests embodied in the Party-state bureaucracy, whose influence invaded every aspect of existence. Even family bonds were not safe from the merciless penetration of ideology. People hid the truth about their loved ones who had been innocently repressed and declared enemies of the people.

Gorbachev opened the country to the world. Soviet people, and then Russians, could freely travel abroad and do business with foreign partners. Many emigrants, deprived of their citizenship, were at last able to return to their homeland. People were no longer afraid to acknowledge their origins and could freely associate with friends or relatives who had previously been regarded as traitors. After many long years of worshipping various "-isms", ordinary human fairness had started to come back to life.

For the new Russia, negotiating the path of democratic reforms was a tortuous process. Although the CPSU had been dissolved, the spirit of the Party's ideology was deeply rooted in many people's consciousness and resisted change. Not everyone viewed freedom and new opportunities as important relative to the hardship of losing the accustomed, guaranteed Soviet "stability". The upheavals were enormous. The country went through some difficult ordeals: the "shock therapy" of Gaidar's reforms, the privatisation of enterprises, the unrelenting battle between the forces embodying the new Russia and the old Party hardliners. People suffered terrible privations and stress. After long years of guaranteed Communist "levelling", people had to adapt to new ways of living, where they decided their own fate rather than the state doing it for them.

Many found this difficult and were forced to rethink their views on life. But, as a result of these difficult trials, Russia became a state that fitted in with the global system of development, with an elected parliament, multiple political parties, a market economy and principles allowing the free development of society.

The Yava factory also entered upon a long and difficult journey. Following privatisation, the Yava-Tabak open joint stock company was formed. A controlling interest was bought by the international tobacco company British American Tobacco (BAT). The enterprise was completely rebuilt, and modern production processes were implemented. As part of an international company, the BAT-Yava factory began to use the latest advances in global management. It was a colossal leap forward. We had to cross the chasm between a Soviet enterprise and a modern business in a single jump. The nature and objectives of our activities changed completely. Whereas before we had wrestled with internal difficulties, battling to fulfil the state plan, now our efforts were focused on appealing to the consumer, increasing the market share of our products and raising efficiency. Other tobacco factories in Russia were also undergoing development. Philip Morris, Reynolds and Liggett & Myers bought controlling shares in large enterprises. Now there was stiff competition on the cigarette market. Shops and kiosks offered a full selection of the best foreign brands. It was a serious test for traditional Soviet products. I am proud to say that only Yava cigarettes managed to survive and remain on the market. The Yava product family was joined by the Yava Gold brand, which achieved great popularity and offered serious competition to the international brands.

Crucially, Yava's staff had been prepared for these changes by its entire past history and greeted the new arrangements with dignity. We proved that we could work as equal partners of an international company. We defended our identity and remained true to ourselves. A symbolic event occurred when descendants of the factory's founder, Samuil Gabay, came to see us. It was in June 2003 that this momentous visit took place. The factory welcomed Irina Olegovna Fokke, her father Oleg Alexandrovich Bayul and her son Oleg Pudikov – the granddaughter, son-in-law and great-grandson of the last owner, Iosif Samuilovich Gabay. We learned a lot first-hand about the fate of that once very influential family. After the Revolution, all the Gabays' property was nationalised. Fortunately, they managed to avoid serious repressions. Polina Nikolayevna, Gabay's wife, was a well-known beautician. After the Revolution she continued to run a fashionable salon on

Stoleshnikov Lane, where her clients included the wives and girlfriends of high-ranking Soviet officials. In the end, however, the Gabays did not avoid the fate of the so-called "disenfranchised" – people who were deprived of personal and political rights because of their non-proletarian origins. An honorary hereditary citizen of Moscow, Iosif Gabay lived first in Sukhumi, then in Tver. Their only daughter, Anna, was unable to obtain a higher education and worked as an accompanist her whole life. Gabay's son-in-law, Oleg Alexandrovich Bayul, recounted a moving story of true love. In 1935 he met Anna in Kislovodsk and fell in love at first sight. They were twenty-one. Oleg worked in the Kremlin as deputy secretary of a Komsomol (Communist Youth) organisation. Marrying the daughter of a former factory owner was out of the question. Nevertheless, he was determined to do just that. When he told his boss, the latter could not believe his ears. "Are you out of your mind?! We'll pretend that you didn't say anything". Despite everything, two years later he and Anna were married. It meant that Oleg had to quit his job. Iosif Samuilovich Gabay lived to quite a ripe old age before he died in 1937 in Tver.

Of course, the Gabays' story is by no means the most tragic example of the family sagas that took place after 1917. Samuil Sadukovich Gabay made a great contribution to the development of manufacturing industry in Russia. Of Karaite descent, born in Crimea, he was an intelligent, enterprising man. By the age of thirty he owned tobacco plantations and a small factory in Kharkov. During the Crimean War[1] he moved to Moscow and began trading in tobacco products. In 1856 he founded a small workshop, which in time grew into a large tobacco factory: the future Yava. His son Iosif became involved in running the factory from the age of eighteen. Under Iosif Samuilovich's leadership the factory became well known throughout the country and supplied products to the Imperial Palace. He maintained a family atmosphere at the factory, treating the workers with compassion. He was respected and loved for his kindness. And now at last, in the new Russia, Gabay's descendants could openly take pride in their provenance as equal citizens. Irina Olegovna told us that her father and son had opened a private business in Moscow in 1992 – and so the Gabay dynasty of entrepreneurs lives on.

---

1 1854–1855.

CHAPTER 15.

NEW RUSSIA

THE TRANSITION TO THE MARKET WAS INEVITABLE

On one of the last days of December 1991, right before New Year, a very important meeting took place in my office. Besides the deputy head of the Rosbakaleya office, Dmitry Dreitsen, it was attended by my closest assistants – the chief accountant, Alla Poloiko, and the head of the legal department, Yury Polisar. The subject of our discussion was a matter of revolutionary significance. Under an edict signed by Yeltsin, prices in Russia were to be freed as from 2 January 1992, effectively signifying a transition to a market economy. Shortly before that, he had signed edicts on the liberalisation of foreign trade and the convertibility of the rouble. With effect from 1 January, restrictions on the purchase of foreign currency were lifted for both individuals and legal entities. All this meant that enterprises would have complete independence in buying materials, organising the production and distribution of finished products, and setting and achieving economic targets. First, however, there was the matter of setting prices for our products. I hardly need say that this was the first time that we had been faced with such a task. It was a highly complex undertaking with many unknowns. We could not simply take the production cost and add a profit margin, as we did not yet know how much our suppliers would be charging us. Nor did we know the exchange rate for converting roubles into hard currency, which made it impossible to estimate the cost of our imports.

We decided, therefore, to approach the problem from a different angle – by working out how much the potential buyers of our products could afford. By the end of 1991, a genuine tobacco market had begun to emerge. Imported cigarettes of such international brands as Marlboro, Kent, Winston, Liggett & Myers, and so on, had appeared in tobacco kiosks. This had been made possible by the first steps towards the liberalisation of foreign trade even before the collapse of the USSR. The State Bank had begun conducting the first currency auctions, widely referred to as "tights and fags" auctions. Businessmen would buy hard currency at market price and import scarce consumer goods and computers. State prices were kept in place for products made by the domestic tobacco industry, while commercial prices could be set for imported cigarettes. The lowest price for a pack of imported cigarettes was around eight roubles. This was quite a large sum, so the people who switched to buying foreign cigarettes were those whose incomes allowed them to do so. After analysing the situation, we decided that, to retain customers for our main product, soft-pack Yavas, a retail price of four roubles per pack would be reasonable. Accordingly, a factory price of three roubles was set, plus a trade mark-up of around 30 per cent Our calculations proved correct. Meanwhile, a rather curious situation arose with Ducat's products. Literally the day before, Ducat had set up the tobacco industry's first joint venture with the American firm Liggett & Myers. The young, ambitious management set a wholesale price of five roubles for filter cigarettes, meaning that they retailed at about six roubles per pack. This caused consternation among smokers, to put it mildly. It was hard to find any justification for such a high price. It even sparked an improbable rumour that the Liggett-Ducat JV had already begun producing international-class cigarettes. However, it very quickly became clear that no changes in quality had occurred, and the cigarettes stopped selling. The price had to be reduced. This foul-up did not do much good for the image of Ducat products.

The freeing of prices completely upended the economic relationships that had prevailed over the years of Soviet rule. Of course, it meant that manufacturers could set prices that reflected the new level of costs. That was essential to encourage production. But for the public, it came as a real shock. In January 1992 prices rose by an average of 3.5 times,[1] slashing the value of private savings. The majority of people were unprepared for this. Foundations had to be laid for life in the new reality.

There are still arguments to this day about whether such draconian measures were justified. I can give an account of my own experience – a view from within, so to speak. During the last few months, we had been operating by inertia, using the remaining stocks of materials in the warehouses. Our regular supplier, the Arkhangelsk Pulp and Paper Plant, had stopped supplying us with

---

1   The inflation rate in 1992 was over 2500 per cent. It went down to 850 per cent in 1993, 215 per cent in 2014 and 131 per cent in 1995.

our allocated quantities of *papirosa* paper. A similar situation had arisen with other materials. The demolition of the command-administrative system was threatening to put enterprises out of operation altogether. Price liberalisation made it possible to revive relationships between buyers and suppliers, only this time on a commercial footing. Immediately after the edict came out, we received a telegram from Arkhangelsk offering to supply us with paper at new prices. Our suppliers had a reason to start producing again. We received similar offers from other suppliers. Tobacco supplies had come from the Union republics, which were now independent states. In this case there was no question that things had to be arranged by commercial means. It is a fact that price liberalisation saved industry from inevitable collapse. The freeing of prices was meant to rebalance the purchasing power of the rouble and incentivise manufacturers to increase production. The state no longer set production targets for enterprises. We made our own plans based on production capacity and sales forecasts. The liberalisation of foreign trade and the convertibility of the rouble opened up Russia's market for imported goods. The reformers were proved right. Gradually, stores filled up with goods and queues disappeared. Manufacturers began to compete to sell their products. The changes on the cigarette market were a good example. Now, kiosk and shop windows displayed row upon row of all kinds of imported cigarettes, and in among them were packs of Yava and Ducat products. No other Russian manufacturers managed to break into the Moscow market.

One of the most acute problems for industry in the USSR had been access to hard currency. Centralised methods did not lend themselves to the efficient use of hard currency. As a result of the economic reforms, hard currency needs could be met through the market. Enterprises began to buy currency from commercial banks using their own money, and the dollar exchange rate was determined by trading on the Moscow Interbank Currency Exchange (MICEX). Under the new legislation, exporters were obliged to sell a portion of their hard currency proceeds on that exchange. The price of the dollar was determined by supply and demand. In January 1992 it rose to 125 roubles (compared to the USSR rate of 0.63 roubles to the dollar). The price continued to rise, reaching over 400 roubles at the beginning of 1993. Enterprises were free to buy hard currency, but now they had to consider whether it made economic sense to do so. Economic factors began to play a key role in decision-making.

The most significant changes occurred in the area of product sales. Instead of shortages, there was suddenly real competition on the market. It became very difficult for Russian products to stand up against the flood of imported goods. The systemic problems of Soviet industry – outdated technology and high production costs – rose to the surface. There was absolutely no experience of operating in a market environment, no flexibility, no focus on the needs of the consumer. These were serious shortcomings which could not be remedied overnight. One of the first sectors to cave in to competition with imports was the consumer goods industry. The introduction of free trade brought about a sharp rise in a new form of entrepreneurial activity carried on by so-called "shuttle traders". They would bring in cheap goods, mainly clothes and shoes, from China and Turkey. These goods were often imitations of well-known international brands, while domestically produced wares were based on old Soviet designs and were priced higher, making it impossible for them to compete. Decreased sales meant that enterprises were deprived of the working capital needed to keep themselves in operation. There were delays in paying wages to workers. Then, wages began to be paid in the form of factory output. Suddenly, you would see people selling blankets, towels, tablecloths and linen along the sides of main roads. Workers tried to sell products themselves in order to turn their wages into cash. It was a sorry picture.

Many enterprises across various industries faced problems with sales. Our neighbour, the once famous Slava Second Watch Factory, faded away before our eyes. Large quantities of imported watches had appeared on the market, distinguished by eye-catching modern designs and low prices. Soviet-made watches had a relatively high reputation for quality, but their designs were dull and unattractive. The factory did not have the technology needed to modernise products and make them cheaper. A watch, after all, is an accessory, an element of personal style, as much as anything else. No attention had been paid to that fact in the USSR. But when imported products appeared, it was the design element that attracted buyers. Sales of Russian-made watches dried up. Gradually, employees were let go, and workshops emptied. Workers began to receive salaries in the form of alarm clocks. To keep afloat, the factory rented its vacated spaces out to commercial entities. The large administrative building was dotted with signs bearing the names of various tenant companies.

In a market environment, the main problem is ensuring that your products sell. If you have sales, you have money coming in to boost your working capital, pay wages to employees and pay your suppliers. But Soviet enterprises, accustomed to working in a "shortage economy", were not ready to face real competition. It was in the area of sales that all the shortcomings of Russian industry were laid bare. Difficulties in finding buyers for their goods typically left enterprises unable to pay each other or their employees. Of course, different industries started from different positions, each having to find its own development path and work out its own approach to operating in the marketplace.

The tobacco industry faced stiff competition from imported cigarettes. This affected different segments of the tobacco market in different ways. The poorest and most conservative consumers continued to smoke unfiltered cigarettes and *papirosy*, so there was little change in those segments. As far as Yava products and the filter cigarette segment were concerned, the factory had to go toe to toe with the foreign brands and fight for its customer base. One might ask, what chance did a Soviet enterprise stand of surviving in the marketplace? But there were two important factors that could be used to the advantage of Russian products. Firstly, the majority of smokers had limited incomes: the household budget made it impossible for them to switch to imported brands. Secondly, and no less importantly, imported cigarettes differed greatly from their Russian counterparts in terms of both flavour and strength, and by no means all smokers were prepared to change their habits. It was on exploiting these advantages that the Yava factory focused its efforts.

How could Yava cigarettes be made cheaper than foreign brands? After all, foreign enterprises had much better technology and much higher efficiency, meaning that they used less raw material and achieved higher labour productivity. Realistically, therefore, one way to keep the price down was to use domestically sourced materials. Prices for Russian-made products were generally lower than for imports. But the factory was compelled to source most of its manufacturing materials – cigarette and tipping paper, filters, and cellophane – from abroad. The only thing left was the tobacco itself. The cost of 1 kg of tobacco blend for the production of the major foreign brands was around four dollars. To achieve an acceptable price for our cigarettes, we needed to keep this down to one dollar. That price could only be secured by arranging supplies from the former Union republics, now member states of the CIS.[1] But there were serious difficulties where this was concerned. Changes in ownership structures and other

---

1   CIS – the Commonwealth of Independent States.

transitional processes in the former republics had caused tobacco production to fall, reducing the reliability of supplies. Some farms had stopped working. Stocks of tobacco in the factory's warehouses were beginning to dwindle.

Yava had found its niche in the market, but we were fully aware of how unstable the situation was. To withstand competition from imported brands, we would need to improve the quality of our cigarettes and bring in new technologies. We did not have the resources to do that. On the contrary, our cost-cutting policy meant that we actually had to reduce the quality of Yava cigarettes. This was mainly due to the need to keep down the cost of the tobacco blend. Whereas in Soviet times the factory had received good-quality imported tobaccos, now we quite often had to resort to the principle of "whatever it takes" just to keep production running. There was even a crisis period in which we had to make do with virtually one tobacco grade for almost a whole month. That was in September-October 1992. Warehouse stocks had fallen to a critical level, and shipments from the new harvest had not yet begun. We cast around desperately for a way out of the situation, realising that the factory was threatened with imminent shutdown. Suddenly, we received an offer to make a barter deal: we would receive a large shipment of tobacco from Azerbaijan in exchange for cigarettes. It turned out that Yava cigarettes had not lost their appeal. The parties fulfilled their respective obligations. Whether smokers noticed the deterioration in flavour, I cannot say, but at least it meant that we kept up supplies of Yava cigarettes to the market.

After the episode with the Azerbaijani tobacco, the problem with supplies of raw material began to resolve itself. Smaller, more mobile foreign firms got wind of the problems faced by Russia's tobacco enterprises and began offering tobacco from Turkey, Greece, Middle Eastern countries and South Africa at reasonable prices. Yava's first import contracts were with a well-known businessman from Zimbabwe, Alvin Pollack. He had had experience of dealing with former socialist bloc countries (Poland, Czechoslovakia) which had faced similar problems in making the transition to market relations. The imported tobacco was of a somewhat low quality, in keeping with its price. But having it enabled us to create a more balanced tobacco blend.

And so, step by step, we endeavoured to overcome the hurdles using all the means at our disposal. The factory had remained a financially stable enterprise after the transition to market relations. We had managed to maintain our output levels, and Yava cigarettes were still in demand. Money from the sale of our products was steadily flowing into the factory's account. At a time when non-payments were rife, Yava settled with its suppliers on time and was never once late in paying wages. People we talked to were impressed at how high these were. But we knew how precarious this situation was. Our equipment and technology were hopelessly out of date. The Mark 8 machines had been used for over twenty-five years. I think that must be something of a world record. The factory was in dire need of major investment. Yava was ready to work with foreign firms. And international companies were interested in getting a firm foothold in the Russian market. Not just to supply their products, but to start manufacturing them in Russia itself. The Russian cigarette market was one of the largest in the world, and at that stage international brands made up only a small percentage of it. The biggest share was accounted for by ordinary Russian cigarettes, which were what the majority of smokers could afford. To establish a presence across all market segments, foreign companies needed to set up production within the country, especially as they had enough spare capital to invest in the development of Russian tobacco factories. It was a rare instance of the interests of international manufacturers wholly coinciding with those of large Russian tobacco enterprises. Now that the lines had been drawn, everyone awaited the acceptance of their privatisation documents.

THE FIRST MONTHS OF THE REAL MARKET. A CHALLENGE JUST TO SURVIVE

Operating in a real economy confronted industry with new, complex challenges. Inflation was galloping. Over 30 per cent of the population was below the poverty line. Enterprises were forced to raise prices, and with real household incomes falling, this led to a sharp fall in consumer demand. Sales of consumer goods declined. In the food industry, output fell by 20 per cent.

The tobacco industry had its own unique factors to contend with. A smoker grows accustomed to a certain daily dose, meaning that, to sustain sales and maintain output, the factory had to keep prices within an affordable range. That was hugely difficult. Suppliers were raising their prices, and the price of the dollar kept on rising. We had our workers to think about too: because of the high rate of inflation we regularly had to increase their wages. And so we operated at a minimal profit. We could not expect to make much in such tight circumstances. Our priorities were to preserve the enterprise's workforce and meet the needs of Yava smokers.

Problems of a particular kind arose in searching for a sales agent. This field of business had proved to be a highly expedient way of generating start-up capital. Besides, it was a time when fundamental shifts had begun to occur in the priorities of the population. Cuts to the funding of state-owned organisations had left the staff of research, educational and government institutions bereft of motivation. They were forced to change occupation and turn their hand to business. Since jobs in manufacturing were mostly taken, many enterprising people headed into sales and distribution despite not having adequate training. "Buy and sell" is what they called the business then. It attracted light-fingered sorts and members of criminal groups. They began grabbing the most profitable areas of trade. The business world became a dangerous place. Seeking protection and security, trade organisations began hiring law enforcement agencies and criminal outfits alike as a *krysha* (or "roof"). Thus, trade became a place where the interests of very different forces came together. For enterprises, this made choosing partners to sell their products a complex and demanding task. Some directors attempted to handle their own sales. But it was difficult to combine production and trading roles. It could be dangerous, too. Intentions in that direction ended tragically for the general director of the famous Cheryomushki bakery and confectionery plant. The plant was the sole producer of the highly popular Charodeika cakes. Evidently, the director had been unhappy with the work of the enterprise's sales agents. One morning as he left his apartment for work, there was a large explosion. He lost his leg and was disabled for life. There were many other cases of gang violence over popular products.

The Yava factory's products still had great appeal. The shortages of old were no longer an issue, and Yava cigarettes were always available in Moscow's retail outlets even though sales were very high. There were many sales agencies with an interest in selling tobacco products. After analysing the situation, we decided to take a cautious approach to this matter – especially as the USSR had had a relatively stable system for the distribution of tobacco products. The Rosbakaleya Moscow office, which had handled wholesale operations for tobacco and confectionery products, was still essentially intact and had been converted into a commercial organisation. It was now the joint stock company

TKS (tobacco, confectionery, salt). Yava sold all its products to TKS at factory prices. TKS in turn had contracts with seven trading firms which bought the cigarettes at wholesale prices. We were satisfied with the arrangement. Our trading partners displayed an interest in developing their business and strictly adhered to a uniform pricing policy. This came to be a highly important factor in keeping retail prices stable. The retail trade system ensured the availability of a whole range of tobacco products all over the city. Cigarettes were sold not only through tobacco kiosks, but also through newsstands and other retail outlets. Everywhere they acted as a key profit-making product.

A distinctive feature of that time (the early 1990s) was the sight of elderly women – *babushkas* – peddling cigarettes beside metro stations and other busy places. In place of a window display they would hold up an assorted set of cigarette packs wrapped in transparent film, while next to them would stand a box containing their wares. Many people bought cigarettes from them not only because they were a little cheaper than in the kiosks and it was convenient to buy cigarettes on the go. There was also a moral factor involved. Everyone knew about the hardships faced by elderly people. This type of trade became so common that purchases "from *babushkas*" began to appear as a separate item in market price surveys.

Cigarette imports occupied a particular place in the scheme of things. It was considered one of the most reliable and profitable lines of activity, and one that was not easy to get into. Initially, it was the preserve of commercial entities with close ties to the government. Later, the government assumed full control over this area of business and effectively began using it as a source of funding for specific social programmes. Quotas for duty-free tobacco imports were granted under presidential edicts to the Russian Fund for Disabled Veterans of the Afghan War, the National Sports Fund, the Fiftieth Anniversary of Victory Fund and the Orthodox Church. These "generous gifts" brought little benefit. Doubts arose about the proper use of the proceeds. Conflicts broke out within the organisations themselves. Bombs went off at the Afghan Veteran Fund and serious abuses were uncovered at the Sports Fund. The association with the sale of tobacco and alcohol inflicted considerable reputational damage on the Church.

Fundamental changes occurred in the banking system. The State Bank of the USSR, which had been in charge of all banking operations in the country, had been dissolved. The Central Bank of the Russian Federation, which was established in its place, was responsible, among other things, for implementing state monetary policy and overseeing the activities of commercial banks. It was the commercial banks that provided services to enterprises and organisations. The creation of private banks could be very lucrative, but equally very risky. They began to multiply like flies. Many of them had neither adequate capital nor suitably qualified staff. They varied in their terms of business and transaction charges. Choosing the right bank became a key factor in organising an enterprise's financial arrangements. We were lucky in this regard. The Frunzensky branch of the USSR State Bank, with which the factory had a long-standing relationship, was reconstituted as the Frunzensky Commercial Bank, managed by the former branch chairman, Tamara Sergeyevna Krushinskaya. The Yava factory was a good client for the bank, too, with its relative financial stability and large daily turnover. The Frunzensky bank had a good knowledge of our enterprise's financial arrangements. This meant that the transition to the new banking system was a comparatively painless process for Yava.

The conversion of the Soviet command economy to a market system was a hugely complex challenge. The risks were immense, the consequences unpredictable. It was rather like leaving a rudderless, unseaworthy ship at the mercy of a raging ocean. It is hardly surprising that the reformers referred to themselves as the "kamikaze government" and set themselves a time limit of no more than a year in which to do their work. The government's first task after freeing prices was to avert a disaster scenario in macroeconomic terms. This required it to pursue tough monetary policies. The first to suffer as a result were Group A enterprises – manufacturers of means of production. Their sales fell sharply as government investment decreased. The situation was exacerbated by the fact that these enterprises had a long operating cycle, and the lack of adequate working capital made it impossible to finance production. High inflation meant that borrowing was virtually out of the question. Group B enterprises were in a better position. Although their output was falling, there was real demand for their products. And by making their goods cheaper, it was possible to carve out a niche in the market. Everything was decided by competition, but not all enterprises could withstand it.

Nevertheless, as a result of the liberalisation policies, the country had begun to live in a real economy. Shop shelves had started filling up with food and goods. Street markets were springing up all over the place. At the same time, it was the most difficult and dangerous period of the reforms. The break-up of the Soviet command-administrative system and the rapid transition to market relations brought devastating consequences. Many enterprises found themselves on the verge of bankruptcy, and most of the population slipped below the poverty line. There were delays in paying workers their wages. A major problem in the economy was that of non-payments between enterprises, which could only be addressed by relaxing monetary policy and increasing subsidies to industrial and agricultural enterprises. Despite all this, the first four months of rigorous stabilisation enabled the economy to come through the most challenging phase of price liberalisation. This was a major triumph for Yegor Gaidar's government. It was with good reason that he personally headed up the Ministry of Economics and Finance, which was at the centre of the process. When I met Gaidar after he left office, I saw at once that Yegor Timurovich had been precisely the man to get the job done. He was a man of unique intellectual abilities. As a brilliant chess player, he could rapidly map out in his mind the various ramifications of his decisions. Not to mention his impeccable honesty.

THE INVOLVEMENT OF INTERNATIONAL COMPANIES IN PRIVATISATION

The industry's first joint stock company with foreign capital was founded in St Petersburg as a partnership between the Uritsky Factory and the American firm Reynolds. The partners had studied each other well, as the question of setting up a joint venture had first arisen back in 1989. A very important consideration where privatisation involving foreign capital was concerned was that the investments had to be fully guaranteed. After all, there were large sums of money involved. The foreign partners usually wanted to have control over the company. Although the share ownership figures were not made public, I am sure that Reynolds received a controlling stake in the enterprise. A key factor was the support given by the St Petersburg city government. The enterprise was certainly in a worrying condition. Once the USSR's leading factory, it was still making outdated products and had lost its influence on the market. On visiting the factory, I had seen what a sorry, neglected state it was in. Bringing it back to life would take major investment, effectively the building of a new plant. The approval of the first joint stock company with the involvement of a major international company in 1992 was a landmark event. Directors of tobacco enterprises were invited to the signing of the agreement. The lavish reception put on at a government residence was attended by the city's leaders. Among them was Vladimir Putin, who at that time was head of the foreign economic relations section of the Mayor's Office. Putin opened the ceremony and read out a welcome message from the mayor, Anatoly Sobchak. Closer to midnight, arriving from some other important event, Sobchak himself appeared together with his wife. Everything was organised to a top-class standard. Reynolds duly honoured its commitments. The resulting joint stock company, RJR-Petro, produced a wide range of tobacco products, including the first successfully selling filter cigarettes to be developed by a foreign company in Russia, Peter I. Plus, of course, the international brands, Camel and Winston.

I returned to Moscow with a full realisation of the momentous significance of the changes that were happening. The industry now had its first joint stock company with foreign capital. The factory would undergo extensive rebuilding with the complete replacement of its equipment. Previously, this would have been unthinkable. It set a real challenge for its competitors. Yava had yet to go down this path, and I felt the heavy weight of responsibility that went with making these decisions. We too were preparing to establish a joint venture and had opted for the second privatisation option, which meant that the state would put up 49 per cent of the shares at auction. This was not something that could be left to chance. It was vital to select an investor in advance, agree on all the details and then decide on the strategy for the investor's participation in the share auction. The Yava factory was one of the most attractive investment targets, and there were plenty of investors who wanted to buy a stake in it. But it was clear to us that only one of the international tobacco companies was realistically capable of bringing in new technology and equipment and modern methods of management.

The situation had not been looking ideal. Reynolds had made a deal with St Petersburg, while Philip Morris was looking at the Krasnodar Tobacco Plant. The company had evidently decided to favour enterprises in the provinces, where it was easier to deal with the local authorities. For all its undeniable advantages, Yava was vulnerable in terms of its prospects for growth. The factory was located in the centre of Moscow, confined within strict boundaries. This made the job of finding a partner all the more difficult.

Suddenly, however, another player appeared on the horizon in the shape of the international tobacco firm British American Tobacco (BAT), one of the Big Three companies (alongside Philip Morris and Reynolds) and the maker of such well-known brands as Kent, Lucky Strike and Pall Mall. This large company, headquartered in London, had never had any ties with the USSR and therefore had no clear idea about the state of tobacco enterprises in Russia. BAT's managers must have realised that they risked leaving it too late to get in on the privatisation of Russian tobacco factories and decided to make up for lost time. To this end, in the summer of 1992, a private plane was dispatched to Russia containing an entire assault force of specialists, who proceeded to visit a number of tobacco factories in various parts of the country. In July they came to Yava and made a close inspection of the plant. It was clear that they had come with specific business intentions. At the end, the leader of the group, Mr Wan Wai, informed us that the factory would very soon receive a visit from the head of BAT, Sir Patrick Sheehy.

That visit took place at the end of August. In the evening I was invited to a business supper at the Olympic Penta, Moscow's first European-class hotel, where BAT had opened a commercial office shortly before. Sir Patrick made a great impression on me. A large, colourful and very open person with an easy manner, he was what people call a "self-made man". He had been with BAT his whole life, working his way up from the very bottom of the ladder. At the beginning of the meeting Sir Patrick seemed troubled. It emerged that he had gone to see Luzhkov that day about establishing a joint enterprise. Yury Mikhailovich had greeted him drily, telling him that they were too late, both Moscow factories already had partners: Ducat had gone into a joint venture with Liggett & Myers, while Yava already had an arrangement with Philip Morris. I was taken aback. Luzhkov must have got mixed up, thinking about earlier plans. I had to clarify the situation, explaining that Yava was indeed looking for a privatisation partner. After that, the conversation assumed a business-like nature and we quickly established a rapport. BAT had attracted our attention on a number of counts. It was a flexible and loyal company without the rigid centralisation that was characteristic of the American firms. Structurally, it consisted of the holding company BAT Industries and a number of largely independent firms: Suza Cruz in Brazil, BAT Deutschland in Germany, BAT UK in Britain, and Brown & Williamson in America. Those companies even had their own separate commercial offices in Moscow, each with its own independent marketing policies. This meant that there was more flexibility over cigarette brands. Besides the well-known international brands, there was an active policy of developing popular local cigarette brands. This was important for us, as we were eager to preserve the uniqueness of Yava as the country's leading cigarette brand.

The following day, we had a meeting at the factory and agreed to do business together. Since the privatisation process in Moscow was only just beginning, we decided to work on setting up a JV. This would allow us to start work straight away, get to know each better and work out proposals on renovation and investment. Once the documents were ready, it would be quicker and easier to set the privatisation process rolling. Before we could start, we had to get approval from the Moscow government. I took a draft letter of intent to the deputy mayor responsible for foreign economic matters, Ordzhonikidze. Iosif Nikolayevich greeted me pleasantly and promised his support. A short time later he informed us that Luzhkov had given his approval. The British side were impressed at how quickly the matter was resolved. BAT was likewise eager to start work sooner rather than later. A letter of intent signing ceremony was scheduled for as early as 2 November 1992. A large delegation came to Moscow to attend the ceremony. Sir Patrick Sheehy was accompanied by two key assistants who had played an important role in progressing the deal: the new development director, Nick Brookes, and the corporate relations director, Michael Prideaux. The ceremony took place in Moscow's swankiest hotel, the Baltschug-Kempinski opposite the Kremlin, which had just opened after refurbishment. The rooms still smelled of fresh paint. Our side was represented by the factory's managers and chief specialists. The director of the Rostabakprom association, Terevtsov, and the former head of Glavtabak, Zverev, were also invited. The "Letter of Intent" was ceremoniously signed by the president of BAT, and on the Russian side by Ordzhonikidze (on behalf of the Moscow government) and your humble servant. After the signing, our people had a chance to mingle with the foreign company's staff, which was important just before the start of a major joint undertaking. Sir Patrick could be seen in animated conversation with Iosif Ordzhonikidze. Later, in London, he joked about having drunk vodka at breakfast on a frosty Moscow morning with Luzhkov's deputy. Strictly speaking, Sir Patrick was a champagne man, but he was not averse to stronger tipples now and then.

As we prepared for privatisation, we realised how much hard work was involved in establishing a joint venture with foreign capital. These were completely new processes for our country, whereas elsewhere in the world they were common practice. The Yava factory needed to hire professional consultants with international experience in supporting such deals. More often than not, such services were provided by special divisions of investment banks, which had also begun looking into new opportunities for doing business in Russia. We received an offer of services from the well-known bank, Credit Suisse First Boston (CSFB). Little did we know when we signed this agreement that the bank would become just about the number one player in the privatisation process in Russia, and our advisers would be Boris Jordan and Leonid Rozhetskin,[1] who went on to play important roles in major privatisation deals. At first, matters were handled by a pleasant, intelligent young man called Leonid Anikeyev. Very soon, however, reinforcements were sent over to Moscow from London. The investment office in Russia was headed by the young, ambitious Boris Jordan, an American citizen and third-generation Russian émigré. His grandfather had been a White officer, his father a naval officer with the American armed forces. Boris had been brought up on love for Russia and its pre-revolutionary traditions – which explains why, after becoming a prominent businessman, he established the Cadet Corps Fund in Russia. In the USA he received a good education, started his business career early and made a success of handling investment deals. Inspired by the dramatic changes happening in Russia, he came to Moscow to get involved in privatisation. Boris thrived on constant activity. Here, happily for him, there were opportunities to satisfy both his professional and spiritual impulses at the same time. I remember when I first saw Boris Jordan in the bank's new headquarters – a freshly renovated building next to the famous McDonald's restaurant on Pushkin Square. Enthused by what was happening in Russia, he paced energetically around his office giving me a lecture on Western approaches to investments. Despite his youth, he was a mature, professional person, focused on his goals. He took personal charge of the Yava-BAT project and we had the opportunity to witness at first hand his great professionalism and fantastic capacity for work. We would be working together intensely for a little under two years.

---

1   Leonid Borisovich Rozhetskin (1966–2008) was actively involved in Russia's business life. He was murdered in mysterious circumstances.

The first phase of work consisted of two main strands. The factory management prepared the set of documents needed to register the joint stock company, while a group of foreign specialists, assisted by the factory's engineers, made a detailed study of the works and drew up a plan for the renovation of the factory and the replacement of its equipment. They prepared an investment programme. Meanwhile, contacts with the management of BAT were further strengthened. The factory was visited by the company's second-in-command, the executive director Martin Broughton, the technical director Ulrich Herter, and other executives.

The question of the establishment of the joint stock company was reviewed by a commission from the Moscow Property Administration Committee. It was a complex, multi-stage process. A lot of economic and technical calculations had to be made. In July 1993, the open joint stock company Yava-Tabak was established with a charter capital of 157 million roubles. 157 million shares were issued at a price of 1 rouble each. We opted for the second privatisation option, whereby investors were brought in through an investment tender. The enterprise's personnel received 51 per cent of the shares, and the Moscow government 49 per cent, of which 25 per cent had to be sold through a public "voucher" auction and 15 per cent went to the winner of the investment tender. Of the remaining 9 per cent, 4 per cent was sold by cash auction and 5 per cent was transferred to the enterprise as a bonus after the successful completion of the process.

PRIVATISATION NOT AS CHUBAIS INTENDED

This was the time of the mass privatisation of industrial enterprises – the grand sell-off of state property. To facilitate public participation, Anatoly Chubais – the key architect of the privatisation process – proposed the use of privatisation "vouchers". Every inhabitant of the country – children included – was issued one voucher, which could be used to buy shares in state-owned enterprises. The face value of a voucher was 10,000 roubles. It was determined by dividing the total book value of the country's fixed assets by the size of the population. This was considered a fair way of ensuring that every inhabitant received the right to an equal portion of state property. This seemed fine in theory, but no realistic mechanism was developed for the fair exchange of an individual person's voucher for shares in enterprises. Since state property was sold through auctions in exchange for vouchers, the auctions themselves were called voucher auctions. It was practically pointless for an individual person with his handful of vouchers to participate in auctions directly. The majority of people had no idea what to do. The concepts of investment and shares were completely new to the minds of Soviet people. Many did not understand the value of vouchers and sold them for pennies or exchanged them for a bottle of vodka. I remember that some intelligent acquaintances of ours were confused by it all and enquired whether they could be exchanged for shares in the Yava factory. But there was a certain swathe of enterprising people who understood what a unique opportunity this was. It allowed valuable property to be bought through state auctions at affordable prices, representing ultra-profitable investments. To participate in voucher auctions, it was essential to have large blocks of vouchers, which were the key to acquiring state property. Demand for vouchers soared, and buying them up from the public became a lucrative business, as shown by the sudden proliferation of voucher investment funds (VIFs). The privatisation ideologists had intended VIFs to act as institutional investors on the securities market. By collecting vouchers from citizens, they would amass large blocks with which to take part in auctions and buy shares in attractive enterprises. Then, as large shareholders, they would ensure that the joint stock companies were run in the interests of the voucher holders. But that was a long-term game, so most funds acted on behalf of large investors. It was much simpler and more lucrative to resell large blocks of vouchers to them or purchase shares in specific enterprises at their request.

In effect, the main activity of the VIFs consisted in voucher manipulation. They became the main point through which vouchers passed from the public into the hands of large investment entities. Many of them ceased to exist after privatisation was completed without ever settling with the voucher holders. According to data, over forty-five million privatisation vouchers were pumped through the funds. Soon, a large part of the country's active population was drawn into the purchase and sale of vouchers. Notices reading "I buy vouchers" were seen hanging at many retail outlets. A special network dedicated to the sale of vouchers appeared. The Central Post Office building on Kirovskaya (now Myasnitskaya) Street, home to the Russian Commodity Exchange (RCE), became a central hub for the trading of vouchers. It was possible to buy large blocks of vouchers there. The government's hopes that vouchers would give every citizen a share in the nation's wealth were not realised. In the absence of any real opportunities to use their vouchers to take part in privatisation, most people were forced to sell them.

The privatisation of many enterprises likewise took place not in the way the Property Administration Committee had planned. Chubais had figured that it would lead to enterprises having more effective owners. But this was by no means always the case. Tight schedules were set for privatisation. Many managers had no time to prepare for the auctions, and local authorities were unable to supervise this important stage in the development of an enterprise. What happened as a result was that random people would turn up to the auctions with suitcases full of vouchers, buy up all the shares on the cheap and then, at best, sell them on to a potential investor, or at worst, strip the enterprise of its assets, driving it to ruin and bankruptcy. Reports appeared in the press about serious abuses committed in connection with privatisation and the improper undervaluation of enterprises at state auctions. Privatisation often led to conflicts between an enterprise's sitting management and the new shareholders – even in Moscow, where oversight of the privatisation process was fairly effective. There was particular controversy over the privatisation of ZIL – the flagship of the domestic car-making industry. The auction to sell the state's shareholding was held in September 1992. Despite the great importance of the enterprise for the country and Moscow, the privatisation failed to bring about favourable conditions for the development of the plant. At the auction, a 24 per cent stake was bought by the trading company Mikrodin, which was far removed from the problems of the automotive industry. After a battle with the plant's administration, the post of general director of ZIL was taken by the head of Mikrodin, Alexander Yefanov. This farcical situation was a hot topic of discussion among enterprise managers. I remember Yefanov stating in an interview about his approach to managing ZIL that he had appointed twenty deputies in charge of different areas of work. Evidently this was his way of compensating for his own lack of competence in the problems of car manufacturing. The confrontation between Yefanov and the former management of ZIL went on for more than a year until the Moscow government stepped in and reached an agreement to buy Mikrodin's stake. All these vicissitudes did no good at all for the plant's development.

Criticism of privatisation was growing more vociferous. One of the first people to speak out openly against "Chubais-style privatisation" was Luzhkov. By this time Yury Mikhailovich had gained absolute power in Moscow, combining the posts of mayor and head of government. Luzhkov's policies in administering Moscow greatly differed from, and sometimes even clashed with, the endeavours of the federal government with its focus on liberal values. People said that he was building "state capitalism" in Moscow. Gaidar believed that the main thing was to give free rein to enterprise, while the involvement of the state should be limited. Luzhkov often voiced opposition to the government's actions. Especially vehement disagreements arose between him and Anatoly Chubais over the privatisation of state property. Luzhkov criticised Chubais for his "laissez-faire" approach to a matter of such critical importance. He accused him of giving away state property and condemned the sale of shares in Moscow enterprises through auctions. He proposed that government-held shares should be distributed among investors who had proven their usefulness to the city. Chubais responded by attacking Luzhkov for the fact that privatisation in the capital was not proceeding in accordance with Russian law. The conflict affected the progress of privatisation in Moscow, which was slower than in the country as a whole.

Luzhkov's approach to privatisation is exemplified in the story of the Ducat factory. As already mentioned, Ducat and the American tobacco company Liggett & Myers had established the USSR's first joint venture back in 1991 under the name Liggett-Ducat. This event had passed without undo fuss. There had not even been a special reception for the staff to mark the establishment of the JV, as was usually done. Time passed, and word got out that nothing was really being done about refurbishing the factory. From there, things got worse. It emerged that the JV had been established on the initiative of the Moscow government, and the American side was interested not in cigarette-making, but in the location of the Ducat factory. Liggett & Myers, which was losing ground in the market, was part of the Brooke Group, which dealt in real estate. Ducat happened to be situated right in the centre of Moscow in a quiet, very prestigious spot on Gashek Street, a stone's throw from Mayakovsky Square. Land in that part of Moscow was already very expensive, and the value was continuing to rise. Brooke's objective, therefore, was not to develop cigarette production, but to take possession of this lucrative site in the centre of Moscow. The Americans had, however, agreed under the terms of the agreement to relocate production away from the city centre by building a modern tobacco factory in another area of Moscow. This also enabled the Moscow government to achieve its aims with regard to the development of the city's infrastructure. The tobacco factory would be moved out of the centre, and in its place the American company would construct modern office buildings. All well and good, it seemed. A mutually beneficial arrangement. The parties to the agreement had both made serious commitments. But suddenly a conflict arose. After the privatisation law was passed, the state's share in Ducat had to be put to auction. The Brooke Group was at risk of having to share its ownership with other shareholders, thus threatening the ability of the Moscow authorities to honour their obligations. Faced with this situation, the Moscow government was compelled to pass a decision to establish (by way of an exception) a closed joint stock company (CJSC) at the Ducat factory. In August 1993, the Moscow government issued a resolution "On bringing the documents governing the activities of the Liggett-Ducat joint venture into line with the current legislation of the Russian Federation". It would be hard to think of a more precise way of expressing the purpose of the document. Control over the factory was transferred to Liggett & Myers. This meant that the enterprise's workforce was deprived of the right to any involvement in the privatisation, and the management lost control over the enterprise. The decision to establish the Liggett-Ducat CJSC was made without consulting the enterprise's workers or managers. I do not know how legal the decision was.

This came as a complete shock to the factory's director, Vladimir Tyumentsev. After receiving the Moscow government's decision, he refused to comply with it and ordered security not to allow any representatives of the American firm onto the factory's premises. The Moscow authorities called in OMON special forces to impose order. Then Tyumentsev barricaded himself in his office and refused to leave it for ten days. The stand-off was widely covered in the press. But it was an uneven contest. In the end, the director was forced to give in. Order was established at the enterprise, and after talks with the factory's new owners Tyumentsev left his post. There the story ended, having caused an immense stir. Privatisation, even when carried out under the government's control, brought conflicts of its own. After all, it concerned the ownership of property whose value was growing and growing.

THE CREATION OF BAT-YAVA OJSC. BRITISH AMERICAN TOBACCO AND SEVENTY MILLION DOLLARS OF INVESTMENT IN YAVA

It was against this complex background that Yava began preparations for the main stage of privatisation – the holding of the voucher auction. First, however, there was the question of distributing 51 per cent of the shares among the factory's employees. This was no simple task: most people were beginning to realise that shares in an enterprise were a valuable and reliable thing to possess. Moreover, Yava was giving the shares out free of charge, as it had formed a big enough privatisation fund to buy them from the state. At many enterprises, conflicts broke out if the workers felt that shares were distributed unfairly. Justifying the proportion of shares allocated to an enterprise's managers was a sensitive issue. We therefore decided to draw up clear criteria for evaluating each employee's contribution to the factory's work and to begin distributing shares on that basis. To do this, we used guidelines published by the State Property Administration Committee. These involved looking at an employee's length of service at the enterprise and his or her direct contribution to its work, which we decided to assess using a proxy measure, namely the employee's average pay. But it was impossible for a particular employee's importance to the enterprise to be captured by formal measures alone. For this reason, the factory's shops and departments were permitted to apply scale-up factors in determining the contribution of individual operators and engineers. The proposals were then reviewed by the workers' council and approved by the management. We decided that we could not forget the contribution of those who had retired. Each of them received an identical fixed number of shares. This approach won approval among the workers. The clear criteria and transparency in making decisions enabled conflicts to be avoided. The factory's management retained the complete trust of the workforce, which was especially important during the process of privatisation.

At the same time, intense discussions were proceeding with representatives from BAT. The involvement of large foreign companies in the privatisation of Russian enterprises was a completely new and unfamiliar phenomenon. Talks held by Russian enterprises with such global industrial giants as General Motors, Siemens and Philip Morris generated much attention and evoked a sense of pride in the public consciousness. On the wave of euphoria, people came to believe that these deals signified the formation of alliances between equal partners. When we signed the letter of intent with BAT, the leading business daily *Kommersant* published an article entitled "Tobacco giants finally reach agreement". The well-known journalist and head of the Top Secret publishing house, Artyom Borovik, made a television series devoted to planned deals between Russian enterprises and large foreign companies. In it, he conducted parallel interviews with the director of a Russian enterprise and with its international partner. The questions were about the principles of doing business. I remember that one of the first programmes involved the general director of AvtoVAZ, Kadannikov, and the head of General Motors. Artyom Borovik also approached me about making a programme with the involvement of Sir Patrick Sheehy. But I politely declined. I regarded myself as Sir Patrick's junior partner and considered that it would be improper to place myself on an equal footing with the head of a gigantic company that did business all over the world.

Deals of this sort were known in world practice as buyouts. The new owner takes over management, refurbishes the plant and restructures the business. Usually, the management is replaced. Similar processes had occurred a little earlier in ex-Soviet bloc countries. Not long before it began talks over Yava, BAT had purchased a factory in Pécs in Hungary. Within half a year, the director resigned and handed management over to BAT. A friend of mine from Prague, Leopold Lev, a cigarette machine designer at Škoda, became general director of a Czech state tobacco company after the fall of the Communist regime. After it had been privatised and sold to Philip Morris, he complained to me that he was left with nothing to do. "I sit in my office and sign ready-made papers with a gold-feathered pen". The actual running of the business was handled by a team from PM. The same thing happened in Russia. In St Petersburg, Sergei Akulov and his immediate team soon left the Uritsky factory, handing over complete control to Reynolds. In Krasnodar, the general director Gennady Tsygankov retired after Philip Morris took control of the factory. We took a different position when we embarked on talks with British American Tobacco. Our objective was to preserve Yava's distinctive character, develop its popular brand of cigarettes and maintain the involvement of the factory's management in the running of the joint stock company. We were against employees selling shares to the investor before the process of establishing the joint stock company had been completed. In our view, having the support of the staff in the first meeting of shareholders would enhance the legitimacy of the changes proposed by BAT.

Our stance took the management of BAT by surprise. The privatisation meant that BAT could count on acquiring 30–35 per cent of shares through the voucher auction and the investment tender, which was not enough for a controlling stake. This was not the way things usually went. There was a period in which the talks temporarily broke down. We got word that representatives of BAT had been speaking to the managers of tobacco factories in Rostov, Yaroslavl and Saratov. However, it was not long before we got back to the negotiating table. It was with Yava that BAT had its heart set on reaching a deal. Moreover, our arguments were rather persuasive. We hoped to work in close collaboration with the BAT team. Besides, we had in-depth knowledge of local realities and enjoyed some clout with the authorities. This was particularly important given that the legislation was often unclear. We guaranteed that if the talks led to an agreement, the workers would support BAT's investment at the first meeting of shareholders. Crucially, BAT's managers took us at our word. Conducting negotiations in this manner was a risk which they decided to accept. And there was a lot at stake, with the investment figure set at seventy million dollars. The talks could have hit a dead end, but we were helped by a number of factors. The BAT managers were intelligent, broad-minded people. It was also significant that they were greatly interested in and supportive of the changes happening in Russia. During our visit to London in early 1993, Sir Patrick recounted how, as a member of the British business elite, he had been at a meeting with the ex-prime minister, Yegor Gaidar: "Just imagine, Yegor Timurovich held forth about the reforms in Russia in perfect English for three whole hours. He literally blew us all away". Sir Patrick often expressed his delight at the changes happening in our country. The company's board members, Nick Brookes and Michael Prideaux, and the executive director, Martin Broughton, all displayed a similar attitude. I think that the enthusiasm they showed for the processes that were happening in Russia influenced the atmosphere of the negotiations and enabled us to move beyond a purely formal framework. There were also purely practical considerations.

We sensed that BAT's managers desperately needed to get an agreement signed with Yava so that they could report to the shareholders that tangible results had been achieved in Russia. It was a very interesting time. An exceptionally professional team formed around the negotiations. We were strongly supported by advisers from Credit Suisse First Boston. Boris Jordan devoted a great deal of attention to the project and made frequent visits to the factory. His authority as a professional businessman and an experienced negotiator was a key factor. This was acknowledged by the British side. BAT had hired the French investment bank Lazard as its consultant. Its Moscow office was headed by the well-known economist and former Fuel and Energy Minister in Gaidar's government, Vladimir Lopukhin. The BAT representative in charge of Yava projects, Roger Alford, was permanently based in Moscow. He made regular trips to London to coordinate matters. Nick Brookes, the director for new business, was in overall charge of the negotiations. The necessary paperwork was prepared, including documents needed for BAT to purchase shares in the Yava-Tabak open joint stock company (Yava OJSC) and tender proposals detailing investment amounts and equipment, technology and technical assistance to be supplied by BAT, as well as a "share subscription agreement" setting out the key policies of the joint stock company once the share acquisition process was completed. This included sections on Yava's obligations, BAT's commitments, the management structure of the new company and, no less importantly, obligations to employees. Reputable international legal companies were engaged to draft the documents: Baker McKenzie for British American Tobacco and White & Case for Yava. This was a complex and pivotal period in our history. We were about to take part in a real share purchase deal carried out to international standards, working with a team of top-class professionals. BAT had a lot of experience of deals of this kind. It had pledged to invest substantial sums in developing Yava. "Our responsibility to the shareholders is very high" was a phrase often repeated by the BAT managers when we met. Where property is concerned, there is no such thing as trivial detail. Every matter was very thoroughly discussed on both sides. People from Baker McKenzie spent several months at the factory and literally turned the accounting office upside down, poring through every agreement. I had to give explanations on some matters. To the credit of the Yava staff, we managed to weather the storm. The lawyers found no serious barriers to the completion of the deal. Boris Jordan, who had a lot of experience in such matters, even called the deal between BAT and Yava one of the cleanest he could remember.

Along the way, there were difficult situations which sometimes demanded unorthodox solutions. We were unhappy with the progress of work on the share subscription agreement. This was a particularly important legal agreement in which virtually every paragraph had to be evaluated and coordinated with both parties to the agreement. Our White & Case advisers were moving very slowly with their work on the text. We raised this issue with the company's management. Things changed completely when a young employee by the name of Leonid Rozhetskin, who had arrived from America, got involved. Born in Leningrad, he had emigrated to the USA with his mother as a child, studied law and worked as an assistant judge. Like other enterprising foreigners with Russian roots, he had decided to come to Russia to get involved in privatisation. White & Case was the first company he worked for in Russia. Leonid quickly built a rapport with the Yava staff and the advisers on the British side. Approval processes began to move forward at an efficient pace. Suddenly, right in the middle of it all, Boris Jordan arrived at the factory looking distraught. It turned out that Rozhetskin had fallen out with the White & Case management and decided to leave the firm. What could we do? Work on the agreement had reached a decisive stage, and Rozhetskin knew the material inside out. Bringing new people in could cause serious delays. On the other hand, having a standalone lawyer work on such a crucial document carried risks of its own. We discussed the situation and decided to conclude a contract with Rozhetskin, sacrificing formalities for the good of the cause. The indignation of the American firm knew no bounds. But time showed that we had made the right decision. A little later Leonid founded his own firm, Rozhetskin & Associates, and gradually rose to become a well-known figure in Moscow. He was involved in numerous projects, including controversial deals involving the privatisation of Svyazinvest and the foundation of Megafon.

The talks with BAT proceeded with difficulty at times, with problems in aligning our positions. Despite the difference in stature, we tried to partake in the discussions on an equal basis, protecting our interests. We managed to secure a very good outcome. BAT undertook to invest seventy million dollars in production development over three years. Yava's management retained its influence in the management of the joint stock company. It was agreed that the board of directors of Yava-Tabak OJSC would have seven members: three of Yava's current managers, three directors from BAT and one independent director, Vladimir Mikhailovich Lopukhin. I would remain as general director and chairman of the board of directors for five years. Another important point was that BAT undertook not to make any redundancies for five years. All in all, it was a package that would ensure the growth of the factory, management stability and job security for the workers.

At the beginning of 1994 Yava was ready for the final stage of share distribution – the holding of the voucher auction. Privatisation in Russia was entering a decisive phase. A lot of new players had entered the field, intent on seizing this rare opportunity to become owners of shares in enterprises. The press carried reports about the blatant undervaluation of shares in major concerns and serious conflicts between shareholders. There were various mechanisms for participating in auctions. For instance, firms appeared that specialised in purchasing shares in companies in which large investors had an interest. To consolidate its shareholding, the investor was forced to buy the shares at a significantly higher price. We had to make provision for all these things.

The conflict between the State Property Committee and the Moscow government continued. At the beginning of 1994 it was resolved in Luzhkov's favour. President Yeltsin signed an edict introducing "special privatisation rules" in Moscow. The Moscow authorities were allowed to exert more influence over outcomes by selecting privatisation options themselves and keeping possession of 20 per cent of the shares in Moscow enterprises. These changes did not affect Yava. The factory's privatisation mechanism had already been approved. However, evidently to allow time to prepare for the introduction of the new rules, Luzhkov temporarily suspended all voucher auctions in Moscow.

In preparing for the voucher auction, we carefully analysed the risks. For BAT, it was crucially important for the investment programme to be supported at the first shareholders' meeting by a qualified majority (meaning 75 per cent of shares). We could not affect the intentions of new shareholders who bought shares through the auction. We were relying on the full support of the workers. The terms of the agreement with BAT were discussed in detail within each of the factory's units. Everyone understood the importance of the investments for the development of the enterprise, the preservation of jobs and the improvement of working conditions. Yava's employees had already had substantial experience of working with foreign partners, so the prospect of working in a joint stock company with foreign capital did not evoke any fear or nervousness. For its part, BAT put faith in the management's influence over the Yava workforce.

We considered an option whereby the workers would grant the administration mandates to vote on their behalf in the shareholders' meeting.

In April Boris Jordan and I paid another visit to the building on Prechistenka Street where the State Property Committee had its office to enquire about the prospects for voucher auctions being held in Moscow. We were told that the first auction after the long hiatus would take place on 6 May. The timing suited us. We wanted to avoid shares being bought by big players. From this point of view, participating in the auction on 6 May struck us as advantageous. The fact that it was the first auction was not ideal, but on the other hand there would be an element of surprise. The auction date fell in the short period between two major public holidays, when the level of business activity dropped. Voucher auctions would be taking place all over Russia on the same day, meaning that some attention would be diverted away from Moscow. Another important factor was that the list of participants in the auction included some rather attractive targets: the Moscow Jewellery Plant, the well-known Zvyozdny bakery plant, the Tsentralnaya hotel right in the centre of Moscow, Ostankino and others. It emerged that the list of enterprises to be auctioned had already been drawn up and preparations for the auction had already begun. However, we understood that there was still a chance to "jump onto the last carriage". When we put the question to the deputy chairman of the Property Committee he replied, "We are the storefront of the Moscow government. Everything depends on the Industry Minister, Yevgeny Alexeyevich Panteleyev". I immediately went to see Panteleyev, whom I knew from when he worked for the Moscow authorities. Just as I got back to the factory, I received word that the directive had come through. Two weeks remained until the auction. It was a race against time. We had to submit all the documents required for the auction and agree the details of BAT's participation. The job of accepting bids for shares had been assigned to Imperial Bank. It was agreed that Credit Suisse First Boston would act as the buyer of shares on behalf of British American Tobacco. This was an important decision, as CSFB had a lot of experience with auctions. Just before the auction was due to take place, an article appeared in *Kommersant*: "Moscow government prepares a last-minute treat for voucher holders". Noting that an auction was being held in Moscow for the sale of shares in several high-potential enterprises at once, the newspaper wrote, "The most attractive target for investors is undoubtedly Yava. Shares in the enterprise represent a good investment both in the long term and from a speculative point of view, given that foreign investors are bound to show an interest in buying shares in the factory". Competition at the auction was high. Of the 25 per cent of shares put up for sale, BAT bought 8 per cent for 253,493 privatisation vouchers. Even based on the face value of a voucher, that amounted to almost 2 billion 535 million roubles. The price of shares in Yava-Tabak OJSC at the auction reached around 200 times the face value. The way the shares were spread among buyers did not arouse any alarm at first. Nothing out of the ordinary seemed to have happened. BAT had received 8 per cent of the shares, as planned. Noticeable quantities had been acquired by three other companies: 4 per cent by MMM-Invest, a subsidiary of the notorious MMM,[1] and 6–7 per cent each by two other unknown firms. The remaining shares were dispersed among small owners (less than 2 per cent each), who posed no danger. MMM Invest's business profile was well known. They were unlikely to have any designs of their own and had probably mostly bought shares in Yava as an enterprise with strong potential. Questions arose over the two unknown companies, which had bought fairly hefty blocks of shares. Only time would tell what their intentions were.

We did not have to wait long. Just a week later, representatives of New Century Holding (NCH), an American investment fund with Latvian roots, appeared in my office. Their names were Grigory Finger and Konstantin Papachristou. NCH had been founded in 1991 specifically for the purpose of participating in privatisation in Russia and the Baltic countries. The fund had a dubious reputation. It openly engaged in share price manipulation at auctions and was not shy of using dirty methods for this purpose. They had put up two dummy companies to buy up around 14 per cent of Yava's shares on their behalf. Now they intended to increase their stake and blackmail BAT by threatening to derail its deal with us. Without batting an eyelid, these fine gentlemen set out to persuade me that with their assistance we could secure better terms for the agreement with BAT. They, after all, knew all about negotiating with international companies. They invited me to act as their ally. All they needed was my assistance in buying shares from employees so that New Century Holding would own a blocking shareholding of 25 per cent plus one share. The real objectives of these visitors and their owners were obvious enough. I

---

1 Founded by Sergei Mavrodi, MMM was a classic financial pyramid (Ponzi) scheme and the largest of its kind in Russia. It was liquidated by the state at the beginning of August 1994.

tried to shift the conversation onto a positive tack, feigning ignorance of their true intentions. I told them about the talks with BAT, about the fact that the investment agreements reached were very significant for Yava's growth and would therefore benefit all shareholders. It was just a question of being patient. I advised them to read the investment prospectus after the investment tender and vote for the deal at the shareholders' meeting. Once the parties had set out their positions, the conversation came to an end in an outwardly positive light.

What followed next, however, was like something out of a crime novel. It upset all our calculations regarding the ownership structure of the Yava-Tabak joint stock company. The visit from NCH's representatives took place towards the end of May. On the afternoon of 3 June, in the changeover period during which the second (evening) shift was arriving just as the day shift was finishing work and preparing to leave, some unknown figures came and dropped a large quantity of leaflets in the factory's foyer. I was immediately called to take a look. The financial investment company Olma was offering to buy shares in the enterprise from Yava's employees at a price of 300 roubles per share (against a face value of 1 rouble). 300 times the face value was quite something! It was obvious that Olma was acting on behalf of the fund. The idea was that this would be too good an offer to turn down. NCH had evidently taken this step in the expectation of pocketing a hefty profit. Our situation had become more than serious. But, as has often been the case in my life, our just cause was helped by favourable circumstances. Our foes had left one important factor out of their equation. The leaflets were distributed on Friday. The way they saw it, the workers would receive the information, digest it over the weekend and race to sell their shares on Monday. But that was not how it turned out. The third of June was the last day before the annual vacation (the factory shut for maintenance in June). The workers were already getting ready to go on leave. They all had their own plans. Very few of them would be staying in Moscow. And so, after receiving the leaflets, they all went away on holiday. That gave us a month in which to plan countermeasures. But our options were limited. Simply persuading people not to take advantage of such a tempting offer was not a realistic plan. There was only one way out of the situation, and that was to come to an agreement with BAT about purchasing the employees' shares. Of course, it was in BAT's interests to increase its shareholding to a controlling stake. I am sure that BAT would in any case have presented the employees with some such option after the shareholders' meeting. But the situation had forced a change of plan, and the issue had to be dealt with as a matter of urgency. This meant preparing a rival share purchase offer and choosing a financial agency to buy shares from Yava employees on BAT's behalf. All this had to be arranged before the beginning of July when the workers were due to return to work after the vacation. After working on the investment project for over one and a half years, we had seen at first hand that at BAT, like any big company, there was a lot of red tape. Decisions required numerous approvals. It soon became apparent that progress was unacceptably slow, so I flew to London to pay a visit to the company's head office. Things sped up after intervention from senior executives. A proposal was drawn up under which BAT would buy the shares at an even higher price of 370 roubles each.

Serious work lay ahead when I got back. The share purchase terms were financially attractive and respectful to the shareholders. A flexible purchase scheme was offered under which employees could, if they wished, sell all their shares in order to give BAT sufficient voting power at the first shareholders' meeting, but would have the option of buying back up to 50 per cent of the shares at the same price after the meeting, thereby remaining shareholders in Yava. The arrangement was beneficial for both parties – investor and shareholders. The overwhelming majority of workers supported BAT's offer. It helped that all the managers acted in solidarity with the workers. We too sold our shares, then bought back 50 per cent. The share purchase process demonstrated the unity and maturity of Yava's workforce and the trust that the workers felt towards the management. This relationship had been built over many years of working together. Only a handful of people had rushed to sell their shares to Olma in June. An offer made by Olma in July to buy shares at 400 roubles each was roundly ignored.

For three weeks, an intensive campaign was conducted in the factory shops from the morning until the end of the evening shift. Each employee signed an individual agreement with BAT. The person authorised to sign the agreements on behalf of BAT was Roger Alford. We joked about this that Roger finally had some proper work to do – signing his name around 3,000 times. Standard Bank was chosen as our financial agent. The bank's young team of managers, headed by Vladimir Tarankov, showed great inventiveness in organising the share purchase. They were keen to expand their business relationship with

Yava, as a financially sound enterprise, and with its workers. The share deal involved substantial amounts of money, and Yava employees were set to be the beneficiaries of the arrangement. Advertising for Standard Bank was hung up all over the factory with an ingenious slogan that used the Yava logo: "*Ya vash bank*" ("I am your bank"). This, then, was how we managed to protect the plan to develop the enterprise. Workers who sold their shares received an average of 10 to 20,000 dollars (depending on their length of service). That was big money in Russia at that time. All in all, the purchase of shares from the workers played a positive role in the subsequent development of the Yava-Tabak joint stock company. It added certainty to the situation. It meant that BAT directly owned a sufficient stake to make decisions at the first shareholders' meeting. Funnily enough, New Century Holding had actually helped things along, acting as a catalyst for the process. Its actions had forced us into the decision to buy the shares and forced BAT into preparing a good offer for the workers. I think the fund itself came off none the poorer, too. BAT negotiated with them and bought up their shares. Of course, NCH was not in such a strong negotiating position as it had hoped to be, but BAT understood that there were risks involved in leaving such an uncooperative shareholder in place. They were forced to make a deal. Such are the laws of international business.

Next came the final stage of the distribution of shares in Yava-Tabak. The investment tender, the winner of which stood to receive 15 per cent of the shares, was to take place in mid-August. Under the regulations, tenders were conducted by special tender commissions formed by local authorities – in our case the Moscow government. Of course, BAT had done a lot of work directly at the factory, assisted by Yava's own specialists, and had examined every facet of its operations. As a result, it had prepared a detailed commercial proposal involving the replacement of all equipment. As already mentioned, it guaranteed to make investments amounting to seventy million dollars over a period of three years. It was unlikely that anyone would be able to come up with a worthwhile rival offer, but the unexpected sometimes happened. Such was the case with the investment tender for the Krasnodar tobacco plant. The privatisation was undertaken by Philip Morris. It was a lengthy process. The company put together a solid proposal and filed an investment bid. It guaranteed substantial investment, comparable with BAT's proposal for Yava. Knowing how PM worked and how adept it was at pushing its interests, I was sure that the company had established a good relationship with the local authorities and had no doubt about the outcome of the tender. But suddenly another proposal was submitted by PM's main competitor, Reynolds. Understanding that it had little chance of winning the tender by objective measures, Reynolds put in an offer that was blatantly intended as a provocation, proposing to invest twice more than PM. They hoped to stir up trouble – and succeeded. As expected, the tender commission awarded the victory to PM. In response, a lot of criticism appeared in the press: how could such a substantial offer of investment have been turned down? The local authorities were virtually accused of a fix-up. But only amateurs could see things that way. PM had worked hard on the project and presented a thorough and detailed proposal based on an optimised cost-benefit ratio. Reynolds, meanwhile, had attempted to derail its competitor's carefully planned deal by conjuring up an investment figure off the top of its head. Fortunately, common sense prevailed.

The Yava tender in Moscow passed off without any nasty surprises. Our arguments were watertight. No one ventured to submit a competing offer.

And that was how, with the difficulties noted, all the stages of the distribution of shares in Yava-Tabak OJSC were completed. The important thing was that we achieved what we had set out to achieve. The aim of privatisation had been to put control of the enterprise into the hands of an effective owner. The controlling interest in the company had been acquired by a reliable investor, one of the top cigarette manufacturers in the world. In our negotiations with BAT we had succeeded in securing substantial guarantees for the workforce. Having received their shares free of charge, the workers sold them to the investor at a good price. I am sure that there were not many enterprises in Russia where ordinary shareholders could have made so much money from selling their shares. The first shareholders' meeting took place on 4 November 1994. At that meeting, the formation of the Yava-Tabak open joint stock company was completed, the BAT investment programme was adopted and the governing body – the board of directors – was elected. Exactly two years had passed since the signing of the Letter of Intent. It had been a period full of dramatic events. It had required us to solve completely new problems and change our way of thinking. In effect, we had been involved in two major processes at the same time: the privatisation of the enterprise and the sale of shares to an international investor. Events proved that the decisive factor in privatisation was a properly prepared strategy. By no means all enterprises were ready for the state sell-offs. In most cases the directors were unable to find a genuine investor with an interest in the development of a joint stock company. There were objective reasons for this. Many enterprises had no obvious growth prospects – besides which, there were not that many investors who were ready to make real investments. Luzhkov's proposal for the Moscow government to take control of the process was not really a solution either. Making government connections a factor in the purchase of state shareholdings led to distortions of a different kind. A prime example of this was Menatep Bank's privatisation activities. Using its lobbying power, the bank bought up shares in numerous enterprises in various sectors. Its dealings were on such a grand scale that it established a dedicated company – Rosprom – to manage them. The director of the Moscow Food Plant, Leontiev, who was a friend of mine, received a "recommendation" from the Moscow government to secure Menatep as an investor. At the same time, it acquired a number of other well-known Moscow food enterprises (including the Koloss conglomerate). Assets were purchased without any clear development plan, and investment programmes were not fulfilled. As a result, once famous enterprises lost their identity, and consumers were left without their favourite products. This was one of many examples of privatisation being carried out to the detriment of business. The risks were substantial.

Many were surprised that Yava's value was higher than that of the majority of the top industrial enterprises from the Soviet period. In a market economy this was natural. The factory made highly popular products that guaranteed reliable sales in the long term. There were plenty of people interested in "capturing" Yava. We had managed to avoid this eventuality by holding serious negotiations in advance with an international tobacco company. Of course, I was full of pride at our success in overcoming all the difficulties, and had not yet given any thought to the no less challenging time that lay ahead, working in a new management team as part of the international giant, British American Tobacco.

A large team headed by Sir Patrick Sheehy arrived in Moscow ahead of the shareholders' meeting. By this time BAT had completed the purchase of a controlling interest in the Saratov tobacco factory. It was decided to hold a joint celebration of these two events. The reception took place in the Savoy restaurant in the centre of Moscow. The guests included VIPs, as they were known by then. In contrast to the ostentatious luxury of the Americans in St Petersburg, the British put on an exquisite party. They had hired a well-known London firm to organise it. The guests all sat at small tables. Everyone was handed a copy of Sir Patrick's speech in Russian. Expressing his great satisfaction at the opportunities that had arisen for doing business in Russia, he said that he hoped that the guests would derive pleasure from the evening spent together. The food had been especially brought over from Britain, and splendid dishes had been prepared by top London chefs. The gastronomic part of the speech ended with the elegant phrase, "But let the wines be French!" It really was a magnificent event. The chatter at the tables was accompanied by wonderful performances of arias by artistes from London theatres as well as the sound of Scottish bagpipes. The guests were bowled over by the atmosphere of the evening.

This was my last meeting with Sir Patrick in his role as president of BAT. Presenting me with a farewell gift, he jokingly pointed out that our relationship was now moving into a different phase. As the experienced Brits rightly said, deals of this kind were like weddings. First the future partners meet, and there is a "courting" period. The groom – meaning the party buying the shares – tries to make a good impression and lavishes compliments. Up to that point they each still have their independence. After the deal is done, everything falls into place. BAT becomes the master, and Yava becomes part of a large multinational company. Of course, I could scarcely have imagined that I would work for over fifteen years as general director, then board chairman of BAT-Yava OJSC.

CHAPTER 16.

WORKING IN AN INTERNATIONAL TOBACCO COMPANY

VERY DIFFERENT CHALLENGES

On visiting London after the investment tender, I was introduced to Mr Tony Johnson, a member of the BAT board of directors and our new manager. He was in charge of the company's BAT-UK division, based in London. Russia came under his responsibility. He in turn introduced me to the top managers appointed by BAT to Yava's board of directors: the English financial director Jim Green and the Costa Rican technical director, Mario Chacon. The Englishman Richard Howe had been appointed BAT's general manager in Russia. As a result of privatisation, the big three international tobacco companies all owned enterprises in Russia. Philip Morris had acquired the Krasnodar tobacco plant, Reynolds the Uritsky factory, and British American Tobacco Moscow's Yava and the Saratov tobacco factory. It meant that there would be serious competition on the market. All three companies intended to make substantial investments in manufacturing operations. There was no time to lose.

BAT's first step was to establish infrastructure in Russia. The company began to be known as BAT-Russia. Tobacco products were manufactured at BAT-Yava and BAT-STF (the Saratov tobacco factory). A company called International Tobacco Marketing Services – with the Russian acronym MUMT – was set up to construct and implement a uniform market strategy. MUMT handled the marketing of all products manufactured at the Moscow and Saratov factories. BAT-Yava and BAT-STF were open joint stock companies. BAT owned controlling interests – around 90 per cent, but just over 10 per cent of each factory belonged to minority shareholders. Global decisions had to be made at shareholders' meetings and expenditures had to be reported and justified to the shareholders. This made for protracted approval processes. For this reason, only manufacturing activities were financed through BAT-Yava and BAT-STF themselves. The financing of BAT-Russia's overall operations took place through MUMT, in which BAT held 100 per cent ownership.

In terms of marketing policy, a goal was set of strengthening the position of mainstream varieties of tobacco products. Everyone understood the inevitability of smokers gradually migrating towards filter cigarettes. The focus would be on producing them at an affordable price. It was in this segment of the market that we expected to face the stiffest competition. By this time, Philip Morris had begun producing Soyuz-Apollo soft-pack cigarettes in Krasnodar. In quality terms they were not a patch on the famous cigarettes once manufactured in the USSR. Nonetheless, it represented an attempt to compete with Yava filter cigarettes. We decided to respond by relaunching Yava cigarettes with a new design and improved flavour qualities. At the same time, it was important to keep these popular cigarettes in the same price band. Serious work began on developing a design and selecting tobaccos for the blend. Of course, the way in which the problem was approached was on an entirely different level. For the first time in our country, focus groups of smokers were used to test the design and flavour qualities of cigarettes. A lot of work lay in store in terms of creating new brands and promoting international brands on the Russian market. Substantial increases in output were planned. BAT-Russia had a multitude of different departments: brand marketing, sales marketing, finance, legal, information technology, human resources and corporate relations. Very soon, the office rented by BAT-Russia on Nikoloyamskaya Street was brimming with employees with a command of English. These were young people of the new generation, raised in the perestroika period. A lot of foreign specialists arrived. There were as many of thirty of them, sometimes even more. Their role was to help implement Western technologies and train Russian workers. BAT was preparing for business in Russia on a grand scale.

Even during the talks with BAT on establishing the joint stock company, I had not quite been able to imagine a situation in which Yava was only part of a larger company. In line with Western practice, the highest management body of BAT-Russia, responsible for key decisions, was the Executive Committee (Ex-Co), which met weekly. The committee consisted of ten people, of whom two were Russian citizens: the head of BAT-Russia's corporate relations department, Vladimir Aksyonov, and me. The board of BAT-Yava, elected at the shareholders' meeting, played what effectively amounted to a decorative role. Obviously, this sort of management structure made it difficult for us to retain our influence. We had to adapt to the new circumstances, develop relationships with the foreign staff ("expats") and defend our professional principles and functional authority. As the British put it, we had to "learn how to work as a team".

There was also a group of foreign technicians from BAT working directly at Yava. Paul Ogborn and Andy Coote were responsible for the implementation of modern technologies and the upgrading and retooling of the factory. Both answered to BAT-Russia's technical director, Mario Chacon. Under the management structure, Mario Chacon and the financial director of BAT-Russia, Jim Green, were also members of the factory's executive board as the financial and technical directors of BAT-Yava. Problems arose between the Yava management and these gentlemen over the division of responsibilities. Effectively the same functions were performed by Yava-appointed directors, with Alla Konstantinovna Poloiko responsible for accounting work and Yury Fyodorovich Trifonov for technical matters. This led to duplication in the handling of the same matters. It was a complicated situation that required a fine balance to be found in dealings between the directors. While Alla Poloiko showed flexibility and managed to make things work with Jim Green, there was ever increasing discord between Yury Trifonov and Mario Chacon.

An intensive schedule had been set for the renovation of the factory and it was essential to get things moving straight away. Preparing for the work required changes to be made to the configuration of certain production areas without stopping production. These matters were dealt with by managers from Mario Chacon's team. After coming up with ideas, they would come to Yury Trifonov to get his approval. Yury Fyodorovich was a highly skilled professional and a man of principle, but he could also be rather stubborn and inflexible. The proposed solutions usually had shortcomings, often failing to take proper account of specific aspects of Yava's operations. He would refuse to approve them. Conflicts would arise, in which I would have to act as arbiter. The technical director, Mario Chacon, would get involved in the dispute. The hot-headed Costa Rican lacked any restraint. In the heat of argument, his team made comments that endangered the spirit of cooperation: "We bought you, and you're trying to oppose us!"

It soon became clear that, far from being a rogue view among individual managers, this reflected a general policy towards the factory's staff. The general manager of BAT-Russia, Richard Howe, was not happy with the influence that the Yava management had over the workers, or with our assertive attitude. The way he saw it, this prevented BAT from establishing total control over the factory. Since, however, our authority was legally enshrined in the share subscription agreement, Howe realised that the problem would have to be addressed gradually, one step at a time. He was fully supported in this by his boss in London, the regional director Tony Johnson. Jim Green and Mario Chacon had their offices on the factory's premises. They were both tough managers with experience of dealing with situations of this kind. They were not particularly choosy about their methods, either. Naturally, conflicts began to arise, giving reason to speak of confrontation between the managements of Yava and BAT.

A distinctive pattern of relationships emerged among members of the BAT-Russia management team. Richard Howe valued commitment to teamwork above all else. In his interpretation this meant having a monolithic managerial team based on unanimity of opinion and solidarity with the general manager. Anyone who failed to meet these criteria was quickly removed. Howe once told us candidly, "The new marketing manager from Paris is being too critical of our market strategy, but I have arranged with Tony (as he sometimes referred to his boss) to have him recalled". Within literally a few days, the critic had left the company. Another eloquent example was the career of David Rivlin. This relatively young, intelligent man had been involved with us since back at the development stage of the Yava investment project. David had made a good impression and established a rapport with the factory's specialists. After the completion of the deal he was appointed general manager of BAT-STF in Saratov. There, too, he succeeded in creating a good working climate, managing the factory efficiently and enjoying the respect of the workers. His management style compared favourably with the monolithic system at BAT-Russia. Evidently, this did not sit well with Richard Howe, especially as David operated with a fair degree of independence. At one of the Ex-Co meetings, therefore, Howe suddenly announced that David Rivlin was leaving the company. David, who was present at the time, could not conceal the fact that he had in no way anticipated this turn of events. It came as a surprise to the Saratov staff, too.

HOW WE FOUGHT BAT BUREAUCRACY

It soon became clear that BAT-Russia was intent on establishing a one-sided approach to resolving matters. The "Tony Johnson in London – Richard Howe in Moscow" axis meant that Howe was able to put his decisions into effect with speed. When it came to the Yava management, however, it was much more difficult, as any changes in our status had to be ratified at the level of the BAT directors. Very soon, on my very first visit to London as the general director of BAT-Yava, I realised that Howe was deliberately working against me. Our new boss, Mr Johnson, expressed no wish to hold a meaningful discussion with me about the progress of Yava's integration into BAT-Russia's work. My schedule had been arranged so that I had no opportunity to raise my doubts with those managers with whom I had formed relationships of trust back in the preparatory stages of the project. At a lunch with the company's technical director, Ulrich Herter, at which Tony Johnson and Richard Howe were present, there was no possibility of entering into a detailed conversation. Herter treated me with respect but, evidently influenced by Johnson, made comments about the need to work more closely as a team to achieve BAT's goals in Russia. I returned from the trip feeling disappointed. I had not been able to discuss the things that worried me. Howe had cleverly blocked my attempts to communicate my concerns to the company's management.

Serious changes were happening at Yava at that time. It was decided to stop producing *papirosy*. Most workers operating the *papirosy* lines had already reached pension age. They were offered a sizeable retirement package. The company honoured its obligations to the workers. Preparations were underway for the arrival of modern cigarette-making lines and the complete replacement of equipment in the primary processing section. Major construction work would be undertaken in the factory's buildings with a view to reconfiguring the production process. BAT had hired the well-known British firm Arup, which did project design and management work all over the world, to draw up the renovation plan. While working on the design, Arup's representatives gave a presentation of the Yava project. Richard Howe left it until after the main parameters had been approved to propose moving BAT-Russia's office onto the factory's site. The company's staff was expanding, and renting a class A office in the centre of Moscow was very expensive. It was decided to convert the vacated *papirosy* production building into a modern office facility. It was a building that had been constructed back in Gabay's time, a very fine-looking example of late nineteenth-century industrial architecture. Howe was in a hurry to relocate, but as yet there was no design and no construction permit. Understanding the importance of the issue for the company, I went to see Industry Minister Yevgeny Alexeyevich Panteleyev, who called up experts from the Moscow appraisal bureau.[1] We talked things through and came to an acceptable solution. Based on a report stating that the building was in a dangerous condition, the bureau issued a permit to carry out emergency construction work to stabilise the building. The general contractor for the factory renovation, McHugh CJSC, could start work.

It then became apparent that there was no comprehensive working design for the renovation of the factory either. In typical fashion, the BAT management team had tried to conceal this fact from the Yava management. We had been told that a working design had been accepted by BAT's people in London, but we had never actually seen it. Mario Chacon's team and Arup tried to organise the work into separate projects, which was a gross violation of Russian law. This led to a new round of confrontation between the BAT-Russia team and the Yava management. I spoke out categorically against such work methods, setting out specific reasons for my position. We were talking about a complex renovation project involving a lot of construction work, including the complete rebuilding of power facilities and the replacement of underground utility lines. The law required us to go through all the necessary stages of approvals. Carrying out work without a construction permit could lead to serious penalties being imposed by the oversight authorities, including closure of the construction site and large fines. That sort of thing could be very detrimental to the company's image. Howe responded with complete incredulity: What? We invest over seventy million dollars and still have to ask for someone's approval? Surely we can do whatever work we want in our own plant? He had to be reminded that the USSR and Russia were civilised, highly developed countries, unlike the African countries where he had worked before. And the fact that BAT was investing money in developing Yava certainly did not free it from the obligation to comply with Russian law. This was a conflict that threatened to wreck the renovation schedule. I decided to turn to BAT-Yava's independent director, Vladimir Lopukhin, for help. Vladimir Mikhailovich fully supported me. Unexpectedly, his resolute stance had an effect on Howe. In Western countries it is customary to pay close heed to the opinion of independent directors. Evidently to avoid

---

1   Part of the Chief Architectural and Planning Authority.

any undesirable consequences, he was forced to prepare a design for approval. This was a time when the BAT-Yava board of directors made a real difference, assisting in the resolution of a matter of fundamental importance.

Working in an international company was a real education for me and my colleagues. We were astonished at the speed with which BAT built its new structure in Russia. It was obvious that the company had a lot of international experience in such matters. The BAT-Russia staff was assembled in the twinkling of an eye. The foreign staff worked in line with the company's time-tested standards founded on the latest management practices. There was good communication between the different units. Every component of the BAT-Russia structure was focused on the end result, as in a well-organised system goals are achieved not so much on account of the individual qualities of managers as by reason of strict observance of instructions laid down by the company. It was particularly important to study BAT's approach to marketing work. For us, this was a completely new field of activity. It was at this time that we completed the relaunch of the "parent" Yava brand, as the company had begun to refer to the famous Yava cigarettes. This notable event coincided with the thirtieth anniversary of the commencement of production of the popular cigarettes in the USSR. The retail release of the cigarettes was preceded by a large-scale advertising campaign. The advertising was designed by the Moscow subsidiary of the well-known British company Grey, a regular partner of BAT. The expression "Yavas from Yava", which had arisen among smokers virtually of its own accord, was used as a tagline. Eye-catching advertising for the new Yava filter cigarettes appeared on Moscow's billboards, which had become one of the features of the new age. The factory put on a presentation for journalists. Smokers responded favourably to the changes in their favourite cigarettes. The price had remained the same, while the quality had improved. While the design retained the style of the Yava brand that had been so popular in the USSR, it had naturally been refreshed and updated. The smoking qualities had improved significantly, something that BAT was well placed to achieve on account of its consummately organised system for purchasing materials. The company purchased tobacco directly from farmers all over the world. Cutting out the brokers enabled it to secure lower prices. As a major customer, BAT also received substantial discounts on paper materials and other manufacturing components.

Fundamental changes were happening in sales strategies for tobacco products. There was now serious competition on the market. People in the regions were still smoking locally made, outmoded products, such as *papirosy* and low-quality unfiltered cigarettes. It was the regions that came to be seen by the multinationals as holding the key to increased sales. The goal was set of expanding sales of BAT-Yava and BAT-STF products to a nationwide level.

This meant radically reorganising the distribution system, expanding it to cover the vast expanses of Russia's provinces and autonomous regions. An ambitious project was launched to build a countrywide BAT distribution network. Direct distribution agreements were signed between MUMT and seven companies that had already been selling the Yava factory's cigarettes in the Moscow region for a number of years. The "group of seven" companies (as the new distributors were referred to) began expanding their operations to new areas. They set up their own warehouse depots, made agreements with local trade networks and aided their development in order to bring the products closer to the customer. They ensured that regional warehouses were constantly supplied with sufficient stocks of products at optimal prices. At the same time, BAT-Russia set up a large sales office division as part of MUMT. Sales offices were opened in all regions of Russia. Around a thousand sales representatives were employed to monitor the progress of product sales. They regularly drove around sales outlets making sure that cigarette packs were properly arranged in display windows. If any brand was missing, they would promptly replenish supplies, ensuring that BAT cigarettes were constantly available to buy. It was a soundly constructed distribution system with effective feedback mechanisms. A lot of attention was devoted to the work of the sales representatives. A large number of Volkswagen cars were bought for them. Their activities were extensively featured in BAT-Russia's internal corporate magazine. The results did not take long to show. The proportion of trade outlets selling BAT brands rose to over 90 per cent The market research company Business-Analytica began regularly publishing data on the status of the cigarette market in Russia's regions. There was now real competition, with Philip Morris and BAT-Russia leading the way. Their market share just kept growing.

There were major changes in our production operations. At last, the Mark 8 machines were replaced by modern Protos lines with a production rate of 8,000 cigarettes per minute. The demand for filter cigarettes was rising all the time. Work began on the complete overhaul of the primary processing facility.

The Bulgarian equipment was replaced with high-technology lines made by the German company Hauni and the British firm Dickinson. After three years (at the end of 1997) the company reported to the Moscow authorities that the investment obligations in relation to Yava-Tabak OJSC had been fulfilled.

The fact that Yava had kept its old management had a positive effect for BAT's image. At a time of widespread conflicts over changes of director at other enterprises, it demonstrated the foreign company's commitment to tradition and flexible approach to management and enhanced its relationship with the authorities. This made the swift and satisfactory resolution of important matters all the easier. The staff, too, had been prepared in advance for work in the new environment, and so the introduction of modern standards of production management proceeded fairly painlessly. However, the atmosphere within the management team remained tense. There was no integration between the Yava and BAT-Russia directors. Richard Howe persisted in his pursuit of total power. He used all the means at his disposal to limit our influence at Yava. At the end of 1995, changes were made to the law that prevented one individual from acting as both general director and chairman of the board of directors. In a conversation with me over this matter, Howe blatantly hinted that he would prefer me to keep the board chairman position. However, I responded that I could be more useful in the role of general director. Since it was my right to choose, he had to accept my decision.

We did everything we could to iron out disagreements and find common ground between the partners. A real crisis erupted after I was informed of a new management structure which had been worked out without our involvement and was presented as a fait accompli. Against all the laws of management, Yava's technical divisions had been placed under the authority of BAT-Russia's technical director, Mario Chacon, who was not answerable to the general director of Yava. It was impossible for things to be properly run under this arrangement. My objections were ignored, and the employees were informed of the new structure. Needless to say, this move had been deliberately planned as the next step towards limiting the functions of Yava's general director. I consulted with my immediate colleagues and we decided that there could be no backing down. Decisive action was needed.

Important changes were occurring in London at that time. Sir Patrick Sheehy had retired, and the new president, Martin Broughton, had presented the next phase of the company's development strategy. Most importantly, this involved an overhaul of BAT's structure. In place of separate companies united under a holding entity, an umbrella structure, BAT Industries, was set up with five regional divisions. Fundamental changes were made to the European business. Whereas European countries had previously been shared between two companies, BAT-UK and BAT-Germany, they were now combined into the "European region". This included Russia, Ukraine and other CIS countries.

There were major shake-ups in personnel. The head of the new European region was the former head of BAT-Germany, Bernd Schweitzer, while Tony Johnson had retired. I personally greeted this news with great relief. I was not acquainted with Bernd Schweitzer, but a more odious figure than Tony Johnson would have been difficult to imagine. The situation demanded urgent action. I wrote a short letter to Schweitzer requesting a meeting. To my surprise, I received an immediate reply. Schweitzer flew out to Moscow and arrived at Yava straight from Sheremetyevo. Our meeting lasted over two hours. He listened to me attentively and asked a lot of questions. He was interested in many aspects of the situation in Russia. Richard Howe was clearly rattled. Sitting in his office on Nikoloyamskaya, he called several times on supposedly important matters. In the evening, we met for dinner.

Schweitzer spent the next day at the BAT-Russia office. As far as I could make out, he had taken our concerns seriously. These related to the need to change the tone of relationships within the company. Only an atmosphere of cooperation, trust and mutual respect could bring success in work. This is precisely what he talked about with BAT-Russia's foreign directors, and later at the Ex-Co meeting with the involvement of Yava's directors. Practical steps were taken. The new management structure was cancelled, and it was decided to introduce a new position of production director, to be held by a foreign specialist who would answer directly to the general director. He would be responsible for integrating BAT management standards into Yava's production operations.

There could scarcely have been a more positive outcome. Once again, of course, we were helped by favourable circumstances. It so happened that Bernd Schweitzer was an intelligent man and a highly professional manager. He immediately realised the seriousness of the situation and took matters in hand. After he left, certain personnel changes were made with a view to improving the atmosphere within the company. Out went Jim Green and Paul Ogborn, giving way to a new financial director, David Graas, and Yava's production director, Jean-Pierre Mamet, who I am sure were given appropriate instructions upon being appointed. Not long afterwards, Ulrich Herter and Bernd Schweitzer came on a visit to Moscow. After a tour of the Yava factory, where Herter attended the opening of the administrative building, a meeting took place involving the enlarged team of BAT-Russia managers. A candid discussion took place, with a particular focus on improving relationships within the company. Answering questions, Herter commented that one of BAT's great merits was its respect for and close attention to the culture and traditions of the countries in which it operated.

The changes made as suggested by London improved the situation. The new financial director, David Graas, was approachable and independent-minded. He clearly fell outside Dick Howe's tight-knit team and brought a breath of fresh air to the Ex-Co's work. Jean-Pierre Mamet established working relationships with the Russian staff. He and I met regularly and coordinated with each other on everything. Sensing the support of the London management, the Russian directors began to behave with greater confidence, showing initiative and working more freely. Many problems with the renovation of the factory had arisen because of a lack of coordination between foreign and Russian specialists, so I decided to take personal charge of the renovation command centre. The issues involved needed to be addressed in a joined-up manner through the combined efforts of all parties. We held weekly meetings, and from that point on the renovation work progressed much more smoothly.

The reorganisation of BAT had a positive impact on the way the regions were managed. We were aware of much closer attention from the centre. The managers of the European region often visited Russia and had a palpable influence on the way things were going. There was a particular focus on promoting new cigarette brands. After the relaunch of the parent Yava brand, there was a need to work out what the next steps in our brand marketing would be and to decide on a portfolio of brands to be manufactured in Russia. The parent Yava brand fell within the low-price band for filter cigarettes. Now that disposable incomes were rising, we expected increased demand for better-quality, higher-price cigarettes. Reynolds had just launched its new Peter I brand of filter cigarettes, which had proved popular. Besides the patriotic name, smokers were attracted by the fact that they offered just the right price-quality ratio. Peter I was effectively the first brand in the new category of "international quality cigarettes at an affordable price", which was set to become the fastest growing segment in Russia's tobacco market.

It was over to the major competitors to make their countermoves. Now that they had started manufacturing cigarettes in Russia, foreign companies were able to make global brand cigarettes at a lower price. Philip Morris decided to launch its popular L&M cigarettes at a price point below that of imported brands. BAT-Russia had two projects up its sleeve: Pall Mall and a new international quality member of the Yava family – Yava Gold. The Yava Gold launch was planned as a direct response to Peter I. We were strongly behind this project, understanding that the appearance on the market of international quality cigarettes would boost the image of the Yava brand and give consumers of the popular cigarettes the option to switch to a more expensive, higher-quality segment.

Oddly, however, Richard Howe took a different view. His proposal was to launch production of Pall Mall in Saratov first, and then move onto making Yava Gold at Yava in Moscow. His reasoning was that it would be impossible to carry out two projects at the same time, and he regarded the Pall Mall launch as having better prospects. This meant putting off the launch of Yava Gold for at least half a year. That was a long time. The cigarette market was moving so fast that the Yava brand could lose a lot of smokers during that period. We were categorically against the idea. We argued that Pall Mall was not yet a well-known brand in Russia and still needed to find its consumer, whereas Yava was a big asset for the company and it was unacceptable to risk losing smokers.

Despite the measures taken by the BAT leadership, Howe persisted in his contrary stand. Evidently, he could not forgive us for our appeal to Bernd Schweitzer. After the production management issue was resolved in our favour, he changed tactics. He began criticising the way we ran the factory, drawing comparisons with the way things were in Saratov. He came up with the idea of relocating some of our Yava cigarette production to the Saratov factory, supposedly as way of cutting costs. To support the plan, he produced calculations of "conversion costs". This was a term used in international accounting to denote the cost of producing a unit of production less the cost of materials, i.e. it directly reflected manufacturing costs. Conversion costs at Yava came out higher than at the Saratov tobacco factory. This was easy enough to explain. Life was more expensive and wages were higher in Moscow than in the provinces. The cost of various services (electricity, water, transport) was also higher for the same objective reasons. His reasoning was therefore disingenuous, especially as there were a number of advantages to manufacturing cigarettes in Moscow: cigarettes made by the Yava factory were psychologically perceived by the consumer as "original products", added to which, transport costs for delivering products to sales outlets were lower.

We knew very well that the idea would not be supported in London, but it reflected a recurring theme in Howe's behaviour. He made attempts to torpedo other plans relating to the Yava factory. He suddenly announced that, because of the excessive costs, the London office had decided to suspend financing for the renovation of some of the factory's facilities. They had ordered work to be limited to the main production building. Inflated figures were cited for amounts already spent. To address these issues, Bernd Schweitzer invited me and Mario Chacon to London. I was asked to give a presentation. I attempted to clarify things, giving a detailed analysis of the state of affairs. I gave the real figures for the renovation costs so far, which were fully in line with the original plan. It was clear from Bernd Schweitzer's reaction that Howe had been misinforming the European management. His idea of partly relocating the production of Yava cigarettes to Saratov could hardly be called well thought-out. As a result of the meeting it was decided to finance the factory renovation in full.

I returned to Moscow in good spirits. At last I had managed to make direct contact and raise my concerns with the company's directors. People at the top were beginning to listen to what I had to say. I remained absolutely convinced that we needed to start manufacturing Yava Gold cigarettes as soon as possible. It was essential in terms of protecting the market position of the entire family of Yava cigarettes – the company's main brand in Russia. But the BAT-Russia management was preparing for the launch of Pall Mall. My attempts to somehow get this decision changed were in vain. At a meeting with BAT-Russia's marketing director, Rolf Bielefeld, I was told plainly that the Pall Mall launch had been approved in London and there was no way anything could be changed.

It was not long after this conversation that the BAT president Martin Broughton came to Moscow along with Bernd Schweitzer. The BAT leadership understood the importance of this moment. What the company did next would determine who would be the top seller in one of the world's largest markets. As usual, on the first day of their visit, presentations were given about the current state of affairs and plans for the future. After the marketing presentation I was called on to speak. Addressing the BAT leaders, I explained my position about the launch of the new cigarette brands. I said that delaying the production of Yava Gold could cost the company a lot of money. To my great surprise, Martin Broughton supported me. That was what settled the issue over the production of Yava Gold cigarettes, which became BAT's most successful project in Russia. Once again, Richard Howe's plans had been defeated. Nevertheless, he stubbornly persisted in pursuing his agenda. It was clear that Howe's work had provoked criticism from Bernd Schweitzer.

All in all, things began to change. New managers appeared, and the old ones were gradually replaced under the influence of the decision-makers in London. There was a new dynamism about the company's work. In 1996 BAT-Russia achieved record figures for cigarette production and sales – over thirty billion sticks. This occasion was marked at the end of December by a concert in the large hall of the Rossiya cinema. It was clear from the spirit and energy of the young employees who gathered there that the company was gathering momentum, that it had the strength to go on and achieve even greater heights. The company had spawned a whole army of sales representatives – young, energetic people who represented Russia's regions. Richard Howe's management style was completely unsuited to the new challenges. Lacking strategic vision, he was driven by an obsessive need to concentrate power in his own hands. Maintaining his confrontational stance, he was now reduced to picking on the most trivial things. We tried not to notice it, immersing ourselves in our work. But things could not go on like this for much longer. Matters came to a head after a visit from the European region's production director, John Lord. On the day he visited the factory, Howe spent a lot of time with him and evidently fed him stories about how badly Yava was run by the general director. He instructed Mario Chacon to show the visitor the production areas as evidence of the chaotic state of the factory. At that time, the renovation was in full swing, and some of the auxiliary units looked rather a mess. I had been expecting to have discussions on important matters, but Howe had made such an impression on Lord that, quite to my surprise, he proceeded to march me around all corners of the factory demanding explanations. There was blatant bias in all this. In the context of the dramatic changes in our main production operations, these problems amounted to nothing more than a temporary inconvenience. I lost my patience and replied in scathing terms. I told John Lord exactly what I thought. I declared that it was impossible to work in an atmosphere like this. Our conversation occurred at the end of the day, just before he left for the airport. It was obvious that Lord would tell London that the confrontation between the managers of BAT-Russia and Yava was still going on, and conclusions would be drawn.

Sure enough, very soon Howe was summoned to London. A nervous wait began. I realised that a major decision would probably be made which would affect my future career as well. A few days later, towards evening I got a call from the general manager's secretary to say that Howe was flying back from London and had asked for all members of the Ex-Co to await his arrival at the office. It was clear that some important information was about to be imparted to us. All the directors assembled in the meeting room. The atmosphere was tense. Arriving straight from the airport, Howe made an announcement: "After discussing the situation with the management in London, I am resigning". In Western companies it is conventional for a manager to announce his resignation to his subordinates in this way. It is a very good rule which allows the person who has been in charge of the workforce to maintain his dignity. The reaction of all those present was very restrained.

This was undoubtedly a great victory for us, but I experienced no feelings of joy. This was not at all how I had envisaged things when I started working for BAT. Everyone understood the reasons for the resignation, but not all employees were happy about it. Of course, the foreign staff might have seen it as a humiliation: a British company director being forced to resign over a conflict with local managers. But no one, not even Richard Howe, discussed the matter with me or picked a quarrel over it. Outwardly, Howe carried himself well. He even bid me a friendly goodbye. The resignation was a defeat for him, but it was no great tragedy. He was a fairly wealthy man and had a new appointment to look forward to. It was at precisely the same time that his wedding took place in Moscow: he married his long-standing flame, the heiress of a noble family from an African country in which he had previously worked. How different this was from Soviet managers, who would take the loss of their job as a crushing blow, after which they would sink into a depression and quietly waste away. At the same time as he announced his resignation, Howe informed us approvingly that the post of general manager would be taken over by Ben Stevens, who had previously worked in Afghanistan and done very well there. It was clear from the reaction of the foreign directors that this figure commanded a lot of respect in the company.

Sure enough, the short time for which Ben (as everyone called him) was with us proved to be the brightest, most fruitful period in BAT-Russia's history. His management style could not have been further removed from Richard Howe's methods. Ben did not go in for high-handed administration. He immediately presented his strategy for the company's development for discussion by the Ex-Co. He did not make a show of fervent activity, clearly preferring to focus on intellectual work. He spent most of his time working in his office. It was unusual to see a general manager sitting at a computer and pondering things over rather than calling meetings. Within a short period, he succeeded in building an effective system for running the company. He treated us with respect and did not differentiate between Russian and foreign directors. During his tenure we gradually forgot about that problem. A new team of managers arrived at BAT-Russia at the same time as Ben Stevens. The Dutchman René Eisenstein was appointed in place of Mario Chacon, while the brilliant young Englishman David Fell took over as marketing director.

"YAVA GOLD". COUNTERSTRIKE

The new management team demonstrated its professional mettle with the launch of Yava Gold cigarettes, which became a landmark event on a national scale. The timing of the launch was very precise. Imported cigarettes had become widely available, and international brands no longer carried the wow factor that they had once enjoyed. Smokers, especially the younger ones, were interested in sampling the high-quality Russian brands. Life had improved in the country, things were settling down – and as a result, a sense of patriotism had begun to kick in. People started asking: why can we not make decent products ourselves? The launch of the famous Yava cigarettes, manufactured to international standards, was a worthy response to this call. The new BAT-Russia team did an admirable job of capturing the mood. It devised an advertising strategy headed "Counterstrike", implying that Yava Gold was striking back against American brands of cigarettes. Spectacular advertising for Yava Gold with the Counterstrike caption appeared on Moscow's streets, featuring the Statue of

Liberty and Manhattan's skyscrapers with a fine-looking packet of Yava Golds flying above them from the direction of the ocean. The advertisement hit like a bombshell. Everyone paid attention to it, even people who had never had any interest in cigarettes. BAT's specialists had made great efforts in developing the flavour qualities and design of the cigarettes, taking full account of the priorities of Russian smokers. The end result was a cigarette that was genuinely capable of competing with international brands. And at a cheaper price than the imports.

Much thought went into the process of promoting the Yava Gold brand. Sales representatives and young employees from other divisions of BAT-Russia travelled around the country, visiting sales outlets and presenting the new cigarettes. The results were impressive. Smokers switched from imports to Yava Golds in their droves, expressing delight at the high quality and pride at the appearance of a worthy new Russian product. Sales exceeded all expectations. For a long time, Yava Golds became the arbiter of fashion, pushing L&M, Philip Morris's popular brand, into second place. The Yava Gold launch took place in the summer of 1997, and in August 1998 Russia was hit by a financial crisis. This prompted a second wave of sales growth for Yava Gold, with many people switching to the brand out of financial considerations.

BAT-Russia's period of success effectively began after the launch of Yava Gold. There was a sense that the company was on the rise. The young staff began to take pride in the fruits of their labour. Although most smokers associated the success of Yava Gold with the Yava factory, BAT-Russia's standing also rose significantly – especially in the halls of power. The Counterstrike slogan became popular in Russia. Our achievements were highly appreciated in London. Russia had become British American Tobacco's most promising, fastest-growing market. The progress made in Russia was held up as an example to other regional divisions. BAT's top executives became frequent visitors to Moscow. Yava Gold became a sort of locomotive for the company's other brands, and the Yava family was the biggest in Russia. Sales topped thirty billion sticks a year. The Yava brand was placed among the top ten brands in various rankings. Yava Gold won several "Product of the year" prizes. The success raised the standing of the factory's directors. Martin Broughton remembered that it was Sinelnikov who had insisted on commencing production of Yava Gold as soon as possible. On one of his visits he pointed this out and apologised for the behaviour of Howe and his team. Ben Stevens decided to move me into an office next to his just off the main reception area. Our influence on decision-making within BAT-Russia increased significantly.

A relationship of partnership and trust was established with the foreign managers. We worked harmoniously with the production director, René Eisenstein, which aided progress in production terms. By the end of 1997, exactly three years after the investment tender, the full replacement of Yava's equipment had been completed. Strict process discipline was observed at the factory. Operations were now organised no differently than at the company's factories in other countries.

As strange as it may sound, the changes in the manufacturing side of things were very visibly manifested in the condition of the factory site. It had always been an affliction of Soviet enterprises that all the deficiencies of the production process were reflected in the functional uses and external appearance of factory yards. They became a dumping ground for poorly processed production waste, making factory grounds look cluttered and unsightly. This in turn had a psychological effect on the workers, instilling a sense of disorderliness and indifference. This was the picture I myself had encountered at Yava when I first joined the factory. Voitsekhovich regularly did the rounds of the factory, bawling at people in his usual heated manner for the mess he found in the outside areas. The question of keeping the site clean was discussed at practically every supervisors' meeting in the director's office, but nothing could be done because the causes of the build-up of excess waste were not addressed. After the factory began making filter cigarettes, which are more material-intensive, the problem grew even worse. Although the factory received modern equipment, process failures continued to occur because of the low quality of materials used. The increased quantity of defective cigarettes meant increased amounts of waste. So that it could be collected, a concrete bunker had to be built right in the middle of the yard to make it easier for the waste to be loaded onto special refuse trucks. This structure was extremely unsightly. It often happened that the trucks did not come when scheduled, so the bunker became overfilled with waste, hampering other transport operations on the factory site. Of course, we paid constant attention to this matter. The technology division made regular checks of waste processing activities, punishing those who breached the regulations, but no actual progress was made. It seemed to be a problem without a solution. On my visits to foreign factories, I looked with envy at the clean, uncluttered yards, functioning solely as a space for trucks to deliver raw materials or collect finished products. All handling operations were performed using forklift trucks and pallets. For us, this picture had seemed an unattainable ideal. So what was the key to solving the problem? As it turned out, it was very simple. Being able to operate strictly in line with process specifications meant that less waste was generated, and modern equipment was brought in to process what there was. The notorious bunker – that symbol of backwardness and disorderliness – was eliminated. The yard began to resemble that of any modern factory: a nice clear tarmac surface with markings for vehicles and traffic regulation signs.

I am reminded in this connection of a chance meeting with the former head of the personnel department, Voitsekhovich's legendary comrade-in-arms, Yevdokia Vasilyevna Monat. Now well into her retirement, she had come to the factory to visit the medical office. Naturally, I enquired about her health. But Yevdokia Vasilyevna immediately shot back with a question of her own: "Lyonya (this was what she had called me since back in the days when she hired me) – tell me, how did you get the yard looking so neat? Mikhail Demyanovich tried so hard, effing and blinding at everyone to do their job. It was never any use". Even long after they had hung up their hats, these people continued to take a lively interest in what was happening at their native factory.

Of course, the arrival of British American Tobacco heralded a new era for us. I have often been asked where I found it harder to work as director: in a Soviet enterprise or as part of a large foreign company. The answer is that they are completely different challenges. In Soviet times, a director had to spur the workforce to fulfil the plan in the most difficult conditions. The materials were not of the proper quality, spare parts were in short supply, and equipment and processes were out of date. The workers blamed all these ills on the enterprise's management. It gave the workers the moral high ground, and the administration was forced to close its eyes to many of their mistakes.

When BAT came in, priorities changed completely. Modern equipment was installed, and there were no problems obtaining proper parts. The focus was on making high-quality products and raising efficiency. The key to achieving these things lay in strict adherence to the production process. The workers understood this. Conditions of pay were good, and social benefits were preserved. Medical insurance was introduced for workers and members of their families. There were all sorts of training and professional development courses. Operators learned how to use new equipment, and engineers could do internships, including at factories abroad. People were eager to hold onto a job that was well paid and carried prestige. In return, workers were required to adhere strictly to operating procedures and faced tough demands. The relationship between management and workers shifted to a wholly business-oriented footing.

The upgrading of BAT-Russia's factories meant that they could produce international cigarette brands belonging to BAT. There was no difference in quality between products made at Yava and in Saratov. Following the launch of Yava Gold at BAT-Yava, the Saratov factory began manufacturing the popular Pall Mall brand. This was followed by the production of Kent cigarettes, a brand well-known in the USSR even before Marlboros appeared. The Kent launch was a real event, accompanied by a vigorous promotional campaign and impressive advertising.

The marketing people continued their work on expanding the Yava cigarette family. Next in line was the Yava Gold Light brand. Advertising for these elegant cigarettes was based around the famous "flying skirt" image of Marilyn Monroe from the romantic comedy film *The Seven Year Itch* (1955, directed by Billy Wilder). Because of the great success of Yava Gold, production volumes of hard-pack filters increased significantly. The factory found itself short of capacity. As a result, production of soft-pack Yavas was moved to the Saratov factory. This time we supported the decision because it made logical sense.

This flurry of activity on the tobacco market helped maintain BAT-Russia's rating. It also increased the standing of the promising young general manager. Soon, we learned that Ben Stevens was to be promoted to a position at the company's London office, Globe House. Bernd Schweitzer was greatly impressed by the atmosphere of trust between foreign and Russian staff that had been created at BAT-Russia and the positive contribution that this relationship had made to the company's performance. It was this criterion, therefore, that drove his search for Ben's replacement. In making his choice he decided to go even further by appointing Sergei Krasnov, a man with Russian roots and an excellent knowledge of the language, as Russian general manager. Krasnov's parents had been forcibly deported to Germany in their youth. After the end of the war, probably fearing that they would face persecution in the USSR, they had settled in Canada. Krasnov had been head of Reynolds in Petersburg for some years and knew the workings of the Russian tobacco business.

Before the appointment was finalised, Bernd invited me to join him and

Krasnov on a tour of the Golden Ring (Yaroslavl, Rostov and Uglich), to help build a rapport. The trip went very well. I got to know Krasnov better in an informal setting. In Yaroslavl we visited the tobacco factory and met the director, Vladimir Galagayev. On returning to the office I sensed that Bernd's initiative had not gone down well with the foreign directors. They appeared irritated that the director of the European region was fraternising with the Russians in this way. It was, admittedly, a little strange that he had flown straight to London after the trip without looking in at the office. Perhaps he wanted to avoid creating an awkward atmosphere given that Krasnov had not yet officially started in his role as general manager. In any case, it struck a nerve with the Brits.

There must have been similar feelings at Globe House, i.e. that he was too openly supportive of local managers. Soon, it was announced that Bernd was leaving the company and retiring very early at the age of fifty-six. His farewell party was for some reason organised in Budapest. Strangely, the only person there from the company's senior management was his close friend Ulrich Herter. However, the managers who attended from former Soviet bloc countries and from Ukraine and Uzbekistan were sincerely sorry to see him go. I feel very grateful towards Bernd. He showed himself to be a true progressive, unfettered by convention. But in this instance, corporate principles won out, and Bernd Schweitzer was forced to retire.

The role of a top manager in an international company is in many ways that of a politician. Numerous factors have to be considered when making any decision. Krasnov, too, was treated warily at first, as something of an outsider. The main critic was David Fell, who had been Ben Stevens' closest associate. It was not long before the 1998 financial crisis struck. Those were desperate times. The rouble fell several-fold against the dollar. The banks were paralysed and temporarily shut down. Money from cigarette sales had to be flown to Moscow in sacks. Every day of work threatened major financial losses. BAT-Russia set up a crisis team consisting of the top managers. We met twice a day, in the morning and evening, to assess how things were going and review sales figures and amounts coming into MUMT's accounts.

YAVA CIGARETTES KEEP BAT AFLOAT IN RUSSIA

BAT-Russia managed to avoid big losses thanks to its balanced portfolio of differently priced brands. During the crisis period, sales of expensive international brands all but came to a halt as disposable incomes plummeted. The chief saviour was the Yava brand, which attracted smokers with its optimal balance of price and quality. Yava Golds and traditional Yavas became the top sellers in the segments of affordable international-standard and mass-market filter cigarettes.

Gradually, things began to settle down. Sergei Krasnov showed political agility. Keeping a cool head, he gradually succeeded in establishing himself as general manager and smoothing out relations within BAT-Russia's management team. Every day he sent reports to London advising them of the state of affairs. The responsibility was immense. The fact that the company managed to get through the crisis without serious losses greatly strengthened his credentials.

This critical period proved a triumph for Yava cigarettes. In effect, it was the famous Soviet cigarette brand that stopped British American Tobacco from going under in Russia. By no means all foreign companies survived the crisis. This was well understood in London. A short while later, BAT's marketing director, the flamboyant Jimmy Rambishevsky, came to Moscow. After getting to know how things stood, he reacted in his usual eccentric style, declaring straight out to the foreign directors, "If it hadn't been for Yava Gold, we'd be out of a job here. We'd be heading straight out of Moscow, and they'd be waving us goodbye".

Soon, BAT-Russia's brand portfolio expanded substantially. In early 1999 British American Tobacco acquired Rothmans, the world's fourth-largest tobacco company. Rothmans made a number of well-known elite brands: Dunhill, Rothmans, and the stylish women's brand, Vogue. Rothmans had also started up business in Russia, establishing a joint venture with Nevo-Tabak OJSC – Rothmans-Nevo CJSC – in 1994. It had been allocated a fine plot of land in a St Petersburg suburb called Konnaya Lakhta on which to build a new factory. Commissioned in September 1997, the factory began producing Dallas (a Rothmans brand) and Hermitage filter cigarettes, especially designed for the Russian market. But competition was stiff, and promoting the new brands was hard going. Things got even worse when the financial crisis took hold. After the purchase of Rothmans was announced, the Rothmans-Nevo factory was taken over by BAT-Russia. I remember the first time I visited the enterprise as part of the management team. It made a very mixed impression. It was a beautiful site with potential for growth: the production buildings, equipment and manufacturing process all reflected the high standards for which Rothmans was well known. But this splendid facility stood virtually idle, working a single shift three days a week. A 200-strong trained workforce was bused in from Petersburg. It was a terrible waste. They had built a factory without giving proper thought to their product range. It had been the wrong time to introduce high-price brands, and they did not have any worthy contenders in the medium-price bracket.

To cut a long story short, the BAT team sorted everything out. In time, the BAT-Neva factory (as it is now called) became BAT's top facility in Russia. It began to produce major international brands. BAT-Russia came out of the crisis with an even stronger position in the market. Things stabilised on the production side of things, too. The renovation work was completed. Technologically and organisationally, Yava was in no way different from BAT's factories in other parts of the world. The day-to-day running of the factory was increasingly handled by the new production director, the Belgian Marc Van Herreweghe. This allowed me to shift my focus towards corporate relations, which had become very important. In 2003 I left the post of general director and was elected chairman of the board of directors of BAT-Yava OJSC.

CHAPTER 17.

CONCLUSION: TOBACCO UP IN SMOKE

STATE REGULATION OF THE TOBACCO INDUSTRY. "KEEP YOUR EAR TO THE GROUND"

Many issues relevant to the creation of a favourable business environment were now addressed in the context of the state regulation of business activity: taxes, regulations on quality standards, conditions for the sale of products on the market, and so on. Companies therefore began to focus heavily on lobbying government institutions to advance their interests. At BAT-Russia, this was the job of the corporate relations department headed by Vladimir Konstantinovich Aksyonov. Since resolving regulatory issues involved representing the company at a particular level and reaching out to government bodies, I had increasingly been called upon to assist with these problems while I was still general director of the famous Yava factory. For its part, the government was keen to take the interests of the business community into account in drafting its laws and regulations. It was to aid this process that industry associations were set up with the authority to liaise with government bodies and present the concerted positions of participants in the market.

In the tobacco industry, an association of this kind, Tabakprom, had been founded back in 1991 in place of the dissolved Rosglavtabak, the chief directorate for the tobacco industry under the Food Ministry of the RSFSR. Virtually every tobacco enterprise in the Russian Federation was a member. The arrival of foreign companies in Russia greatly increased the authority of Tabakprom. The creation of industry associations was an essential practice in global business. Foreign companies began to attach great importance to involvement in Tabakprom's activities.

The leading Russian-owned factories – Donskoy Tabak in Rostov, Balkanskaya Zvezda in Yaroslavl and Nevo-Tabak in Petersburg – strengthened their positions and began to play an even more prominent role. These enterprises took an active part in Tabakprom's affairs. In line with the organisation's charter, the interests of multinational companies were represented by the tobacco factories which they owned, i.e. BAT-Yava and BAT-STF for BAT-Russia, Philip-Morris-Kuban (the Krasnodar factory) for PM, and Liggett-Ducat for Liggett & Myers. The directors of these companies and of the three leading Russian-owned factories were on the board of Tabakprom.

Tabakprom's main task was to liaise with government bodies and keep them up to date on matters in order to give the government and lawmakers the guidance they needed in developing regulatory measures relating to tobacco production. And tobacco manufacturers were facing increasingly tough requirements. In Russia, as in other countries, there was active discussion of issues surrounding cigarette consumption, such as reducing the harmful effects of smoking on public health, preventing smoking among minors and combating counterfeit products and illegal imports of cigarettes from neighbouring countries (Belarus, Ukraine and Kazakhstan). The issue of the pricing of tobacco products was kept under review as a factor that could help limit consumption and make them less accessible to young people.

The process by which laws were made had changed. Bills were submitted by the government to the State Duma, where they were first discussed by specialist committees, then put to plenary sessions. Deputies themselves could also propose their own laws or make amendments to bills. Public organisations now played a major role. For some deputies, the tobacco theme became a convenient plank on which to make a display of initiative. Newly formed anti-tobacco organisations and movements advocated tough measures against the tobacco industry and smokers. The danger was that this approach was in large measure driven by populism and ill-thought-out proposals that threatened to damage positive developments in tobacco production and the tobacco market. The task of the board of directors of Tabakprom, therefore, was to formulate the objective position of the professional community.

We were aided in this endeavour by the fact that trends in the tobacco industry and market in Russia were naturally moving in the direction of positive solutions to important economic and social problems. Over the years, output of filter cigarettes had dramatically increased, while consumption of unfiltered kinds had dropped. This was an important factor in reducing the harmful impact of smoking on public health. All enterprises owned by foreign companies, as well as the major Russian-owned factories, had upgraded their plants, implemented modern processes and fitted out their quality testing laboratories with imported equipment. This allowed enterprises to manufacture products meeting prescribed quality parameters and enabled lawmakers to introduce limits on tar and nicotine content. The tremendous progress made in reducing harmful factors in smoking was plain to see. Despite this, serious disagreements arose over the approaches to setting limits on tar and nicotine content in cigarette smoke. Populists and opponents of smoking insisted on the introduction of European standards. The tobacco companies supported a gradual lowering of the levels of these substances, arguing that the Russian consumer was accustomed to stronger cigarettes, and a sudden drop in nicotine content could result in disgruntled smokers. Besides, it could deliver a painful blow to smaller companies which made unfiltered cigarettes and were not yet in a position to operate to European standards.

The pricing of tobacco products became a topic of fierce debate. Cigarette prices in Russia were substantially higher than in Soviet times but still a long way behind global levels. This situation was criticised by opponents of smoking, who argued that low prices were fuelling the spread of tobacco use in the country and proposed that they be raised to European levels. The tobacco companies advocated moderate, gradual price rises. Disposable incomes in Russia were much lower than in European countries. It was very important to harmonise tobacco prices with those in neighbouring countries so as to prevent any increase in contraband trade. Global practice showed that high prices led to increased volumes of illicit, counterfeit products. An example of this was the UK, where high prices had led to a situation in which illicit imports from Europe made up over 20 per cent of cigarettes sold. This resulted in a substantial loss of government revenue.

All these factors had to be taken in consideration in formulating measures to regulate the market. To its credit, the Russian government took a balanced approach regarding tobacco consumption. A large part in this was played by the consistent position of the professional community. The Tabakprom board met regularly, with agendas covering the most burning issues of the day. We tried to take a proactive role. I, like other members of the board, found myself frequenting high offices together with the general director, Terevtsov, and addressing meetings of specialist committees of the State Duma. Gradually, Tabakprom grew in stature and began to play an important role in shaping government policy on the production and consumption of cigarettes. Government institutions attached particular importance to combating illicit and counterfeit products.

Illicit tobacco products began appearing after the collapse of the USSR, when government authority in the country was weakened. The bulk of tobacco products in Russia came from former Soviet state enterprises. But a number of semi-clandestine factories began to materialise, operating out of ill-suited facilities with substandard equipment. They acquired outdated, worn-out machinery, primarily from ex-Soviet bloc countries (the Czech Republic, Bulgaria and Poland). Some such factories were set up in the Moscow region. The products they produced – *papirosy* and unfiltered cigarettes – were of a poor quality. Obviously enough, the income of these enterprises was wholly dependent on the avoidance of taxes. But that was not so hard. The Tax Service was only just being formed, tax bases had not yet been defined and tax evasion was common among new businesses. This situation did not last long. The state began to strengthen controls. The scope for the existence of the semi-legal factories was gradually narrowed. The introduction of excise stamps (based on international practice) in 1994 put up a serious barrier to illicit trade. To obtain stamps, businesses had to be registered with the tax authorities and file tax returns. The presence of a stamp on a cigarette pack acted as proof that the contents were legal. To deter forgery, the stamps had multiple security features. As government papers, they were made by Goznak, the specialised state enterprise responsible for printing banknotes.

The situation on the tobacco market changed. The appearance of large distribution companies enabled greater control over compliance with government standards on cigarette trade. Philip Morris engaged Megapolis as its exclusive distributor, while British American Tobacco used SNS. They maintained a close relationship with the manufacturers. Russia now had a civilised tobacco industry. There was a whole variety of cigarette brands on sale, spanning different price segments. Around 90 per cent of the total volume was made by large tobacco companies. Official sources put the proportion of illegal products at 3–4 per cent. This was a low figure even by international standards.

Despite this, the issue of illicit products on the tobacco market continued to be whipped up in certain quarters. The industry as a whole produced over 400 billion cigarettes a year, equating to 20 billion packs requiring the same quantity of excise stamps. These figures attracted the attention of the special authorities, who were keen to establish control over large financial flows, especially as turnover in cigarette retail now totalled over six billion dollars. Data protection agencies with close ties to the FSB[1] began developing proposals for protecting the alcohol and tobacco market against counterfeit products. There was a deliberate stoking up of tension around these matters. The government and the State Duma would periodically receive reports from the FSB and the Interior Ministry giving blatantly inflated figures on the levels of illicit tobacco trade. The same reports proposed measures to impose order by strengthening controls over the manufacture and distribution of alcohol and tobacco products: for example, by introducing stamps with ultra-modern holographic security features. It was becoming an increasingly expensive issue, with the more sophisticated technology pushing up the cost of stamps. The proposals won support among a certain group of officials and deputies. They were prepared to take control over the manufacture of the stamps, but they could not get round the government decree of 14 April 1994 defining the status of excise stamps as "government papers", meaning that they could only be made by a specialised state enterprise. Experts confirmed that the technology used by Goznak provided all the necessary protection.

While the tobacco community had succeeded in proving the high level of legitimacy in its market, the alcohol market really was rife with criminality. The proponents of hardline measures therefore succeeded in persuading the State Duma to pass a law requiring liquor manufacturers to register with the EGAIS tracking system. The idea was that full information on products manufactured would be entered in the system while they were still being made, allowing items to be tracked right up to the point of sale on the market. The source of the information would still be a special stamp made by Goznak.

Theoretically, it was possible to track the movement of every individual bottle up to the point at which it was sold at retail. But who was going to sort through such a huge volume of information? The onus of combating counterfeit production fell mainly on the alcohol market itself. There was little change in the situation: the alcohol market remained largely uncontrolled.

The reason I am dwelling on the EGAIS system like this is that the same forces made persistent efforts to impose it on the tobacco industry. We had to fight them off as best we could.

---

1 FSB − *Federalnaya Sluzhba Bezopasnosti* − the Federal Security Service.

We had to work hard to defend ourselves against all sorts of attacks. But there was one time when we were literally one step away from defeat. The assailant on this occasion was, strangely enough, the Moscow government. The Moscow authorities were sometimes prone to acting without consulting federal laws. For example, at the government's suggestion, the Moscow City Duma passed a law "On Symbols in Moscow". The list of symbols included the majority of the city's sights. The law stated that the owner of these assets was the government of Moscow, and any use of them by commercial entities in their logos, advertising, and so forth had to be approved in advance by the city authorities. In actual fact, legally speaking many of Moscow's well-known features were federal property, and the rights to use images of them were owned by private individuals. But no one seriously attempted to challenge the law. Everyone accepted the conditions laid down by the Moscow authorities.

BAT-Russia came up against this problem while working on the next phase of its advertising for Yava Gold cigarettes. The marketing director, David Fell, came to me for help. The design firm Grey had come up with an impressive advertisement. It featured a close-up image of Vera Mukhina's famous *Worker and Kolkhoz Woman* statue (filling the whole billboard) in which the figures are holding up a pack of Yava Gold in their raised hands instead of a hammer and sickle. David set great store by this advertisement, believing that it aptly built on the idea at the heart of the Counterstrike campaign. But it misfired with the Moscow authorities. A special commission set up by the Moscow government refused to approve it on the grounds that it played too fast and loose with one of the city's most famous symbols. David hoped that I could use my contacts within the government to resolve this important matter for the company.

Before contacting anyone in the government, I decided to consult with an intellectual property expert, Alexander Lvovich Gorodissky, to find out how legally sound the commission's decision was. The experts examined the documents and established that the owner of the legal rights to Mukhina's artistic legacy was her son, who lived in St Petersburg. After conferring, we decided not to make any further application to the Moscow authorities, but to secure the right to use the image through the artist's heir, which was the proper thing to do. The company's lawyers contacted Mukhina's son, travelled to Petersburg and sorted out an agreement. It was just at the time when the 1998 financial crisis struck. BAT took advantage of the temporary fall in advertising prices, and posters featuring the *Worker and Kolkhoz Woman* went up on billboards all over Moscow. Evidently reeling from the financial crisis, Moscow's government made no immediate response. After coming round, it presented us with a rather sternly worded demand for explanations. But after we produced the agreement with the heir, the matter was quietly dropped. There was nothing they could say. We found it particularly satisfying to have defended our interests by purely law-based methods.

The next round of confrontation with the Moscow authorities involved the saga over the "Moscow stamp for cigarettes". This time, the story involved all suppliers of cigarettes to the Moscow market, meaning mainly international tobacco companies. This did not deter the Moscow government. It was virtually one step away from achieving what the mighty security authorities had failed to achieve. Again based on falsified data about the quantity of illicit tobacco products on the Moscow market, they dreamed up another panacea against forgery. It was proposed that every pack of cigarettes sold in Moscow should be required to bear, in addition to the government excise stamp, a special Moscow stamp endowed with advanced security features. The main initiator of the plan was Vladimir Ivanovich Malyshkov, the Moscow government minister in charge of the Department for the Consumer Market and Services. The legality of the action was highly questionable: federal legislation did not grant individual regions the power to establish their own rules on the sale of excisable goods. But the central authorities made no serious attempt to block what was effectively an unlawful measure. There were reasons for this.

It was a period in which central authority was weakened. After the financial crisis, the political situation in the country had become unstable. Serious opposition to Yeltsin emerged in the State Duma. For a long time, the country remained without a confirmed prime minister. The president was often absent due to illness. Luzhkov, on the other hand, had grown in stature and influence. There was a sense that he had outgrown Moscow. The city was vigorously strengthening ties with the regions, giving them all kinds of financial and technical assistance. Many governors saw Yury Mikhailovich as a new leader. The Moscow mayor began advancing political initiatives of nationwide import.

The mayor's efforts culminated in the creation in 1996 of the Fatherland-All Russia party, of which he became co-chairman. Many people started talking about Luzhkov as a possible successor to Yeltsin. Given these factors, the

Moscow government felt no pressing need to seek approval from the centre for its intentions. The tobacco companies did not take the initiative seriously at first. It sounded just too ridiculous. Nowhere in the world had there been any precedent of two stamps being placed on one pack of cigarettes. What was the point? They had not even worked out the technical aspects. We put forward all these arguments in discussions with Moscow bodies. They were so convincing that the Moscow government's industrial policy department issued an adverse opinion on the introduction of a second stamp. But we soon realised that our attempts to change the Moscow leadership's mind were useless. The Moscow government simply decided to go ahead and impose what amounted to an additional tax on sales of tobacco products in the capital. It was a flagrant violation of Russian law.

We tried appealing to the federal authorities, but the reaction there was surprisingly passive. They were seemingly too busy with other things, while the Moscow authorities were taking huge liberties. The machinery for the decision was set in motion. A series of articles about the heinous state of affairs on the tobacco market appeared in the Moscow press. They included a lot of improbable claims, such as that investigators had stumbled upon a room piled high with false excise stamps for cigarettes.

We got word that a Moscow government order introducing the Moscow stamp had been drafted ready for approval. The situation was exactly like in Soviet times: it was obvious what was going on, but there was nothing that could be done. An instruction had come from the top, and no arguments were accepted. The only chance that remained was to appeal to Luzhkov himself. As always, the tobacco companies maintained a unified position, with Tabakprom acting as their mouthpiece. But since the matter concerned the Moscow market, the bulk of the burden was borne by the management of BAT-Yava OJSC. Although a number of large companies were affected, it was with Yava that the supply of cigarettes in the capital city was traditionally associated. All discussions of technical issues took place at the factory, which meant that head of corporate relations Vladimir Aksyonov and I were fully involved in the process and felt the weight of responsibility. It was such an important issue that it took up all our attention. The proposed measures effectively created special conditions for the sale of cigarettes in Moscow, different from those in the rest of the country. What impact might that have on the market? The implications of the decision were almost incalculable.

There was no time to lose, so we took the matter of appealing to Luzhkov into our own hands. We decided to start with Sergei Yastrzhembsky, one of the mayor's closest associates. Vladimir Aksyonov knew him from when they had worked together at the Foreign Ministry. Despite this, Sergei Vladimirovich received us with emphatic formality. He confirmed that a decision in principle had already been made on the matter in question. We had decided in advance what line to take. Mindful of Yastrzhembsky's involvement in handling Luzhkov's political activities, we drew his attention to the consequences that the planned move might have for Yury Mikhailovich's image abroad. The introduction of the Moscow stamp could be construed as a protection racket arranged by the Moscow authorities against foreign manufacturers operating in Russia. We handed him a letter addressed to Luzhkov from the directors of multinational companies requesting an audience to discuss the issue. Yastrzhembsky was clearly thrown off balance by our visit.

The response soon came: a meeting was scheduled with Luzhkov. Taking place in the Moscow city council building on Tverskaya, it was attended by general managers and corporate relations directors of multinational companies. The general director of Tabakprom, Terevtsov, was invited. The Moscow government was represented mainly by officials of the consumer market department. Yury Mikhailovich opened the meeting in an assured manner, painting a brief picture of the situation. His whole demeanour indicated that he viewed the problem as clear-cut and had no intention of consulting with representatives of the tobacco industry. Then he gave the floor to the director of the consumer market department, Malyshkov. Vladimir Ivanovich was in charge of a very complex area of activity. The whole capital was one big marketplace. Conflicts arose all the time. Malyshkov had gained a reputation as a leader with whom it was difficult to negotiate. In defending the city's business interests, he was not especially picky about the methods he chose to prove his point. On this occasion, unphased by the fact that there were tobacco professionals sitting in the room, he reiterated and even enlarged on his thoughts about the tobacco market. He did not say a word about the problems that the introduction of the Moscow stamp might bring. Again, no dialogue ensued. For some reason, the managers of the tobacco companies, who were deeply concerned about the problem, sat passively, not saying a word. It was as if the delicate foreigners were unnerved by the self-assurance of the Moscow leaders as they brazenly distorted the facts.

Keeping up the pressure, Luzhkov gave his summing-up. After the minister's speech, he said, what doubts could there be? It was imperative to introduce the Moscow stamp and put a stop to the outrages occurring on Moscow's tobacco market. After that, a pause hung in the air. I was on pins and needles. I realised that this was the decisive moment, the last chance to inject a note of discord into this skilfully executed charade. I asked for permission to speak. Addressing Luzhkov, I said, "Yury Mikhailovich, minister Malyshkov is misleading you. Why do you not consult with the professionals? The tobacco companies have a greater interest than anyone in seeing a reduction in levels of illicit products. A lot is already being done to achieve that. But the introduction of the Moscow stamp could give rise to a whole range of serious negative consequences". My speech was very emotional. I sat down in a state of inner turmoil, so I do not remember the reaction of those around me. After a short pause, Luzhkov declared, "Well then, before we go any further, let's set up a group of experts to consider all possible aspects of the issue". It was impossible to fathom the reasons for this sudden U-turn. I left the room with my spirits raised. In all honesty, it was hard to imagine what might have happened had I not stood up and spoken. I happened to bump into Malyshkov, who said reproachfully, "How could you drop me in it like that in front of the mayor?" For whatever reason, however, there was no malice in his attitude. It was clear that he was ready to talk.

Literally the next day, Vladimir Ivanovich invited Moscow factory directors and Terevtsov to discuss the matter. Liggett-Ducat was represented by the deputy general director Anatoly Veniaminovich Levi, the former director of the Rosbakaleya Moscow office and an experienced professional in the field of trade. In a calm, business-like atmosphere we managed to convey all our concerns about the consequences of the introduction of the Moscow stamp. And with that, the reckless scheme, as I will not shy away from calling it, came to an end just as suddenly as it had descended on us. After the meeting with Malyshkov, the Moscow government drew a curtain over the matter. To this day, I cannot understand why Luzhkov made the decision he made. Despite aberrations of this sort, I remain grateful to Yury Mikhailovich for the many occasions on which he gave us his constructive support. As a man of action himself, he always stood up for real business. I think it was only thanks to his support that Yava was able to continue operating in the centre of Moscow for such a long time.

THE SCHISM IN THE TOBACCO COMMUNITY AND THE STATE DUMA

The Moscow stamp was the last problem on which the tobacco companies acted as a united front. A schism occurred in the course of discussions about a new excise tax. The excise tax was introduced in Russia in 1992 after the transition to the market economy. Since excise is an indirect tax and the cost of paying it is effectively passed onto the consumer, it is perfectly natural for a higher rate to be imposed on more expensive goods. Accordingly, the rates of excise tax for cigarettes were set using the system established in the USSR for dividing tobacco products into classes. Differential specific rates were applied: the highest rate for class I cigarettes, as the most expensive, and the lowest for products in the cheapest segment – class V. It all seemed quite logical, but the lawmakers had failed to consider that in what was now a competition-based market, the old Soviet technical standards, known as GOST, were out of step with the changes that had occurred in the tobacco industry. There were fundamental differences. For example, GOST set the composition of the tobacco blend for each class of cigarettes, whereas in a market environment the tobacco blend was developed by each individual company, constituting its unique know-how and a key competitive factor in the industry.

Effectively, products made in Russia no longer conformed to the Soviet GOST. Despite this, factories that continued to produce Soviet-era brands were obliged to label each pack with the appropriate cigarette class. The discrepancy with the standards was ignored, as people understood that the labelling was for excise purposes. Although Yava was producing its famous cigarettes using new technology, therefore, it continued to print "class II cigarettes" and "class IV cigarettes" on hard and soft packs of Yava cigarettes respectively. The factory paid excise tax at the rates set for those classes. But then a loophole appeared. Tobacco companies gained the right to create new cigarette brands based on "technical specifications". Since no excise rates were set for these products, this became a common way of evading excise tax in the tobacco industry. Companies went in for tricks, carrying out "rebrandings" of Soviet products which involved little more than a change of name. They registered the cigarettes as being manufactured under "technical specifications" and stopped paying excise tax. This helped many provincial enterprises stay in business. International cigarette brands manufactured in Russia could not be classified under GOST either, so they too were legally manufactured under "technical specifications". This meant that revenues from the tax were ridiculously low. At the end of the 1990s this matter attracted a lot of intense criticism. Figures were quoted for comparison about the very high level of excise revenues from cigarettes in developed countries. The facts spoke for themselves. The government set about developing new principles for the calculation of excise tax that better reflected the new realities.

Since the tobacco industry in Russia now differed little from that in developed countries, the lawmakers looked at international practice, in which there were two main systems for calculating excise tax. America applied a single specific rate for all kinds of cigarettes, while the European Union applied a mixed rate comprised of specific and *ad valorem* components. The *ad valorem* part was set as a percentage of the cigarette price. This meant that price was a factor in the calculation of tax. This was very important for Russia. Whereas in America the price differences between different cigarette brands were negligible, in Russia prices for unfiltered cigarettes were several times lower than those for international brands. This meant that the introduction of a single specific rate would deal a devastating blow to Russian enterprises. It was around these different approaches to the selection of an excise taxation system that major disagreements broke out among cigarette manufacturers. Philip Morris, as a manufacturer of expensive cigarettes, naturally favoured a flat rate. British American Tobacco and all Russian factories that manufactured cigarettes falling in a range of price segments began lobbying for a mixed rate. PM stood to gain a major competitive advantage from the adoption of a specific rate. With a mixed rate, on the other hand, tax on expensive brands would shoot up because of the *ad valorem* component. The mixed rate reflected the interests of consumers of cheap cigarettes, who belonged to the most socially disadvantaged groups in society. It meant that the price of expensive cigarettes would rise to a greater degree, which was in keeping with the principle of social fairness, in that consumers of high-price cigarettes would bear a greater proportion of excise tax.

This was what divided opinion among the members of Tabakprom. It was a very serious issue. The choice of excise taxation system would to a large extent determine the future development of the tobacco industry. At first, the Tabakprom board tried to find a compromise and come up with a united position.

The majority were in favour of a mixed rate structure. Only two international companies – Philip Morris and Japan Tobacco – were pushing for a specific rate. It was impossible to overcome these differences. PM had lobbied for a purely specific tax system in all the countries where it operated. For the first time in Tabakprom's history, its member companies began voicing different positions.

It should be mentioned that this was a time when parliamentary forms of political wrangling were in the ascendancy. The second and third State Duma convocations included parties and single-mandate deputies of various political orientations. There were many issues on which they opposed the policies of the president and the proposals of the government. In 1998 it took three attempts to secure approval for Sergei Kirienko's appointment as head of government. In May 1999, the deputies initiated an impeachment process against Yeltsin. Many of the government's proposals were rejected and sent back for revision. Its strong, principled voice made the State Duma a force to be reckoned with. The government was forced to listen closely to the opinions of the deputies. The State Duma became a political platform for the development of legislative initiatives on important matters affecting the country's future.

Reflecting the multifaceted nature of the problem, several ministries – those for finance, tax and economic development, as well as the Agriculture Ministry as the relevant industry body – were brought into the process of drafting the excise tax law. A number of State Duma committees – budget and taxes, economic policy and entrepreneurship, and agriculture – were also involved. And to complicate things further, the tobacco companies espoused differing views. Tabakprom found itself in a difficult position. It was impossible for the association's position on such an important matter to be decided by a simple majority vote. As a specialist, Terevtsov supported the mixed rate system, but as chairman he had a duty to consider the views of all members of Tabakprom. Essentially, the Russian legislative authorities were being lobbied by two opposite camps over the issue of the excise tax on cigarettes. On one side were British American Tobacco and Russian manufacturers, and on the other were Philip Morris and Japan Tobacco.

Gradually, the press was drawn into the excise tax issue, and it became one of the biggest political topics of the day. The disagreements within the tobacco community began to be read as a battle for leadership of the tobacco market between the two international giants – BAT and Philip Morris. Of course, the proponents of the mixed system had persuasive arguments. With such a wide range of cigarette prices, introducing a single flat rate was out of the question. It would artificially drive cheap cigarettes out of the market, bankrupt many Russian enterprises and hit the pockets of low-income groups. Adopting a mixed rate structure would preserve the existing balance of interests in the market for both consumers and manufacturers of cigarettes of all price segments and protect the principle of social fairness.

On the face of it, the advocates of the specific rate appeared to have no chance. But Philip Morris, as a seasoned fighter of corporate battles, managed to find an advantage to latch onto. It concerned the ease of collection of the excise tax. It was true that having a purely specific system made it very simple to monitor payment of the tax. A single rate was set per thousand cigarettes sold. There were certain difficulties involved in the mixed system. The *ad valorem* component was calculated on the basis of the price of cigarettes. The retail price was variable: it was set by sales outlets directly and depended on the sales region. It could not be used as a basis for calculating the tax. The factory price was also found to be vulnerable. Opponents of the mixed system argued that tobacco factories might artificially lower the tax base through so-called transfer pricing arrangements. They could structure their cigarette sales system to include a chain of intermediaries, which would enable them to reduce the factory price and, accordingly, the amount of tax payable to the budget. The specific system, on the other hand, would ensure that the treasury received the full amount due. And this was paramount at a time when the country was running a budget deficit. Philip Morris spent a lot of effort on pushing this line. As a result, the opinions of the deputies were divided.

PM's position unexpectedly received support from deputies promoting the interests of the oil companies. These companies made extensive use of transfer pricing and did not want to see extra attention being drawn to this issue by the adoption of a mixed excise tax on cigarettes. It became clear that the main battle would be over tax collectability. The heads of tobacco companies sensed the importance of this moment. A lot was riding on the State Duma's decision, including the very existence of a large number of companies and the preservation of a level playing field on the market. This very real threat forced the tobacco companies to unite their efforts. They formed a team of managers who actively worked together on the issue of excise taxation.

It was clear that we needed to strengthen our case regarding the advantages of the mixed excise tax system. It was decided to arrange for a group of deputies to visit Brussels to gain a practical insight into how the mixed system worked in the European Union. The trip was organised under the aegis of the Tabakprom association. It was one of the most efficiently organised trips I have ever known. The group of Russian parliamentarians was accorded a high-level reception. Over the course of three days they had meetings with relevant committees of the European Parliament as well as officials from the Belgian Finance Ministry and tax and customs authorities. The discussions mainly centred around the collection of excise tax and measures against contraband tobacco. It became clear why the mixed excise tax had been chosen when the European Union was formed. Cigarette prices differed significantly from one European country to another, depending on living standards. They were higher in Germany, France and Belgium than in Spain, Greece and Portugal. Imposing a single specific tax would therefore be detrimental to countries with lower household incomes. The situation was similar to Russia's, but on the scale of the united countries of Europe.

The question of the administration of excise tax was examined in great detail. Transparency in the calculation of tax had been achieved by introducing the concept of a "maximum retail price" for a pack of cigarettes. The maximum retail price was set by the manufacturer and printed on each pack. Vendors did not have the right to sell cigarettes above that price (but were permitted to sell them at lower prices). The maximum retail price was used as the tax base for the calculation of the *ad valorem* component and made the taxing process transparent. It was set in line with the interests of real competition on the market. It was not in the interests of tobacco companies to set it too low, as that would lead directly to losses on cigarette sales.

The Russian deputies, accustomed to the routine flouting of trade laws in their own country, could not immediately understand how these rules worked in real terms, and even asked, "But supposing someone did actually sell the cigarettes at a higher price?" The question was so unexpected that the European Union's representative could not answer it straight away. Once he had grasped what was meant, he responded in a surprised tone, "But that would be against the law. And in any case, customers are well-informed and would not buy cigarettes at a higher price". The information the deputies received convinced them of the wisdom of adopting a mixed excise tax structure. Even the issue of the transparency of tax assessment was resolvable, but it would mean getting the trade sector to behave more responsibly. That was essential in any case.

A complete transformation occurred in the views of Gennady Vasilyevich Kulik. Before the trip he had been inclined to support the introduction of a purely specific tax. Gennady Vasilyevich – a major expert in agriculture – was one of the most professional parliamentarians. His opinion was very important, as the conclusions of the agriculture committee would be taken into account in making the final decision. He carried a lot of weight in the budget committee, too. After the Brussels trip he had no qualms about changing his opinion. Kulik believed that the deputies would not yet be ready to come to a decision about the introduction of a maximum retail price. A thorough review would be needed to make sure that the retail system was ready for such a measure. And so the agriculture committee, headed by Kulik, submitted a proposal to the State Duma for the introduction of a mixed rate structure with the factory price as the tax base. Eventually, however, a transition would have to be made to a maximum retail price.

As the vote on the excise tax law drew closer, tensions reached fever pitch. The introduction of the mixed rate system was supported by such influential figures as the speaker of the State Duma, Gennady Nikolayevich Seleznyov, and Vyacheslav Viktorovich Volodin, a rising political force. But this was no guarantee of victory. A true pluralism of opinions (as Mikhail Gorbachev liked to call it) arose in the State Duma. In the government, too, opinion was divided. The specific rate was supported by the Ministry for Taxes and Levies, for whom the priority was to simplify the tax collection process.

In the end, however, the arguments of the mixed rate proponents proved more persuasive. As a result, by a slender majority, the budget committee recommended the adoption of a mixed excise tax on cigarettes. That as good as sealed the victory. The law introducing the mixed tax was passed by the State Duma in the third reading and signed by President Putin. It took effect from January 2003.

Soon after the law was passed, it became clear that Philip Morris had not given up hope of a return to a specific tax. As early as mid-2003, the chairman of the budget and taxes Committee, Alexander Zhukov, submitted a request to the Accounts Chamber to review the effectiveness of the mixed rate system for cigarettes and the use of transfer pricing in the assessment of tax. The very haste with which the review was set up (long before the end of the tax period) betrayed the biased nature of the exercise. It was not difficult to predict the outcome. The Accounts Chamber concluded that selling cigarettes through trading houses allowed tobacco factories to set an artificially low factory price and thereby reduce the amount of excise tax paid to the state.

The results of the review were sent to the government, the State Duma and the Federation Council. The Accounts Chamber's recommendation to the Ministry of Finance was to return to a wholly specific tax system. Russian factories disagreed with the Chamber's findings. Unlike in the oil industry, where chains of intermediate sellers were set up specifically to reduce tax liability, the tobacco industry had been using trading houses to sell tobacco products long before the introduction of the mixed tax. Accusing tobacco firms of a deliberate transfer pricing ruse was therefore somewhat far-fetched. The conclusions of the Accounts Chamber once again whipped up a media debate about excise tax on cigarettes. The reasons behind the rushed review soon revealed themselves. Philip Morris had planned to use the Chamber's report to trigger a renewed review of the specific tax system in 2004. But the government did not agree with the Chamber's conclusions. Even the Tax Ministry was satisfied with the amount of revenue being generated. A government proposal to index the mixed rate of excise tax for 2004 was passed by the State Duma in the first reading.

A line was finally drawn under the confrontation in 2007. With the agreement of all parties, a maximum retail price was incorporated into law as the basis for calculating the *ad valorem* component of the excise tax. It remains in place to this day. By that time, the retail sector was wholly ready for this measure. Excise receipts grew rapidly, amounting to around 150 billion roubles in 2010, which was several times higher than in 2003.

In my view, the process of the consideration and adoption of the law on cigarette excise tax was a shining example of the rise of parliamentarism in Russia. As the well-known Russian proverb goes, "Truth is born in argument". It is possible that not all the parties involved were completely sincere and guided solely by the general interest. There were no doubt other factors in play – political considerations, one might say. BAT spoke out against the specific system, which is apparently why, after completing its review of the payment of tax by tobacco factories, the Accounts Chamber decided to carry out an additional inspection of BAT's Saratov factory. When the company's lawyers analysed the contents of the inspection questionnaire, they concluded that the Chamber was exceeding its authority. The law on the Accounts Chamber allowed it to audit enterprises which received government funds or enjoyed tax reliefs. BAT did not fall into either of those categories. It was therefore decided to refuse the inspection and lodge a suit against the Chamber. The Moscow Commercial Court upheld the claim filed by the Saratov Tobacco Factory (BAT-STF) against the Chamber. The auditors did not have the right to inspect a commercial business. The ruling set an important precedent. It was the first time a business had won a court case against the Accounts Chamber.

All these things were indicative of the development of democratic institutions in Russia. By no means everyone was happy about this. Viewed in the context of today's public attitudes, I suspect that the above account of the process of the introduction of the tobacco excise tax might meet with disapproval. Rather than so much precious time being spent by important public bodies, would it not have been simpler to reach a decision in government offices and then have it passed by an obedient parliament? This puts me in mind of a speech that Viktor Stepanovich Chernomyrdin[1] made at an important event. It happened in Zurich in 2008 at an annual discussion of economic cooperation between Russia and Switzerland, attended by members of the Swiss government, a number of Russian officials and business representatives from both countries. Noting Russia's economic successes, Viktor Stepanovich complained, "When I was chairman of the government, so much valuable time had to be spent on settling matters with the State Duma, persuading deputies. Things are much simpler and more efficient now that there is full agreement between the government and deputies". He made this comment in the presence of representatives of one of the most democratic countries in the world. Viktor Stepanovich was undoubtedly an intelligent and highly experienced leader, but how deeply entrenched in him was that belief in the virtues of centralised authority! It is a feature of the Russian mentality that has been shaped over the entire course of the country's history.

The election of Vladimir Putin ushered in a period of political stabilisation in the country. In the first term of his presidency he succeeded in combining the strengthening of state power with the preservation of effective political

---

1   Viktor Stepanovich Chernomyrdin (1938–2010) – chairman of the Russian government from December 1992 to March 1998.

institutions. The creation of a monolithic "party of power" in the State Duma was the first step towards the establishment of a rigid vertical power structure. It was believed that this would improve the governability of the country and make it easier for important decisions to be made at the highest level. As before, however, this was a profound mistake. Progress can only be achieved through the development of civil society. And there is only way to do that – by introducing democratic institutions and freedoms. Making the transition from an authoritarian regime to a democratic one is very difficult. But sooner or later that transition has to be made. There is no alternative.

THE FRAMEWORK CONVENTION ON TOBACCO CONTROL. WHAT WILL BECOME OF SMOKING?

I never thought that I would witness such changes in attitudes to smoking throughout the world. Even in Russia, where people are fairly conservative in their habits, cigarette consumption is falling. Questions about the harmful effects of smoking on human health have been around for a long time. In the 1970s the industry responded by making light and ultra-light cigarettes. In the early 1990s, new research concluded that reducing tar and nicotine levels in cigarette smoke did not lessen the risks from smoking, and advertisements for light and ultra-light cigarettes were misleading. Accusations that tobacco companies had concealed information about the dangers of smoking from consumers, resulting in health problems, formed the basis of prominent court cases in the USA with claims running into millions of dollars. All this triggered a new phase in the war on smoking. The governments of a number of countries began introducing measures aimed at restricting cigarette consumption. These mainly involved increasing cigarette prices through rises in excise tax, banning advertising, sponsorship and other forms of promotion and requiring a greater part of the display area of cigarette packs to be occupied by health warnings and even images of human organs damaged by smoking. Rigorous measures were introduced to limit smoking areas in order to protect non-smokers against tobacco smoke (passive smoking). Norway and Australia led the way in the adoption of anti-tobacco laws. These measures presented serious challenges for the tobacco industry, requiring correctives to all aspects of the business. In developing their strategy, the tobacco companies acknowledged the probability that these trends would form the basis of tobacco control policy in the twenty-first century.

Initially, the introduction of anti-tobacco laws was fragmented and depended on attitudes to smoking in individual countries. The pharmaceutical industry had the most to gain from the globalisation of the anti-smoking movement. The World Bank took an active stand on the issue. Numerous non-governmental organisations trumpeted demands for tougher measures, up to and including a complete ban on smoking. The idea of uniting anti-smoking efforts via the World Health Organisation (WHO) took some time to gain traction. Although the WHO adopted a resolution to begin developing a framework convention on tobacco control in 1996, little progress was made on the issue.

With the appointment of Gro Harlem Brundtland as Director-General of the WHO in 1998, work on the convention was revived. In May 1999, the Fifty-Second World Health Assembly adopted a resolution establishing a working group to prepare the text of the Framework Convention on Tobacco Control (FCTC) and an intergovernmental negotiating body (INB). The working group, which was open to all WHO member states, was tasked with preparing the proposed draft elements of the FCTC. In May 2000, the draft was presented at the Fifty-Third World Health Assembly. It reflected the positions of the countries involved on the regulation at a global level of the following areas related to tobacco consumption: tax policy and international harmonisation of cigarette pricing, education about the harmful effects of smoking, advertising and sponsorship, the sale of cigarettes to minors, illicit trade and contraband, and passive smoking. Each delegation involved in drafting the document could make its own suggestions about what it should contain. Since the views of the countries ranged from draconian to moderate, the final document included multiple proposed options for each clause of the convention. The task of the INB was to select one of these options in each case and finalise the text of the convention as a whole. Like other countries, Russia had to formulate a position on each clause of the convention and appoint a delegation to participate in the INB.

Although the FCTC was designed to combat smoking as a serious risk to health, its implementation had major implications for many aspects of the economy and the social sphere. This being so, the decision could not be left at the mercy of medical circles. It was to voice this concern that the general director of Tabakprom, Terevtsov, and I went to see the deputy chairman of the government, Vladimir Nikolayevich Shcherbak, at the White House. As an experienced official, he took the matter seriously and issued appropriate instructions. As a result, the process of preparing Russia for involvement in the development of the FCTC was set in motion. An interdepartmental working group was set up which, aside from the Health Ministry, included representatives of the Tax Ministry, the Education Ministry, the Agriculture Ministry and the customs committee. The Chief Medical Officer and first deputy health minister, Gennady Grigoryevich Onishchenko, was appointed chairman of the group. We thought it perfectly natural that representatives of the tobacco industry, as legal manufacturers of cigarettes, should be involved in the negotiating process.

Shcherbak gave an official order for my inclusion in the Russian delegation to the negotiations as a representative of Tabakprom. This allowed me to take part in the negotiation process throughout the entire period of the development of the FCTC, which lasted three years and was completed in May 2003.

In October 2000, shortly before the INB began its work, large-scale hearings on the proposed framework convention were conducted at the International Conference Centre in Geneva. Representatives of the tobacco industry were also invited to take part. I was accredited as a member of the board of directors of Tabakprom. The hearings enabled the interested parties to set out their positions. The tone of the speeches was set by representatives of non-governmental organisations. Describing smoking as the "plague of the twentieth century", they called for the text of the convention to be toughened with a view to eradicating smoking altogether within twenty years. They placed all the blame for the spread of smoking on the global tobacco companies and called for them to be banned from taking part in the negotiation process or in any advisory, research or executive organisations connected with the framework convention. The tobacco companies presented balanced viewpoints. Openly acknowledging the harmful impact of smoking on people's health, they were amenable to discussions about imposing restrictions. The accusations against them were unreasonable. It is the purpose of every business to operate on the market and promote their products. Introducing restrictions on the consumption of a particular product is the prerogative of the state. Tobacco companies are legal businesses operating within the laws of the countries in which they manufacture and sell their products. The proposal for legitimate producers to be excluded from the discussion of measures to restrict the production and consumption of cigarettes was greeted with bemusement, to put it mildly. But the extremist position won the day. A large role in this was played by the Director-General of the WHO, Gro Harlem Brundtland. A doctor by profession, she had previously been the prime minister of Norway, a country with some of the toughest anti-smoking policies in the world. Under her leadership, the WHO itself had become the first large employer to make non-addiction to tobacco a requirement for recruitment. An atmosphere of irreconcilable intolerance towards tobacco and towards cigarette manufacturers was created around the negotiations over the FCTC. The WHO made a strong recommendation to participating countries not to include representatives of tobacco companies in their delegations. As a result, of all the participants in the negotiation process I was probably the only representative of the tobacco industry.

Under the regulations on the development of the framework convention, the World Health Organisation was not a party to the negotiations. The WHO's functions consisted in organising the process and providing technical support. There were 191 sovereign countries involved in the INB. The negotiation process took place in several phases. For each phase, a chairperson was elected from the representatives of the participating countries. Under their leadership, discussions were held about each clause of the convention in turn. The delegations were free to present proposals regarding the text. There was no voting. After each phase ended, dates would be set for the next session, in time for which the chairperson and the working group would prepare a new version of the text of the convention, revised for the proposals made by the delegations in the preceding phase. It was planned that the parties would, in this way, gradually reach a consensus and hammer out a final version of the convention.

The difficulty lay in the fact that the countries were all in different situations with regard to restrictions on smoking. This meant that their negotiating positions varied significantly. They depended on public attitudes to smoking, the influence of the tobacco industry on the economy, and cultural traditions. As a rule, the prevalence of smoking depended on a country's overall level of development. Some countries, as prominent tobacco exporters, were concerned about the fall in demand for raw tobacco. Even highly developed countries had difficulty formulating their positions. For the European Union delegation, the problem was that smoking cultures varied across the different European countries. In the case of the USA, although it had achieved progress in restricting smoking, some clauses of the convention conflicted with its laws. Japan found itself in a delicate position. The government was the main shareholder in the tobacco company JTI, which made them wary about any provisions that might damage the company's business. There was particular concern over demands for the terms "light", "ultra-light" and "mild" to be excluded from the names of cigarettes. The adoption of this provision could jeopardise JTI's right to continue producing its most famous brand, Mild Seven.

In Russia, many elements of the convention had already been resolved or were the subject of serious public discussion. Television advertising of tobacco products had been banned in 1996. There was active debate about restricting outdoor advertising, which was prohibited altogether in 2007. In 2003 a new excise law was passed, and tax rates were indexed upwards on a yearly basis. Limits on tar and nicotine content were brought closer to European standards. The tobacco companies supported measures to educate the public, prevent smoking among minors and protect people against passive smoking. They adhered to the position that "Smoking is a conscious choice made by adults" and opposed excessively stringent measures which might unreasonably restrict the rights of the smoking population.

The USSR, and then Russia, had a strong culture of smoking. There were therefore serious misgivings about some of the proposed clauses of the convention. How would smokers, accustomed to the pleasant feel of a packet of cigarettes in their hands, take to being confronted with grim warnings (blazoned over almost the whole pack) about the effects of smoking, not to mention disturbing images of damaged human organs? There was no doubting the need to raise cigarette prices by increasing excise tax. But it had to be done gradually, so that smokers could buy cigarettes in line with their income level. Pricing policy played a significant role in combating smuggling and illicit trade. To protect a country's economic interests, it was essential for its tax policies to be harmonised with those of its neighbours. These matters were at the centre of the FCTC negotiations. I am sure that, even though representatives of the tobacco industry were not involved in the negotiations, the delegations were compelled to take their opinions into account. You could not simply exclude a whole industry from the equation at the stroke of a pen. Despite the diversity of positions among the INB parties, work on the convention progressed. The framework convention comprised a general system of guiding principles on which the delegations gradually managed to align their positions. Specific obligations regarding individual sections were developed in so-called "protocols" to the framework convention. Accession to the protocols was a separate process which took place after the adoption of the FCTC.

The business-like atmosphere was disturbed only by the hysteria whipped up by the NGOs. They were a constant presence at the negotiations, taking up position in separate areas of the INB conference hall. Under the regulations, they were allotted a certain amount of time for speeches. Presenting scary statistics about the casualties of smoking, they pressed for tougher wording in the convention. They tried to exert direct pressure on the delegations. Over 170 NGOs united to form the Framework Convention Alliance. In the breaks between sessions they literally forced various propaganda materials into delegates' hands. The Alliance published a daily bulletin commenting on the progress of the negotiations. They often made disparaging comments about those countries which they believed were taking an insufficiently tough stance on this or that part of the convention. And yet, despite this overwhelming pressure, the talks proceeded in a business-like way. In contrast to the one-sided position of the NGOs, the delegations had to contend with a range of specific issues that could have significant economic and social implications for their respective countries.

The Russian Federation also gradually formulated its position. This involved considering major changes in specific economic parameters relating to various aspects of the production and consumption of tobacco products. Before each new session of the INB, Gennady Onishchenko would convene the Interdepartmental Working Group (IWG) and the various ministries and departments would present their proposals regarding the clauses of the new version of the convention. After the IWG's discussions the Russian delegation would receive a government assignment for the next stage of the negotiation process. It should be said that Russia supported all the provisions of the convention in principle, but advocated gradual implementation based on the individual interests of each country. This was achievable. After the convention was signed, the countries committed themselves to all the principles set out in it, but specific restrictions on smoking were imposed through laws passed by each individual state.

The nucleus of the Russian delegation consisted of representatives of medical circles. For the entire period of the negotiations the delegation was headed by the director of the Preventive Medicine Institute, academician Rafael Gegamovich Oganov. The Health Ministry was represented by Galina Borisovna Tkachenko, coordinator of the Tobacco Control Centre, and Olga Nikolayevna Priyezheva. Nikolai Pavlovich Napalkov, a highly authoritative oncologist, academician, and honorary director of the Petrov Institute of Oncology in St Petersburg, served as expert advisor. The great erudition of the eminent scholars, Oganov and Napalkov, helped promote a broad-minded attitude to the problem of tobacco control among the Russian delegation, which was far removed from extremist dispositions and had a respectable look about it. This did not go amiss when it came to adopting a position that accorded with the country's interests in the matter of anti-smoking policy. The delegation even put forward an initiative to coordinate with other CIS countries on those elements of the convention that affected mutual relations between neighbouring countries. The initiative was approved in Moscow. An interesting evolution occurred in the attitude of the well-known anti-smoking warrior, Galina Borisovna Tkachenko, who shifted away from her hardline stance over the course of the negotiations. It was not that she changed her views, but she realised just how complex the issues surrounding the adoption of anti-smoking measures were.

For me, too, it was a highly educational experience. I saw for myself the process by which major international agreements are made – the "inner workings", so to speak. Although the tobacco companies were kept out of the negotiations, they kept an attentive eye on their progress. A number of provisions in the convention caused them concern. A particular sore point was the section about the disclosure of the content of the tobacco blend. Not because, as is commonly thought, cigarette manufacturers use banned components in their cigarettes. Tobacco companies are very responsible. But the tobacco blend is a proprietary design, and disclosure of its composition goes against the principles of know-how protection.

At the start of the negotiations it was difficult to imagine how it would be possible, in such a large auditorium and with such differing interests among the participants, to reach agreement on the text of the convention. But international experience in the development of global documents made it possible to have the FCTC ready for adoption within three years. The idea was that the INB would be considered to have completed its work once all objections expressed by the delegations had been eliminated. The further the negotiations progressed, the more intense they became. I remember the final agreement being reached at four o'clock in the morning before the last day of the sixth and final session of the negotiations. The full text of the convention was considered by the Fifty-Sixth World Health Assembly in May 2003 and passed by a secret ballot of the participating countries. The Convention on Tobacco Control was one of the most swiftly adopted international agreements. Within a year it had been signed by almost 90 per cent of the countries involved in the negotiations. It remained for the convention to be ratified by individual parliaments. On 27 February 2005, after it had been ratified by forty states, it entered into force. Russia officially acceded to the FCTC on 11 May 2008.

The goal, it seemed, had been achieved: a global strategy to reduce smoking had been devised. Moreover, even the tobacco industry did not find the convention too objectionable. While the anti-smoking measures noted above had been included in the final text, the need for compromises to be reached among the countries concerned meant that some provisions had been watered down relative to the original version. Furthermore, individual countries were permitted to delay the passage of national laws on certain articles that required preparatory measures.

Once it had been passed, the tobacco industry supported countries' accession to the FCTC. It was in its interest to operate in strict accordance with international laws. Clarity is very important in the business world. This was reiterated by representatives of Tabakprom and multinational tobacco companies operating in Russia at an FCTC roundtable which took place in Moscow in November 2004. Getting things done required all the parties involved to work together. But the WHO leadership continued to pursue a policy of ostracising the tobacco sector. The leaders of national medical groups received instructions from Geneva not to have any contact with representatives of tobacco companies. This was seized upon by hardline anti-smoking warriors, who proceeded to launch an unprecedented and mendacious hate campaign against the tobacco companies. They accused them of putting pressure on lawmakers to slow down the adoption of tobacco control measures. Even the fact that it had taken Russia until 2008 to ratify the treaty was laid at their door, although the real cause had been nothing other than bureaucratic dilly-dallying in the government machinery.

Reports about my participation in the INB meetings were like something out of a crime novel. On the internet I am characterised as a sort of spy who infiltrated the Russian delegation. In fact, I was included in the delegation at the instruction of the First Deputy Premier, Shcherbak, who acted fully within his powers. And when Vladimir Nikolayevich retired a year later, his successor in that lofty post, Alexei Vasilyevich Gordeyev, reconfirmed my authority. Claims that I could have substantially influenced the position of our delegation are absolutely baseless. All I did was convey the opinions of Tabakprom members to the members of the steering committee. My participation in the negotiations drew no objections from members of the delegation or of the steering committee, with whom I had a constructive relationship. I think that the Russian leadership was within its rights to include a representative of the tobacco industry in its delegation. It was only to avoid ruffling feathers that it had been decided to present me as an expert from the Ministry of Agriculture. When, therefore, at the last session of the INB, Sinelnikov was "exposed" by NGO activists as one of BAT's top managers in Russia, the Russian delegation paid no attention to the matter.

There was a changed atmosphere after the adoption of the FCTC. People who worked for tobacco companies began to be treated as personae non gratae in medical circles. I was greatly surprised at the statement made by Gennady Grigoryevich Onishchenko that he regarded the inclusion of a representative of the tobacco industry in the Russian delegation as a disgrace. This was despite the fact that we had worked closely and constructively together on the steering committee. I had thought that Gennady Grigoryevich, himself a man of great wit, was more broad-minded than that. It seemed that the identification of the tobacco industry as public enemy number one and smokers as second-class citizens had become an important factor in tobacco control.

There is, in general, a lot of dogmatism as far as this issue is concerned. The way in which the medical profession treats smoking has changed dramatically. Before, doctors would take a flexible approach to the smoking habits of a particular patient. They took account of individual physical characteristics. In many cases, heavy smokers would be advised to try cutting down. Nowadays, any such "dissent" is out of the question. A doctor must order his patients to quit smoking altogether. No one would deny that smoking can be the cause of a number of serious diseases, but there is a great deal of populism and inaccurate information in anti-smoking propaganda. Claims that five million people die each year from smoking lack credibility. Loss of health results from the impact of multiple factors on a person's body, so it is improper to make a judgment about the influence of smoking without considering other causes. Moreover, supposed "expert assessments" are steeped in subjectivity. In the INB conference hall in Geneva there was an electronic display with rapidly changing digits, which was intended to convey in real time the number of people dying from tobacco addiction. The implication was that while we sat there in our meeting, people outside were dying from tobacco, so we needed to get a move on. It is highly unlikely that this attempt to exert psychological pressure on the negotiation participants was based on accurate data.

In actual fact, the problems associated with smoking are much more complex. For a long time, cigarettes, like alcohol, were the most common natural tranquilisers, which had a major influence on the emotional and psychological state of society. Attempting to ban smoking upsets the prevailing balance and summons new products into existence. Psychological pressure and prohibitive measures have driven many smokers to take up electronic cigarettes, whose impact on health has not yet been studied. For young people especially, the way is left open for the rapid proliferation of drugs and "smoking mixes". Now that really is a plague, and one that has swept across our entire planet. But no one seems to think about that. You stop believing that the world's leading governments and public institutions are capable in their current state of addressing global problems that pose a real threat to society. You cannot help but wonder about this as you observe global political processes in the world today.

I am particularly anxious about the situation with regard to smoking in Russia. After all, the population lived through all the hardships of the twentieth century with tobacco in its midst. Where will anti-smoking policies lead us? What I see at the moment is that lawmakers and society take an overly simplified view of the problem, overlooking the fact that it affects the interests of tens of millions of living people for whom smoking has become a part of everyday life. For the first time since the formation of the USSR, then Russia, we are seeing a fall in cigarette consumption. There are no loud protests, however. It appears that smokers are adapting to the changes and keeping a low profile. The important thing is that their customary cigarettes are freely available to buy. The biggest restrictions relate to the places where smoking is forbidden. As always, these bans were blithely imposed without a second thought to the interests of smokers, who are also people with rights. There are few suitable places for smoking these days. But smokers are gradually adapting, especially since, in Russia, the government's traditional lack of respect for the people is evened out by a slack approach to enforcement of the law. The ban on advertising, sponsorship and product promotion is more of a problem for the tobacco industry. But the tobacco companies are adapting too. Since cigarettes are largely discredited as a consumer product, they are refocusing their research onto the creation of new types of products which imitate smoking without the burning of tobacco. The challenge for tobacco companies is to keep developing their business.

In the immediate term, the thorniest issue is the price of cigarettes. Opponents of smoking maintain that it is high prices that will force a large proportion of the population to quit the habit. In my view, if you look at people's real disposable incomes, the price has reached a critical level. But the WHO leadership and certain hot-headed deputies are calling for the proportion of excise tax in the price of cigarettes to be raised to the European level of 75 per cent with immediate effect. This would more than double the price and make cigarettes unaffordable for a large proportion of the population. They think that by doing this they will be able to slash the number of smokers in one go. But by no means all smokers are willing to quit, and further rises in prices could have serious consequences. Giving up smoking is a personal choice which is ultimately made by the consumers themselves. Leaning too hard on smokers may have counterproductive effects.

Even now, for instance, there is evidence of increased smuggling of cigarettes from neighbouring countries. In Belarus and Kazakhstan, Russia's partners in the Customs Union, cigarettes are cheaper because of the lower excise tax, while the borders are fairly transparent. If cigarette prices continue to rise, people will naturally seek their own solutions. Some might even switch to smoking self-grown tobacco, especially in rural areas. It is hard to imagine that people in Russia's remote provinces will take to smoking electronic cigarettes. Also rather dubious are the arguments that raising prices will protect young people from getting addicted. There is another, more serious danger here. Whereas teenagers used to mess about with cigarettes, now they experiment with drugs.

In my view, it is time to put dogmatism aside and take a realistic look at the problems. It sometimes feels as if tobacco control has been elevated into the principal challenge of the modern age – as if vanquishing tobacco would resolve all the nation's health issues. How we love our little crusades! In fact, smoking is only one of a whole range of problems that have to be addressed. It is time to take a sober look at things and be realistic about where smoking lies in the overall battle for a healthier nation.

The overwhelming conclusion is that the global effort to reduce smoking is timely and necessary. But it is essential to take a balanced approach and recognise that the problem cannot be resolved by prohibitive measures alone. Many adult smokers do not want to quit smoking. Their choice must be respected, and they must be given that option. The important thing is not to allow the smoking population to be swelled by young people taking up the habit. This will require coherent policies over a range of different areas. Those hoping for a quick and easy solution to this complex problem will, as in many other such matters, be disappointed.

A BRIEF AFTERWORD

In December 2010 I finished working at BAT-Russia. I felt that this was a natural step to take for a number of reasons. According to BAT's internal policies, management teams in end markets are changed every three to four years. Over the time I had worked for the company, there had been seven general managers in Russia and, accordingly, the same number of management teams. There had been four different presidents in the London office. Practically no one remained of those with whom we had started out and navigated our way through the most difficult years.

In 2009 the government issued a decree "On the Compulsory Purchase of Shares from Minority Shareholders". The company took advantage of the opportunity. BAT became the 100 per cent owner of BAT-Yava OJSC and BAT-STF. The role of board chairman became purely symbolic. In addition, the Yava factory's position in the centre of Moscow grew increasingly precarious. Our neighbour, the Second Watch Factory, had been shut down and its site purchased by Vozrozhdeniye Bank, which planned to build a large business centre there. Yava was the only enterprise left in the industrial zone. My efforts to have the factory moved out of the centre of Moscow were not supported in London. I accepted that decision with a full inner realisation that my mission was at an end.

Indeed, it was only a short time later, in mid-2011, that BAT announced the closure of the Yava factory and the relocation of production to St Petersburg and Saratov. I cannot say that the decision came as a complete surprise, but to witness the closure of the enterprise to which one has devoted one's whole life is, believe me, not an easy thing. Most of all, it was the people I thought about. Many of the staff had reached an age at which it is difficult to find decent work. Although the company granted sizable severance packages, it was hard to get by without a job. And then there was the psychological factor. Most of the workers had linked their lives to the factory. The Yava "collective" had become a sort of community in its own right.

The closure of the factory strengthened my resolve to set my memories down in writing. After all, that small area of land had served as the manufacturing home for very important products, seen passions run high and watched several generations of workers come and go. It struck me as unjust that the lives of those people and the events, often dramatic, that had accompanied them should be condemned to oblivion. I had been a young man when I came to work at the factory. I had been a witness to and participant in all the significant events that had befallen it. I was practically the only person left who could write about it.

Of course, Yava was a part of the Soviet tobacco industry and a fragment of an enormous country. When I began to write these memoirs, I realised that the events that took place at the factory could not be separated from what was happening in the country at large – especially as it was a period of history that coincided with fundamental, one might even say revolutionary, changes. Over a matter of fifty years (a short period in historical terms), the country travelled the entire path from Communism to a capitalist economic system. I began my career under a centrally planned system and ended it as part of a multinational tobacco company operating in a market economy. There are probably few people who can make such a claim.

One might say that our generation happened to live through a unique and unparalleled period of history. And yet, it appears that age-old national traditions cannot be changed in such a short time. There is a lot of truth in the popular saying that "whatever we try to build in Russia, we still end up with the CPSU". Even our capitalism is of a distinctive, home-made variety, with the monopolisation of power and business, the decisive role of government connections (the notorious "administrative resource"), the stranglehold of officialdom, corruption... in short, the complete absence of what is needed for a democratic, developed civil society.

Unfortunately, we have failed to make good use of the fundamental advantages offered by the modern world: freedom of enterprise and the development of competition. International rankings on the ease of doing business place Russia far behind developed countries. There has been no leap forward in terms of developing domestic industry and creating new technologies. We continue to buy industrial equipment and know-how from the West. Our main export is energy commodities, which nature has generously bestowed on us. Russia's reputation as a commodity exporter remains firmly in place. Because of the lack of demand for innovation, our science is stagnating. Granted, the notorious shortages of the Soviet period have been overcome – but by importing goods rather than making our own. Despite our vast lands, we even contrive to import potatoes – a Russian staple. There are certain strategic areas in which we are firmly hooked on imports, which is very worrying. The pharmaceutical industry is a primary case in point.

No qualitative changes have occurred compared with Soviet times, and tentative advances towards democracy have been halted by the excessive centralisation of power. In the USSR, it was the central planning system that impeded economic development; in Russia this has been replaced by the phenomenon of "administrative resource". The winners have been the elite and government officials, who have used their proximity to power to amass personal fortunes beyond the wildest dreams of Soviet Party functionaries. As a result, economic stratification in society is growing. Ordinary people have received no tangible advantages, yet at the same time have lost the social guarantees they enjoyed under the Soviet regime. The Soviet Union proved unviable, but the current course has no future either. A huge country with colossal internal resources cannot remain subdued for long. Today's elite would do well to wake up to that fact.

So, were the efforts invested in perestroika and the transition to the market economy all for nothing? I think that, when it comes to it, the country has tasted freedom, and a forward course has been set. And historical memory remains. The search for a way out of the impasse must go on. It is time for the country to turn to its people, because it is only through trust in individual initiative that foundations for real growth can be laid.

There are many talented people in Russia. They have to be given real opportunities to realise their potential.